Frommer's®

Jamaica & Barbados

Here's what the critics say about Frommer's:

"Amazingly easy to use. Very portable, very complete."
—*Booklist*

♦

"The only mainstream guide to list specific prices. The Walter Cronkite of guidebooks—with all that implies."
—*Travel & Leisure*

♦

"Complete, concise, and filled with useful information."
—*New York Daily News*

♦

"Hotel information is close to encyclopedic."
—*Des Moines Sunday Register*

Other Great Guides for Your Trip:

Frommer's Caribbean

Frommer's Caribbean from $60 a Day

Frommer's Caribbean Cruises

Frommer's Caribbean Ports of Call

Frommer's Born to Shop Caribbean

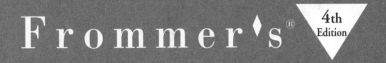

4th Edition

Jamaica
& Barbados

**by Darwin Porter
& Danforth Prince**

MACMILLAN • USA

ABOUT THE AUTHORS

A native of North Carolina, **Darwin Porter** was a bureau chief for *The Miami Herald* when he was 21, and later worked in television advertising. A veteran travel writer, he is the author of numerous best-selling Frommer guides, notably to England, France, Italy, and the Caribbean. He is assisted by **Danforth Prince,** formerly of the Paris bureau of the *New York Times.* For years, they have been frequent travelers to Jamaica and Barbados, and have become intimately familiar with what's good there and what isn't. In this guide, they share their secrets and discoveries with you.

MACMILLAN TRAVEL

A Simon & Schuster Macmillan Company
1633 Broadway
New York, NY 10019

Find us online at **www.frommers.com**

ISBN 0-02-862265-0
ISSN 1061-9429

Editor: Lisa Renaud
Production Editor: Chris Van Camp
Photo Editor: Richard Fox
Design by Michele Laseau
Digital Cartography by Ortelius Design
Page Creation by John Bitter, Jena Brandt, Jerry Cole, Natalie Hollifield, and Dave Pruett

SPECIAL SALES

Bulk purchases (10+ copies) of Frommer's and selected Macmillan travel guides are available to corporations, organizations, mail-order catalogs, institutions, and charities at special discounts, and can be customized to suit individual needs. For more information write to Special Sales, Macmillan General Reference, 1633 Broadway, New York, NY 10019.

Manufactured in the United States of America

Contents

List of Maps   viii

1   The Best of Jamaica & Barbados   1

1 The Best Beaches 1
2 The Best Water-Sports Outfitters 2
3 The Best Golf Courses 3
4 The Best Tennis Facilities 3
5 The Best Natural Attractions 4
6 The Best Honeymoon Resorts 5
7 The Best Family-Friendly Resorts 6
8 The Best Places to Get Away from It All 7
9 The Best All-Inclusives 8
10 The Best Restaurants 9
11 The Best Shopping Buys 10
12 The Best After-Dark Fun 11

2   Getting to Know Jamaica   13

1 The Natural Environment 14
2 The Regions in Brief 16
3 Jamaica Today 17
4 History 101 18
★ Dateline 18
5 The Jamaican People & Their Culture 25
★ Ganja 28
6 Calypso, Reggae & Rap: The Rhythms of Jamaica 29
7 A Taste of Jamaica 33

3   Planning a Trip to Jamaica   35

1 Visitor Information, Entry Requirements & Customs 35
2 Money 37
★ The Jamaican Dollar, the U.S. Dollar & the British Pound 38
3 When to Go 39
★ Jamaica Calendar of Events 41
4 The Active Vacation Planner 43
5 Health & Insurance 46
6 Tips for Travelers with Special Needs 47
★ Tying the Knot in Jamaica 50
7 Package Tours 52
8 Flying to Jamaica 54
9 Cruises 57
10 Getting Around 60
11 Tips on Accommodations 62
12 Renting Your Own Condo, Cottage, or Villa 66
13 Tips on Dining Out 67
14 Tips on Shopping 70
★ Meeting the Jamaicans 71
★ Fast Facts: Jamaica 72

4   Montego Bay   75

1 Where to Stay 75

2 Where to Dine 88

3 Hitting the Beach, Hitting the Links & Other Outdoor Pursuits 94

4 Seeing the Sights 96

★ The White Witch of Rose Hall 97

5 Shopping 99

6 Montego Bay After Dark 101

7 A Side Trip to Falmouth 101

5   Negril, the South Coast & Mandeville   104

1 Introducing Negril 106

2 Getting There 107

3 Where to Stay 107

★ Ann Bonney & Her Dirty Dog 112

4 Where to Dine 118

5 Scuba Diving & Snorkeling 122

6 Negril After Dark 123

7 A Side Trip to the South Coast 123

8 Mandeville 126

6   The North Coast Resorts: Runaway Bay, Ocho Rios & Port Antonio   129

1 Runaway Bay 130

2 Ocho Rios 135

★ Noël's Folly 150

3 Port Antonio 154

7   Kingston & the Blue Mountains   165

1 Where to Stay 165

2 Where to Dine 170

3 Exploring Kingston 173

★ Cays & Mangroves 174

4 Shopping 175

5 Kingston After Dark 177

6 Side Trips to Spanish Town & Port Royal 177

★ The Wickedest City on Earth 179

7 Exploring the Blue Mountains 180

8   Getting to Know Barbados   184

1 The Regions in Brief 184

★ Did You Know? 185

2 Barbados Today 189

3 History 101 190

★ Dateline 190

4 Calypso! 192

★ Miss Rachel & the Prince 193

5 A Taste of Barbados 194

9   Planning a Trip to Barbados   196

1 Visitor Information, Entry
   Requirements & Customs 196

2 Money 197

3 When to Go 197

★ The Bajan Dollar, the U.S.
   Dollar & the British Pound 198

★ Barbados Calendar of Events 198

4 Package Tours 200

5 Flying to Barbados 201

6 Cruises 202

★ The Babe Ruth of Barbados 204

7 Getting Around 204

★ Fast Facts: Barbados 206

10   Where to Stay & Dine on Barbados   210

1 Where to Stay 210

★ Family-Friendly Hotels 214

2 Where to Dine 228

★ Family-Friendly Restaurants 233

11   Exploring Barbados   243

1 Beaches 243

2 Outdoor Pursuits 244

★ Frommer's Favorite Barbados
   Experiences 247

3 Seeing the Sights in Bridgetown
   248

4 A Driving Tour Around
   the Island 251

5 Exploring Inland 256

6 Cruises & Tours 258

7 Shopping 260

8 Barbados After Dark 263

Index   266

General Index 266

Accommodations Index 273

List of Maps

Jamaica   14
Jamaica Accommodations   64
Jamaica Dining   68
Montego Bay   76
Negril   105
Ocho Rios   137
Port Antonio   155

Kingston Area   166
Barbados   186
Barbados Accommodations   212
Barbados Dining   230
Bridgetown   249
Driving Tour—
    Around Barbados   253

AN INVITATION TO THE READER

In researching this book, we discovered many wonderful places—hotels, restaurants, shops, and more. We're sure you'll find others. Please tell us about them, so we can share the information with your fellow travelers in upcoming editions. If you were disappointed with a recommendation, we'd love to know that, too. Please write to:

Frommer's Jamaica & Barbados
Macmillan Travel
1633 Broadway
New York, NY 10019

AN ADDITIONAL NOTE

Please be advised that travel information is subject to change at any time—and this is especially true of prices. We therefore suggest that you write or call ahead for confirmation when making your travel plans. The authors, editors, and publisher cannot be held responsible for the experiences of readers while traveling. Your safety is important to us, however, so we encourage you to stay alert and be aware of your surroundings. Keep a close eye on cameras, purses, and wallets, all favorite targets of thieves and pickpockets.

WHAT THE SYMBOLS MEAN

✪ Frommer's Favorites

Our favorite places and experiences—outstanding for quality, value, or both.

The following abbreviations are used for credit cards:

AE	American Express	EURO	Eurocard
CB	Carte Blanche	JCB	Japan Credit Bank
DC	Diners Club	MC	MasterCard
DISC	Discover	V	Visa
ER	EnRoute		

The following abbreviations are used in hotel listings:

MAP (Modified American Plan) usually means room, breakfast, and dinner, unless the room rate has been quoted separately, and then it means only breakfast and dinner.

AP (American Plan) includes your room plus three meals.

CP (Continental Plan) includes room and a light breakfast.

EP (European Plan) means room only.

FIND FROMMER'S ONLINE

Arthur Frommer's Outspoken Encyclopedia of Travel (**www.frommers.com**) offers more than 6,000 pages of up-to-the-minute travel information—including the latest bargains and candid, personal articles updated daily by Arthur Frommer himself. No other Web site offers such comprehensive and timely coverage of the world of travel.

The Best of Jamaica & Barbados

Y ou're flying off to Jamaica or Barbados to relax and have a good time—not to waste precious vacation hours searching for the best deals and experiences. So take us along and we'll do the work for you.

We've tested the best beaches, reviewed countless restaurants, inspected the hotels, sampled the best scuba diving, and taken the best hikes. We've found the best buys, the hottest nightclubs, and even the best places to get away from it all when you want to escape the crowds. Here's our very opinionated selection, compiled after years of traveling through these islands.

1 The Best Beaches

Both Jamaica and Barbados are known for white, sandy beaches—that's what put them on the tourist map in the first place. And best of all, the beaches on both islands are open to the general public. So even though the top resorts have naturally grabbed the prime coastal real estate, you can still enjoy their beaches, even if you have to walk across the resorts' grounds to reach them.

- **Doctor's Cave Beach** (Montego Bay, Jamaica): This 5-mile stretch of white sand made "Mo Bay" a tourist destination. Waters are placid and crystal clear, and there are changing rooms and a beach bar. This one is a family favorite. See chapter 4.
- **Cornwall Beach** (Montego Bay, Jamaica): Although it's often too crowded, this beach is covered in soft, white, sugary sand that's deep enough to really sink your toes into. The water is clean and warm, and it's a place to take your family. The admission charge entitles you not only to swim and sunbathe, but also to use the changing room. The beach is near the main tourist strip and close to the popular and larger Doctor's Cave Beach (see above). The "higglers"—as local vendors are called—will seek you out and try to sell you everything from black coral jewelry to drugs. See chapter 4.
- **Negril Beach** (Negril, Jamaica): On the island's West Coast, this beach stretches for 7 miles along the sea. It was once the haunt of the Caribbean's most notorious pirates. In the background are some of the most hedonistic resorts in the Caribbean, mixed in with a few family favorites. Many strips of these golden sands are

fine for families, although there are several nudist patches where guests bare all. The nude beach areas are sectioned off, even though some new oceanfront resorts have Peeping Tom views of these areas. See chapter 5.

- **Booby Cay** (Negril, Jamaica): Although it's X-rated, the aptly named Booby Cay is the haunt of snorkelers as well as nude sunbathers. Many folks come here from Hedonism II, Jamaica's answer to Club Med. Once they've landed by motor launch or even kayak, bathers in the buff—mainly male/female couples—disperse to seek out their own little white sandy patch of private heaven. See chapter 5.

- **Boston Beach** (Port Antonio, Jamaica): It's known not only for its white sands, but for its jerk pork stands. You can enjoy your unique beach barbecue while gazing out upon the incredibly clear waters of the bay. The beach has the biggest waves in Jamaica, and young men will rent you surfboards and even give you lessons. See chapter 6.

- **Treasure Beach** (South Coast, Jamaica): Tired of fighting the crowds for your place in the sun? Head for Treasure Beach on Jamaica's dry, sunny, and isolated South Coast, a real hideaway that's a secret among young Jamaicans. There are drawbacks here, and the undertow can be dangerous, so swimming is a bit tricky. These secluded sands are gray, and waves crash into the shore: It's one of the most dramatic beachscapes in Jamaica. Local residents you encounter often have café au lait complexions, a slight Scottish accent, blue eyes, and blondish hair—they're descended from Scottish seamen who wrecked offshore. See chapter 5.

- **Crane Beach** (Barbados): This southern beach—one of the most photographed and fabled in the West Indies—has big Atlantic waves of incredibly blue waters rolling in, but lifeguards are standing by. The beach is filled with pink-tinged coral sand. If you dig into it with your fingers, it's like reaching into a bowl of sugar. The sweeping ocean views are the most panoramic in Barbados, and water sports and lounge chairs are available. In the unlikely event you tire of all this beautiful sand, you can retreat to the nearby Crane Beach Hotel for a refreshing drink. See chapter 11.

- **The Beaches of St. James** (Barbados): Whether it's called "the Platinum Coast" or "the Gold Coast," this fabled strip along the Caribbean Sea along the western side of Barbados is a beachcomber's paradise. Against a backdrop of some of the most exclusive hotels in the West Indies, you can stroll for miles along this strip of white sand, taking in the natural beauty of the coastline and the clear blue sea. Local families come here to picnic on Sunday, roasting their breadfruit or frying fish over open fires, and fishers can be seen drying their nets. You'll find plenty of beach cricket games. Our favorite spots along the strip are Paradise Beach, Brighton Beach, and Brandon's Beach, a strip of white sandy beaches at Fresh Water Bay, directly south of Payne's Bay. See chapter 11.

2 The Best Water-Sports Outfitters

- **Negril Scuba Centre** (Negril, Jamaica; ☎ **800/818-2963** in the U.S., or 876/957-9641): This is the best-equipped dive facility in this popular resort area. It has one of the most professional staffs on the island, all certified instructors. They'll take you for dives into a bay once frequented by some of the most notorious pirates (male and female) in the West Indies. See chapter 5.

- **Buccaneer Scuba Club** (Port Royal, Jamaica; ☎ **876/924-8148**): Based at Morgan's Harbour Hotel and Beach Club, this operator is unique in the

Caribbean. It offers the widest range of dive sites in Jamaica, including the *Texas* wreck, an American naval ship that sank in 1944. Other sites include South East Cays, a reef that runs alongside the south of Jamaica, and Sandra's Buoy, one of the largest reefs and filled with marine life, including coral growth. You can spot turtles, dolphins, and rays. See chapter 7.

- **The Dive Shop** (Barbados; ☎ **246/426-9947**): Offering the best scuba diving on the island, the staff of qualified instructors will take you to intriguing dive sites where 50 varieties of fish are found. Off Sandy Beach are found sea fans, corals, gorgonians, and dozens of rainbow-hued reef fish. Asta Reef, with a drop of 80 feet, has coral, sea fans, and reef fish galore as well. See chapter 11.

3 The Best Golf Courses

Jamaica has far greater golf courses than Barbados. An official PGA golf destination, it has some of the most challenging courses in the West Indies, with a dozen championship links.

- **Wyndham Rose Hall Golf & Beach Resort** (Montego Bay, Jamaica; ☎ **800/ 822-4200** in the U.S., or 876/953-2650): Wyndham has been called one of the top five courses in the world. That may be a bit of an exaggeration, but it is an unusual and challenging seaside and mountain course built on the shores of the Caribbean. The 10th fairway abuts the family burial grounds of the Barretts of Wimpole Street, and the 14th passes the vacation home of singer Johnny Cash. The 300-foot-high 13th tee offers a rare panoramic view of the sea and the roof of the hotel, and the 15th green is next to a 40-foot waterfall, once featured in a James Bond movie. See chapter 4.
- **Tryall Golf, Tennis & Beach Club** (Montego Bay, Jamaica; ☎ **800/238-5290** in the U.S., or 876/956-5660): Jamaica's finest course, Tryall is the site of the annual Johnnie Walker World Championship. A par-71, 6,680-yard course, it crosses hills and dales on what was once sugarcane farmland. Some ruins, including an old waterwheel, remain. Wind direction can change suddenly, making the course more intriguing. One golfer we interviewed confessed he's played the course 50 times, and "each game was different." See chapter 4.
- **Half Moon Golf, Tennis & Beach Club** (Montego Bay, Jamaica; ☎ **800/ 626-0592** in the U.S., or 876/953-2211): The island's second championship course was designed by Robert Trent Jones Sr. in 1961. Played by the likes of former U.S. President George Bush, the course has manicured and diversely shaped greens, but it's not as challenging as the one at Tryall. See chapter 4.
- **Royal Westmoreland Golf & Country Club** (Barbados; ☎ **246/422-4653**): The premier golf course on Barbados dates from 1994. On the West Coast, near its twin Pemberton properties, Glitter Bay and Royal Pavilion, it is a private residential community. The course can be played only by guests of certain hotels. Serious golfers will want to book into one of these hotels (a wide price range) to be granted the privilege of playing this course, designed by Robert Trent Jones, Jr. The $30 million, 27-hole course is spread across 500 acres, overlooking the western Gold Coast, the island's fabled beach strip. See chapter 11.

4 The Best Tennis Facilities

- **Half Moon Golf, Tennis & Beach Club** (Montego Bay, Jamaica; ☎ **800/ 626-0592** in the U.S., or 876/953-2211): Half Moon has Jamaica's best tennis—13 state-of-the-art courts, seven of which are lit for night games. The head pro offers a clinic with a video playback. See chapter 4.

- **Wyndham Rose Hall Golf & Beach Resort** (Montego Bay, Jamaica; ☎ **800/822-4200** in the U.S., or 876/953-2650): Wyndham Rose Hall features six hard-surfaced courts, each lit for night games. Hotel guests play for free; others must pay a fee. There's also a resident pro on hand to offer lessons. See chapter 4.

- **Tryall Golf, Tennis & Beach Club** (Montego Bay, Jamaica; ☎ **800/822-4200** in the U.S., or 876/956-5660): Tryall is rivaled only by the Half Moon Club in Jamaica. It has nine hard-surface courts, three of which are lit for night games. Four pros on site will help improve your skills. See chapter 4.

- **Ciboney Ocho Rios** (Ocho Rios, Jamaica; ☎ **800/333-3333** in the U.S., or 876/974-1027): This Radisson franchise offers three clay surfaces and three hard-surface courts, all lit for nighttime play. There's a lot of emphasis here on tennis, including Pan-Caribbean competitions and even pan-parish tournaments. Twice-a-day clinics are sponsored, both for beginners and more advanced players. See chapter 6.

- **Sandy Lane Hotel** (Barbados; ☎ **800/225-5843** in the U.S., or 246/432-1311): Sandy Lane places more emphasis on tennis than any other resort on Barbados. It offers five courts with an open-door policy to nonresidents. Two of the five courts are lit for night games. See chapters 10 and 11.

5 The Best Natural Attractions

- **The Black River** (South Coast, Jamaica): You can explore what feels like real Tarzan country, with mangrove trees and crocodiles in the wild, on an outing with **South Coast Safaris** (☎ 876/965-2513). At the mouths of the Broad and Black rivers, saltwater meets freshwater, and extensive red mangroves are formed with aerial roots of some 40 feet. Lots of wild things grow in these swamps. Birders look for ring-necked ducks, whistling ducks, herons, egrets, and even the blue-winged teal. See chapter 5.

- **Somerset Falls** (Port Antonio, Jamaica): This sun-dappled spot is not as touristy as Dunn's River. The waters from Daniels River race down a deep gorge split through a rain forest. Flowering vines, waterfalls, and foaming cascades form the lush backdrop. You can swim in the deep rock pools. See chapter 6.

- **Dunn's River Falls** (Ocho Rios, Jamaica): A favorite of cruise-ship passengers, these 600 feet of clear, cold mountain waters race over a series of stone steps. Visitors (and we mean *lots* of visitors) splash in the waters at the bottom of the falls or drop into the cool pools higher up between cascades of water. It's the best way to cool off on a hot day in Jamaica. Visitors hold hands climbing the falls and trust that the human chain won't have a weak link! See chapter 6.

- **Welchman Hall Gully** (Barbados): This lush tropical rain forest is operated by the Barbados National Trust. Occasionally you'll spot a wild green monkey (though we can't give you any guarantees). You'll definitely see specimens of plants flourishing just as they did when the first English settlers arrived in 1627: tree fern, cacao, nutmeg, and clove. You can commune with nature and experience the island's most serene tranquillity. See chapter 11.

- **Harrison's Cave** (Barbados): This series of limestone caverns with a 40-foot waterfall and subterranean streams is viewed as one of the finest cave systems in the world and is the leading tourist attraction of Barbados. Visitors can view the caves aboard an electric tram and trailer. Bubbling streams, tumbling cascades, stalagmites rising from the floor, and deep pools are just part of the attraction. See chapter 11.

6 The Best Honeymoon Resorts

Many hotels in Jamaica or Barbados will help you get married, doing everything from arranging the flowers and the photographer to applying for the marriage license (see chapter 3 for more information about Jamaica or chapter 9 for Barbados). Regardless of where you decide to hold your wedding, both Jamaica and Barbados offer romantic destinations for post-wedding wind-downs and honeymoons.

- **Sandals** (Montego Bay, Negril, and Ocho Rios, Jamaica; ☎ **800/SANDALS** in the U.S.): These resorts for male/female couples pride themselves on providing an all-inclusive environment where food and drink are spread out in abundance and you never have to carry cash or worry about tipping. Enthusiastic members of the staff bring heroic amounts of community spirit and enthusiasm to any weddings celebrated on-site. All of these resorts can provide a suitable setting, but the most favored ones are Sandals Royal Jamaican at Montego Bay and Sandals Dunn's River at Ocho Rios. See chapters 4, 5, and 6.
- **Half Moon Golf, Tennis & Beach Club** (Montego Bay, Jamaica; ☎ **800/ 626-0592** in the U.S., or 876/953-2211): This resort offers honeymooners deluxe ocean-view rooms fronting a near perfect crescent-shaped beach. Newlyweds who didn't blow all their money on the wedding opt for one of the large private "cottages," complete with their own swimming pool. Although there are plenty of nooks and crannies where you can retreat for romantic interludes, this is also the resort of choice for honeymooners who want lots of activities, such as aerobics, tennis, swimming, and most definitely golf. See chapter 4.
- **Trident Villas & Hotel** (Port Antonio, Jamaica; ☎ **809/993-2602**): Here you can follow in the footsteps of that perpetual honeymooner, the late actor Errol Flynn. Poet Ella Wheeler Wilcox called Port Antonio "the most exquisite on earth," and if you're here there's no better hideaway than this posh hotel, enjoying a 14-acre setting on a rocky bluff at the edge of the Caribbean. White cottages and villas are staggered about the property to ensure maximum privacy. The main building has an English country-house tradition with formal service; the bedrooms feel very private and quiet, with only the sounds of the pounding surf, a large paddle fan, and pillow talk. See chapter 6.
- **Jamaica Inn** (Ocho Rios, Jamaica; ☎ **800/837-4608** in the U.S., or 876/ 974-2514): At one of the great hotels of the island, the "White Suite" is secluded on the brink of a promontory (Winston Churchill slept here), and it's quite a swanky place for a honeymoon if you can afford it. Otherwise, there are plenty of other spacious and classic rooms in which to begin your married life. The resort opens onto a private cove with powdery champagne-colored sand. The inn, with its colonial aura and a certain degree of formality, is a real contrast to the more free-for-all Sandals properties where anything (well, almost) goes. See chapter 6.
- **Ciboney Ocho Rios** (Ocho Rios, Jamaica; ☎ **800/333-3333** in the U.S., or 876/974-1027): The honeymoon villas at this stately, plantation-style spa and beach resort are set on lush hillside acreage and are perfect private retreats for newlyweds. Each has a private attendant and pool. Guests are pampered here

with complimentary massages, pedicures, and manicures. A private beach is reached by shuttle as the resort is not on the water. The resort is all inclusive and there's a range of sports facilities, such as tennis courts—but you'll be able to find some privacy to be with your new spouse. See chapter 6.

- **The Enchanted Garden** (Ocho Rios, Jamaica; ☎ **800/847-2535** in the U.S., or 876/974-1400): The island's most romantic retreat seems to have been designed just for honeymooners looking for their own Garden of Eden. Tropical plants and flowers are spread across some 20 acres of gardens, along with a series of waterfalls and streams. The rooms may be a bit small, but 30 come with their own private plunge pool. A shuttle will transport you to the nearest beach. Some of the resort's drinking and dining choices evoke the *Arabian Nights,* which should put you in a romantic mood. See chapter 6.
- **Sandy Lane** (Barbados; ☎ **800/225-5843** in the U.S., or 246/432-1310): For years, this has been the most luxurious choice on the island for a romantic interlude. A satisfying sense of tradition has always pervaded this venerable British-inspired hotel, which is set on one of the island's best beaches, with acres of well-maintained grounds. But note, however, that the hotel will be closed from April to at least September 1998, to complete a lavish $75 million renovation, including a complete refurbishment of the rooms and the addition of a host of new facilities, including a 45-hole golf course, seven new tennis courts, and a spa. The renovation had not begun as of press time, but if it will be completed when you're ready to honeymoon, Sandy Lane promises to be better than ever. See chapter 10.
- **Royal Pavilion** (Barbados; ☎ **800/223-1818** in the U.S., 800/268-7176 in Canada, or 246/422-5555): Imagine that your honeymoon breakfast or lunch can be served alfresco at your oceanfront suite. Children are discouraged, at least in the winter, so the resort becomes something of a couples-only retreat. There are plenty of activities to occupy your day, if you're so inclined, including tennis courts and water sports (golf is available nearby), followed by supper-club entertainment—and then it's off to bed. See chapter 10.

7 The Best Family-Friendly Resorts

Jamaica has some of the most family-oriented resorts in the Caribbean. Some accommodations, especially in the winter, discourage children under 12, but the hotels below aggressively pursue the family market and offer plenty of extra advantages for booking with them.

- **Coyaba** (Mahoe Bay, Little River, Montego Bay, Jamaica; ☎ **800/237-3237** in the U.S., or 876/953-9150): With a graceful British colonial atmosphere, this small all-inclusive resort offers children 11 and under a 50% discount. This oceanfront retreat is intimate and inviting, and occupies a bucolic site a 15-minute drive east of the center of Montego Bay, opening onto a lovely strip of sandy beachfront. There's a nanny service to help you keep the little ones fed and entertained. See chapter 4.
- **Beaches Negril** (Negril, Jamaica; ☎ **800/BEACHES** in the U.S. or 876/957-9274): New in 1997, this is the family-oriented wing of the Sandals chain, whose resorts usually cater only to male/female couples. A roster of child and teen activities awaits youngsters on a highly desirable 20-acre lot studded with palms and sea grapes adjacent to a sandy beach. This resort's five separate restaurants include a grill only for children. See chapter 5.

- **FDR (Franklyn D. Resort;** Runaway Bay, Jamaica; ☎ **800/654-1FDR** in the U.S., or 876/973-4591): The FDR is the north coast family favorite. All meals and activities are included in one net price, and families are housed in Mediterranean-style villas on the grounds 17 miles west of Ocho Rios. A personal attendant does all the cooking, cleaning, and child care, and many programs are provided to keep your kids entertained. The Kiddies' Centre features everything from computers to arts and crafts. There are dinners for tots as well. See chapter 6.
- **Sandy Beach Hotel** (Barbados; ☎ **246/435-8000**): This is one of the island's most family-oriented resorts, allowing children under 12 to stay free in their parents' room. The resort contains only one- and two-bedroom suites, each with a fully equipped kitchenette and private balcony or patio. Bajan buffets are popular with the entire family, and the resort reserves a play area for children, plus a wading pool. See chapter 10.
- **Almond Beach Village** (Barbados; ☎ **800/4-ALMOND** in the U.S., or 246/422-4900): This all-inclusive resort, located on 30 acres of prime beachfront property 15 miles north of Bridgetown, boasts one of the best children's programs on the island. It offers a club just for children, with videos, Nintendo, a computer lab, books, and board games, plus two children's playgrounds, a kiddies' pool, an activity center, beach games, nature walks, water sports, treasure hunts, story time, arts and crafts, and even evening entertainment. See chapter 10.

8 The Best Places to Get Away from It All

- **Good Hope** (Falmouth, Jamaica; ☎ **800/OUTPOST** in the U.S., or 876/954-3289): Montego Bay is hardly a place to escape from the tourist hordes, but this romantic 18th-century Great House in the nearby mountains above Falmouth is just the sort of place where you can run away and hide. It is set on a 2,000-acre plantation with lush gardens. Our impresario, Chris Blackwell—who specializes in sylvan retreats—owns this choice property, which offers hiking along country trails, horseback riding, tennis, and swimming. The main house is furnished with antiques. In the evening after a family-style classic Jamaican dinner, you hear only the sounds of the night lulling you to sleep. See chapter 4.
- **Treasure Beach Hotel** (South Coast, Jamaica; ☎ **876/965-2305**): Lying on a lushly landscaped hillside above a sandy beach on Jamaica's unhurried South Coast, this is a place where no one will ever find you. It hardly competes with the grand megaresorts of Jamaica, but Treasure Beach offers tranquillity and a laid-back attitude. Bedrooms are in a series of outlying cottages, offering complete privacy. There's a freshwater pool, but most activities are those you organize yourself. It's cheap, too. See chapter 5.
- **Navy Island Marina Resort** (Port Antonio, Jamaica; ☎ **876/933-2667**): Once owned by the late actor Errol Flynn, this resort and marina is Jamaica's only private island getaway. Part of Flynn's hedonism still prevails, especially at the clothing-optional beach called Trembly Knee Cove. Accommodations are in studio cottages or villas, and ceiling fans and trade winds recapture the romantic aura of Jamaica's past. See chapter 6.
- **Strawberry Hill** (Blue Mountains, Jamaica; ☎ **800/OUTPOST** in the U.S., or 876/944-8400): This highland retreat has been called "a home-away-from-home for five-star Robinson Crusoes." Lying 3,100 feet above the sea, it's our favorite

accommodation in all of eastern Jamaica. Set in a well-planted botanical garden, it is a cottage complex built on the site of a 17th-century Great House. Multimillionaire Chris Blackwell is the owner, and he's created a memorable, lush retreat. See chapter 7.

- **Kingsley Club** (Barbados; ☎ 246/433-9422): On the hidden-away east coast of the island, this property opens onto the turbulent Atlantic Ocean and seems a world removed from Barbados' overbuilt West Coast beach strip. Here you can return more to the laid-back life of Barbados of 30 years ago. It's just a simple, unpretentious West Indian inn lying in the foothills of the little hamlet of Bathsheba. Its rooms are clean and comfortable, and the Bajan food is good, too. It's a very reasonable place to stay, although the beach is not suitable for swimming. Come here to beachcomb. See chapter 10.

9 The Best All-Inclusives

It seems that every resort in Jamaica is going all-inclusive—offering everything (or almost everything), including food and drink, for one flat price. The trend is catching on in Barbados, too. Lavish buffets, evening entertainment, and fun and games in the sun characterize these resorts. The major drawback is that they are virtually fenced-in compounds, completely isolating guests and discouraging them from having a true experience with Jamaican or Barbadan life. But it is this very sense of retreat that many vacationers seek, especially those who don't want to face a lot of hidden extra costs at the end of their trips.

- **Sandals Montego Bay** (Montego Bay, Jamaica; ☎ 800/SANDALS in the U.S., or 876/952-5510): This is a honeymoon haven in spite of the nearby airport and its zooming planes. This 19-acre all-inclusive resort (catering only to male/female couples) is one of the most popular in the Caribbean. Everything's included, even those notorious toga parties. It's mainly for couples wanting to have a good time. Guests tend to be extroverted and gregarious, and they usually eat and drink their money's worth here. We think it's outclassed by some of the better resorts of Ocho Rios, but many vacationers prefer this Mo Bay location. See chapter 4.
- **Grand Lido** (Negril, Jamaica; ☎ 800/859-7875 in the U.S., or 876/957-5010): This hedonistic resort is a class act. It's the grandest and most architecturally interesting along Negril's beach strip. Adjacent to the often raunchy Hedonism II, the Grand Lido is upscale and discreetly elegant. The smaller of its two beaches is reserved for nudists. Unlike many of Jamaica's resorts, it is not a male/female couples–only joint; it also welcomes singles and same-sex couples. It entertains and treats all guests in a grand style, which is far superior to the typical Club Med in the Caribbean. The dining options are the best in Negril. See chapter 5.
- **Ciboney Ocho Rios** (Ocho Rios, Jamaica; ☎ 800/333-3333 in the U.S., or 876/974-1027): This Radisson franchise is the leading all-inclusive resort in the Greater Ocho Rios area. Its accommodations are in one-, two-, or three-bedroom villas, each with its own pool and fully equipped kitchen. The dining choices are the best of any of the competing resorts, including one restaurant with a menu of healthy haute cuisine. It's not directly on the beach, but there's a beauty spa and a health and fitness center. A nearby private beach club offers an array of water sports. See chapter 6.
- **Couples Ocho Rios** (Ocho Rios, Jamaica; ☎ 800/268-7537 in the U.S., or 876/975-4271): "Any man and woman in love" are pampered and coddled during their stay at Couples. The resort offers its own private island where

couples can bask in the buff. Couples is more upscale and, we think, a little classier than either of the Sandals resorts in the Ocho Rios area. Accommodations are first class, and the food is among the best in the area, with a choice of four restaurants featuring widely varied cuisine. See chapter 6.

- **Almond Beach Club** (Barbados; ☎ **800/4-ALMOND** in the U.S., or 246/ 432-7840): On the island's swanky West Coast, Almond Beach Club was established in 1991 as the first all-inclusive resort on Barbados. Accommodations are in seven low-rise three-story buildings, and everything's included. To break the monotony of dining in one place every night, an eat-around option exists at neighboring hotels. Lively nightly entertainment is offered, followed by days spent enjoying a trio of freshwater swimming pools, a fitness center, fishing, windsurfing, kayaking, or even banana boating. See chapter 10.

- **Almond Beach Village** (Barbados; ☎ **800/4-ALMOND** in the U.S., or 246/422-4900): Set on 30 acres of prime beachfront property 15 miles north of the capital of Bridgetown, this is a companion resort to the also all-inclusive Almond Beach Club (see above). Rooms are spread among seven three- or four-story buildings. Best are the units lying along the beach with views of the Caribbean. The resort offers four different restaurants and five bars, including our favorite, Enid's, for a typically Bajan cuisine. Lively entertainment is presented, along with an array of sports, including a water-sports kiosk and nine freshwater swimming pools. See chapter 10.

10 The Best Restaurants

- **Norma at the Wharfhouse** (Montego Bay, Jamaica; ☎ **876/979-2745**): In a coral stone warehouse, this is Mo Bay's finest adventure in dining out. It's the domain of Norma Shirley, the foremost female restaurateur in Jamaica. With a view of Montego Bay glittering in the background, Ms. Shirley serves a nouvelle Jamaican cuisine that is without equal in the area. From Caribbean lobster steamed in Red Stripe beer (the island's local brew) to jerk chicken with flambéed mangoes, from chateaubriand larded with pâté in a peppercorn sauce to grilled deviled crab backs, Ms. Shirley sets a table that keeps them coming back for more. See chapter 4.

- **Sugar Mill Restaurant** (Montego Bay, Jamaica; ☎ **876/953-2314**): In the Half Moon Club, this is the premier restaurant at any of the megaresorts in the Mo Bay area. Chef Hans Schenk may be from Switzerland, but he pioneered a style of cookery using local ingredients that is innovative for the island. For example, he'll take a classic Dijon mustard and blend it with the island's local pick-me-up, Pickapeppa, creating unique taste sensations. His smoked north-coast marlin is without equal, and he makes his own version of bouillabaisse à la Jamaican that is the island's finest. See chapter 4.

- **The Pork Pit** (Montego Bay, Jamaica; ☎ **876/952-1046**): It may look like a dump, but The Pork Pit is a classic, the best place on Jamaica's north coast for the famous jerk pork or jerk chicken. The highly spiced meat is barbecued slowly over wood fires until crisp and brown. Its taste is unique, and will make you forget about any so-called barbecues you might have sampled elsewhere. Of course, only a Red Stripe beer would do to wash it all down. See chapter 4.

- **Evita's Italian Restaurant** (Ocho Rios, Jamaica; ☎ **876/974-2333**): Evita's reigns supreme in an area not noted for having top-notch restaurants outside of the hotels. Evita (actually Eva Myers) is a local culinary star, devoting at least half her menu to pastas. Her recipes are wide ranging, from the north to the south of

Italy. Try her snapper stuffed with crabmeat or the lobster and scampi in a buttery white cream sauce—everything washed down with a good Italian vino. See chapter 6.

- **Blue Mountain Inn** (near Kingston, Jamaica; ☎ 876/927-1700): The continental and Caribbean cuisine matches the elegant setting on the grounds of a coffee plantation from the 18th century, high on the slopes of Blue Mountain, which produces the world's best and most expensive coffee. Steaks and seafood dominate the repertoire, and the chef is never better than when preparing his lobster thermidor or his tender chateaubriand with a classic Béarnaise sauce. See chapter 7.
- **Carambola** (Barbados; ☎ 246/432-0832): Standing on the upper edge of a sea-side cliff, with one of the most dramatic and panoramic terraces in the Caribbean for dining, this is the island's most romantic dining spot, and serves some of the best food, a unique blend of Thai and continental cuisine among other influences and inspirations. See chapter 10.
- **The Cliff** (Barbados; ☎ 246/432-1922): Opened in 1995, The Cliff quickly became one of the island's premier dining choices. It's an open-air restaurant blasted into a coral-stone cliff and set on four levels. The menu, a combination of West Indian and international creations, is of the highest level. The grilled snapper, drizzled in three types of coriander sauce, is just one of the innovative touches to this all-too-familiar dish. Sushi is presented when available, and the fresh local tuna is terrific. See chapter 10.
- **Olives Bar & Bistro** (Barbados; ☎ 246/432-2112): Olives Bar & Bistro occupies the site of the first two-story house ever built in Holetown. Its historic status, however, is not why savvy foodies flock here. The Mediterranean and Caribbean cuisine is unique on the island, and in honor of its name, only olive oil is used to prepare these savory dishes. One of the many stellar examples in the chef's repertoire is yellowfin tuna marinated and seared rare, then served on a bed of roast garlic mashed potatoes with grilled ratatouille. See chapter 10.
- **The Orchid Room** (Barbados; ☎ 246/422-2335): In the Colony Club Hotel, this dining room offers a plantation-house ambience complete with white-glove service. It's one of the most formal and elegant dining venues on the island, to be savored and reserved for that special evening. Sparkling chandeliers and period furnishings form the mere backdrop for this successful blend of a French and West Indian cuisine. Gallic flair is brought to the fresh and often home-grown local ingredients. A cold lettuce soup with peppercorns may not sound like much, but the chefs manage to bring out natural flavors in all their dishes. Their grilled dorado—laid on a puree of eggplant and potato and dressed with olive oil and lime—is worth crossing the island to sample. See chapter 10.
- **Bagatelle Restaurant** (Barbados; ☎ 246/421-6767): Housed in one of the island's most historic buildings, this is fine Barbadian dining at its best, special-izing in a French-influenced Caribbean cuisine. Candles and lanterns illuminate the ancient place, forming a backdrop for such delectable fare as homemade duck liver pâté, deviled Caribbean crab backs, and smoked flying-fish mousse. The service is as gracious as the setting. See chapter 10.

11 The Best Shopping Buys

Jamaica and Barbados aren't the serious shopping meccas of the Caribbean in the way that San Juan, St. Thomas, and St. Maarten are. But there are some good deals here, on both islands, especially in arts and crafts.

- **Art:** Its paintings may never rival that of Haitian artists when they are at their finest, but Jamaica is at least the second-best center for art in the Caribbean. Prices are still reasonable, too, even when the artist has a certain renown. Although paintings are sold all over the island, the finest art is found in Kingston at either the **Frame Centre Gallery** or the **Mutual Life Gallery,** the two leading display showcases for the best of the island's artistic talent. See chapter 7.

   In Barbados, art is displayed at many sources, with quality work showing up at the **Art Foundry** at Heritage Park (☎ **246/426-0714**). See chapter 11.

- **Handcrafts:** If you see something you like, either in Barbados or Jamaica, you'd better purchase it on the spot, as it isn't likely to turn up again. Many Jamaicans produce unique creations, a one-time carving or a one-time straw basket, then vary their pattern if they make it again. Crafts come in many forms, ranging from alabaster carvings to wood carvings and weavings. Some wood carvings show extreme style and others are so hideous you wonder why they were carved in the first place. Any outlet of **Things Jamaican,** including one in Montego Bay (see chapter 4), displays a good assortment of Jamaican crafts, as does **Harmony Hall** outside Ocho Rios on the north coast (see chapter 6). In Bridgetown, the capital of Barbados, **Articrafts** (☎ **246/427-5767**) has the most impressive display of Bajan arts and crafts (see chapter 11).

- **Fashions:** Many artisans in both Jamaica and Barbados produce quality resort wear. (On many other islands, the clothing is inferior and often tacky.) Both Jamaican and Bajan women are known as good seamstresses, and they often make quite passable copies based on the works of top designers and sell them at a fraction of the original's price. Some of the best resort wear—for both men and women—is found in Jamaica at **Caribatik Island Fabrics,** a famous outlet outside Falmouth (see chapter 4). In Barbados, **Colours of De Caribbean** has a very individualized display of tropical clothing (see chapter 11).

- **Jewelry and Watches:** Sometimes watches at various outlets in Jamaica sell for 20% to 40% off stateside prices. Major international brands are sold, but you must buy from a reliable dealer—not from vendors hustling so-called gold Rolex watches. Seiko watches in Barbados are often priced 20% below stateside prices.

   Jamaican gemstones include coral agate and black coral, and many fashionable pieces are made from these stones. Handmade necklaces are sold everywhere, even on the beach. Dozens of outlets in both Jamaica and Barbados, especially at shopping malls, sell a vast array of jewelry and watches, but you must shop carefully.

12 The Best After-Dark Fun

Jamaican reggae and Bajan calypso are never better than when heard on their own turf. Yet there's a surprising lack of nightclubs outside of the hotels on these islands—that is, clubs that are reasonably safe for tourists to visit. (Many visitors don't want to take their chances traveling potholed and often dangerous roads at night.) So the diversions, especially live bands, come to the hotels instead. Nearly all major hotels feature entertainment in the evening, maybe even fire-eaters and limbo dancers.

But there are some nighttime diversions outside the hotels, including the following:

- **An Evening Cruise Aboard the** *Calico* (Montego Bay, Jamaica; ☎ **876/ 952-5860**): This 55-foot wooden ketch sails from the Montego Bay waterfront. From Wednesday through Saturday, there is no better or more romantic way to spend an evening at Mo Bay than by taking this cruise. From 5 to 7pm you sail into the sunset while enjoying drinks and the sound of reggae. See chapter 4.

- **Combo at Lollypop on the Beach** (Montego Bay, Jamaica; ☎ **876/953-5314**): A half mile west of Tryall at Sandy Bay forms the setting for this event staged every Wednesday beginning at 7:30pm. You get not only a zesty Jamaican dinner of seafood and jerk meats, but a robust evening program of dancing, including reggae and the limbo. See chapter 4.

- **Baxters Road** (Barbados): This entire street in Bridgetown, the capital, is where Bajans go "caf crawling": hopping from bar to bar while listening to records, often the scratchy recorded voice of Billie Holiday. Enid's is the most famous cafe to check out. The joint's jumping after 11pm, especially on a Friday or Saturday night. See chapter 11.

- **1627 and All That** (Barbados; ☎ **246/428-1627**): Combining entertainment and dancing, 1627 and All That is the most exciting choice on a Thursday night in Barbados. Sample a large buffet of Bajan food and then sit back to watch a historic and cultural presentation. See chapter 11.

- **Plantation Restaurant and Garden Theatre** (Barbados; ☎ **246/428-5048**): Here you'll find the best evening dinner theater and Caribbean cabaret on the island. You get lots of exotic costumes, plenty of reggae and calypso, and the inevitable limbo. Dinner and show are presented every Wednesday and Friday night. See chapter 11.

Getting to Know Jamaica   **2**

Most visitors already have a mental picture of Jamaica before they arrive: its boisterous culture of reggae and Rastafarianism, its white sandy beaches, and its jungles, rivers, mountains, and clear waterfalls. Jamaica's art and cuisine are also remarkable.

Jamaica can be a tranquil and intriguing island, but there's no denying that it's plagued by crime and drugs. There is also palpable racial tension here. But many visitors are unaffected; they're escorted from the airport to their hotel grounds and venture out only on expensive organized tours. These vacationers are largely sheltered from the more unpredictable and sometimes dangerous side of island life. Those who want to see "the real Jamaica," or at least to see the island in greater depth, should be prepared for some hassle. Vendors on the beaches and in the markets can be particularly aggressive.

Most Jamaicans, in spite of hard times, have unrelenting good humor and genuinely welcome visitors to the island. Others, certainly a minority, harm the tourism business, so that many visitors vow never to return. Jamaica's appealing aspects have to be weighed against its poverty and problems, the legacy of traumatic political upheavals that have characterized the island in past decades, beginning in the 1970s.

So should you go? By all means, yes. Be prudent and cautious— just as if you were visiting New York, Miami, or Los Angeles. But Jamaica is worth it! The island has fine hotels and terrific food. It's well-geared to couples who come to tie the knot or celebrate their honeymoon. As for sports, Jamaica boasts the best golf courses in the West Indies, and its landscape affords visitors a lot of activities that often aren't available on other islands, like rafting and serious mountain hiking. The island also has some of the finest diving waters in the world.

This country lies 90 miles south of Cuba, with which it was chummy in the 1970s (when much of the world feared that Jamaica was going Communist). It's the third largest of the Caribbean islands, with some 4,400 square miles of predominantly green, lush land; a mountain ridge that climbs to 7,400 feet above sea level; and many beautiful white-sand beaches with clear blue sea.

Jamaica

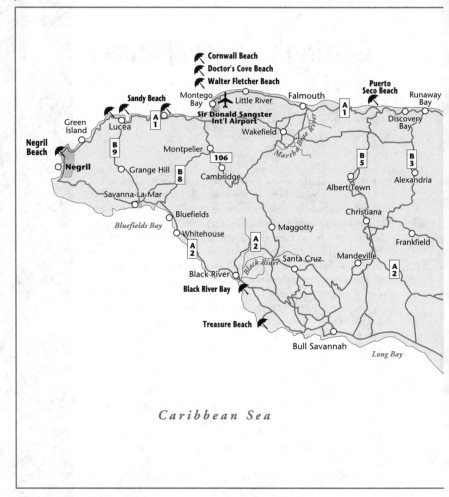

1 The Natural Environment

Jamaica and the rest of the West Indian archipelago are summits of a submarine string of mountains, which in prehistoric times probably formed a land bridge between modern Mexico and Venezuela. Although not the area's largest island, Jamaica offers a diverse landscape.

Covering about 4,240 square miles, Jamaica is approximately the size of Connecticut. The island is some 146 miles long, with widths of 22 to 58 miles.

Millions of years ago, volcanoes thrust up from the ocean floor, forming mountains, ranging to 7,402 feet high, which are loftier than any along the eastern seaboard of North America. These mountains, located in an east-to-west line in central Jamaica, contain more than 120 rivers and many waterfalls as well as thermal springs. In the high mountains of the east, the landscape features semi-tropical rain forest and copses of mist-covered pines.

The mountains are bordered on the north and east by a narrow coastal plain fringed with beaches. The flat, arid southern coastline reminds visitors of African savanna or Indian plains, whereas the moist, fertile north coast slopes steeply from hills down to excellent beaches.

Much of Jamaica is underlain by limestone, dotted with dozens of caves that store large reservoirs of naturally filtered drinking water.

Almost everything grows in Jamaica, as proved by colonial British botanists who imported flowers and fruits from Asia, the Pacific, Africa, and Canada. The island contains unique kinds of orchids, ferns, bromeliads, and varieties of fruit, like the Bombay mango, that don't flourish elsewhere in the Western Hemisphere. Birds, insects, and other animals are also abundant.

Framing the capital of Kingston, the Blue Mountains dominate the eastern third of the island. This is the country's most panoramic area, and it's split through with a network of paths, trails, and bad roads—a paradise for hikers. From this region comes Blue Mountain coffee, the most expensive in the world.

Younger than the Blue Mountains, the John Crow Mountains rise at the north-eastern end of the island. Only the most skilled mountain climbers or advanced hikers should attempt this rugged karst terrain. It rains here almost daily, creating a rain-forest effect.

Jamaica's longest river is called Black River, and it's bordered by marshes, swamps, and mangroves where bird and animal life, including reptiles, flourish. Black River, which is also the name of a small port, is in the southwestern section, lying east of Savanna-La-Mer and reached along route A2.

2 The Regions in Brief

Montego Bay   The second-largest city in Jamaica, Montego Bay serves as the capital and has a busy airport served by international flights. Here's where you'll find the greatest concentration of resorts and some of the island's finest beaches and golf courses. Tourists come to "Mo Bay" for its duty-free shopping, good restaurants, late-night discos, museums, historic buildings, and tours of nearby rum distilleries.

Negril   Situated near Jamaica's relatively arid western tip, Negril enjoys a repu-tation as the nudist center of the West Indies, with a kind of gently provocative do-as-you-please attitude. Its 7-mile beach is one of the longest uninterrupted stretches of sand in the Caribbean. Because of a boom in hotel construction, the Negril region is no longer the hippie hideaway it was during the 1960s and early '70s. The area has become big business and mainstream, competing aggressively for tourist dollars once headed almost exclusively to Montego Bay and Ocho Rios.

The South Coast   The little-visited South Coast, lying east of Negril along the A2 (the road to Kingston), is undiscovered Jamaica—although it's getting better known all the time. Contrary to the island's lush, tropical image, this area is dry and arid. Hotels are few and far between, and they are frequently of the mom-and-pop persuasion. The chief draw here is **Treasure Beach,** tucked away on the secluded coast. Savvy locals—many descended from Scottish seamen wrecked off the coast—consider their beachfront a secret on the verge of being discovered by the general public. Regrettably, undertow makes swimming a bit tricky, but the beach is secluded and tranquil, and dramatic waves crash into the gray sands.

Mandeville   Located in south-central Jamaica, Mandeville is the country's highest-altitude town, and is built in a style strongly influenced by the English. A gateway for tours of the Blue Mountains, Mandeville was the first community in Jamaica to receive tourists on a large scale (Victorian English visitors looking for a cool mountain retreat). It is now the center of the island's noted coffee cultivation. A sense of slow-paced colonial charm remains a trademark of the town.

The North Coast   The region's primary natural attractions include the steeply sloping terrain, which has challenged the architectural skill of Jamaica's most sophisticated hotel developers and provided the setting for panoramic public gardens and dramatic waterfalls.

Beginning directly west of Ocho Rios is the satellite town of **Runaway Bay,** which boasts a handful of resorts opening onto some good beaches and has the distinct advantage of not being overrun, as many parts of Ocho Rios are.

Set on a deep-water harbor easily able to accommodate cruise ships, **Ocho Rios** boasts a dense concentration of resort hotels and other vacation spots. A relative newcomer to the tourist trade, the community lures visitors with its natural beauty and the aura of history left behind by Spanish colonists.

The hub of verdant eastern Jamaica, **Port Antonio** has retained a sense of glamour ever since financier J. P. Morgan and actors Bette Davis, Ginger Rogers, and Errol Flynn took their vacations—and their paramours—here many years ago. Frequently photographed for its Victorian/Caribbean architecture (with slightly rotted gingerbread), the town is refreshing and not as touristy as Negril, Ocho Rios, and Montego Bay.

Kingston & Spanish Town   Located on the southeast coast, Kingston is Jamaica's capital, largest city, and principal port. There are also extensive poverty-stricken areas in Kingston, though, and it's not the safest place to be—it's not really a tourist destination. Nearby are the remains of **Port Royal,** once an infamous lair of pirates and renegades, most of whom were unofficially pressed into service to the English Crown. Port Royal was superseded by Kingston after being destroyed by earthquakes in 1692 and again in 1907. Kingston is a cosmopolitan city with approximately 650,000 residents in its metropolitan area. It serves as the country's main economic, cultural, and government center. Residents proudly say it is the world's reggae capital as well. The city's northern district, called New Kingston, includes most of the capital's high-rises, showcase modern buildings, upscale hotels, and upscale private homes.

Twenty minutes by car west of Kingston is **Spanish Town,** the country's capital from 1534 to 1872. It was the second town built by Spanish colonists in Jamaica after Nueva Sevilla (now abandoned). The slow-paced village today contains the Cathedral of St. James (early 16th century)—one of the oldest Spanish churches in the West Indies—and memorials to English colonization.

The Blue Mountains   A land of soaring peaks and deep valleys with luxuriant vegetation, the Blue Mountain range rises to the north of Kingston. Mountain roads wind and dip, and they are in bad repair, so don't try to visit on your own. Road signs do not exist in most places, and it's easy to get lost. However, travel agents in Kingston can hook you up with tours through this area, with its coffee plantations and rum factories. Maintained by the government, the prime part of the mountain range is the 192-acre Blue Mountain–John Crow Mountain National Park. The most popular climb begins at Whitfield Hall (see chapter 7), a high-altitude hostel and coffee estate 6 miles from the hamlet of Mavis Bank. The summit of Blue Mountain Peak towers at 3,000 feet above sea level.

3 Jamaica Today

Those who haven't been to Jamaica in a long time are in for some surprises. The island has changed a lot, and 1997 saw a healthy 11% increase in tourism on an island that now boasts 20,000 hotel rooms. Though visitors were once frightened away by drug-related crime and aggressive hustlers, there has been a mass return of adventurers, nature lovers, sports enthusiasts (especially golfers), and honeymooners—even a jet-setter or two.

More and more visitors in the late '90s are visiting Jamaica by cruise ship. Cruise passenger arrivals to the island in 1997 were up 10% over the previous year. Part of Ocho Rios' increase can be attributed to the recently completed harbor-dredging project that now permits entry of larger-draft vessels.

Agriculture and mining, the traditional ways that Jamaicans have earned money, have declined in relation to tourism. If anything, Jamaica approaches the millennium almost too heavily dependent on tourism. If the world economy grows shaky and its visitors diminish, Jamaica will be unduly affected.

Jamaica's economy is battered, and export earnings continue a downward spiral. With little money to keep them in state-of-the-art or even passable condition, its highways and city streets, especially those in Kingston, are potholed and pitted. Imported goods and food undercut local farmers, making it tougher for them to eke out a living. And even though its soil is extremely fertile, the island has had severe summer droughts.

Jamaica's many problems remain, but the government is taking strong action to handle its problems, especially crime, since it cannot afford to let a negative image impact on much-needed tourism dollars.

On March 8, 1997, one of the most charismatic figures in Jamaica died: Michael Manley, the island's former premier, who dominated Jamaican politics for a generation and became a spokesman for Third World causes. Forced to step down in 1992 because of failing health, Manley was born to wealth and privilege but earned world fame as an advocate for the impoverished. His father was Norman Washington Manley, who led Jamaica to independence and was prime minister from 1955 to 1962. The younger Manley sought a closer relationship with Cuba, which strained his ties with the United States.

Under Michael Manley, many of Jamaica's young doctors, educators, and other professionals left the country in the '70s for careers in the United States or England. But under Manley's successors, Prime Minister Edward Seaga and later P. J. Patterson, some came back to rekindle new enterprises.

Politics today remain as volatile as ever. In fact, right before Christmas in 1997, island-wide parliamentary elections, often notoriously violent, opened in the old-fashioned way: with gunfire. In this election only a dozen were wounded. (In 1980, elections claimed the lives of some 800 citizens.)

In spite of the election gunfire, Jamaica is large enough to allow the more or less peaceful coexistence of all kinds of people, everyone from expatriate English aristocrats to dyed-in-the-wool Rastafarians. Despite its long history of social unrest, political turmoil, unemployment, drugs, and crime, Jamaica remains one of the most interesting islands in the Caribbean to visit. The allure of Jamaica has always been there: the tumbling waterfalls, the tropical rain forests, the wildflower-covered mountains, the plantation Great Houses, and best of all, the warm people—now a multiracial mix of some 2.5 million souls.

4 History 101

Dateline

- ca. 6000 B.C. Indian groups settle Jamaica.
- ca. A.D. 600 Arawak Indians come to the island.
- 1494 Columbus visits Jamaica.
- 1503–04 Columbus is stranded on the north coast.
- 1509 Spain establishes colony at St. Ann's Bay.
- 1513 First enslaved Africans arrive.
- 1520 Sugarcane cultivation introduced.

continues

IN THE BEGINNING   Jamaica has long been viewed as one of the most desirable islands of the West Indies, richer and more diverse than many of the sandier, smaller, and less dramatic islands that lie nearby. Attempts by outsiders to control Jamaica have influenced much of its history.

Jamaica was settled around 6000 B.C. by Stone-Age people about whom little is known. They were displaced around A.D. 600 by the Arawak, Indians who originated in northern South America (probably in the area of modern Guyana). Skillful fishers and crafters of pottery and bead items, they had copper-colored skin and lived in thatch-covered huts similar to those used in parts of Jamaica today. The Arawak made flint knives and spears tipped with sharks' teeth, but they never developed the bow and arrow. They lived mainly on a diet of fish and turtle steak. The Arawak were completely unprepared for the horrors brought by the Spanish conquest.

A CRUEL COLONY In 1494, during his second voyage to the New World, Christopher Columbus visited Jamaica and claimed the island for the Spanish monarchy. Although he quickly departed to search for gold and treasure elsewhere, he returned accidentally in 1503 and 1504, when he was stranded with a group of Spanish sailors for many months off Jamaica's northern coastline while they repaired their worm-eaten ships.

Beginning in 1509, Spaniards from the nearby colony of Santo Domingo established two settlements on Jamaica: one in the north (Nueva Sevilla, later abandoned) in modern St. Ann Parish and another in the south, San Jago de la Vega (St. James of the Plain), on the site of present-day Spanish Town. Pirates estimated the Arawak population in Jamaica at the time to be about 60,000.

In 1513 the first African slaves reached Jamaica, and in 1520 sugarcane cultivation was introduced. In the 1540s the Spanish Crown grudgingly offered the entire island to Columbus's family as a reward for his service to Spain. Columbus's descendants did nothing to develop the island's vast potential, however. Angered by the lack of immediate profit (abundantly available from gold and silver mines in Mexico and Peru), the Spanish colonists accomplished very little other than to wipe out the entire Arawak population. Forced into slavery, every last Arawak was either executed or died of disease, overwork, or malnutrition.

RAISING THE UNION JACK After 146 years as a badly and cruelly administered backwater of the Spanish Empire, Jamaica met with a change of fortune when a British armada arrived at Kingston Harbour in 1655. The fleet had sailed on orders from Oliver Cromwell, but it had failed in its mission to conquer the well-fortified Spanish colony of Santo Domingo. Almost as an afterthought, it went on to Jamaica. Within a day, the Spaniards surrendered the whole island to the British, who allowed them to escape. Most of the Spaniards immigrated to nearby Cuba, although a handful remained secretly on the island's north coast.

- **1655** British troops overrun Jamaica.
- **1658** English repel Spanish invaders.
- **1661** Major English colonization begins.
- **1670** Hundreds of privateers given royal protection in Jamaica.
- **1692** Earthquake destroys Port Royal.
- **1739** Rebellious Maroons sign treaty with English.
- **1800** Census reveals huge majority of blacks in Jamaica.
- **1808** Slave trade abolished by Great Britain.
- **1838** Slavery ended.
- **1866** Jamaica becomes a British Crown Colony.
- **1930** Jamaicans push for autonomy.
- **1943** Bauxite mining begins.
- **1944** Universal adult suffrage instituted.
- **1960s** Tourist industry grows.
- **1962** Jamaica achieves independence on August 6.
- **1970s** Bob Marley and reggae gain world fame.
- **1972** Michael Manley, a socialist, becomes prime minister.
- **1980** Edward Seaga, a moderate, succeeds Manley.
- **1980s** High unemployment spreads, though tourism thrives.
- **1988** Hurricane Gilbert devastates Jamaica.
- **1989** Manley, now moderate, returns to power.
- **1992** P. J. Patterson becomes prime minister.
- **1997** Patriarch Michael Manley dies; elections retain Patterson and People's National Party.

Six months later, British colonists arrived, but many died from poisoning and disease. In 1657, Spaniards based in Cuba initiated a last-ditch effort to recapture

Jamaica. Two of the fiercest and biggest battles in Jamaican history pitted the Spanish against the English. The defection from the Spanish by some Maroons (escaped slaves and their descendants living in the Jamaican mountains) led to the permanent exit in 1660 of Spanish troops from Jamaica. Humiliated, these soldiers escaped to Cuba in canoes.

In 1661 the British began to colonize Jamaica in earnest. They appointed a governor directly responsible to the Crown, with orders to create a governing council elected by the colonists. All children born of English subjects in Jamaica became free citizens of England. In 2 years the population of Jamaica grew to more than 4,000. Hostilities between England and Spain continued, with occasional skirmishes and richly successful raids by the English on Spanish colonies in Cuba and Central America.

The Maroons formed an important subculture in Jamaica. They lived independently in the mountainous interior, often murdering every white person who transgressed their boundaries. In the coastal areas, the population swelled with the importation of many slaves from Africa and the immigration of more than 1,000 settlers from Barbados. Additional settlers came from the ranks of semiautonomous bands of privateers, who with the full approval of the British Crown plundered any ship or settlement belonging to nations hostile to England. Under Gov. Thomas Modyford, Britain initiated a policy of full protection of privateers at Port Royal, near Kingston. Modyford simultaneously encouraged cacao, coffee, and sugarcane cultivation, tended by an increasing number of slaves.

A few years later, Britain committed one of the most cynical, yet practical, acts in the history of Jamaica when it appointed the notorious privateer, Welsh-born Henry Morgan, as the island's lieutenant governor. Morgan's previous bloody but profitable exploits had included plundering Panama City and Porto Bello on the Isthmus of Panama, both laden with treasure from the mines of Peru awaiting shipment to Spain. Despite the well-known torments and atrocities he had inflicted on non-English colonists throughout the Caribbean, Morgan was buried with honors in 1688 at Port Royal. By then more than 17,000 persons lived in Jamaica. Port Royal reveled in its reputation as "the wickedest city on earth." It likely contained more houses of dubious repute than any other contemporary city in the Western Hemisphere.

EARTHQUAKES, FIRES & PROSPERITY   British interest in Jamaica grew as opportunities for adding profits and territory increased. In 1687, Sir Hans Sloane, physician to powerful aristocrats of Britain and namesake of London's Sloane Square, wrote two influential scholarly books on the geography, flora, fauna, and people of Jamaica. The volumes helped convince Britain to continue its investments in the island.

In 1690 a slave rebellion was crushed by the British, who executed its leaders. Some participants escaped to the mountains, where they joined the independent Maroons.

On June 7, 1692, just before noon, one of the most violent earthquakes in history struck the city of Port Royal. In less than 20 minutes the three shocks, ascending in intensity, caused the sea to recede and then rush back with terrible force, drowning the virtuous and wicked alike. Much of the city actually dropped into the sea. A handful of survivors attempted to rebuild parts of the city, but in 1704 a great fire destroyed every building except a stone-sided fort.

Although the centerpiece of Jamaica had disappeared, the countryside was becoming one of the world's great producers of sugar. This corresponded neatly with the increasing demand in England for sugar to sweeten the flood of tea imported from Asia. Within 4 years of the destruction of Port Royal, Jamaica contained more than 47,000 inhabitants. They were divided into three main classes: white property owners (planters, traders, and professionals, many of whom prospered), slaves from Africa and their descendants (the largest by far in number but with little power), and white indentured servants.

In 1694 a French fleet led by Admiral Du Casse invaded the north shore of Jamaica, at Carlisle Bay. At the time France and Britain were at war in Europe as well, and the French plan was meant to divert English warships from Europe. Although the French were eventually driven back to their ships, they destroyed at least 50 sugar plantations and captured some 1,300 slaves. Six years later the French fleet was counterattacked by the English off the coast of Colombia, but after 5 days of concentrated fighting, the battle ended in a draw. Back in Kingston, the captains responsible for the early withdrawal of the British fleet from the fighting were convicted of misconduct and shot.

POWER STRUGGLES   The struggle for control of Jamaica intensified over the next 50 years as the island became one of the most profitable outposts of the British Empire, despite hurricanes, pirate raids, and slave rebellions. For ease of government, it was divided into 13 parishes, whose boundaries remain today.

Most troublesome for the English were the Maroons, who escaped control by fleeing into the mountains and forests. In 1734, in one of many dramatic battles, the English captured the Maroon stronghold of Nanny Town, destroying its buildings and killing many of its inhabitants. The survivors committed suicide by jumping off a cliff, preferring death to enslavement. By 1739, however, both the English and the Maroons recognized the virtues of increased cooperation, and they signed a series of peace agreements. The Maroons were given tax-free land in different parts of the island. They were allowed to govern themselves and to be tried and punished by their own leaders, who could not, however, sentence a subject to death. Also very important, the Maroons agreed to capture all runaway slaves and return them to their masters, and to assist in suppressing any slave rebellion.

In 1741 the British navy used Jamaica as a base of operations for mostly unsuccessful military strikes against Spanish strongholds in Cartagena, Colombia, and on the Isthmus of Panama. Caused by harsh conditions, slave rebellions in 1746 and 1760 led to many deaths. The British ended both revolts, killing many, and sending most survivors to Honduras to work in swamps and sweltering timberlands.

By the time of the American Revolution, the population of Jamaica had reached almost 210,000, some 193,000 of whom were slaves. After 1776 some Loyalist residents of the United States moved to Jamaica. France, which sided with the Americans against the British, sent an opportunistic militia to the West Indies. It captured many British islands in the eastern Caribbean, and Jamaicans trembled with anticipation of a French invasion. Admiral Horatio Nelson, later famous for defeating Napoléon's French fleet at the Battle of Trafalgar, drilled the Jamaican garrisons to repel the expected attack. It never came, however.

Naval skirmishes among the British, Spanish, and French continued offshore, with Jamaica usually serving as the stronghold for British forces. In 1782, Admiral George Brydges Rodney defeated a huge French force off Dominica, killing more than half of the 6,000 men intended for an invasion of Jamaica. Rodney brought the captured French ships to the rebuilt Port Royal. Appreciative colonists voted to spend £3,000 to erect a statue in his honor, and the British government made him a peer.

In 1793, Britain tried to influence a rapidly disintegrating situation in nearby Haiti, a dependency of France. Although several Haitian cities were captured by English troops, an outbreak of disease and the fierce opposition of the noted leader Toussaint L'Ouverture (who later ruled all Haiti) soon ended the venture.

Also in 1793, some 5,000 British troops equipped with specially trained bloodhounds imported from Cuba fought another bloody war against the Maroons in the Jamaican highlands. The British sent the captured Maroons first to Canada, then to Sierra Leone, in West Africa. Those not involved were allowed to remain in Jamaica.

An official census in 1800 revealed a Jamaican population of 300,000 blacks and 20,000 whites. This disparity was not lost upon either the powers in London or the leaders of the increasingly politicized blacks.

Despite revolts by blacks and military expeditions to neighboring islands, Jamaica in 1803 exported the largest sugar crop in the country's history. In part the island's wealth resulted from acts of Parliament that imposed high tariffs on sugar imported into Britain from Cuba, Haiti, Martinique, Guadeloupe, and other areas. The Jamaican planters maintained one of the best-organized political machines in London, lobbying hard and spending great amounts of money to retain the trade barriers that kept sugar prices artificially high in England. Adding to the wealth was coffee; in 1814 the island exported a record crop.

After Nelson defeated Napoléon at Trafalgar in 1805, the huge sums expended by Jamaica to defend against French raiders decreased dramatically. At the same time, Jamaica's role as a depot for smuggling contraband British goods to Cuba and Spanish colonies of South America also diminished. Within 20 years the island's economy worsened considerably, signaling an end to a great era of Jamaican prosperity.

SLAVERY & PROSPERITY END   After the United States became independent in 1776, Britain imposed an embargo on U.S. products and cut off trade between North America's eastern seaboard and Jamaica, a condition that caused great hardship throughout the island.

Adding to Jamaica's woes was increasing popular sentiment in Britain against the slave trade. The importation of forced laborers from Africa was outlawed in 1807, and in 1838 slavery itself was made illegal in all British dependencies, including Jamaica. Parliament voted £20 million to compensate the slave owners. Partly because of Jamaica's influence in Parliament, almost £6 million of that money was designated for the island's slave owners. Freed blacks celebrated throughout Jamaica, with credit for the legislation going (rightly or wrongly) to Queen Victoria.

The problem now arose of finding workers for the labor-intensive sugar plantations. Planters offered blacks only low wages (about 9 pence a day) for the difficult labor, and in addition many former enslaved persons refused to work under any circumstances for their former owners. As a result, the large sugar industry declined.

The Jamaica Railway opened in 1845, having been built by inexpensive laborers from India. Any benefits the line might have offered the sugar planters, however, was quickly undercut by passage in 1847 of the Free Trade Act. Designed to encourage untaxed trade in the British Empire, the act removed the protection enjoyed by Jamaican sugar in Britain, placing it on even par with the plentiful, cheap sugar produced in other parts of the Caribbean.

Between 1850 and 1852 epidemics of Asian cholera and smallpox ripped through the island's overcrowded shantytowns, whose sanitation facilities were minimal. More than 32,000 people died from the maladies brought from other parts of the British Empire. At the same time, Jamaica suffered from an exodus of creative entrepreneurs, a lack of funds to run the government, and a continuing decline of the agricultural base. The island's workforce vehemently protested low wages and competition from cheap labor brought in from British dependencies in India and China.

REVOLTS & REFORMS   As a result of the American Civil War fought between 1861 and 1865, many vital shipments formerly brought to Jamaica from North America were blocked or rendered very expensive. During this period, the lieutenant governor of the colony, at odds as usual with both planters and laborers, publicly described the colony as being "in a state of degeneration." Labor unrest, attempts by blacks to overturn the government, and interference in Jamaican affairs by committees of English Baptists and London-based liberals plagued the planters. In 1866, Jamaican laborers mounted an extremely bloody revolt, which was put down by English troops. Many changes were initiated thereafter, however, including the recall of the very unpopular lieutenant governor of the island. Eventually, a more liberal form of government emerged, and island residents had a larger voice in Jamaican affairs. The police and judicial systems were reorganized into a fairer system directly responsible to the British Crown, rather than to local potentates who had often abused their power. Also, administrative divisions of the island's parishes were changed and their numbers reduced.

Meanwhile, telegraph communication with Europe was established in 1869, the Jamaica Railway was extended, and nickel coins, guaranteed by the Bank of England, were issued for the first time. The educational system was improved, great irrigation works were initiated, and the dependency became known for the enlightened application of British ways. Hurricanes seemed to demolish parts of the island at regular intervals, however, and the power struggle between British authorities in London and local administrators in Kingston went on.

British tourism to Jamaica began in the 1890s, and a quintet of hotels was built to house the administrators and investors who showed keen interest in developing the island's fertile land. A Lands Department was organized to sell government-held land to local farmers cheaply and on easy terms. The island's teachers were organized into unions, and the railroad was extended to Jamaica's northeast tip at Port Antonio. New bridges and improved roads also helped open the island. Frustrated by low sugar prices, Jamaican planters invested heavily in the production of bananas.

On January 14, 1907, another great earthquake shattered much of the city of Kingston, destroying or damaging just about every building. More than 800 lives were lost, and total damage was estimated at £2 million. It seemed to be a repeat of the earthquake that had shattered Port Royal 215 years earlier. Parliament and the Church of England sent massive funds to rebuild Kingston. The new street plan remains the basis for the city's layout today.

JAMAICA IN THE WORLD WARS   During World War I, Jamaica sent about 10,000 men to fight with British forces. They were eventually deployed in Palestine, where they battled heroically against the Ottoman Empire. Many ships used in peacetime to export Jamaican agricultural products were commandeered for use in European waters. Martial law was imposed on Jamaica, and local volunteers were organized to defend the island from attack. In 1915, 1916, and 1917 the war effort was complicated by hurricanes that devastated the island's banana crop. But some progress was made: In May 1917, Jamaican women were given the right to vote.

In 1938, Alexander Bustamante organized Jamaica's first officially recognized labor union. At first imprisoned but later freed and knighted by the British, he is today regarded as a founder of modern Jamaica.

At the outbreak of World War II in 1939, Jamaica was placed under rigid control, and the governor set prices and censored the press, the telephones, the telegraph, and international mail. In 1940, the United States was granted the right to establish army and navy bases in British territories, including Jamaica, where two bases were quickly built. By 1943, many Jamaicans had moved to the United States to work in munitions factories. In the same year, bauxite, the raw material for making much-needed aluminum, was mined for the first time in St. Ann Parish. The next year a new constitution provided for universal adult suffrage.

In 1947, after the war, Jamaica served as the meeting place for discussions concerning the amalgamation of English-speaking lands of the Caribbean area into a single political unit. The countries sending representatives to the meetings included Barbados, Trinidad and Tobago, the Leeward Islands, the Windward Islands, British Guiana (now Guyana), and British Honduras (now Belize). The union never developed fully, however, mainly because of political infighting and local attachments.

FREEDOM ARRIVES In 1950, newly formed Radio Jamaica Ltd. (RJR) provided an outlet for the ideologies rapidly being shaped in Jamaica.

In 1951 the worst hurricane in almost 100 years completely demolished Port Royal for the third time. No serious attempt was made thereafter to rebuild the city, which had played a vital part in developing Jamaica.

In 1957, Jamaica attained full internal self-government under a system based on well-established English models. Lengthy celebrations marked the event. The same year, nearly 17,000 Jamaicans emigrated to England to find work because the island's economy was not growing as fast as the population. Concurrently, bauxite and alumina (processed bauxite) exports surged, and the government demanded and received a higher percentage of profits from the mining companies. With the advent of the intercontinental jet airliner, Jamaica's tourist industry also expanded at this time, and hotels were built to accommodate visitors from North America and Europe.

After the rise to power in 1959 of Fidel Castro, Jamaica cut many ties with Cuba, and established trade and cultural links with other islands, especially Puerto Rico. In 1959, Montego Bay airport was opened, and Kingston airport was expanded to handle the flood of visitors. Despite economic growth, however, large-scale emigration to Great Britain continued.

In 1961, Jamaica withdrew from the Federation of the West Indies, which had been formed in 1958, after Jamaicans voted to seek independence as a separate nation. The next year, on August 6, Jamaica achieved its independence, although still recognizing the British monarch as the formal head of state and maintaining other ties as a member of the Commonwealth of Nations. Sir Alexander Bustamante, head of the Jamaica Labour Party (JLP), became the country's first prime minister. Also in 1962, the Royal Hampshire Regiment— the last British troops in Jamaica—departed the island, thus ending the colonial era begun in 1655.

RECENT TIMES In 1966, Haile Selassie I, emperor of Ethiopia, came to Jamaica on a 3-day state visit. The stay sparked national interest in the emperor's life, and as a result there was a notable increase in Jamaican converts to Rastafarianism, a religion that venerates the late emperor, known earlier as Ras Tafari (see "Rastafarianism" later in this chapter). During the 1970s, the popularity of

Rastafarian musician Bob Marley and other Jamaican reggae performers spread around the world, giving the country an important role on the international music stage.

In 1972, Michael Manley, a trade unionist who headed the left-wing People's National Party (PNP), was sworn in for the first of what would eventually be several terms as Jamaica's prime minister. For many historians, this marked the beginning of full-scale ideological battles for the heart and soul of the Jamaican people. Jamaicans argued vehemently over whether the young nation should embrace socialism, and over its relationship with the United States. A noteworthy event of Manley's Democratic Socialism occurred in 1977, when Cuban President Fidel Castro paid a 6-day official visit to Jamaica, which led to a perception in Washington that Jamaican politics were increasingly shifting leftward. Despite Manley's political prowess, the months leading up to the 1980 elections were particularly violent, with episodes of civil disobedience and numerous deaths on both sides. The elections were won by the moderate, free-enterprise JLP, led by relatively conservative Edward Seaga, who became prime minister. Shortly afterward, Jamaica broke diplomatic ties with Cuba. Seaga's mandate was solidified in the 1983 elections, which the PNP claimed were unfairly run. Seaga attempted to promote economic growth and cut inflation, but with little success. Unemployment rose, as did violent crime.

In September 1988, the island was devastated by Hurricane Gilbert, which destroyed some 100,000 homes.

A much more moderate Manley returned to power in 1989. This time he sought friendly ties with the United States.

In the early 1990s Jamaica continued to face daunting economic difficulties, as unemployment hovered near 18% of the workforce. In Kingston there was gang violence, some reputedly tied to the country's main political parties. Tourism boomed, however. Manley retired in 1992 because of ill health and was succeeded by an associate, Percival J. Patterson, also a moderate. Patterson was confirmed in office when his PNP won 53 of 60 seats in the House of Representatives in elections in March 1993.

In the elections of 1997, Patterson continued his reign over Jamaica, consolidating his power. The Peoples National Party continued to hold the loyalty of the majority of voters.

The island also laid to rest one of its all-time major power brokers, the controversial former premier Michael Manley, who became prime minister in 1969, succeeding his father, Norman Manley. His left-wing politics, and especially his ties with Fidel Castro, brought an increasing strain with the United States. Manley later accused the U.S. of "overreacting" to his friendship with Castro. Manley also became one of the most forceful boosters of the Black Power movement that swept the Caribbean in the '70s and '80s.

5 The Jamaican People & Their Culture

RASTAFARIANISM

Although relatively small in number (it had about 14,000 firm adherents in the early 1980s), Rastafarians have had wide-ranging influence on Jamaican culture. Their identifying dreadlocks (long, sometimes braided, hair) can now be seen at virtually every level of Jamaican society.

To understand the origins of Rastafarianism, it's necessary to introduce Marcus Garvey. Born in 1887 in Jamaica's St. Ann Parish, Garvey did much to build black pride in the United States as well as in the West Indies. To combat the vast cultural upheavals wrought by slavery, Garvey founded the Universal Negro Improvement Association (UNIA) to raise the consciousness of blacks about a diaspora unmatched since the scattering of the Jews. Advocating a "back to Africa" kind of self-reliance, he aroused the loyalty of blacks and the hostility of whites. Garvey died in London in 1940, almost forgotten, but his body was later returned to Jamaica, where he received a hero's burial.

None of the power of Garvey, however, could match the later revival of African consciousness by the Rastafarians. Stressing the continuity of black African culture throughout history, Rastas believe in their direct spiritual descent from King Solomon's liaison with the queen of Sheba. Rastafarianism, according to some, is based on an intuitive interpretation of history and scripture—sometimes with broad brush strokes—with special emphasis on the reading of Old Testament prophecies. Rastafarians stress contemplation, meditation, a willingness to work inwardly to the "I" (inner divinity), and an abstractly political bent. Their assumptions are enhanced through sacramental rites of ganja (marijuana) smoking, Bible reading (with particular stress on references to Ethiopia), music, physical exercise, art, poetry, and cottage industries like handcrafts and broom making. Reggae music developed from Rasta circles and produced such international stars as the fervently religious Bob Marley. Jamaica's politicians, aware of the allure of Rastafarianism, often pay homage to its beliefs.

A male Rastafarian's beard is a sign of his pact with God (Jah or Jehovah), and his Bible is his source of knowledge. His dreadlocks are a symbol of his link with the Lion of Judah and Elect of God, the late Emperor of Ethiopia Haile Selassie, who while a prince was known as Ras Tafari (hence the religion's name). During the emperor's 1966 visit to Jamaica, more than 100,000 visitors greeted his airplane in something approaching religious ecstasy. The visit almost completely eclipsed Queen Elizabeth's a few months earlier. Rastas believe Haile Selassie to be their personal savior.

LANGUAGE

The official language of Jamaica is English, but the unofficial language is a patois. Linguists and a handful of Jamaican novelists have recently transformed this oral language into written form, although for most Jamaicans it remains solely spoken— and richly nuanced. Experts say that more than 90% of its vocabulary is derived from English, with the remaining words largely borrowed from African languages. There are also words taken from Spanish, Arawak, French, Chinese, Portuguese, and East Indian languages.

Although pronounced similarly to standard English, the patois preserves many 17th- and 18th-century expressions in common use during the time of early British colonial settlement of Jamaica. This archaic and simplified structure, coupled with African accents and special intonation, can make the language difficult to understand. Some linguists consider it a separate language, whereas others view it as just an alternate form of English. Some of the most interesting anecdotes and fables in the Caribbean are usually told in the patois, so understanding its structure can add to your insight into Jamaican culture.

Proverbs and place-names express some of the vitality of Jamaican language. For "Mind your own business," there is "Cockroach no business in fowl-yard." For being corrupted by bad companions, "You lay wid dawg, you get wid fleas." And for the pretentious, "The higher monkey climb, the more him expose." Both British and biblical place-names abound in Jamaica. Examples include Somerset and Siloah, Highgate and Horeb. One also sees Arawak names like Linguanea, Spanish ones like Oracabessa, Scottish names like Rest-and-Be-Thankful, and entirely Jamaican names like Red Gal Ring.

A final note: The patois has been embellished and altered with the growth of Rastafarianism. Rastas have injected several grammatical concepts, one of the most apparent being the repeated use of "I"—a reminder of their reverence of Ras Tafari. "I" is almost always substituted for the pronoun "me." It is also substituted for many prefixes or initial syllables. Thus, "all right," becomes "I're," "brethren" becomes "Idren," and "praises" becomes "Ises." The Rastafarian changes of Jamaica's patois are a recent phenomenon, and have not always been adopted by non-Rastas.

FOLKLORE

Nothing shaped the modern culture of the Caribbean more than the arrival of slaves from various parts of Africa. They brought gods, beliefs, superstitions, and fears with them. Although later converted to Christianity, they kept their traditions vibrant in fairs and festivals. Jamaican cultural and social life revolved mostly around the church, which was instrumental in molding a sense of community. Storytellers helped maintain ties to the past for each new generation, since little was written down until the 20th century. Since the advent of television, however, Jamaicans rarely gather to hear stories of the old days.

The folklore and ancient oral traditions of Jamaicans have fascinated English colonizers as well as modern-day visitors searching for a pattern to the mysticism that sometimes seems to pervade the countryside. Oral tradition forms a powerful undercurrent in this devoutly religious island; many folk beliefs were brought from Africa by slaves during the 17th and 18th centuries. Despite the later impact of Christian missionaries, a strong belief in magic remains, as does a wide array of superstitions.

Some folk beliefs are expressed in music, notably in the lyrics of reggae. Others are expressed in rhythmic chanting, whose stresses and moods once accompanied both hard labor and dancing. Other beliefs can be found in fairy tales and in legends concerning the island's slaves and their owners. The telling of oral narrations is a highly nuanced art form. Repetition and an inspired use of patois are important features.

Healing arts make use of Jamaican tradition, especially in the "balm yard," an herb garden-cum-healing place where a mixture of religion and magic is applied by a doctor or "balmist" of either sex. Some medicines brewed, distilled, or fermented in the yard are derived from recipes handed down for many generations and can be effective against ailments ranging from infertility to skin disease. A balm yard is usually encircled by a half-dozen thatch-covered huts, which house supplicants (patients). Bright red flags fly above each hut to chase away evil spirits. Ceremonies resembling revival meetings are held nightly, with a "mother" and a "father" urging the crowd to groan ecstatically and in unison. The threat of damnation in hellfire may be mentioned as punishment for anyone who doesn't groan loudly enough or believe fervently enough. Prayer and supplications to Jesus and various good and evil spirits will help relieve the sick of their ailments, it is believed.

The two most famous spirits of Jamaica are Obeah and the jumbie. Originating in the southern Caribbean, Obeah is a superstitious force that believers hold responsible for both good and evil. It is prudent not to tangle with this force, which might make trouble for you. Because of a long-established awareness of Obeah, and an unwillingness to tempt it with too positive an answer, a Jamaican is likely to answer, "Not too bad," if asked about his or her health.

Ganja

Marijuana use is the island's biggest open secret, and you'll no doubt encounter it during your vacation. (To be honest, it's the big draw for some visitors.) Vendors seem to hawk it at random, often through the chain-link fences surrounding popular resorts.

Ganja is viewed with differing degrees of severity in Jamaican society, but it's still officially illegal. We should warn you that being caught by the authorities with marijuana in your possession can lead to immediate imprisonment or deportation.

Marijuana and Jamaica have long endured a love-hate relationship. The plant was brought here by indentured servants from India in the mid-19th century. Revered by them as a medicinal and sacred plant, and referred to by the British as "Indian hemp," it quickly attracted the attention of the island's plantation owners because its use significantly reduced the productivity of those who ingested it. Legislation against its use quickly followed—not for moral or ethical reasons, but because it was bad for business.

During the 1930s, the slow rise of Rastafarianism (whose adherents believe marijuana use is an essential part of their religion) and the occasional use of marijuana by U.S. bohemians, artists, and jazz musicians led to a growing export of the plant to the United States. A massive increase in U.S. consumption occurred during the 1960s. Since the mid-1970s, after more stringent patrols were instituted along the U.S.–Mexico border, it is estimated that between 75% and 95% of all marijuana grown in Jamaica is consumed in the United States.

Cultivation of the crop, when conducted on the typical large scale, is as meticulous and thorough as that of any horticulturist raising a prize species of tomato or rose. Sold illegally by the quart, seeds must first be coaxed into seedlings in a greenhouse, then transplanted into fields at 2-foot intervals. Popular lore claims that the most prolific seedlings are raised in Jamaica's red, bauxite-rich soil and nurtured with all-organic fertilizers such as bat dung or goat droppings. As the plants mature, tattered scarecrows, loud reggae music,

There is no agreement on the nature of a jumbie. It's been suggested that it is the spirit of a dead person that didn't go where it belonged. Some islanders, however, say that "they're the souls of live people, who live in the bodies of the dead." Jumbies are said to inhabit households and to possess equal capacities for good and evil. Most prominent are Mocko Jumbies, carnival stilt-walkers seen in parades.

One folk tradition that can while away hours of a Jamaican's time is reciting Anansi stories. Such narration is an authentic performing art, which celebrates the nuances of Jamaican patois as well as the cunning, or lack thereof, of the stories' protagonists. Partly reflecting the tellers, the richly funny stories can include repeated key phrases whose rhythms add dramatic effect. Some stories concern Anansi, the spider-man. Like ancient Greeks, Africans invested the spider with human characteristics and intelligence. Whereas the Greeks linked the spider with Arachne, who taught humans to weave and spin, Africans emphasized the wiles and craft of a poisonous and vaguely repulsive eight-legged animal. By the time the tradition reached Jamaica, the spider had become a spider-man, and had been given both a name (Anansi) and a distinctive personality.

fluttering strips of reel-to-reel recording tape, and slingshots manned by local laborers are used to fend off the birds that feed off the seeds.

Even more feared than natural predators, however, are the Jamaican police. The constables periodically raid fields and destroy the crop by burning it or spraying it with herbicide.

Marijuana plants reach maturity 5 to 6 months after transplanting, often with a height of about 9 1/2 feet. Stalks and stems are then pressed for hash oil; leaves are dried for smoking, baking into pastries, or use in herbal teas. Most seeds are saved for the next planting.

Various types of ganja can be grown in a single field, each identified by names like McConey, Cotton, Burr, Bush, Goat's Horn, Lamb's Breath, and Mad. Bush and Mad are the least potent of the crop, whereas the strongest are acknowledged to be Lamb's Breath, Cotton, and Burr. The last three are marketed in the United States under the name of sinsemilla (Spanish for "without seeds"). Rastafarians typically prefer specific types of marijuana, much the way a gastronome might prefer specific types of caviar or red wine. To each his own.

Smuggling of the dried and packaged final product is disconcertingly efficient. A small plane lands at any of the country's hundreds of outlaw airstrips, which are sometimes disguised immediately before and after use by huts and shacks, moved into place by crews of strong-armed men. The planes then whisk away the crop, much of it to Florida. Undoubtedly, in a country with chronically low wages and constant fear of unemployment, the temptation to accept bribes among government officials in both high and low positions runs high.

Now that we have told you all we know about ganja, we remind you again that marijuana is illegal in Jamaica despite its widespread presence. Whatever you choose to do while you're on the island, we implore you above all not to try to buy a bag and bring it home to the United States—drug-sniffing dogs are employed at the airports, and we don't want you to end your vacation in jail.

A notorious trickster, with a distinctly Jamaican humor, Anansi manipulates those around him and eventually acquires whatever spoils happen to be available. In one well-known story, Anansi steals sheep from a nearby plantation; in another, he pilfers half of every other person's plantain. Among the funniest are episodes in which Anansi exposes the indiscretions of an Anglican priest. Anansi's traits include a lisp, a potent sense of greed, and a tendency to be wicked. The stories are sometimes funny, sometimes poignant, sometimes sexually suggestive. They often are parables, teaching a basic lesson about life. Each narrative has a well-defined and often charming ending, which tends to be followed by an explosion of laughter from the storyteller. Several collections of Anansi stories have been published.

6 Calypso, Reggae & Rap: The Rhythms of Jamaica

Many people visit Jamaica just to hear its authentic reggae. Reggae is now known around the world and recognized in the annual Grammy awards run by the U.S. music industry.

The roots of Jamaica's unique reggae music can be found in an early form of Jamaican music called **mento.** This music was brought to the island by African slaves, who played it to help forget their anguish. Mento is reminiscent of the rhythm and blues that in the mid-20th century swept across North America. It was usually accompanied by hip-rolling dances known as dubbing, with highly suggestive lyrics to match. Famous Jamaican mento groups reaching their prime in the 1950s included the Ticklers and the Pork Chops Rhumba Box Band of Montego Bay.

In the late 1950s, Jamaican musicians combined boogie-woogie with rhythm and blues to form a short-lived but vibrant music named **ska.** Jamaican artists in this form included Don Drummond, Roland Alphanso, Lloyd Knibbs, Theophilus Beckford, and Cluet Johnson. The five often played together during a vital chapter in Jamaica's musical history. It was the politicization of ska by Rastafarians that led to the creation of reggae.

CALYPSO

No analysis of Jamaican music would be complete without the inclusion of Jamaican-born musician, actor, and political activist Harry Belafonte. Recognizable to more North American and British listeners than any other Jamaican singer in the 1950s and early '60s, he became famous for his version of the island's unofficial anthem, "Jamaica Farewell," in which the singer leaves a little girl in Kingston Town. Although he worked in other musical forms, Belafonte is particularly known for his smooth and infectious calypsos. *Note:* Some purists in the crowd will point out that calypso is really a product of Trinidad, but it remains very popular in Jamaica (and Barbados).

REGGAE

The heartbeat of Jamaica, reggae is the island's most distinctive musical form, as closely linked to Jamaica as soul is to Detroit, jazz to New Orleans, and blues to Chicago. The term *reggae* is best defined as "coming from the people." It is taken from a song written and performed in the late 1960s by Jamaica-born "Toots" Hibbert and the Maytals ("Do the Reggay"). With a beat some fans claim is narcotic, it has crossed political and racial lines and temporarily drained the hostilities of thousands of listeners, injecting a new kind of life into their pelvises, knees, fingertips, and buttocks. It has influenced the music of international stars like the Rolling Stones, Eric Clapton, Paul Simon, the B-52s, Stevie Wonder, Elton John, and Third World as well as lesser-known acts like Black Uhuru, Chicago's Blue Riddim Band, and rap groups. Most notably, it propelled onto the world scene a street-smart kid from Kingston named Bob Marley. Today, the recording studios of Kingston, sometimes called "the Nashville of the Third World," churn out hundreds of reggae albums every year, many snapped up by danceaholics in Los Angeles, Italy, and Japan.

Reggae's earliest roots lie in the African musical tradition of mento. Later, the rhythms and body movements of mento were combined with an improvised interpretation of the then-fashionable French quadrille to create the distinctive hip-rolling and lower-body contact known as dubbing. Lyrics became increasingly suggestive (some say salacious) and playful as the musical form gained confidence and a body of devoted adherents.

In the 1950s calypso entered Jamaica from the southern Caribbean, especially Trinidad, whereas rhythm and blues and rock 'n' roll were imported from the United States. Both melded with mento into a danceable mixture that drew islanders into beer and dance halls throughout Jamaica. This music led to the powerful but short-lived form called ska, made famous by the Skatalites, who peaked in the mid-1960s. When their leader and trombonist, Drummond, became a highly politicized convert to Rastafarianism, other musicians followed and altered their rhythms to reflect the African drumbeats known as kumina and burru. This fertile musical tradition, when fused with ripening political movements around 1968, became reggae.

Leading early reggae musicians included Anton Ellis and Delroy Wilson. Later, Bob Marley and (to a lesser degree) Jimmy Cliff propelled reggae to world prominence. Marley's band, the Wailers, included his Kingston friends Peter Mac-Intosh (later known as Peter Tosh), Junior Brathwaite, and Bunny Livingston (now known as Bunny Wailer). Since the death of Marley in 1981, other famous reggae musicians have included his son Ziggy Marley, Roy Parkes, Winston "Yellowman" Foster, and Roy Shirley. Among noteworthy bands are Third World and The Mighty Diamonds.

One of the most recent adaptations of reggae is **soca,** which is more upbeat and less politicized. Aficionados say that reggae makes you think, but soca makes you dance. The music is fun, infectious, and spontaneous—perfect for partying—and often imbued with the humor and wry attitudes of Jamaican urban dwellers. Soca's most visible artists include Byron Lee and the Dragonaires. A skillful entrepreneur and organizer, Lee is the force behind the growing annual Jamaica Carnival, which draws more than 15,000 foreign visitors.

RAP

After 1965, the influx of Jamaican immigrants to North America's ghettos had a profound (and profitable) influence on popular music. Such Jamaican-born stars as Clive Campbell, combining the Jamaican gift for the spoken word with reggae rhythms and high electronic amplification, developed the roots of what eventually became known as rap. Taking on a street-smart adaptation of rhyming couplets, some of which were influenced by Jamaica's rich appreciation of word games and speech patterns, he organized street parties where the music of his groups— Cool DJ Herc, Nigger Twins, and the Herculords—was broadcast to thousands of listeners from van-mounted amplifiers.

Designed to electrify rather than soothe, and reflecting the restlessness of a new generation of Jamaicans bored with the sometimes mind-numbing rhythms of reggae, popular Jamaican music became less awestruck by Rastafarian dogmas, less Afro-centric, and more focused on the urban experiences of ghetto life in New York. Music became harder, simpler, more urban, and more conscious of profit-searching market trends. Dubbed dance-hall music, the sounds seemed inspired by the hard edge of survival-related facts of life ("girls, guns, drugs, and crime") on urban streets.

One of the major exponents of the new form is Super Cat (William Maragh), who wears his hair cut short ("bald-head") in deliberate contrast to the dreadlocks sported by the disciples of Marley. The sounds are hard and spare, the lyrics as brutal and cruel as the ghetto that inspires them. Super Cat's competitors include Kris Kross, an Atlanta-based rap duet who affect Jamaican accents and speech patterns, and Shabba Ranks, known for often blatant sexual references and unconcealed black machismo. Whereas Marley during the peak of his reggae appeal sold mainly to young whites, the new sounds appeal mostly to young black audiences who relate to the sense of raw danger evoked by dance-hall music's rhythms and lyrics. During some of Shabba Ranks's concerts, audiences in Jamaica have shown their approval by firing gunshots into the air in a gesture known locally as a "salute of honor."

RECOMMENDED RECORDINGS

Jamaica's culture is indicative of and certainly can be defined by its main musical export—reggae. The undisputed king of reggae, the late Bob Marley, popularized the genre, which is musically stylized by percussive guitar riffs and lyrically peppered with political and social actions.

Legend (Best of Bob Marley and the Wailers) chronicles the late artist's career of work. Termed as a poet and a prophet, Marley brought reggae into the American conscience and mainstream. The album features a collection of hits such as "Get Up, Stand Up," "Jamming," "One Love," and perhaps his biggest hit, "Stir it Up." *Legend* was released in 1984, and has already outsold such megahits as Michael Jackson's *Thriller,* The Beatles' *Sgt. Pepper's Lonely Hearts Club Band,* and Pink Floyd's *Dark Side of the Moon.* (Tuff Gong/Island Records, 422846210-2.)

Honorary Citizen, a three-CD box set, covers the career of Marley's contemporary, Peter Tosh, a reggae legend in his own right. Termed also as a poet, prophet, preacher, and philosopher, *Honorary Citizen* brings out the best of Tosh's work, including some unreleased and live tracks with artists such as Marley, Bunny Wailer (of the Wailers), and Mick Jagger and Keith Richards. Tracks include "Fire Fire," "Arise Blackman," and "Legalize It." (Columbia/Legacy, C3H 65064.)

Liberation by Bunny Wailer is another important album of the reggae movement. When *Newsweek* selected the three most important musicians in the Third World, Bunny Wailer was among them. He has controlled his artistic development, despite tragedies in his career, while avoiding any compromising of his vision. (Shanachie Records, 43059.)

One Love by Bunny Wailer, Bob Marley, and Peter Tosh (Three Greats) offers the three biggest legends of reggae together on one album, a "Three Tenors" of reggae. This compilation is the first chronological and definitive study of Bob Marley and the Wailers and Peter Tosh in their formative years. The music, the cornerstone of the ska era, includes previously unreleased alternate takes and rarely recorded Jamaican singers. (Heartbeat Records, CDH111/112.)

Ziggy Marley and the Melody Makers, Best of 1988–1993 spans the successful and ongoing career of one of Bob's many children. Ziggy is largely responsible for reggae's 1990s mainstream acceptance, penning such crossover hits as "One Bright Day," "Joy and Blues," and "Brothers and Sisters," which are contained in this collection. His debut album, *Conscious Party,* is still his best work. (Virgin, 724384490821.)

Liberation—The Island Antology by Black Uhuru is a box set of collective works from the band's 1980s Island Records catalog. The 1980s were still dominated by the Marley effect, and Black Uhuru was the band that passed the reggae torch along to Ziggy Marley. (Island Records, 314518282-2.)

The Lee "Scratch" Perry Arkology is another recent box set release of another "old skool" reggae artist from "back in the day." Covering his entire career, it contains recordings from the many different bands he formed, as well as solo works, including two never-before-released tracks. (Island/Jamaica, 61524 3792.)

In Concert—Best of Jimmy Cliff is a recording of a legendary pedigree. Produced by legends Andrew Loog Oldham and Cliff, this album features Ernest Ranglin on lead guitar and Earl "Baga" Walker on bass. Includes the classic, "Many Rivers to Cross" and "The Harder They Come." (Reprise, 2256-2.)

Jah Kingdon by Burning Spear is known for its strongly political lyrics. This record could serve as a definition for hard-core reggae. Includes "World Power" and "Land of My Birth." (Mango/Island Records, 162539915-2.)

Too Long in Slavery is an album by one of Ziggy Marley's contemporaries, Culture. All songs were written and performed by J. Hill, K. Daley, and A. Walker. (Virgin, CDFL9011.)

The recordings by the Marleys, Tosh, and the Wailers are considered to be the purist reggae, defined as such today because of reggae's splintering into many different forms such as dance/house music and rap.

Best Sellers by Mikey Dread is a compilation album spanning the career of Dread, Jamaica's best-known DJ. With material ranging from 1979 to 1990, it was Dread (along with the band Maxi Priest) who ushered reggae into the new dance movement. (Rykodisc Records, 20178.)

Many Moods of Moses by Beenie Man is the latest release by an artist whose political lyrics maintain all the criteria for purist reggae, but instead adds a dance beat heard only from the likes of Dread before the 1990s. Tracks from this album include "Who I Am (Zim Zamma)" and "Oysters and Conch." (VP Records, VPCD1513-2.)

Sawuri, the self-titled release by Sawuri, offers a Creole taste to the Jamaican sound. It features the Caribbean artists Marcel Komba and Georges Marie. If you have trouble finding this record in your favorite store, try **www.worldmusic.com,** a site devoted to promoting world music that is yet to become mainstream. (Dom Records, CD 1067.)

Militant, by newcomer Andrew Bees, is a signal that the purist reggae will always remain *en vogue* in Jamaica. Tracks such as "Struggle and Strive," "Militant," and "Life in the Ghetto" evoke modern realizations of the same themes Marley, Tosh, and Wailer sung about in the past—except now with mounting frustrations of citizens from a Third World society. (Ras Records, ML 81811-2.)

7   A Taste of Jamaica

A visit to Jamaica doesn't mean a diet of just local cuisine. The island's restaurants employ some of the best chefs in the Caribbean, hailing from the United States and Europe, and they can prepare a sumptuous cuisine of elegant French, continental, and American dishes.

When dining in Jamaica, try some fish, which is often delectable, especially dolphin (the game fish, not the mammal), wahoo, yellowtail, grouper, and red snapper. These fish, when broiled with hot lime sauce as an accompaniment, may represent your most memorable island meals. With no claws and a tail full of sweet-tasting meat, Caribbean lobster is not to be confused with the Maine variety.

Except for soup, appetizers don't loom large in the Jamaican kitchen. The most popular appetizer is *stamp and go,* or saltfish cakes. *Solomon Gundy* is made with pickled shad, herring, and mackerel, and seasoned with onions, hot peppers, and pimiento berries. Many Jamaicans begin their meal by enjoying plantain and banana chips with their drinks.

The most famous soup, pepperpot, is an old Arawak recipe. It is often made with callaloo, okra, kale, pig's tail (or salt beef), coconut meat, yams, scallions, and hot peppers. Another favorite, ackee soup, is made from ackees (usually from a dozen ripe open pods), flavored with a shin of beef or a salted pig's tail. Pumpkin soup is seasoned with salted beef or a salted pig's tail. Red pea soup is also delicious (note that it's actually made with red beans).

Tea in Jamaica can mean any nonalcoholic drink, and fish tea, a legacy of plantation days, is made with fish heads or bony fish, along with green bananas, tomatoes, scallions, and hot pepper and other spices.

Because Jamaica is an island, there is great emphasis on seafood, but many other tasty dishes are also offered. Rock lobster is a regular dish on every menu, presented grilled, thermidor, cold, or hot. *Saltfish and ackee* is the national dish, a mixture of salt cod and a brightly colored vegetablelike fruit that tastes something like scrambled eggs. *Escovitch* (marinated fish) is usually fried and then simmered in vinegar with onions and peppers.

Among meat dishes, curried mutton and goat are popular, each highly seasoned and likely to affect your body temperature. Jerk pork is characteristic of rural areas, where it is coated in spices and barbecued slowly over wood fires until crisp and brown.

Apart from rice and peas (really red beans), usually served as a sort of risotto with added onions, spices, and salt pork, some vegetables may be new to you. They include *breadfruit,* originally brought here from the South Pacific; *callaloo,* rather like spinach, used in pepperpot soup (not to be confused with the stew of the same name); *cho-cho,* served boiled and buttered or stuffed; and green bananas and plantains, fried or boiled and served with almost everything. Then there is pumpkin, which goes into a soup, as mentioned, or is served on the side, boiled and mashed with butter. Sweet potatoes are part of main courses, and there is also a sweet potato pudding made with sugar and coconut milk, flavored with cinnamon, nutmeg, and vanilla.

You'll also come across the intriguing *dip and fall back,* a salty stew with bananas and dumplings, and *rundown,* mackerel cooked in coconut milk and often eaten for breakfast. The really adventurous can try *manish water,* a soup made from goat offal and tripe said to increase virility. Patties (meat pies) are a staple snack; the best are sold in Montego Bay. Boiled corn, roast yams, roast saltfish, fried fish, soups, and fruits are available at roadside stands.

As mentioned above, "tea" is used in Jamaica to describe any nonalcoholic drink, a tradition dating back to plantation days. Fish tea is often consumed as a refreshing pick-me-up, and is sometimes sold along the side of the road. *Skyjuice* is a favorite Jamaican treat for a hot afternoon. It's sold by street vendors, but beware: Their carts are not always sanitary. It consists of shaved ice with sugar-laden fruit syrup and is offered in small plastic bags with a straw. Coconut water is refreshing and is safe to drink when a roadside vendor chops the top off a nut straight from a tree.

Rum punches are available everywhere, and the local beer is Red Stripe. The island produces many liqueurs, the most famous being Tía Maria, made from coffee beans. Rumona is another good one to bring back home with you. Bellywash, the local name for limeade, will supply the extra liquid you may need to counteract the tropical heat.

Blue Mountain coffee is considered among the world's best coffees—it's also very expensive. Tea, cocoa, and milk are also usually available to round out a meal.

Planning a Trip to Jamaica

3

This chapter will give you all the nuts-and-bolts information about your trip to Jamaica—what you need to do before leaving home. We'll answer questions such as when to go, how to get the best airfare or package deal, what to take along, and what documents you'll need.

Some of the information in this chapter applies to Barbados as well as to Jamaica, especially those sections on health, insurance, and tips for travelers with special needs. If you're going to Barbados, these sections are for you, too.

1 Visitor Information, Entry Requirements & Customs

VISITOR INFORMATION

Before you go, you can obtain information from the Jamaica Tourist Board (JTB) in the following U.S. cities. **Atlanta:** 300 W. Wienca Rd., Suite 100A, Atlanta, GA 30342 (☎ **770/452-7799**); **Chicago:** 500 N. Michigan Ave., Suite 1030, Chicago, IL 60611 (☎ **312/527-1296**); **Miami area:** 1320 S. Dixie Hwy., Suite 1101, Coral Gables, FL 33146 (☎ **305/665-0557**); **Los Angeles:** 3440 Wilshire Blvd., Suite 1207, Los Angeles, CA 90010 (☎ **213/384-1123**); **New York:** 801 Second Ave., New York, NY 10017 (☎ **212/856-9727**); and **Philadelphia:** 842 S. 2nd St., Suite 328, Philadelphia, PA 19147 (☎ **215/922-0643**).

In Canada, obtain information in **Toronto:** 1 Eglinton Ave. E., Suite 616, Toronto, ON M4P 3A1 (☎ **416/482-7850**). The JTB can also be reached via the toll-free number 800/233-4582 in both the U.S. and Canada.

In **London,** contact the tourist board at 1–2 Prince Consort Rd., London SW7 2BZ (☎ **0171/224-0505**).

Once in Jamaica, you will find tourist board offices in **Kingston:** 2 St. Lucia Ave., Kingston (☎ **876/929-9200**); **Montego Bay:** Cornwall Beach, St. James, Montego Bay (☎ **876/952-4425**); **Negril:** Shop no. 20, Adrija Place, Negril, Westmoreland (☎ **876/957-4243**); **Ocho Rios:** Ocean Village Shopping Centre, Ocho Rios, St. Anne (☎ **876/974-2582**); **Port Antonio:** City Centre Plaza, Port Antonio (☎ **876/993-3051**); and **Black River:** 2 High St. in Hendricks Building, Black River (☎ **876/965-2074**).

You might also check out "The Unofficial Web Site on Jamaica" (**http://home. navisoft.com/xkcom/jam.htm**), the best all-around site, with some good pointers, cultural tidbits, a patois primer, and plenty of humor. This is one of the few Jamaica Web pages that isn't either a blatant ad, or just somebody's homepage with a few vacation pictures. "City.Net" (**www.city.net/countries/jamaica/**) also has pointers to several of the more official, and generally more staid, Jamaica sites on the Web. The Jamaica Tourist Board and the U.S. Government weigh in here.

ENTRY REQUIREMENTS

DOCUMENTS   U.S. and Canadian residents do not need passports, but must have proof of citizenship (or permanent residency) and a return or ongoing ticket. A passport is the best bet, but an original birth certificate (or a certified copy) plus photo ID will usually suffice. A voter registration card is acceptable in some cases, but only if you have a notarized affidavit of citizenship, plus photo ID. Always double-check with your airline, though: Sometimes they won't accept a voter registration card. Do check on the latest entry requirements before you travel, as the rules can change. Our advice is to always bring a passport when you're going to another country.

Other visitors, including British citizens, need passports that are good for a maximum stay of 6 months.

Immigration cards are given to visitors at the airport arrivals desks. Hold onto it, as you will need to surrender the document to Jamaican Customs when you leave the country.

Before leaving home, make two copies of your most valuable documents, including the identification pages of your passport, your driver's license, or any other identity document; your airline ticket; and hotel vouchers. If you're taking prescribed medication, make copies of prescriptions.

CUSTOMS

Generally, you're permitted to bring in items intended for your personal use, including tobacco, cameras, film, and a limited supply of liquor, usually 40 ounces.

U.S. CUSTOMS   Generally, returning U.S. citizens can bring home U.S.$600 worth of goods for each 48-hour visit without paying any duty. And, to make it even more attractive, items made in Jamaica such as hand carvings or whatever are completely duty-free. The same liberal terms also apply to Barbados as well. You're allowed 1 liter of alcohol, 200 cigarettes, and 200 cigars.

Collect receipts for all purchases made abroad. Sometimes merchants suggest a false receipt to undervalue your purchase, but be aware that you might be involved in a sting operation—the merchant might be an informer for U.S. Customs. You must also declare on your Customs form the nature and value of all gifts received during your stay abroad. It's prudent to carry proof that you purchased expensive cameras or jewelry on the U.S. mainland. If you purchased such an item during an earlier trip abroad, you should carry proof that you have previously paid Customs duty on the item.

For more specifics, write to the **U.S. Customs Service,** 1301 Constitution Ave., P.O. Box 7407, Washington, DC 20044, (☎ **202/927-6724**) and request the free pamphlet *Know Before You Go* or check the U.S. Customs Web site at www.customs.ustreas.gov1.

CANADIAN CUSTOMS   The exemptions that Canadians are granted by their government are dependent on the time they've spent outside the borders of Canada.

Canadians who have spent 24 hours or less outside the country are allowed a (CAN) $50 exemption from taxation on goods they've bought, but any tobacco or liquor products purchased abroad are subject to the Canadian tax code. For Canadians who have spent more than 48 hours outside the Canadian border, a (CAN) $300 exemption is granted on goods they've purchased, and they're allowed to bring back duty-free 200 cigarettes, 200 grams of tobacco, 40 imperial ounces of liquor, and 50 cigars. For Canadians who have spent 7 days or more outside the borders of Canada, the exemption is raised to (CAN) $500, and the same quantities of tobacco and liquor mentioned above can be brought in duty-free.

In addition to the exemptions noted above, and regardless of the amount of time they spend away from Canada, Canadians are allowed to mail gifts from abroad to friends, clients, and relatives in Canada (but not to themselves), at the rate of (CAN) $60 per day, provided the gifts are unsolicited and aren't alcohol or tobacco products. Be sure to write "Unsolicited gift, under $60 value" on the outside of the package.

All valuables such as expensive cameras and jewelry should be declared on the Y-38 Form before your departure from Canada, and whenever it's possible, with the notation of the article's serial number. When serial numbers aren't available, as in the case of jewelry, it's wise to carry a photocopy of either the original bill of sale or a bona fide appraisal.

For more information, contact **Revenue Canada,** 2265 St. Laurent Blvd., Ottawa ON K1G 4K3 (☎ **613/993-0534**), and ask for the free booklet *I Declare.* You can also check the agency's Web site at http://rc.gc.can.

BRITISH CUSTOMS On returning from the Caribbean, if you either arrive directly in the United Kingdom or arrive via a port in another EC country where you did not pass through Customs controls with all your baggage, you must go through U.K. Customs and declare any goods in excess of the allowances. These are: 200 cigarettes or 50 cigars or 250 grams of tobacco; 2 liters of still table wine and 1 liter of spirits or strong liqueurs over 22% volume, or 2 liters of fortified or sparkling wine or other liqueurs; 60cc (ml) of perfume; 250cc (ml) of toilet water; and £145 worth of all other goods, including gifts and souvenirs. (No one under 17 years of age is entitled to a tobacco or alcohol allowance.) Only go through the green "nothing to declare" line if you're sure that you have no more than the Customs allowances and no prohibited or restricted goods.

For further details on U.K. Customs, contact **H.M. Customs and Excise Office,** Dorset House, Stamford Street, London SE1 9PY (☎ **0171/202-4227;** fax 0171/202-4216). You can also get more information from their Web site at www.open.gov.uk/customs/c&ehome.htm.

2 Money

The unit of currency in Jamaica is the Jamaican dollar, with the same symbol as the U.S. dollar, "$." There is no fixed rate of exchange for the Jamaican dollar. It is traded publicly and is subject to market fluctuations.

Visitors to Jamaica can pay for any goods in U.S. dollars. *But be careful!* Unless clearly stated, always insist on knowing whether a price is quoted in Jamaican or U.S. dollars.

In this guide, we quote most prices in both Jamaican and U.S. dollars, though U.S. dollars are listed alone for the most part, because the Jamaican dollar tends to fluctuate widely, and U.S. dollar values give a better indication of costs. Prices given in Jamaican dollars are indicated by "J$"; U.S. dollars are indicated by "U.S.$."

The Jamaican Dollar, the U.S. Dollar & the British Pound

Jamaican currency is issued in banknotes of J$10, J$20, J$50, J$100, and J$500. Coins are available in denominations of 5¢, 10¢, 25¢, 50¢, J$1, and J$5. Five-dollar banknotes and 1-cent coins are also in circulation, but are increasingly rare.

The chart below gives rounded-off U.S. dollar and British pound value for Jamaican prices. The chart's exchange rate of J$35 to U.S.$1, and J$55 to U.K.£1 were in effect as this edition was printed, but may be slightly different when you visit the island. Stated differently, J$1 equals about 2.85 U.S. cents and about 1.8 British pence.

Jamaican $	U.S. $	U.K. £
5	0.14	0.09
10	0.28	0.18
25	0.70	0.45
50	1.40	0.90
75	2.10	1.35
100	2.80	1.80
200	5.60	3.60
300	8.40	5.40
400	11.20	7.20
500	14.00	9.00
750	21.00	13.50
1,000	28.00	18.00
5,000	140.00	90.00
10,000	280.00	180.00

Many British travelers prefer to use U.S. dollars in Jamaica, especially if they also plan to visit Puerto Rico, the U.S. Virgin Islands, or the U.S. mainland.

There are Bank of Jamaica exchange bureaus at both international airports (Montego Bay and Kingston), at cruise-ship piers, and in most hotels.

There is no limit to the amount of foreign currency you can bring in or out of Jamaica.

Whenever you leave your hotel, take along some small bills and coins. They will come in handy, since tips are generally expected for any small service rendered.

ATM NETWORKS Plus, Cirrus, and other networks connecting automated-teller machines operate in Jamaica and Barbados. For locations of Cirrus abroad, call ☎ 800/424-7787. For Plus usage abroad, call ☎ 800/843-7587. These are global information lines that will help you find local ATMs.

If your credit card has been programmed with a PIN number, it is likely that you can use your card at Caribbean ATMs to withdraw money as a cash advance on your credit card.

These services exist in such places as Montego Bay and Bridgetown, but don't count on it in the remote villages. Before going, check to see if your PIN number must be reprogrammed for usage in Jamaica and Barbados.

TRAVELER'S CHECKS Although it's now possible to use ATMs around the world to access your own bank account back home, some travelers still prefer the security of carrying traveler's checks so that they can obtain refunds if their checks are stolen.

Most large banks sell traveler's checks, charging fees averaging 1% to 2% of the value of the checks you buy, although some banks, in rare instances, have charged as much as 7%. If your bank wants more than a 2% commission, it sometimes pays to call the traveler's check issuers directly for the addresses of outlets where commissions will be lower. Issuers sometimes have agreements with groups to sell checks commission free. For example, American Automobile Association (AAA) offices sell American Express checks in several currencies without commission.

American Express (☎ **800/221-7282** in the U.S. and Canada, with many regional representatives around the world) is one of the largest issuers of traveler's checks. No commission is paid by members of AAA provided that checks are purchased at AAA offices. American Express platinum card holders get traveler's checks issued commission free at American Express offices or through the American Express service number (☎ **800/553-6782**). Gold card holders can get commission-free checks only through the American Express service number; other cardholders pay a commission.

Citicorp (☎ **800/645-6556** in the U.S. and Canada, or 813/623-1709, collect, from other parts of the world) is another major issuer. **Thomas Cook** (☎ **800/223-7373** in the U.S. and Canada, or 609/987-7300, collect, from other parts of the world) issues MasterCard traveler's checks, and **Interpayment Services** (☎ **800/221-2426** in the U.S. and Canada, or 212/858-8500, collect, from other parts of the world) sells Visa traveler's checks.

CREDIT & CHARGE CARDS   Credit cards are widely used in Jamaica and Barbados. Visa and MasterCard are the major cards, although the American Express card and, to a lesser extent, Diners Club, are also popular.

3 When to Go

HIGH SEASON VS. LOW SEASON: SOME PROS & CONS

With its fabled weather balmy all year, Jamaica is more and more a year-round destination. Nevertheless, it has a distinct **high season** running roughly from mid-December to mid-April. Hotels charge their highest prices during this peak winter period, when visitors fleeing from cold north winds crowd onto the island. (We've quoted each hotel's rack rates throughout this guide, but you don't have to pay *that* much, even in the high season, if you book a package instead of calling the hotel directly.) And let's face it: When it's snowy and 10° in Chicago, sometimes it's worth any price to save your sanity and go bask on a warm, sunny beach.

Reservations should be made 2 to 3 months in advance during the winter. At certain hotels it's almost impossible to book accommodations for the Christmas holidays and in February.

The **off-season** in Jamaica (roughly from mid-April to mid-December, with variance from hotel to hotel) amounts to a summer sale. In most cases, hotel rates are slashed a startling 20% to 60%. Some package-tour charges are as much as 20% lower, and individual excursion airfares are reduced from 5% to 10%. And airline seats and hotel rooms are much easier to come by. It's a bonanza for cost-conscious travelers, especially families who like to vacation together. In the chapters ahead, we'll spell out in dollars the specific amounts hotels charge during the off-season.

There are other advantages to off-season travel as well. Resort boutiques often feature summer sales, hoping to clear merchandise not sold in February to accommodate stock for the coming winter. After the winter hordes have left, a less hurried way of life prevails on the island. You'll have a better chance to appreciate the food, culture, and local customs. Swimming pools and beaches are less crowded, sometimes not crowded at all. There's no waiting for a rental car (only to be told none are available), no long tee-up for golf, no queuing for tennis courts and water sports. You can often walk in unannounced at a top restaurant and find a seat for dinner that in winter would have required reservations far in advance. Also, when waiters are less hurried, they give better service.

The atmosphere is more cosmopolitan in the off-season than in the winter, mainly because of the influx of Europeans and Japanese. You'll no longer feel as if you're at a Canadian or American outpost. Also, the Jamaicans themselves travel in the off-season, and your holiday becomes more of a people-to-people experience.

Summer is also the time for family travel, not often possible during the winter season.

But let's not paint too rosy a picture, as there are disadvantages of off-season travel to consider. Sometimes services are curtailed—perhaps major restaurants at a resort will be closed because of lack of business. Entertainment, including bands and folkloric shows, will be greatly curtailed or may not exist at all until the winter season. Also, when business slows down in summer, many hotels use this time to renovate or even to launch new construction for the coming season. You're also taking a chance that the sun will just be broiling—and the hurricane season in the Caribbean officially lasts from June 1 to November 30. Finally, a minus for singles, there are just fewer people, lowering your chances to meet Mr. Right or Ms. Right.

CLIMATE

Jamaica has one of the most varied climates of any Caribbean island.

Along the seashore where most visitors congregate, the island is air-conditioned by the northeast trade winds, and temperature variations are surprisingly slight. Coastal readings average between 71° and 88°F all year. The Jamaican winter is usually like May in the United States or northern Europe, however, and there can be really chilly times, especially in the early morning and at night. Winter is generally the driest season, but can be wet in mountain areas; you can expect showers especially in northeast Jamaica.

Inland, Jamaica's average temperatures decrease by approximately 1°F for every 300 feet increase in elevation. Temperatures atop the highest of the Blue Mountains might descend to a chilly 50°F, although most visitors find that a light jacket, sweater, or evening wrap is adequate for even the coldest weather on the island. In some cases, a wrap is a good idea even on the beach because of nighttime breezes or strong drafts from a dining room's air conditioner.

Average yearly precipitation in Jamaica is more than 80 inches. Rainfall is heaviest along the eastern edge of the island's north coast, with Port Antonio receiving some of the most intense downpours. The island has two rainy seasons, May and October–November, although with the recent trend toward global warming, there have been less strict seasonal variations.

THE HURRICANE SEASON   The curse of Jamaican weather, the hurricane season officially lasts from June 1 to November 30. But there's no need for panic. Satellite weather forecasts generally give adequate warning so that precautions can be taken.

If you're heading for Jamaica during the hurricane season, you can call your nearest branch of the National Weather Service, listed in the phone directory under *U.S. Department of Commerce.*

An automated way to receive information about the climate conditions in the city you plan to visit involves contacting the information service associated with

The Weather Channel. It works like this: Dial ☎ **800/WEATHER** and listen to the recorded announcement. When you're prompted, enter the account number of a valid Visa or MasterCard. After the card's validity is approved, at a rate of 95¢ per query, punch in the name of any of 1,000 cities worldwide whose weather is monitored by The Weather Channel. The report that's delivered might help you in knowing what to wear and how to pack.

HOLIDAYS

Jamaica observes the following public holidays: New Year's Day (January 1), Ash Wednesday, Good Friday, Easter Monday, National Labor Day (late May), Independence Day (a Monday in early August), National Heroes Day (third Monday in October), Christmas Day (December 25), and Boxing Day (December 26).

JAMAICA CALENDAR OF EVENTS

January

- **Accompong Maroon Festival,** St. Elizabeth. Annual celebration by the Maroons in Western Jamaica, with traditional singing and dancing. Maroon feasts and ceremonies, blowing of the Abeng, and playing of Maroon drums. The festival dates back to the 19th century. Contact Kenneth Watson at ☎ **876/952-4546.** January 6.
- **Jamaica Sprint Triathlon,** Negril. Hundreds participate in a three-part competition joining swimming, cycling, and running in one sweat-inducing endurance test. Contact the Jamaica Tourist Board for details (see "Visitor Information," earlier in this chapter). January 23 to 25.

February

- **Tribute to Bob Marley—Symposium in Music,** Ocho Rios. Seminars for students of music as well as players of drums, guitar, and wind instruments. Contact the Jamaica Cultural Development Commission at ☎ **876/926-5726.** February 4 to 6.
- **Bob Marley Birthday Bash,** Montego Bay. Annual celebration of Bob Marley's birthday with a concert featuring popular reggae artists. Contact Marjorie Scott, at the Bob Marley Foundation, at ☎ **876/978-2991.**
- ✪ **Reggae Sunsplash,** Ocho Rios. Annual reggae festival featuring internationally acclaimed reggae musicians. Contact Rae Barrett, Reggae Sunsplash International, at ☎ **876/960-1904.**

March

- **Spring Break,** at Negril, Montego Bay, and Ocho Rios, an annual program for students vacationing in Jamaica. Discounted rates at selected hotels, attractions, restaurants, and nightclubs. Featured are reggae concerts with live bands and beach volleyball competitions; entry to concerts is free with valid student ID. Contact the Jamaica Tourist Board at ☎ **800/233-4582.**
- **Montego Bay Yacht Club's Easter Regatta.** An annual sailing event with several races staged along the north coast over a 4-day period at Easter time. Contact the Montego Bay Yacht Club (☎ **876/952-8262**).

April

- **Carnival in Jamaica,** Kingston, Ocho Rios, and Montego Bay. Weeklong series of fetes, concerts, and street parades, with flamboyantly costumed groups of all ages dancing through the streets of Ocho Rios, Kingston, and Montego Bay. Local tourist offices will provide more details. First week of April.

May

- **Portland Annual Flower Show at Crystal Springs,** Portland. Displays of plants, arts, and craft items in a garden setting at the beautiful Crystal Springs. Contact the Jamaica Tourist Board at Port Antonio at ☎ **876/993-3051.** Call for actual date (different every year).

June

- **Ocho Rios Jazz Festival** in both Ocho Rios and Montego Bay. International performers from Great Britain, Europe, Japan, and the United States and the Caribbean perform here along with Jamaican jazz artists. A series of jazz concerts is presented, along with jazz lunches, jazz teas, jazz feasts on the river, and even jazz barbecues. Contact the Jamaica Tourist Board office worldwide at ☎ **800/233-4582.** June 8 to 15.

July

- **National Dance Theatre Company's Season of Dance,** Kingston. At the Little Theatre in Kingston, the island's internationally celebrated dance company presents this major cultural event. Creative dancers explore both traditional and modern choreography. The season also features notable singers. July 25 to August 8.
- ✪ **Reggae Sunsplash,** at Chukka Cove, St. Ann. An annual and internationally famous reggae festival, featuring top local and international reggae performers. Contact RADOBAR Holdings at ☎ **876/960-1914.**

August

- **Reggae Sumfest,** at Catherine Hall, Montego Bay, an annual 5-day music festival featuring international singers and top local talent. Call ☎ **876/952-0889** for more information. August 5 to 9.
- **Portland Jamboree,** Port Antonio. This port city comes alive with excitement and fun when an exposition of the town's cultural expression is held for 9 days. Activities include a float parade, church service, street dancing, selling of local foods and crafts—the entire spectacle culminating on the final day with a show featuring well-known singers. Contact ☎ **876/993-3051** for more information. End of August, beginning of September (dates vary).

September

- **Falmouth Blue Marlin Tournament.** Although this fishing tournament outside Montego Bay attracts many world-class fishers, the big event remains in Port Antonio in October (see below). Nevertheless, in September, when there is little activity on the Jamaican calendar of events, it's somewhat of a big deal locally. For more information, contact ☎ **876/952-4425.** September 25 to 27.

October

- ✪ **Port Antonio Blue Marlin Tournament.** One of the oldest and most prestigious sportfishing events in the Caribbean, with participants from Europe and North America. Contact Sir Henry Morgan Angling Association at ☎ **876/923-8724.** October 13 to 17.

November

- **Air Jamaica Jazz & Blues Festival,** Montego Bay. Internationally acclaimed musicians and recording artists perform in a series of concerts at Rose Hall Great

House over a long weekend. Call ☎ **876/926-4377** for more information. November 7 to 9.

December

• **Motor Sports Championship Series,** Dover Raceway, St. Ann. Prestigious championship event which features local, regional, and international motoring enthusiasts. Contact Motor Sports Ltd. at ☎ **876/978-2430.** December 1.

4 The Active Vacation Planner

If sports are important to you, you may want to learn more about the offerings of particular parts of Jamaica before deciding on a resort. Jamaica is so large that it isn't much fun to undertake a long day's excursion just to play golf, for example. The cost of most activities is generally the same throughout the island.

Below is a summary to get you going and help you choose the destination that's right for you.

BEACHES

Many visitors want to do nothing more sporting than lie on the beach. For specific recommendations, refer to the regional chapters that follow and section 1 of chapter 1, "The Best Beaches." On the whole, the best beaches are the 7-mile stretch of sand at Negril, with many sections reserved for nudists (see chapter 5); Walter Fletcher Beach at Montego Bay, with especially tranquil waters (see chapter 4); the unfortunately crowded Doctor's Cave Beach, also at Montego Bay, with water sports and changing rooms (see chapter 4); and San San Beach, at Port Antonio on the north coast, with clean white sand, plenty of water sports, and a favorite picnic area (see chapter 6).

BIRDING

Victor Emanuel Nature Tours (☎ **800/328-8368**) offers weeklong birding trips to Jamaica, costing U.S.$1,995 per person. Jamaica is home to some 30 species of birds found nowhere else in the world. Trips are conducted by a Jamaican ornithologist. Visits are to the Blue Mountains (north of Kingston, the capital) and to the ponds and lagoons of Mandeville in the southwest.

DEEP-SEA FISHING

The waters off north Jamaica are world-renowned for game fish, including dolphin, kingfish, wahoo, blue and white marlin, sailfish, tarpon, Allison tuna, barracuda, and bonito. **The Port Antonio International Marlin Tournament** lures fishers from around the world every October. Most major hotels from Port Antonio to Montego Bay offer deep-sea fishing, and there are many charter boats. See chapters 4 and 6.

GOLF

Jamaica has the best golf courses in the West Indies, with Montego Bay alone sporting four championship links. Those at **Wyndham Rose Hall Golf & Beach Resort** (☎ **876/953-2650**) are ranked as one of the top five golf courses in the world, according to an expert assessment. It is an unusual and challenging seaside and mountain course, built on the shores of the Caribbean.

The excellent course at **Tryall Golf, Tennis & Beach Club** (☎ **876/956-5660**) is the site of the Jamaica Classic Annual.

The **Half Moon** (☎ 876/953-2560) at Rose Hall features a championship course designed by Robert Trent Jones. **The Ironshore Golf & Country Club** (☎ 876/953-2800) is another well-known 18-hole golf course with a 72 par. See chapter 4 for details about these Montego Bay courses.

On the north shore, there's **SuperClub's Runaway Golf Club** (☎ 876/973-2561) at Runaway Bay and **Sandals Golf & Country Club** (☎ 876/974-0119) at Ocho Rios. See chapter 6.

In Mandeville, **Manchester Country Club,** Brumalia Road (☎ 876/962-2403), is Jamaica's oldest golf course but with only nine greens. Beautiful vistas unfold from 2,201 feet above sea level. See chapter 7.

HIKING

Jamaica has some of the most varied and unusual topography in the Caribbean, including a mountain range laced with rough rivers, streams, and waterfalls. The 192,000-acre **Blue Mountain–John Crow Mountain National Park** is maintained by the Jamaican government.

The mountainsides are covered with coffee fields, producing a blended version that's among the leading exports of Jamaica. But for the nature enthusiast, the mountains reveal an astonishingly complex series of ecosystems that change radically as you climb from sea level into the fog-shrouded peaks.

The most popular climb begins at Whitfield Hall, a high-altitude hostel and coffee estate about 6 miles from the hamlet of Mavis Bank. Reaching the summit of Blue Mountain Peak (3,000 feet above sea level) requires between 5 and 6 hours, each way. En route, hikers pass through acres of coffee plantations and forest, where temperatures are cooler (sometimes much cooler) than you might expect, and where high humidity encourages thick vegetation. Along the way, watch for an amazing array of bird life, including hummingbirds, many species of warblers, rufous-throated solitaires, yellow-bellied sapsuckers, and Greater Antillean pewees.

The best preparation against the wide ranges of temperature you'll encounter is to dress in layers and bring bottled water. If you opt for a 2am departure in anticipation of watching the sunrise from atop the peak, carry a flashlight as well. Sneakers are usually adequate, although many climbers bring their hiking boots to Jamaica solely in anticipation of their trek up Blue Mountain. Be aware that even during the dry season (from December to March), rainfall is common. During the rainy season (the rest of the year), these peaks can get up to 150 inches of rainfall a year, and fogs and mists are frequent.

You can always opt to head out alone into the Jamaican wilderness for hiking expeditions on your own, but considering the dangers of such an undertaking, and the crime you might encounter en route, it isn't completely advisable. A better bet involves engaging one of Kingston's best-known specialists in ecosensitive tours, **Sunventure Tours,** 30 Balmoral Ave., Kingston 10, Jamaica, W.I. (☎ 876/960-6685). The staff here can always arrange an individualized tour for you or your party, but if you're interested in their mainstream roster of offerings, two of the options include the following: Their Blue Mountain Sunrise Tour involves a camp-style overnight in one of the most remote and inaccessible areas of Jamaica. For a fee ranging from U.S.$80 to U.S.$115 per person, participants are retrieved at their Kingston hotels, driven to an isolated ranger station, Wildflower Lodge, that's accessible only via four-wheel drive vehicle, in anticipation of a two-stage hike that begins at 4:30pm. A simple mountaineer's supper is served at 6pm around a camp-fire at a ranger station near Portland Gap. At 3am, climbers hike by moonlight and flashlight to a mountaintop aerie that's selected because of its view of the sunrise over the Blue Mountains. Climbers stay aloft until around noon that day, before heading back down the mountain for an eventual return to their hotels in Kingston by 4pm.

A second popular offering involves an excursion from Kingston "Y's Waterfall" on the Black River, in southern Jamaica's Elizabeth Parish. Participants congregate in Kingston at 6:30am for a transfer to a raft and boating party near the hamlet of Lacovia, and an all-day waterborne excursion to a region of unusual ecological interest. Depending on the number of participants, fees range from U.S.$80 to U.S.$100 per person, a price that includes lunch.

HORSEBACK RIDING

The best riding is on the north shore. Jamaica's most complete equestrian center is **Chukka Cove Farm and Resort** (☎ 876/972-0814), at Richmond Llandovery, less than 4 miles east of Runaway Bay (see chapter 6). The best ride here is a 3-hour jaunt to the sea, where you can unpack your horse and swim in the surf. See chapter 6.

Another good program is offered at the **Rocky Point Riding Stables** (☎ 876/953-2286), Half Moon Club, Rose Hall, Montego Bay, which is housed in the most beautiful barn and stables in Jamaica (see chapter 4).

SCUBA DIVING

Diving is sometimes offered as part of all-inclusive packages by the island's major hotels. There are also well-maintained facilities independent of the hotels.

Jamaica boasts some of the finest waters for diving in the world, with depths averaging 35 to 95 feet. Visibility is usually 60 to 120 feet. Most diving is on coral reefs, which are protected as underwater parks. Fish, shells, coral, and sponges are plentiful on them. Experienced divers can also see wrecks, hedges, caves, drop-offs, and tunnels.

Near Montego Bay, **Seaworld Resorts** (☎ 876/953-2180), at the Cariblue Hotel, Rose Hall Main Road, offers scuba-diving excursions to offshore coral reefs among the most spectacular in the Caribbean. There are also PAIC-certified dive guides, one dive boat, and all necessary equipment for either inexperienced or certified divers. See chapter 4.

Outside Kingston, the **Buccaneer Scuba Club,** Morgan's Harbour, Port Royal (☎ 876/967-8061), is one of Jamaica's leading dive and water-sports operators. It offers a wide range of dive sites to accommodate various divers' tastes—from the incredible *Texas* wreck to the unspoiled beauty of the Turtle Reef. See chapter 7.

Negril is a hotbed of diving. **Negril Scuba Centre** (☎ 800/818-2963 or 876/957-9641), in the Negril Beach Club Hotel, Norman Manley Boulevard, is the area's most modern, best-equipped scuba facility. Equally as good is **Scuba World,** a PADI-approved five-star dive shop located at Orange Bay (☎ 876/957-6290). See chapter 5.

TENNIS

All-Jamaica Hardcourt Championships are played in August at **the Manchester Country Club,** Brumalia Road, P.O. Box 17, Mandeville (☎ 876/962-2403). The courts are open for general play during the rest of the year. See chapter 7.

Ciboney Ocho Rios, Main Street, Ocho Rios (☎ 876/974-1027), focuses more on tennis than any other resort in the area. It offers three clay-surface and three hard-surface courts, all lit for nighttime play. Residents play free either day or night, but nonresidents must call and make arrangements with the manager. See chapter 6.

In Montego Bay, you'll find excellent tennis facilities at **Wyndham Rose Hall Golf & Beach Resort,** at Rose Hall (☎ 876/952-2650); **Half Moon Golf, Tennis & Beach Club** (☎ 876/953-2211); and **Tryall Golf, Tennis & Beach Club,** St. James (☎ 876/956-5660). See chapter 4.

5 Health & Insurance

STAYING HEALTHY

Traveling to Jamaica should not adversely affect your health. Finding a good doctor in Jamaica is no real problem, and all of them speak English. The following health and insurance information generally also applies to Barbados.

Before leaving home, you can obtain a list of English-speaking doctors from the **International Association Medical Assistance to Travelers** (IAMAT), in the United States at 417 Centre St., Lewiston, NY 14092 (☎ **716/754-4883**); in Canada at 40 Regal Rd., Guelph, ON N1K 1B5 (☎ **519/836-0102**).

If you have a chronic medical condition, always talk to your doctor before leaving home. For problems like epilepsy, a heart condition, diabetes, or an allergy, wear a **Medic Alert identification tag.** For a lifetime membership, the cost is a well-spent U.S.$35 if steel, U.S.$45 if silver-plated, and U.S.$60 if gold-plated. In addition there's a U.S.$15 annual fee. Contact Medic Alert Foundation, P.O. Box 1009, Turlock, CA 95381-1009 (☎ **800/825-3785;** fax 209/669-2495). Medic Alert's 24-hour hot line enables a foreign doctor to obtain your medical records.

Although tap water in Jamaica or Barbados is considered safe, it's better to drink bottled mineral water. Avoid iced drinks in local dives; however, first-class and deluxe hotels often make ice with purified water.

Many visitors suffer from diarrhea, even if they follow precautions. It usually passes quickly without medication, if you moderate your eating habits and drink only bottled mineral water until you recover. If symptoms persist, consult a doctor.

The Caribbean sun can be brutal, especially if you've come from a winter climate and haven't been exposed to a strong sun in some time. Limit your time on the beach the first day. If you do overexpose yourself, stay out of the sun until you recover. If your exposure is followed by fever or chills, a headache, nausea, or dizziness, see a doctor.

Mosquitoes are a nuisance. One of the biggest menaces is the "no-see-ums," which appear mainly in the early evening. Even if you can't see these tiny insects, you sure can "feel-um," as many Jamaicans or Bajans will agree. Screens can't keep these critters out, so you'll need to carry your favorite bug repellent.

Malaria-carrying mosquitoes in the Caribbean are confined largely to Haiti and the Dominican Republic, less so in Jamaica or Barbados. If you're going into the "wilds" of Jamaica, consult your doctor for antimalarial medication at least 8 weeks before you leave.

Take along an adequate supply of any prescription medications you require. Also, for safety's sake, bring along a written doctor's prescription that uses the generic name of the medicine—not the brand name. You may want to bring such over-the-counter items as first-aid cream, insect repellent, aspirin, and Band-Aids.

INSURANCE

Before purchasing insurance, check your current homeowner's, automobile, and medical insurance policies, and reread the membership contracts of automobile and travel clubs and credit cards.

Many credit-card companies insure their users in case of travel accidents when they pay for the travel with their card. Sometimes fraternal organizations have policies that protect members in case of sickness or accidents abroad.

Many homeowner's insurance policies cover theft of luggage during foreign travel and loss of such documents as a passport or an airline ticket. Coverage is usually limited to about U.S.$500. To submit a claim, you'll need police reports or a statement from a local medical authority that you did in fact suffer a loss or experience an illness. Some policies provide cash advances or arrange for immediate funds transfers.

If you need additional insurance, check with the following companies: **Travel Guard International,** 1145 Clark St., Stevens Point, WI 54481-9970 (☎ **800/826-1300** outside Wisconsin, or 715/345-0505), offers a comprehensive travel protection policy that covers lost luggage, emergency assistance, accidental death, trip cancellation, and medical coverage abroad. Package costs start at U.S.$45 and are based on your total trip cost. Children under 16 are automatically covered if accompanying adults have purchased a policy.

Travelers Insurance PAK, Travel Insured International, P.O. Box 280568, East Hartford, CT 06128-0568 (☎ **800/243-3174**), offers illness and accident coverage costing from U.S.$10 for 6 to 10 days. For lost or damaged luggage, U.S.$500 worth of coverage costs U.S.$20 for 6 to 10 days. Trip-cancellation insurance is U.S.$5.50 per U.S.$100 of coverage to a limit of U.S.$10,000 per person.

Wallach and Co., 107 W. Federal St., P.O. Box 480, Middleburg, VA 20118-0480 (☎ **800/237-6615** or 540/687-3172), offers coverage for between 10 and 120 days at U.S.$4 per day; this policy includes accident and sickness coverage up to U.S.$250,000. Medical evacuation is also included, along with U.S.$25,000 accidental death and dismemberment compensation. Provisions for trip cancellation can also be written into this policy at a nominal cost.

Travelex, P.O. Box 9408, Garden City, NJ 11530 (☎ **800/228-9792**), offers insurance packages priced from U.S.$10 to U.S.$59 per person for a trip lasting between 1 and 31 days. These packages include travel-assistance services and financial protection against trip cancellation, trip interruption, flight and baggage delays, accident-related medical costs, and medical evacuation coverages. An application for insurance can be arranged over the phone with a major credit or charge card.

If you book a package tour, do think about purchasing travel insurance, especially if the tour operator asks you to pay up front. But don't buy your insurance from the tour operator! If they don't fulfill their obligation to provide you with the vacation you've paid for, there's no reason to think they'll fulfill their insurance obligations, either. Get travel insurance through one of the independent agencies recommended above.

6 Tips for Travelers with Special Needs

FOR TRAVELERS WITH DISABILITIES

Hotels rarely give much publicity to the facilities, if any, they offer persons with disabilities, so it's always wise to contact the hotel directly, in advance. Tourist offices probably won't be able to help you with such questions.

For names and addresses of operators of tours specifically for visitors with disabilities, and other relevant information, contact the **Society for the Advancement** of Travel for the Handicapped (SATH), 347 Fifth Ave., Suite 610, New York, NY 10016 (☎ 212/447-7284; fax 212/725-8253). Yearly membership dues in the society are U.S.$45, or U.S.$30 for senior citizens and students. Send a self-addressed, stamped envelope. SATH will also provide you with hotel/resort accessibility for Caribbean destinations.

Travelers with disabilities may also want to consider joining a tour that caters specifically to them. One of the best operators is **Flying Wheels Travel,** 143 W. Bridge (P.O. Box 382), Owatonna, MN 55060 (☎ 800/525-6790). They offer various customized, all-inclusive vacation packages and cruises in the Caribbean, as well as private tours in minivans with lifts. Another good company is **FEDCAP Rehabilitation Services,** 211 W. 14th St., New York, NY 10011. Call ☎ 212/727-4200 or fax 212/721-4374 for information about membership and tours.

Vision-impaired travelers should contact the **American Foundation for the Blind,** 11 Penn Plaza, Suite 300, New York, NY 10001 (☎ 800/232-5463), for information on traveling with seeing-eye dogs.

You can obtain a free copy of *Air Transportation of Handicapped Persons,* published by the U.S. Department of Transportation. Write for Free Advisory Circular No. AC12032, Distribution Unit, U.S. Department of Transportation, Publications Division, 3341Q 75th Ave., Landover, MD 20785 (☎ 301/322-4961; fax 301/386-5394).

For a U.S.$25 annual fee, consider joining **Mobility International USA,** P.O. Box 10767, Eugene, OR 97440 (☎ 541/343-1284 voice and TDD; fax 541/343-6812). It answers questions on various destinations and also offers discounts on its programs, videos, and publications. Their quarterly newsletter, *Over the Rainbow,* provides information on Caribbean hotel chains, accessibility, and transportation.

TIPS FOR BRITISH TRAVELERS   The **Royal Association for Disability and Rehabilitation (RADAR),** Unit 12, City Forum, 250 City Rd., London, EC1V 8AF (☎ 0171/250-3222; fax 0171/250-0212), publishes holiday "fact packs," three in all, which sell for £2 each or all three for £5. The first one provides general information, including planning and booking a holiday, insurance, finances, and useful organization and holiday providers. The second outlines transportation available when going abroad and equipment for rent. The third deals with specialized accommodations.

FOR GAY & LESBIAN TRAVELERS

Jamaica and Barbados have repressive laws to contend with. Homosexuality is illegal in Barbados, and there is often a lack of tolerance here in spite of the large number of gay residents and visitors. Jamaica is the most homophobic island in the Caribbean, with harsh anti-gay laws, even though there is a large local gay population. One local advised that it's not smart for a white gay man to wander the streets of Jamaica at night.

Many all-inclusive resorts, notably the famous Sandals of Jamaica, have discriminatory policies. Although Sandals started off welcoming "any two people in love," they quickly switched to allowing only male/female couples. Gays are definitely excluded from their love nests. However, not all all-inclusives practice such blatant discrimination. Hedonism II, a rival of Sandals in Negril, is a "couples-only" resort, but any combination will do here. The Grand Hotel Lido, a more upscale all-inclusive in Negril, will welcome whatever combination shows up (even singles, for that matter).

There are a few publications and organizations that will help you learn about gay and lesbian travel in the Caribbean. Men can order *Spartacus* (U.S.$32.95), the international gay guide, or *Odysseus, The International Gay Travel Planner* (U.S.$27), an annually published guide to international gay accommodations. Both lesbians and gay men might want to pick up a copy of Ferrari Travel Planner (U.S.$16). These books and others are available from **Giovanni's Room,** 1145 Pine St., Philadelphia, PA 19107 (☎ **215/923-2960**).

Our World, 1104 N. Nova Rd., Suite 251, Daytona Beach, FL 32117 (☎ **904/441-5367**), is a magazine devoted to options and bargains for gay and lesbian travel worldwide. It costs U.S.$35 for 10 issues. *Out and About,* 8 W. 19th St., Suite 401, New York, NY 10011 (☎ **800/929-2268**), has been hailed for its "straight" reporting about gay travel. It profiles the best gay or gay-friendly hotels, restaurants, gyms, clubs, and other places, with coverage of destinations throughout the world. The cost is U.S.$49 a year for 10 information-packed issues, plus four events calendars. It aims for the more upscale gay male and lesbian traveler, and has been praised by everybody from *Travel and Leisure* to the *New York Times.* Both these publications are also available at most gay and lesbian bookstores.

International Gay and Lesbian Travel Association (IGLTA), 4331 N. Federal Hwy. #304, Ft. Lauderdale, FL 33308 (☎ **800/448-8550** or 954/776-2626), encourages gay and lesbian travel worldwide. With more than 1,300 member agencies, it specializes in networking, providing the information travelers would need to link up with the appropriate gay-friendly service organization or tour specialist. It offers quarterly newsletters, marketing mailings, and a membership directory that's updated four times a year. Travel agents who are IGLTA members will be tied into this organization's vast information resources.

FOR SENIORS

Write for a free booklet called *101 Tips for the Mature Traveler,* available from **Grand Circle Travel,** 347 Congress St., Suite 3A, Boston, MA 02210 (☎ **800/221-2610** or 617/350-7500). This tour operator offers extended vacations, escorted programs, and cruises that feature unique learning experiences for seniors at competitive prices.

The Mature Traveler, a monthly 12-page newsletter on senior-citizen travel is a valuable resource. It is available by subscription ($30 a year) from GEM Publishing Group, Box 50400, Reno, NV 89513-0400. GEM also publishes *The Book of Deals,* a collection of more than 1,000 senior discounts on airlines, lodging, tours, and attractions around the country; it's available for U.S.$9.95 by calling ☎ **800/460-6676.**

SAGA International Holidays, 222 Berkeley St., Boston, MA 02116 (☎ **800/343-0273**), books senior citizens on cruises to the Caribbean, offering them good value. To participate, persons must be 50-plus. Medical insurance is included in the net price of the cruise-ship booking.

Information on travel for seniors is also available from the **National Council of Senior Citizens,** 8403 Colesville Rd., Suite 1200, Silver Spring, MD 20910 (☎ **301/578-8800;** fax 301/578-8999). A nonprofit organization, the Council charges a membership fee of U.S.$13 per person or per couple, for which you receive monthly issues of a newsletter and membership benefits, including travel services and discounts on hotels, motels, and auto rentals.

Golden Companions, part of the larger Travel Companion Exchange, has helped travelers 45 and older find compatible companions since 1987. The organization offers a 6-month introductory membership for U.S.$99. The membership includes a bimonthly newsletter, with travel tips for singles and listings of others seeking travel partners. Newsletter-only subscriptions cost U.S.$48 for 12 months.

Tying the Knot in Jamaica

In high season, some Jamaican hotels celebrate several weddings a day. Many of the larger resorts, such as Sandals (call ☎ **800/SANDALS**), can arrange for an officiant, a photographer, and even the wedding cake and champagne. Some resorts will even throw in your wedding with the cost of your honeymoon at the hotel. Both the Jamaica Tourist Board and your hotel will assist you with the paperwork. Participants must reside on Jamaica for 24 hours before the ceremony. Bring birth certificates and affidavits saying you've never been married before, or, if you've been divorced, bring copies of your divorce papers, or in the case of widows and widowers, a copy of the deceased spouse's death certificate. The cost of the license and stamp duty is U.S.$230. The cost of the ceremony can range from U.S.$50 to U.S.$200, depending on how much legwork you want to do yourself. You may apply in person at the **Ministry of National Security and Justice,** 12 Ocean Blvd., Kingston, Jamaica (☎ **876/922-0080**).

For a free brochure, write **Golden Companions,** P.O. Box 833, Amityville, NY 11701 (☎ **800/392-1256** or 516/454-0170).

   Elderhostel, 75 Federal St., Boston, MA 02110-1941 (☎ **617/426-7788**), maintains an array of postretirement study programs, several of which are in the Caribbean, primarily in Jamaica and The Bahamas. Programs do vary throughout the year, but some, like the one offered at Hofstra University's Marine Laboratory in St. Anne's Bay, Jamaica, are usually scheduled several times during the year. Participants in this U.S.$1,126, 12-day, all-inclusive (except airfare) program study marine biology including snorkeling in the morning course. The afternoon course includes hiking and bus trips to natural history sites, and in the evening, guest lecturers present local cultural histories. Most courses last 2 or 3 weeks and are a good value, considering that hotel accommodations in student dormitories or modest inns, all meals, tuition, and activities are included. Courses involve no homework, are ungraded, and center mostly on the liberal arts. Participants must be age 55 or older. However, if two members go as a couple, only one member needs to be 55 or over. Write for their free newsletter and a list of upcoming courses and destinations.

   In addition, many major airlines, including American, United, Continental, US Airways, and TWA all offer discount programs for senior travelers—be sure to ask whenever you book a flight.

FOR FAMILIES

Jamaica and Barbados are two of the top family vacation destinations in the Caribbean. The smallest toddlers can spend blissful hours on sandy beaches and in the shallow seawater or in swimming pools constructed with them in mind. There's no end to the fascinating pursuits offered for older children, ranging from boat rides to shell collecting to horseback riding, hiking, and dancing. Some children are old enough to learn to snorkel and to explore an underwater wonderland. Skills such as swimming and windsurfing are taught, and there are a variety of activities unique to the islands.

   Many of the island's resorts realize that Mom and Dad's idea of fun may not be quite what the kids had in mind. So they offer perks like daily supervised children's activities, baby-sitters, family discounts, and kid's meals, helping your kids to have a great vacation while their parents gain some freedom to relax, too.

Boscobel Beach Resort in Ocho Rios, not too far from Jamaica's famous land-mark, Dunn's River Falls, was the island's first all-inclusive hotel designed specifi-cally for the family. This resort offers parents the atmosphere of a country club, and children aged 14 and under always stay free.

Regrettably, we think the hotel hasn't been well maintained lately, and many readers have complained—justifiably—about the state of their rooms. So, in spite of the wide publicity this resort gets, we don't feel we can recommend them in this edition. However, there are still many other family-oriented places in better shape.

Just a half hour to the west of Ocho Rios is Runaway Bay (see page 000), home of the **Franklyn D. Resort,** Jamaica's all-suite, all-inclusive family resort. F.D.R. offers families an incredible service—a nanny is assigned to each one-, two-, and three-bedroom suite. This warm, friendly Jamaican woman will look after both parents and children while they're at F.D.R. She will cook, clean, and act as companion to the children day or night. And, if the kids want to mingle with other youngsters, they may do so at the resort's fully supervised "Mini Club," complete with satellite television, Nintendo, and other diversions. And best of all, children under 16 sharing their parents' room stay, eat, and play completely free.

Montego Bay, on the northwest coast, is the resort capital of Jamaica, so it's no surprise to find here three special resorts that welcome families on vacation.

A member of the Elegant Resorts group, the **Half Moon Golf, Tennis & Beach Club** (see page 75) welcomes children to their new Children's Activity Centre, which features an array of indoor/outdoor recreational and educational games and activities including a kiddies' swimming pool, duck pond, thatched play houses, a horseshoe court, and tennis courts. Trained professionals will guide children in arts and crafts, nature walks, tennis and golf lessons, treasure hunts, and culinary lessons among other activities. The centre caters to children ages 3 to 14 and is open from 8am to noon and from 2 to 6pm. Daytime and evening nanny service is also available for an additional cost.

Handsomely situated on an old sugar plantation, the **Wyndham Rose Hall Golf & Beach Resort** (see page 80) keeps children entertained in their "Kids Klub," while parents enjoy their four restaurants, three cocktail bars, and complete athletic facility. The Kids Klub at Wyndham operates Monday through Saturday, from 10am until 4pm with separate activities offered for children according to their age group—5 to 8 years or 9 to 12 years. The facility runs activities such as building sand castles, a mini-Olympics, movies, volleyball, and swim races. The resort also features an expanded kid's menu and gives families discounts of up to 50% off if you book your kids an adjoining or separate room.

Holiday Inn SunSpree (see page 85) is located just 10 minutes from Montego Bay's airport, and after a massive renovation program, now has a new emphasis on families with children. The resort's innovative Kids Spree Vacation Club welcomes youngsters from 6 months to 12 years absolutely free. Granny's Nursery (for those up to 2 years old) will feature trained Jamaican nannies—noted for having a way with children—who will rock a restless little guest to a local lullaby. From there on up, different activities are planned for children in different age groups that include nature walks, story times, reggae dance lessons, and pizza parties.

Within a 20-minute drive of all the attractions and activities of Montego Bay is **Comfort Inn & Suites** (see page 81), a luxury all-suite resort set on 14 acres over-looking the Caribbean. This resort offers one-, two-, or three-bedroom units, and as part of the Kiddies Club, fully trained nannies are on hand to keep children busy.

Amenities for children 2 to 11 years include a "Kiddie" restaurant, an arts and crafts pavilion, and a video room. Teens will find advanced video games, a billiards room, a music video room with snacks, and a self-service soda fountain.

Moving to the west in Negril, where 7 miles of uninterrupted white-sand beach grace Jamaica's coast, lies a wonderful beachfront property. The **Poinciana Beach Hotel** (see page 117) offers a variety of activities in its "Kiddie's Club," designed for children aged 3 to 12. Poinciana lets everyone create his or her own personal vacation experience. Separate arrangements can be made for infant care and for baby-sitting on a daily, nightly, or weekly basis. Under Poinciana's all-inclusive family plan, there is no extra cost for a child under 12 sharing a room or villa with an adult.

Nestled among the private coves of Negril's Bloody Bay, the 256-unit **Point Village Resort** (see page 111) is an all-inclusive family resort. Coupled with the casual, laid-back flavor of Negril, Point Village pays special attention to the needs of their littlest of guests. Point Village has a "Kiddie's Club," with fully trained nannies on hand to keep children busy. Amenities for children include a "Kiddie" restaurant, an arts and crafts pavilion, and a video room. Teens find advanced video games, a music video room with snacks, and more.

Jamaica's newest family resort, **Beaches Negril** (see page 115) opened in February 1997. Located on 20 acres of lush landscape, with more than 1,400 feet of white-sand beach, Beaches Negril has a total of 225 rooms including beach-front suites. There are five restaurants including the Beach Grill, which features live entertainment and caters to children only from 5pm to 9pm; parents may be included at the child's special invitation. The resort offers an endless variety of land and water sports, and child-oriented activities for kids as well as facilities catering specifically for teens. There are two freshwater pools—one of which has a swim-up soda fountain and a toddler's paddling pool.

7 Package Tours

Package tours are not the same thing as escorted tours. They are simply a way of buying your airfare and accommodations at the same time.

And for popular destinations like Jamaica, they are really the smart way to go, because they save you a ton of money. In many cases, a package that includes airfare, hotel, and transfers to and from the airport will cost you less than just the hotel alone if you booked it yourself. That's because packages are sold in bulk to tour operators, who resell them to the public. Economy and convenience are the chief advantages of a package tour; everything's neatly tied up with a single price tag. There are extras, of course, but in general you'll know in advance the rough cost of your vacation, and can budget accordingly. The disadvantage is that you may find yourself in a hotel room you dislike, yet are virtually trapped there because you've already paid for it.

Packages can vary a great deal. Some offer a better class of hotels than others. Some offer the same hotels for lower prices. And some offer flights on scheduled airlines while others book charters. In some packages, your choices of accommodations and travel days may be limited. Some packages let you choose between escorted vacations and independent vacations; others will allow you to add on just a few excursions or escorted day trips (also at prices lower than if you booked them yourself) without booking an entirely escorted tour. The time you spend shopping around will be well rewarded.

The easiest place to start looking is the travel section of your local Sunday newspaper. Also check the ads in the back of national travel magazines like *Travel & Leisure, National Geographic Traveler*, and *Condé Nast Traveler.*

To save time comparing the price and value of all the package tours out there, you can call **TourScan Inc.,** P.O. Box 2367, Darien, CT 06820 (☎ **800/962-2080** or 203/655-8091). Every season, the company gathers and computerizes the contents of about 200 brochures containing 10,000 different vacations in the Caribbean, The Bahamas, and Bermuda. TourScan selects the best value at each hotel and condo. Two catalogs are printed each year. Each lists a broad-based choice of hotels on most of the islands of the Caribbean, in all price ranges. (The scope of the islands and resort hotels is amazing.) Write to TourScan for their catalogs (U.S.$4 each; the price is credited to any TourScan vacation).

You can often get great package deals through the airlines. Most prominent among these is the tour desk at **American Airlines Fly-Away Vacations** (☎ **800/321-2121**). Holding an impressive array of vacant hotel rooms in inventory, American often sells Caribbean hotel bookings at prices substantially lower than similar rooms booked by an individual traveler. The packages are available only to passengers who simultaneously purchase transit to the Caribbean on American Airlines.

It's best to remain flexible in your departure and return dates, because greater savings might be available to those willing to shift preferred dates slightly to take advantage of an unsold block of nights at a hotel. For details and more information, ask for the tour desk at American Airlines. (Many hotels they might offer are reviewed in this guidebook.) The telephone representative can sometimes also arrange a discounted rental car for however many days you specify.

Other leading tour operators to the Caribbean include:

Caribbean Concepts, 1428 Brickell Ave., Suite 402, Miami, FL 33131 (☎ **888/741-7711** in the U.S., or 305/373-8687; fax 305/373-8310), offering all-inclusive low-cost air-and-land packages to the islands, including apartments, hotels, villas, or condo rentals.

Consider also **Delta's Dream Vacations** (☎ **800/872-7786**), which offers customized trips to Jamaica or Barbados lasting from 2 to 20 days, including airfare, accommodations, and transfers. Tickets are refundable, and you can cancel for any reason.

If you're seeking just general independent packages, consider:

Renaissance Vacations, 2655 LeJeune Rd., Suite 400, Coral Gables, FL 33134 (☎ **800/468-3571** in the U.S.), offers all-inclusive deals to Ocho Rios, but books only hotels—not flights. **Horizon Tours,** 1634 Eye St. NW, Suite 301, Washington, DC 20006 (☎ **800/395-0025** or 202/393-8390; fax 202/393-1547), specializes in all-inclusive upscale resorts on both Jamaica and Barbados. **Apple Vacations East** (☎ **800/727-3400**) offers some 40 resorts in Jamaica, ranging from Ocho Rios to Negril, from European-plan resorts to all-inclusives, but it deals only with travel agents. Your travel agent can book through Apple.

Despite the proliferation of the many bucket shops advertising special deals to the Caribbean (and Jamaica), your best bet might involve simply walking into the nearest office of North America's largest chain of travel agencies, **Liberty Travel,** whose outlets are concentrated primarily on the Atlantic seaboard. Depending on their inventory and marketing priorities at the time of your call, deals may or may not be attractive. There's no overall toll-free number for the chain, as each branch operates as a semi-independent unit. Consult your telephone directory or call directory assistance for the number of the branch nearest you. You won't get much in the way of service, but you will get a good deal.

American Express Vacations (☎ **800/241-1700**) is another option.

FOR BRITISH TRAVELERS

Caribbean Connection, Concorde House, Forest Street, Chester CH1 1QR (☎ **01244/341131**), offers all-inclusive packages (airfare and hotel) to the Caribbean and customizes tours for independent travel. It publishes two catalogs of Caribbean offerings, one featuring more than 160 properties on all the major islands, and a 50-page catalog of luxury all-inclusive properties.

Other Caribbean specialists operating out of England include **Kuoni Travel,** Kuoni House, Dorking, Surrey RH5 4AZ (☎ **01306/740-888**). **Caribtours,** 161 Fulham Rd., London SW3 6SN (☎ **0171/581-3517**), is a small, very knowledgeable specialist, tailoring itineraries to meet your demanding travel requirements.

8 Flying to Jamaica

We strongly suggest that you read section 7, above, on package tours before you try to book your own airfare separately from your hotel. A package is really the way to go.

There are two **international airports** in Jamaica: Donald Sangster outside Montego Bay (☎ **887/952-4300**) and Norman Manley (☎ **876/924-8331**) outside Kingston. That means you can fly directly to the resort areas via Montego Bay without having to go to Kingston at all.

The most popular routings to Jamaica are from New York or Miami, and several airlines make connections through those cities convenient and easy. Remember to reconfirm all flights, going and returning, no later than 72 hours before departure.

Flying time from Miami is 1¼ hours; from Los Angeles, 5½ hours; from Atlanta, 2½ hours; from Dallas, 3 hours; from Chicago and New York, 3½ hours; and from Toronto, 4 hours.

One of the most popular services to Jamaica, partly because of its dozens of connections to other parts of its vast North American network, is provided by **American Airlines** (☎ **800/433-7300**). Passengers in the U.S. Northeast can opt for American's nonstop flight departing from New York's Kennedy International Airport every morning. It touches down first in Montego Bay, then it continues on to Kingston. On its return to New York, it usually departs from Montego Bay, touches down in Kingston for additional passengers, then continues nonstop back to Kennedy.

American Airlines passengers from other parts of North America usually will connect at Miami, where at least four daily flights depart throughout the day and evening for both Kingston and Montego Bay.

Air Jamaica (☎ **800/523-5585** in the U.S.), the national carrier, operates about 13 flights a week from New York's JFK, most of which stop at both Montego Bay and Kingston. They offer even more frequent flights from Miami. The airline has connecting service within Jamaica through its reservations network to a small independent airline, **Air Jamaica Express,** whose planes usually hold between 10 and 17 passengers. They fly from the island's international airports at Montego Bay and Kingston to small airports around the island, including Port Antonio, Boscobel (near Ocho Rios), Negril, and Tinson Pen (a tiny airport near Kingston).

US Airways (☎ **800/428-4322**) is a newer carrier in the Jamaica market, offering two flights daily from New York's La Guardia to Montego Bay. One of these flights stops in Charlotte, North Carolina, to pick up extra passengers; the other makes a stopover in Philadelphia, also picking up extra passengers. They both have early morning departures.

Canadians who prefer to fly their national carrier, **Air Canada** (☎ 800/776-3000 in the U.S., or 800/268-7240 in Canada), can depart for Jamaica either from Toronto or Montréal. Flights from Toronto leave four to seven times a week, depending on the season, touching down at both Montego Bay and Kingston. Flights from Montréal's Mirabel Airport depart twice a week (usually on Saturday and Sunday) for Montego Bay. Montréal-based travelers bound for Kingston transfer in either Toronto or Montego Bay, depending on the schedule. Connections on Air Canada link both Toronto and Montréal to virtually every other airport in Canada.

In addition, **Northwest Airlines** (☎ 800/225-2525) flies directly to Montego Bay daily from Minneapolis and Tampa.

Travelers based in Britain usually opt for one of the flights operated by the country's premier airline, **British Airways** (☎ 800/247-9297). Aircraft fly three times a week nonstop between London's Gatwick and Montego Bay, touching down briefly in Kingston before continuing back to London. **Air Jamaica** (see above) also began flying to London in 1996.

American and its competitors usually match dollar-for-dollar each other's fares to Jamaica—this is a fiercely competitive market.

GETTING THE BEST DEAL

Airlines generally charge different fares according to season. **Peak season,** which means winter in Jamaica, is most expensive; **off-season,** during summer, offers the least expensive fares. **Shoulder season** refers to the spring and fall months in between.

Some airlines (including American) offer special rates at a number of Jamaica's most interesting hotels, but only if you pay for them at the same time you buy your airline ticket. Most hotels participating in American's program are recommended separately in this guidebook, and the savings of simultaneous air and hotel book-ings can at times be substantial. (See also "Package Tours," above.)

It's important to watch your local newspaper for special promotional fares, which come and go with frequency and carry stringent requirements like advance pur-chase, minimum stay, and cancellation penalties. Any promotion could make the price of airfare to Jamaica even lower, depending on market conditions. Land arrangements (prebooking of hotel rooms) are often tied to promotional fares.

BUCKET SHOPS   Consolidators resell blocks of tickets consigned by major car-riers. They act as a clearinghouse for blocks of tickets that airlines discount and con-sign during normally slow periods of air travel. In the case of Jamaica, that usually means from mid-April to mid-December. Their prices are much better than the fares you could get yourself, and are often even lower than what your travel agent can get you. You see their ads in the small boxes at the bottom of the page in your Sunday travel section. Some of the most reliable consolidators include **1-800-FLY-4-LESS** or **1-800-FLY-CHEAP.** Another good choice, **Council Travel** (☎ 800/226-8624), caters especially to young travelers, but their bargain-base-ment prices are available to people of all ages.

TFI Tours International, 34 W. 32nd St., 12th floor, New York, NY 10001 (☎ 212/736-1140 in New York State, or 800/745-8000 elsewhere in the U.S.), offers tickets on both TWA and American Airlines from New York to such islands as St. Thomas, St. Croix, Puerto Rico, Jamaica, St. Maarten, and the Dominican

Republic at prices that usually averaged around 10% less than those offered by the airlines to anyone who phoned them directly.

REBATORS To confuse the situation even more, in the past few years rebators have begun to compete in the low-cost airfare market. Rebators are outfits that pass along to the passenger part of their commission, although many assess a fee for their services. And although they are not the same as travel agents, they sometimes offer roughly similar services. Some rebators sell discounted travel tickets, and also offer discounted land arrangements, including hotels and car rentals. Most rebators offer discounts averaging anywhere from 10% to 25%, plus a U.S.$25 handling charge.

Travel Avenue, 10 S. Riverside Plaza, Suite 1404, Chicago, IL 60606 (☎ **800/333-3335** in the U.S., or 312/876-6866), is one of the oldest agencies of its kind. It offers up-front cash rebates on every airline ticket over U.S.$350 it sells. It sells airline tickets to independent travelers who have already worked out their travel plans. Also available are tour and cruise fares, plus hotel bookings.

Another major rebator is **The Smart Traveller,** 3111 SW 27th Ave. (P.O. Box 330010), Miami, FL 33133 (☎ **800/448-3338** in the U.S., or 305/448-3338; fax 305/443-3544). This agency offers discounts on package tours, Caribbean cruises, dive packages, and villa and condo rentals.

FINDING BARGAINS ON THE WEB Increasingly, travel agencies and companies are using the Web as a medium to offer everything from vacations to plane reservations to budget airline tickets on major carriers.

There are too many companies now to mention, but a few of the better-respected ones are **Travelocity** (**www.travelocity.com**), **Microsoft Expedia** (**www.expedia.com**), and **Yahoo's Flifo Global** (**http://travel.yahoo.com/travel/**). Each has its own little quirks—Travelocity, for example, requires you to register with them—but they all provide variations of the same service. Just enter the dates you want to fly and the cities you want to visit, and the computer looks for the lowest fares. The Yahoo site has a feature called "Fare Beater," which will check flights on other airlines or at different times or dates in hopes of finding an even cheaper fare. Expedia's site will e-mail you the best airfare deal once a week if you so choose. Travelocity uses the SABRE computer reservations system that most travel agents use, and has a "Last-Minute Deals" database that advertises really cheap fares for those who can get away at a moment's notice.

Great last-minute deals are also available directly from the airlines themselves through a free e-mail service called **E-savers.** Each week, the airline sends you a list of discounted flights, usually leaving the upcoming Friday or Saturday, and returning the following Monday or Tuesday. You can sign up for all the major airlines at once by logging on to **Epicurious Travel** (**http://travel.epicurious.com/travel/c_planning/02_airfares/email/signup.html**), or go to each individual airline's Web site.

Airlines that maintain their own sites include **American Airlines** (www.americanair.com), **United Airlines** (www.ual.com), **Delta Air Lines** (www.deltaair.com), **Northwest Airlines** (www.nwa.com), **Air Jamaica** (www.airjamaica.com), **US Airways** (www.usairways.com), **Air Canada** (www.aircanada.ca), and **British Airways** (www.british-airways.com). These sites are the best way to check for day-to-day fares to get the very best deal on the flight of your choice.

9 Cruises

If you'd like to sail to Jamaica, in a home with an ocean view, a cruise ship might be for you. Some 300 passenger ships ply the Caribbean all year, and in January and February the number increases by 100 or so. You might want to pick up a copy of *Frommer's Caribbean Cruises 99* for more detailed information, or *Frommer's Caribbean Ports of Call,* 2nd edition.

Vacations to Go, 1502 Augusta Dr., Suite 415, Houston, TX 77057 (☎ **800/338-4962** in the U.S.), provides catalogs and information on discount cruises through the Atlantic, the Caribbean, and the Mediterranean. Annual membership costs U.S.$6.95 per family.

How should you book your cruise and get to the port of embarkation before the good times roll? If you have a travel agent you trust, by all means, leave the details to the tried and true. Many agents will propose a package deal that includes airfare to the cruise-departure point. It's possible to purchase your air ticket on your own and book your cruise ticket separately, but in most cases, you'll save money by combining the fares into a package deal.

If you don't have a regular travel agent, contact a cruise specialist. He or she will be likely to match you with a cruise line whose priorities and style are compatible with your needs and wants, and also steer you toward any of the special promotions that come and go as frequently as Caribbean rainstorms.

Some of the most likely contenders include the following: **Ambassador Tours,** 120 Montgomery St., Suite 400, San Francisco, CA 94104 (☎ **800/989-9000** or 415/357-9876); **Cruises Inc.,** 5000 Campuswood Dr. E., Syracuse, NY 13057 (☎ **800/854-0500** or 315/463-9695); **Cruises of Distinction,** 2750 S. Woodward Ave., Bloomfield Hills, MI 48304 (☎ **800/634-3445** or 810/332-3030); **Cruise Fairs of America,** Century Plaza Towers, 2029 Century Park E., Suite 950, Los Angeles, CA 90067 (☎ **800/456-4FUN** or 310/556-2925); **Kelly Cruises,** 1315 W. 22nd St., Suite 105, Oak Brook, IL 60521 (☎ **800/837-7447** or 708/990-1111); and **Hartford Holidays Travel,** 626 Willis Ave., Williston Park, NY 11596 (☎ **800/828-4813**). Any of these stay tuned to last-minute price wars brewing between such megacarriers as Carnival, Princess, Royal Caribbean, Holland America, and Premier.

Carnival Cruise Lines (☎ **800/327-9501**) offers some of the biggest and most brightly decorated ships afloat. It's the richest, boldest, brashest, and most successful mass-market cruise line in the world. One of its vessels (*Celebration*) departs from New Orleans for 7-day circuits through the western Caribbean that include stopovers at Montego Bay en route from Cozumel/Playa del Carmen and Grand Cayman. Carnival itineraries that depart from the coast of Florida include stopovers at Western Caribbean ports that include Ocho Rios, Jamaica, en route to Grand Cayman and the beaches of Mexico's Yucatán. Of the three Carnival vessels (*Destiny, Paradise,* and the slightly older *Imagination*) departing from Miami for Jamaica, the one that's likely to attract special notice is the supermegaship *Destiny.* Launched in 1996 and weighing in at a staggering 101,000 tons, and exceeded only by a vessel within the Princess fleet, it's one of the two largest cruise ships in the world. Even newer is the Carnival *Paradise,* which although classified as a megaship at 70,367 tons, is equivalent to the size of most of the other vessels within the Carnival fleet. Most of the company's Caribbean cruises offer good value, last between 4 and 16 days (most are 7 days), and feature nonstop activities, lots of glitter, and the hustle and bustle of passengers and crew members embarking and disembarking at every port. Food and tropical drinks are plentiful, although with vessels of this size, might convey a hint of being mass produced. The overall atmosphere is comparable to a floating theme park with hordes of visitors, loaded with whimsy and nonstop partying. Lots of single passengers, some of them with gleams in their eyes, opt for this line, and some actually get lucky. Despite the presence of lots of unattached or loosely attached adults, the line makes special efforts to amuse and entertain children between 2 and 17. The average onboard age is a relatively youthful 42, although ages range from 3 to 95.

Celebrity Cruises (☎ 800/437-3111) maintains five newly built, medium-to-large–size ships offering cruises of between 7 and 15 nights. Although many of them cruise through various regions of the Caribbean during part of the year, one in particular, *Century,* focuses exclusively on year-round circuits from Fort Lauderdale to the Western Caribbean. Ports of call include Key West, Cozumel, Grand Cayman, and Ocho Rios, Jamaica. Despite a recent merger of Celebrity with the larger and better-financed RCCL, Celebrity plans on maintaining its own identity and corporate structure within the larger framework of RCCL. The niche this line has created is unpretentious but classy, especially considering its relatively competitive prices. Accommodations are roomy and well equipped, and the cuisine is among the best in the business.

Costa Cruise Lines (☎ 800/462-6782), the U.S.-based branch of a cruise line that has thrived in Italy for about a century, maintains hefty to megasize vessels that are newer than those of many other lines afloat. Two of these offer virtually identical jaunts through the western Caribbean on alternate weeks, each of them departing from Fort Lauderdale. Itineraries through the western Caribbean include stopovers at, depending on the schedule, either Ocho Rios or Montego Bay in Jamaica, Grand Cayman, Key West, and Cozumel. There's an Italian flavor and lots of Italian design on board here, and an atmosphere of relaxed indulgence. The ships—*CostaRomantica* and *CostaVictoria*—feature tame versions of ancient Roman Bacchanalia as well as such celebrations as *Festa Italiana,* and focaccia and pizza parties by the pool.

Commodore Cruise Line (☎ 800/237-5361) has only one ship, a small, solid, not particularly glamorous, but highly seaworthy vessel (*Enchanted Isle*) that was renovated in 1997. It operates out of New Orleans. Despite a cheerful staff and lots of onboard activities, it's not quite up there with many of the newer vessels being launched by more affluent lines (don't expect state-of-the-art facilities). But the prices are extremely affordable. Passengers who embark from New Orleans for jaunts through the western Caribbean usually spend 3 full days of their 7-day cruise at sea, occupying the remaining 4 days at ports in Montego Bay, Jamaica; Grand Cayman; Cancun; or Cozumel. Theme cruises are popular with this line: Big Band music, Irish folklore, wine-tasting, and so on.

Holland America Line–Westours (☎ 800/426-0327) is the most high-toned of the mass-market cruise lines, with eight respectably hefty and good-looking ships, one of the newest and fanciest of which (*Veendam*) makes frequent stopovers in Ocho Rios. These occur at 14-day intervals during 9 months of the year, in conjunction with 7-day cruises that stop at such other western Caribbean ports as

Playa del Carmen and Cozumel, Mexico; Grand Cayman; and Half Moon Cay, the company's private island in The Bahamas. Maintaining its individual identity despite full ownership by Carnival Cruise Lines, HAL usually offers solid value, with very few jolts or surprises, and an overall sense of squeaky-clean thrift and respectability. Expect mature travelers on board who expect (and get) returns for their dollar. Late-night revelers and serious partiers might want to book cruises on other lines such as Carnival.

Premier Cruises (☎ **800/990-7770**) was formed in 1997 after a complicated merger. Although its name is most closely associated with short cruises from the coast of Florida to The Bahamas aboard the company's child-friendly Big Red Boat, the reorganized Premier, at least since 1997, has become a cost-effective competitor in the Jamaica-bound cruise market as well. Don't expect much glamour or cutting-edge technology, as this reconfigured line's ships are oldies but goodies, but you'll get extremely good value for the dollars you'll invest. Premier's *Ocean Breeze* is a 21,000-ton much-renovated semi-antique with smallish cabins and an impressive pedigree. (It's one of very few non-naval ships in the world that was christened by Queen Elizabeth II personally.) Known for its relatively inexpensive rates, it uses Montego Bay as home port for 7-day cruises that travel as far as the first lock of the Panama Canal. En route it includes visits to Colombia (Cartagena), Panama (the San Blas Islands), and Costa Rica (Puerto Limón). Despite the line's preference for older, oft-rebuilt, and sometimes idiosyncratic ships that often have distinct personalities and sometimes old-fashioned architectural features, Premier is a specialist at offering cost-effective, and sometimes free, hotel packages that allow participants to extend their holiday in Jamaica, either before or after their cruise experience.

Princess Cruises (☎ **800/421-0522**) has a large and far-flung fleet that during the life of this edition will total between 8 and 10 megavessels, at least two of which sail in Caribbean waters. Itineraries that include stopovers in Jamaica are offered aboard either the *Sun Princess* or the even newer *Sea Princess,* a state-of-the-art vessel scheduled for launching in October of 1998. Departing from Fort Lauderdale, the cruise ship schedules daylong stopovers at the beaches of the company's private island in The Bahamas, then moves on for calls at Ocho Rios, Jamaica; Grand Cayman; and Cozumel, Mexico. The company is one of the very few in the world offering luxury accommodations and upscale service as a standard feature aboard its megaships. These usually carry a smaller number of passengers than similarly sized vessels at less elegant lines. The company's clientele is upscale and relatively conservative, with an average passenger age of 55 or over.

Royal Caribbean Cruise Line (RCCL) (☎ **800/327-6700**) leads the industry in the development of megaships. Most of this company's dozen or so vessels weigh in at around 73,000 tons, are among the largest of any line afloat, and have more impressive hardware than many national navies. This rather mainstream line encourages a restrained house-party atmosphere that's a bit less frenetic than the more raucous Carnival cruises. The company is well run, and there are enough onboard activities to suit virtually any taste and age level. Though accommodations and accouterments are more than adequate, they are not all that upscale, and cabins aboard some of the line's older vessels tend to be a bit more cramped than the industry norm. At least three of the line's ships (*Enchantment, Majesty,* and

Splendour of the Seas) make it a point to stop in Jamaica as part of their midwinter itineraries, most of which last for 7 days, and some of which stretch out for 11 days. RCCL cruises that pay calls in Jamaica usually include visits to Grand Cayman, Playa del Carmen/Cozumel, and Key West as part of the same trip.

10 Getting Around

BY RENTAL CAR

Jamaica is big enough—and public transportation is unreliable enough—that a car is a necessity if you plan to do much independent sightseeing. Unfortunately, prices of car rentals in Jamaica have skyrocketed, and it is now one of the most expensive rental scenes in the Caribbean.

Subject to many variations depending on road conditions, driving time from Montego Bay to Negril (about 52 miles) is 1½ hours; from Montego Bay to Ocho Rios (67 miles), 1½ hours; from Ocho Rios to Port Antonio (66 miles), 2½ hours; from Ocho Rios to Kingston (54 miles), 2 hours; from Kingston to Mandeville (61 miles), 1½ hours; and from Kingston to Port Antonio (61 miles), 2 hours.

Road Mileage Chart

	Black River	Falmouth	Kingston	Mandeville	Montego Bay	Negril	Ocho Rios	Port Antonio	St. Anne's Bay
Black River	0	62	107	43	46	49	94	156	87
Falmouth	62	0	91	53	23	75	44	110	37
Kingston	107	91	0	61	119	153	54	61	59
Mandeville	43	53	61	0	70	92	72	117	62
Montego Bay	46	23	119	70	0	52	67	133	60
Negril	49	75	153	92	52	0	117	181	110
Ocho Rios	94	44	54	72	67	117	0	66	7
Port Antonio	156	110	61	117	133	181	66	0	73
St. Anne's Bay	87	37	59	62	60	110	7	73	0

In all likelihood, you can book a rental car as part of a package tour, but if you're reserving one on your own, here are some tips.

Car-rental rates vary even more than airline fares. The price depends on the size of the car, the length of time you keep it, where and when you pick it up and drop it off, where you take it, and a host of other factors.

Asking a few key questions could save you hundreds of dollars. For example, weekend rates may be lower than weekday rates. Ask if the rate is the same for pickup Friday morning as it is Thursday night. If you're keeping the car 5 or more days, a weekly rate may be cheaper than the daily rate. Some companies may assess a drop-off charge if you do not return the car to the same renting location; others, notably National, do not. Ask if the rate is cheaper if you pick up the car at the airport or a location in town. If you see an advertised price in your local newspaper, be sure to ask for that specific rate; otherwise you may be charged the standard (higher) rate. Don't forget to mention membership in AAA, AARP, frequent-flyer programs, and trade unions. These usually entitle you to discounts ranging from 5% to 30%. Ask your travel agent to check any and all of these rates.

And most car rentals are worth at least 500 miles on your frequent-flyer account! Don't forget to have your account credited.

There are Internet resources that can make comparison shopping easier. For example, Yahoo's partnership with Flifo Global travel agency allows you to look up rental prices for any size car at more than a dozen rental companies in hundreds of cities. Just enter the size car you want, the rental and return dates, and the city where you want to rent, and the server returns a price. It will even make your reservation for you. Point your browser to **http://travel.yahoo.com/travel/** and then choose "Reserve car" from the options listed.

On top of the standard rental prices, other optional charges apply to most car rentals. First of all, there's a hefty 15% government tax. The Collision Damage Waiver (CDW), which requires you to pay for damage to the car in a collision, is covered by many credit card companies. Check with your credit card company before you go so you can avoid paying this fee, although it's mandatory if you rent in Jamaica from Budget.

The car-rental companies also offer additional liability insurance (if you harm others in an accident), personal accident insurance (if you harm yourself or your passengers), and personal effects insurance (if your luggage is stolen from your car). If you have insurance on your car at home, you are probably covered for most of these unlikelihoods. If your own insurance doesn't cover you for rentals, or if you don't have auto insurance, you should consider the additional coverage (the car-rental companies are liable for certain base amounts, depending on the state).

Since accident claims may be difficult to resolve, and since billing irregularities can occur even in the best of companies, it's best to stick to branches of U.S.-based rental outfits.

Avis (☎ **800/331-1084** in the U.S.) maintains offices at the international airports in both Montego Bay (☎ **876/952-4543**) and Kingston (☎ **876/924-8013**).

Budget is represented in Jamaica by Sun Tours Car Rental (☎ **876/952-5185** for reservations and information, or call 876/952-3838 at the Montego Bay airport). A daily collision damage waiver of U.S.$12 to U.S.$15 is mandatory. In the event of an accident, renters are still responsible for the first U.S.$1,000, plus tax, worth of damage to a rented car. A security deposit of the above amount is therefore required for a rental agreement to be completed.

Hertz (☎ **800/654-3001** in the U.S.) operates branches at the international airports in both Montego Bay (☎ **876/979-0438**) and Kingston (☎ **876/924-8028**). A collision damage waiver costs U.S.$12 to U.S.$15 extra per day, and reduces (but does not eliminate) the customer's responsibility for accident damage to the car. (Without the waiver, you'll be liable for the full cost of the car; with the waiver, the amount of your liability is reduced to between U.S.$1,200 and U.S.$1,500.)

DRIVING RULES *Driving in Jamaica is on the left side of the road*, not on the right side as in the United States, Canada, and Europe. You should exercise more than usual caution because of the unfamiliar terrain and be especially cautious at night. Speed limits in towns are 30 m.p.h., and outside towns, 50 m.p.h. Gas is measured by the imperial gallon (a British unit of measurement that is 25% more than a U.S. gallon); most stations don't accept credit cards. Your valid driver's license from home is acceptable for short-term visits to Jamaica.

ROAD MAPS The major highways of Jamaica tend to be well-marked and easily discernible because of their end destination, which is often adequately signposted. More complicated are secondary roads, urban streets, and feeder roads, whose markings sometimes are infuriatingly unclear. Recognizing this problem, the Jamaica Tourist Board has issued one of the best maps of the island available anywhere, the "Discover Jamaica" road map. Conforming to international cartographical standards, it contains a detailed overview of the entire island, as well as blowups of the Kingston, Montego Bay, Negril, Mandeville, Spanish Town, Port Antonio, and Ocho Rios areas. The map includes a very useful street index to Kingston. A copy of the map is usually available from any branch of the Jamaica Tourist Board, or from car-rental agencies. It's best to obtain one before your visit (see "Visitor Information," above), as local branches might be out of stock.

AUTO BREAKDOWNS   In case of breakdowns, telephone your car-rental agency for assistance. The staff will contact the nearest garage with which it has an affiliation, and a tow truck or mechanic will be dispatched to help you.

BY TAXI & BUS

Taxis in Kingston don't have meters, so agree on a price before you get in the car. In Kingston and the rest of the island, special taxis and buses for visitors are operated by JUTA (Jamaica Union of Travellers Association) and have the union's emblem on the side of the vehicle. All prices are controlled, and any local JUTA office will supply a list of rates. JUTA drivers do nearly all the ground transfers, and some offer sightseeing tours. We've found them pleasant, knowledgeable, and good drivers. There are many companies offering sightseeing tours of the island. Most cabs are old vehicles made in the United States.

BY MOTORBIKE & SCOOTER

Motorbikes and scooters can be rented in Montego Bay. You'll need a valid driver's license. **Montego Honda/Bike Rentals,** 21 Gloucester Ave. (☎ **876/952-4984**), rents Hondas for U.S.$30 to U.S.$35 a day, plus a U.S.$300 deposit. Bikes cost U.S.$35 a day, plus a U.S.$200 deposit. Deposits are refundable if the vehicles are returned in good shape. Hours are 7:30am to 5pm daily.

11 Tips on Accommodations

Because of the island's size and diversity, Jamaica offers a wider array of accommodations than anywhere else in the Caribbean.

Accommodations can range from intimate inns, with no more than six or seven rooms (and the very visible on-site presence of the owner/manager), to giant megahotels with an enviable array of services and such facilities as tennis compounds, therapeutic spas, and golf courses.

One increasingly popular option is the **all-inclusive resort.** Well-publicized, solidly financed, and boasting a wealth of facilities, these tend to be large resorts where all your drinking, dining, and sporting diversions are offered within the hotel compound as part of one all-inclusive price. Although they tend to limit your exposure to local life, they are undeniably convenient; they usually operate as self-sufficient planets with few incentives to travel beyond the fences that surround them. For carefree vacations, however, they're hard to beat, especially since your total cost will be made explicitly clear before you ever leave home.

An equally attractive option might be a **European-style hotel.** Jamaica offers many of these, a few of which are the finest in the Caribbean. There, on any given day, you'll be given an option of dining either within the hotel or at any of the small and charming restaurants that flourish nearby. Although you'll have to arrange evening transportation between your hotel and these independent restaurants, a battalion of taxis is almost always available throughout the evening to carry you there and back.

Other options include renting a **self-catering villa or apartment,** where you can save money by making your own meals in your own kitchen. See section 12, later in this chapter.

Also noteworthy are Jamaica's simple but decent **guest houses,** where low costs combine with a maximum exposure to local life. Unfortunately, these sometimes tend to lie far from beaches and offer almost none of the diversions and activities that vacationers seem to crave, and will probably not appeal to clients who insist on problem-free luxury.

Regardless of what you select, be assured that every choice has its own style, flavor, and methods of operating. Any will contribute richly to your understanding of the kaleidoscopic tapestry that is Jamaica.

HOTELS & RESORTS

There is no rigid classification of Jamaican hotels. The word "deluxe" is often used—or misused—when "first class" might be a more appropriate term. First class itself often isn't apt. We've presented fairly detailed descriptions of the properties mentioned in this book, so you'll get an idea of what to expect once you're there. Even in deluxe and first-class properties, however, don't expect top-rate service and efficiency. "Things," as they are called in Jamaica, don't seem to work as well in the tropics as they do in certain fancy resorts of California or Europe. When you go to turn on the shower, sometimes you get water and sometimes you don't. You may even experience island power failures.

Facilities often determine the choice of a hotel. For example, if golf is your passion, you may want to book into a hotel resort such as Tryall outside Montego Bay. If scuba diving is your goal, then head, say, for Negril. Regardless of your particular interest, there is a hotel catering to you.

One of the most common hotel and resort rates is **MAP,** meaning Modified American Plan. MAP usually includes room, breakfast, and dinner, unless the room rate has been quoted separately, and then it covers only breakfast and dinner. CP means Continental Plan—room and a light breakfast. **EP** is European Plan, room only. **AP,** American Plan, is the most expensive rate, because it includes room plus three meals a day. Nevertheless, you can save money by booking the AP rate. See "Tips on Dining Out," below, for some advice on making your choice.

GUEST HOUSES

An entirely different type of accommodation is the guest house, where most of the Jamaicans themselves stay when they travel. In Jamaica, the term "guest house" can mean anything. Sometimes so-called guest houses resemble simple motels built around swimming pools. Others are made up of small individual cottages with kitchenettes, constructed around a main building often containing a bar and a restaurant serving local food. Some are surprisingly comfortable, often with private baths and a swimming pool. You may or may not have air-conditioning. The rooms are sometimes cooled by ceiling fans, or breezes entering through open windows at night.

The guest house can't be topped for value. You can usually go to a big beach resort to enjoy its seaside facilities for only a small charge. Although bereft of frills, the guest houses we've recommended are clean and safe for families or single women. On the other hand, the least expensive are not places where you'd want to spend much time, because of their simple furnishings, diversions, and amenities.

Jamaica Accommodations

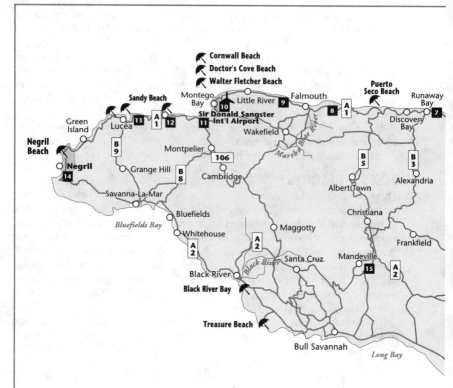

- Cornwall Beach
- Doctor's Cove Beach
- Walter Fletcher Beach
- Sandy Beach

Green Island
Negril Beach
Negril **14**

Lucea **13** **A 1** **12**
B 9
B 8
Grange Hill
Montpelier
106
Cambridge
Savanna-La-Mar
Bluefields
Bluefields Bay
Whitehouse
A 2
Black River
Black River Bay

Montego Bay **10** Little River **9**
Sir Donald Sangster Int'l Airport **11**
Wakefield
Falmouth
Martha Brae River

Puerto Seco Beach
Runaway Bay
8 **A 1**
Discovery Bay **7**
B 5
Albert Town
Alexandria
Christiana
Frankfield
B 3

Maggotty
A 2
Santa Cruz
Black River
Mandeville **15**
A 2

Treasure Beach
Bull Savannah
Long Bay

Caribbean Sea

Banana Shout **14**	De Montevin Lodge Hotel **2**	Half Moon Golf, Tennis, & Beach Club **9**
Beaches Negril **14**	Devine Destiny **14**	Hedonism II **14**
Belvedere **11**	Doctor's Cave Beach Hotel **10**	Hibiscus Lodge Hotel **6**
Blue Cave Castle **14**	Dragon Bay **2**	High Hope Estate **6**
Blue Harbour **10**	Drumville Cove Resort **14**	Holiday Inn Sun Spree **9**
Bonnie Vue Plantation Hotel **2**	Eaton Hall Beach Hotel **7**	Home Sweet Home **14**
Breezes Montego Bay **10**	El Greco Resort **10**	Hotel Astra **15**
The Caves **14**	The Enchanted Garden **6**	Hotel Four Seasons **1**
Charela Inn **14**	F.D.R. (Franklin D. Resort) **7**	Indies Hotel **1**
Ciboney Ocho Rios **6**	Fern Hill Club **2**	Jack Tar Grand Montego Beach Resort **10**
Club Jamaica Beach Resort **6**	Firefly Beach Cottages **14**	Jackie's on the Reef **14**
Comfort Inn & Suites **10**	Foote Prints **14**	Jamaica Grande Renaissance Resort **6**
Coral Cliff Hotel **10**	Goblin Hill Villas at San-San **2**	Jamaica Inn **6**
Couples Ocho Rios **5**	Goldeneye **3**	Jamaica Palace Hotel **2**
Courtleigh Hotel **1**	Good Hope **8**	
Coyaba **10**	Grand Lido **14**	
Crystal Waters **14**	Grand Lido Sans Souci **4**	

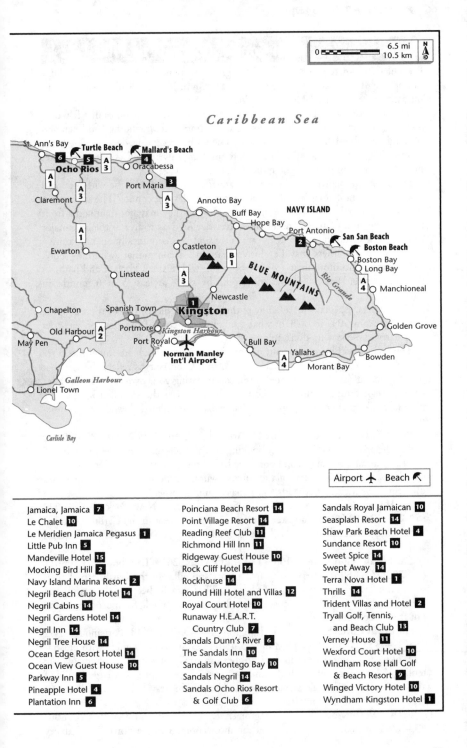

Caribbean Sea

0 ——— 6.5 mi / 10.5 km

N

St. Ann's Bay
Turtle Beach
Mallard's Beach
6
Ocho Rios 5 A3 4
A1 Oracabessa
A3 Port Maria 3
Claremont
A1 Annotto Bay
Ewarton Buff Bay
Linstead Hope Bay
NAVY ISLAND
Port Antonio 2
Castleton **San San Beach**
B1 **Boston Beach**
A3 Boston Bay
Newcastle Long Bay
BLUE MOUNTAINS
Rio Grande
A4 Manchioneal
Chapelton Spanish Town
1 **Kingston**
Old Harbour A2 Portmore *Kingston Harbour*
Port Royal Golden Grove
May Pen Bull Bay
Norman Manley Int'l Airport
Yallahs
A4 Bowden
Galleon Harbour Morant Bay
Lionel Town
Carlisle Bay

Airport ✈   Beach 🏳

Jamaica, Jamaica 7
Le Chalet 10
Le Meridien Jamaica Pegasus 1
Little Pub Inn 5
Mandeville Hotel 15
Mocking Bird Hill 2
Navy Island Marina Resort 2
Negril Beach Club Hotel 14
Negril Cabins 14
Negril Gardens Hotel 14
Negril Inn 14
Negril Tree House 14
Ocean Edge Resort Hotel 14
Ocean View Guest House 10
Parkway Inn 5
Pineapple Hotel 4
Plantation Inn 6

Poinciana Beach Resort 14
Point Village Resort 14
Reading Reef Club 11
Richmond Hill Inn 11
Ridgeway Guest House 10
Rock Cliff Hotel 14
Rockhouse 14
Round Hill Hotel and Villas 12
Royal Court Hotel 10
Runaway H.E.A.R.T.
    Country Club 7
Sandals Dunn's River 6
The Sandals Inn 10
Sandals Montego Bay 10
Sandals Negril 14
Sandals Ocho Rios Resort
    & Golf Club 6

Sandals Royal Jamaican 10
Seasplash Resort 14
Shaw Park Beach Hotel 4
Sundance Resort 10
Sweet Spice 14
Swept Away 14
Terra Nova Hotel 1
Thrills 14
Trident Villas and Hotel 2
Tryall Golf, Tennis,
    and Beach Club 13
Verney House 11
Wexford Court Hotel 10
Windham Rose Hall Golf
    & Beach Resort 9
Winged Victory Hotel 10
Wyndham Kingston Hotel 1

65

12 Renting Your Own Condo, Cottage, or Villa

Particularly if you're going as a family or group of friends, a housekeeping holiday can be one of the least expensive ways to vacation in Jamaica. Self-catering accommodations are now available at many locations.

The more upscale villas have a staff, or at least a maid who comes in a few days a week, and they also provide the essentials for home life, including bed linen and cooking paraphernalia. Condos usually come with a reception desk and are often comparable to life in a suite in a big resort hotel. Nearly all condo complexes provide swimming pools (some more than one).

Some private apartments in Jamaica are rented, either with or without maid service. This is more of a no-frills option than the villas and condos. The apartments may not be in buildings with swimming pools, and they may not maintain a front desk to help you. Cottages are the most freewheeling way to live in the four major categories of vacation homes. Most are fairly simple, many ideally opening onto a beach, although others may be clustered around a communal swimming pool. Many contain no more than a simple bedroom with a small kitchen and bath. In the peak winter season, reservations should be made at least 5 or 6 months in advance.

The savings, especially for a family of three to six people, or two or three couples, can range from 50% to 60% of what a hotel would cost. If there are only two in your party, these savings don't apply.

The savings will be on the rent, not on the groceries, which are sometimes 35% to 60% more costly than on the U.S. mainland. Grocery tabs reflect the fact that much foodstuff must be imported. Even so, preparing your own food will be a lot cheaper than dining around, as most restaurants, even the so-called inexpensive places, are likely to be more expensive than what is considered cheap in your hometown.

Villas of Distinction, P.O. Box 55, Armonk, NY 10504 (☎ **800/289-0900** or 914/273-3331), is one of the best booking agencies offering "complete vacations," including airfare, rental car, and domestic help. Some private villas offer two to five bedrooms, and almost every villa features a swimming pool. Islands on which you can rent villas include Barbados and Jamaica, among others.

At Home Abroad, Suite 6-H, 405 E. 56th St., New York, NY 10022 (☎ **212/421-9165**), has a roster of private homes for rent in the Caribbean, often with maid service included. All the Barbados and Jamaican villas have cooks and maids.

Caribbean Connection Plus Ltd., P.O. Box 261, Trumbull, CT 06611 (☎ **203/261-8603**), offers many apartments and villas in the Caribbean. This is one of the few reservations services whose staff has actually been on the islands and seen the various properties. Hence, the staff can talk to people from experience and not from a computer screen.

Hideaways International, 767 Islington St., P.O. Box 4433, Portsmouth, NH 03801-4433 (☎ **800/843-4433** or 603/430-4433), provides a guide with illustrations of its accommodations in the Caribbean so you'll get some idea of what you're renting. Most of its villas, which can hold up to three couples or a large family of about 10, come with maid service. You can also ask this travel club about discounts on plane fares and car rentals.

VHR, Worldwide, 235 Kensington Ave., Norwood, NJ 07648 (☎ **800/ 633-3284** or 201/767-9393), offers the most comprehensive portfolio of luxury villas, condominiums, resort suites, and apartments for rent not only in the Caribbean, but also in The Bahamas, Mexico, and the United States, including complete packages with airfare and car rentals. The company's more than 4,000 homes and suite resorts are hand-picked by the staff, and accommodations are generally less expensive than comparable hotel rooms.

Heart of the Caribbean Ltd., 17485 Peinbrook Dr., Brookfield, WI 53045 (☎ 800/231-5303 or 414/783-5303), is a villa wholesale company offering travelers a wide range of private villas and condos on several islands. Accommodations range from one to six bedrooms, and include modest villas and condos, as well as palatial estates. Homes have complete kitchens.

Rent-a-Home International, 7200 34th Ave. NW, Seattle, WA 98117 (☎ 800/488-RENT or 206/789-9377), maintains an inventory of several thousand properties, specializing in condos and villas with weekly rates ranging from U.S.$700 to U.S.$50,000. It arranges weekly or longer bookings. For their color catalog including prices, descriptions, and pictures, send U.S.$15, which will be applied to your rental.

Sometimes local tourist offices will also advise you on vacation-home rentals if you write or call them directly.

13 Tips on Dining Out

The bad news is that dining in Jamaica is generally more expensive than in either the United States or Canada. Restaurant prices are in tune with Europe rather than America. Virtually everything must be imported, except the fish or Caribbean lobster that is caught locally, and some fruits and vegetables. Service is automatically added to most restaurant tabs, usually 10% to 15%. Even so, if service has been good, it's customary to tip extra.

To save money, many visitors prefer the Modified American Plan (MAP), which includes room, breakfast, and one main meal per day, nearly always dinner. You can then have lunch somewhere else, or if your hotel has a beach, order a light à la carte lunch at the hotel, the cost of which is added to your bill. The American Plan (AP), on the other hand, includes all three meals per day. Drinks, including wine, are usually extra.

If you want to eat your main meals outside the hotel, book a Continental Plan (CP), which includes only breakfast. To go one step further, choose the European Plan (EP), which includes no meals.

Before booking a hotel, it's wise to have a clear understanding of what is included in the various meal plans offered.

In the summer, only the most sophisticated and posh establishments require men to wear jackets.

Check also to see if reservations are required. In the winter, you may find all the tables gone at some of the more famous places. At all places, wear a cover-up if you're lunching; don't enter a restaurant attired in a bikini.

To save money, stick to regional food whenever possible. For a main dish, that usually means Caribbean lobster or fish (see "A Taste of Jamaica," in chapter 2). You may want to avoid too much red meat; it's probably flown in and may have been waiting on the island long before you arrived on the beach.

Frankly, it's difficult for first-time visitors driving rented cars to navigate the unsatisfactory Jamaican roads at night looking for a special little restaurant. The restaurant's food may be good, but getting there can be dangerous, because roads

Jamaica Dining

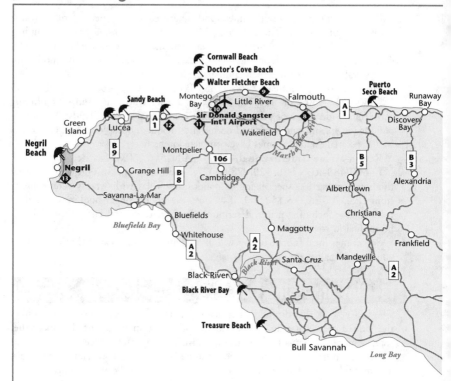

Alexander's **1**
Almond Tree Restaurant **7**
Ambrosia **11**
Blue Mountain Inn **1**
Bounty **3**
The Brewery **11**
Café au Lait/Mirage Cottages **13**
Calabash Restaurant **10**
The Casanova **6**
The Castles **6**
Chelsea Jerk Center **1**

Chicken Lavish **11**
Choices **11**
Cosmo's Seafood Restaurant & Bar **13**
De Montevin Lodge Restaurant **2**
Devonshire Restaurant/
  The Grogg Shoppe **1**
Double V Jerk Centre **7**
El Dorado Room **1**
Evita's Italian Restaurant **7**
Fern Hill Club **5**
Georgian House **10**

Glistening Waters Inn
  & Marina **8**
The Hot Pot **1**
Hungry Lion **13**
Indies Pub and Grill **1**
Jade Garden **1**
Julia's **10**
Le Vendôme **13**
Little Pub Restaurant **7**
Mandeville Hotel **14**
Margueritaville **13**

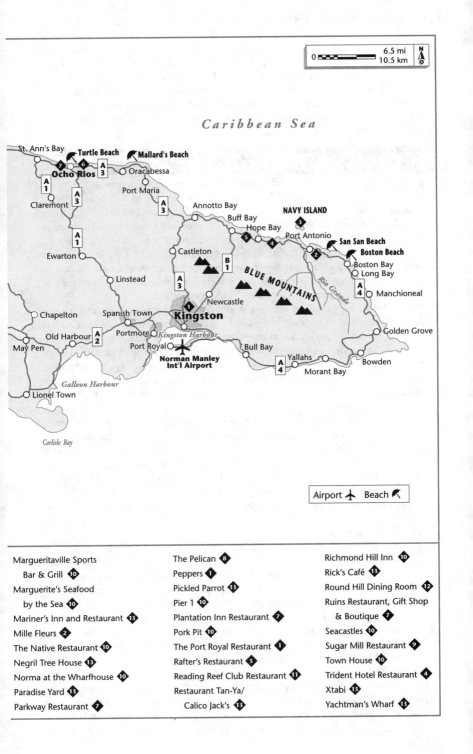

Caribbean Sea

St. Ann's Bay
Turtle Beach
Mallard's Beach
Ocho Rios
Oracabessa
A1
Claremont
A3
Port Maria
A3
Ewarton
A1
Linstead
Castleton
B1
Chapelton
Spanish Town
A3
Newcastle
BLUE MOUNTAINS
Old Harbour
A2
Portmore
Kingston
May Pen
Port Royal
Kingston Harbour
Norman Manley
Int'l Airport
Bull Bay
Yallahs
A4
Morant Bay
Lionel Town
Galleon Harbour

Annotto Bay
Buff Bay
Hope Bay
NAVY ISLAND
Port Antonio
San San Beach
Boston Beach
Boston Bay
Long Bay
A4
Manchioneal
Rio Grande
Golden Grove
Bowden

Carlisle Bay

Airport ✈ Beach ◤

Marqueritaville Sports
  Bar & Grill 🔟
Marguerite's Seafood
  by the Sea 🔟
Mariner's Inn and Restaurant ⓭
Mille Fleurs ❷
The Native Restaurant 🔟
Negril Tree House ⓭
Norma at the Wharfhouse 🔟
Paradise Yard ⓭
Parkway Restaurant ❼

The Pelican ❽
Peppers ❶
Pickled Parrot ⓭
Pier 1 🔟
Plantation Inn Restaurant ❼
Pork Pit 🔟
The Port Royal Restaurant ❶
Rafter's Restaurant ❸
Reading Reef Club Restaurant ⓫
Restaurant Tan-Ya/
  Calico Jack's ⓭

Richmond Hill Inn 🔟
Rick's Café ⓭
Round Hill Dining Room ⓬
Ruins Restaurant, Gift Shop
  & Boutique ❼
Seacastles 🔟
Sugar Mill Restaurant ❾
Town House 🔟
Trident Hotel Restaurant ❹
Xtabi ⓭
Yachtman's Wharf ⓭

are narrow and not well lit. To complicate matters for Americans, Canadians, and Europeans, Jamaicans drive on the left side of the road, as in Great Britain. If you go out for dinner, consider taking a taxi; all taxi drivers know the badly marked roads well. Once at the restaurant, you can arrange for the taxi to pick you up at an agreed-on time or else have the restaurant call the taxi when you are ready to leave. Some upscale restaurants will arrange to have a minivan pick you up and return you to your hotel if you call in advance.

14 Tips on Shopping

If your shopping tastes run toward the electronic, you might discover an occasional bargain in audio equipment in the marketplaces of Jamaica, as well as a scattering of wristwatches, discounted gold chains, and a small appliance or two. Much more appealing, however, are the thousands of handcrafted items whose inspiration seems to spring from the creative depths of the Jamaican soul.

The arts are not a new tradition in Jamaica. During the 1700s, Jamaican wig holders, combs, boxes, and art objects were considered charming decorative objects as far away as London. Today, the tradition of arts and handcrafts continues to flourish, with a far greater array of purchasable possibilities.

In Jamaica, as everywhere else, the distinction between what is art and what is merely a craft is often a matter of personal preference. However varied your artistic background and tastes may be, an estimated 50,000 artisans labor long and hard to produce thousands of paintings, wood carvings, textiles, and whatnots, any of which might serve as an evocative reminder of your Jamaican holiday. It is estimated that there are at least 500 wood-carving stands set beside the road between Montego Bay and Ocho Rios, and many dozens of others scattered throughout the rest of Jamaica as well.

Usually chiseled from either mahogany or a very hard tropical wood known as lignum vitae, **wood carvings** run the gamut from the execrably horrible to the delicately delightful, with many works of power and vision in between. Frequently, pieces have been carved with such crude tools as antique iron chisels, and (sometimes) nothing more than a graduated set of pocketknives and nails. Also available are all sizes of **baskets** woven from palm fronds or the straw of an island plant known as the jipijapa, calabash (gourds) etched with illustrations of hummingbirds and vines, and hammocks woven into designs handed down from the time of the Arawak Indians.

Although many of Jamaica's crafts are distributed by entrepreneurial middlepeople, it always (at least for us) gives a purchase an especially subjective memory when the purchase is made directly from the hands that crafted it.

The island's inventory of wood carvings and weavings is supplemented by establishments selling **leather goods** (sandals and shoes are often a good buy), locally made jewelry fashioned from gold, silver, onyx, and bone, and garments (especially casual wear and sportswear) whose light textures nicely complement the heat of the tropics. Also noteworthy are the many handbags woven from straw or palm fronds, which are sometimes rendered more ornate through colorful embroideries applied by any of the island's "straw ladies."

Many people head home with several bottles of the heady **spices** whose seasonings flavor the best of Jamaica's dishes. Vacuum-sealed plastic containers filled with **Blue Mountain coffee** are enviable gifts for loved ones after your return home, as well as any of the bottles of specialty rums whose flavors (orange, coconut, and

Meeting the Jamaicans

The Jamaica Tourist Board operates a **Meet-the-People program** in Kingston and the island's five major resort cities and towns. Through the program, visitors can meet Jamaican families who volunteer to host them free for a few hours or even a whole day.

More than 650 families are registered in the project with the tourist board, which keeps a list of their interests and hobbies. All you need to do is give the board a rough idea of your interests, and they will arrange for you to spend the day with a similar family. You go along with whatever the family does, sharing their life, eating at their table, accompanying them to a dinner party. You may end up at a beach barbecue, afternoon tea with neighbors, or just sitting and expounding theories, arguing, and talking far into the night. The program does not include overnight accommodation.

If you have a particular interest—birds, butterflies, music, ham radio, stamp collecting, or spelunking in Jamaica's many caves—the tourist board will find you a fellow enthusiast. Lasting friendships have developed because of this unique opportunity to meet people.

Although the service is entirely free, your hostess will certainly enjoy receiving flowers or a similar token of appreciation after your visit.

In Jamaica, apply at any of the local tourist board offices (see "Visitor Information," earlier in this chapter).

Another program is offered by **World Learning,** founded in 1932 as The U.S. Experiment in International Living, Kipling Road, P.O. Box 676, Brattleboro, VT 05302-0676 (☎ **800/336-1616** or 802/257-7751). Their College Semester Abroad program in Jamaica focuses on women and development, and life and culture in Jamaica. Participants become one of the family, taking part in its daily activities, while studying in the region. The program includes field work and an independent study project.

coffee, among others) can evoke the heat of Jamaica even during a snow-blanketed northern winter.

Especially noteworthy are the handful of **art galleries** that stock the paintings of local artists. Jamaica's impressive inventory of painters has been well-documented in art galleries throughout Europe and North America. You'll probably find dozens of paintings for sale. Some critics say the island's most valuable export, after aluminum, is its art. These paintings range from the banal and uninspired to richly evocative portrayals of universal themes. If the painting speaks to you, consider buying it. Before investing in a major purchase, however, we suggest you consult with an expert at one of the island's better-known galleries, where paintings can easily cost several thousand dollars. Lesser works, or works by as-yet unknown artists, are sometimes available for as little as U.S.$20 each on sidewalks throughout the country.

Polite and good-natured **bargaining** is usually expected, especially in the informal markets. In fact, if you bargain with goodwill and humor, you might get some pleasant insights into the interpersonal dynamics that are part of the island's daily life. And you should get a discount of around 15% to 20%. In more formal environments, bargaining often will simply not work. The aura projected by the owner or salesperson will quickly communicate the degree to which bargaining is welcomed.

Although shopping possibilities abound in virtually every tourist resort, every serious shopper should visit an outlet of the government-funded **Things Jamaican.** The quality of inventory varies widely from outlet to outlet, but they all offer a sampling under one roof of some of the best products of the island. (Addresses of Things Jamaican are listed in chapter 4 of this guide.)

FAST FACTS: Jamaica

Airports   See "Flying to Jamaica" and "Getting Around" in this chapter.

Business Hours   Banks are open Monday through Friday from 9am to 5pm. Store hours vary widely, but as a general rule most business establishments open at 8:30am and close at 4:30 or 5pm Monday through Friday. Some shops are open on Saturday until noon.

Car Rentals   See "Getting Around," earlier in this chapter.

Climate   See "When to Go," earlier in this chapter.

Currency   See "Money," earlier in this chapter.

Currency Exchange   There are Bank of Jamaica exchange bureaus at both international airports (near Montego Bay and Kingston), at cruise-ship piers, and in most hotels.

Doctor   See "Hospitals," below. Many major resorts have doctors on call. If you need any particular medicine or treatment, bring evidence, such as a letter from your own doctor.

Documents Required   See "Visitor Information, Entry Requirements & Customs," earlier in this chapter.

Driving Rules   See "Getting Around," earlier in this chapter.

Drugstores   In Montego Bay, try **Overton Pharmacy,** 49 Union St., Overton Plaza (☎ **876/952-2699**); in Ocho Rios, **Great House Pharmacy,** Brown's Plaza (☎ **876/974-2352**); and in Kingston, **Moodie's Pharmacy,** in the New Kingston Shopping Centre (☎ **876/926-4174**). Prescriptions are accepted by local pharmacies only if issued by a Jamaican doctor. Hotels have doctors on call. If you need any particular medicine or treatment, bring evidence, such as a letter from your own physician.

Electricity   Most places have the standard electrical voltage of 110, as in the U.S. However, some establishments operate on 220 volts, 50 cycles. If your hotel is on a different current from your U.S.-made appliance, ask for a transformer and adapter.

Embassies   Calling embassies or consulates in Jamaica is a challenge. Phones will ring and ring before being picked up, if they are answered at all. Extreme patience is needed to reach a live voice on the other end. The Embassy of the **United States** is at the Jamaica Mutual Life Centre, 2 Oxford Rd., Kingston 5 (☎**876/929-4850**). The High Commission of **Canada** is in the Mutual Security Bank Building, 30–36 Knutsford Blvd., Kingston 5 (☎**876/ 926-1500**), and there's a Canadian Consulate at 29 Gloucester Ave., Montego Bay (☎**876/952-6198**). The High Commission of the **United Kingdom** is at 28 Trafalgar Rd., Kingston 10 (☎ **876/926-9050**).

Emergencies   For police and air rescue, dial ☎ **119;** to report a fire or call an ambulance, dial ☎ **110.**

Holidays   See "When to Go," earlier in this chapter.

Hospitals   In Kingston, the **University Hospital** is at Mona (☎ **876/ 927-1620**); in Montego Bay, the **Cornwall Regional Hospital** is at Mount Salem (☎ **876/952-5100**); and in Port Antonio, the **Port Antonio General Hospital** is at Naylor's Hill (☎ **876/993-2646**).

Information   See "Visitor Information, Entry Requirements & Customs," earlier in this chapter.

Mail   Instead of going to a post office, you can, in most cases, give mail to your hotel's reception desk. Most hotels sell postage stamps. A hotel worker will give your mail to a postperson at the time of mail pickup or include them in the hotel mail when a staff member goes to the post office. Parcels can often be mailed by a hotel worker. Allow about 1 week for an airmail postcard or letter to reach the North American mainland. Increases in postal charges can be implemented at any time, so find out the current rate before depositing mail. Call ☎ **876/ 922-9430** in Kingston for any problems or questions about mail in Jamaica. If you want to be sure of delivery, consider using a courier service like DHL or Federal Express.

Maps   See "Getting Around," earlier in this chapter.

Newspapers and Magazines   Jamaica supports three daily newspapers (*Daily Gleaner, The Jamaica Record,* and the *Daily Star*), several weekly periodicals, and a handful of other publications. U.S. newsmagazines, such as *Time* and *Newsweek,* as well as occasional copies of *The Miami Herald,* are available at most newsstands.

Nudity   Nude sunbathing and swimming are allowed at a number of hotels, clubs, and beaches (especially in Negril), but only where signs state that swimsuits are optional. Elsewhere, law enforcers will not even allow topless sunbathing.

Police   Dial ☎ **119.**

Radio & TV   Jamaica is served by two major radio broadcasters, both of which are instantly recognizable to thousands of island residents. Radio Jamaica (RJR) is the more popular of the two, partly because of its musical mix of reggae, rock 'n' roll, and talk show material of everyday interest to Jamaicans. The broadcaster is owned by the Jamaican government, its employees, and members of the Jamaican community. RJR's two island-wide services are known as Supreme Sound and FAME FM. The second broadcaster is Jamaica Broadcasting Corporation (JBC), run by a board appointed by the government. JBC also operates the island's only television station (JBC-TV, established in 1963), which transmits from at least two different points on the island.

The availability of Jamaican radio and TV stations does not prevent many island residents from tuning in TV and radio programming from the U.S. mainland, South America, and other Caribbean islands. Many of Jamaica's better hotels offer Cable News Network (CNN) and other satellite broadcasts. Hotels also offer in-house video movies transmitted from a central point in the establishment.

Safety   You can get into a lot of trouble in Jamaica or you can have a carefree vacation—much depends on what you do and where you go. Major hotels have security guards to protect the grounds. Under no circumstances should you accept an invitation to see "the real Jamaica" from some stranger you meet on the beach. Exercise caution when traveling around the country. Safeguard your valuables and never leave them unattended on a beach. Likewise, never leave luggage or other valuables in a car's passenger compartment or trunk. Many private residences on the island have protected their windows with iron grills and guard dogs are commonplace—even some beaches have guards hired by the resorts to protect their clients from muggers. For the latest advisories, call the **U.S. State Department** (☎ **202/647-5225**).

Taxes   The government imposes a 12% room tax, per room, per night. You will also be charged a J$500 (U.S.$14.25) departure tax at the airport, payable in either Jamaica or U.S. dollars. Car rentals are subject to a 15% government tax.

Taxis   See "Getting Around," earlier in this chapter.

Telephone, Telex, & Fax   All overseas telephone calls are subject to a government tax of 15%. Most calls can be made from the privacy of your hotel room or, in some budget or moderate hotels, from the lobby. Even the island's smallest hotels maintain their own fax machines. For telexes, and in case your hotel isn't equipped with suitable phone or fax equipment, contact the local branch of **Telecommunications of Jamaica,** the country's telecommunications operators. In Kingston, its address is 47 Halfway Tree Rd. (☎ **876/926-9700**).

Time   In the winter, Jamaica is on eastern standard time. When the United States is on daylight saving time, however, it's 6am in Miami and 5am in Kingston, because Jamaica does not switch to DST.

Tipping   Tipping is customary in Jamaica. Typically, 10% or 15% is expected in hotels and restaurants on occasions when you would normally tip. Most places add a service charge to the bill. Tipping is not allowed in the all-inclusive hotels.

Useful Telephone Numbers   Ambulance, 110; fire, 110; police, 119; time, 117; toll operator and telephone assistance on local and intra-island calls, 112; overseas calls operator, 113; and **Post and Telegraph Department,** ☎ **876/922-9430.**

Water   It's usually safe to drink tap water island-wide, as it is filtered and chlorinated; however, it's prudent to drink bottled water, if available.

Weather   See "When to Go," earlier in this chapter.

Montego Bay $\boxed{4}$

Montego Bay made its first appearance on the world's tourism stage in the 1940s when wealthy travelers discovered the warm, spring-fed waters of Doctor's Cave Beach. Now Jamaica's second largest community, the town of Mo Bay—as the locals call it—lies on the northwest coast of the island. In spite of its large influx of visitors, Montego Bay retains its own identity. A thriving business and commercial center, it functions as the main market town for most of western Jamaica. It supports cruise-ship piers and a growing industrial center at the free port.

Montego Bay is served by its own airport, Donald Sangster International, so vacationers coming to Jamaica have little need to visit Kingston, the island's capital, unless they want to see its cultural and historical attractions. Otherwise, you will find everything in Mo Bay, the most cosmopolitan of Jamaica's resorts.

Some 23 miles east of Montego Bay, the small 18th-century port town of **Falmouth** is one of the most interesting morning or afternoon excursions from Mo Bay. (Ocho Rios and Runaway Bay are other good choices; they're covered in chapter 6.) Falmouth is not really a tourist town. The community revolves around farming and fishing; more than any resort town, it is the "real" Jamaica. We'll take you there at the end of this chapter.

1 Where to Stay

The Montego Bay region boasts a superb selection of hotels, ranging from very expensive world-class inns to notable bargains.

There's also an amazing selection of all-inclusive resorts, which are all reviewed together for easy comparison at the very end of this section.

VERY EXPENSIVE

Half Moon Golf, Tennis & Beach Club. Rose Hall (P.O. Box 80), Montego Bay, Jamaica, W.I. ☎ **800/626-0592** in the U.S., or 876/953-2211. Fax 876/953-2731. 418 units. A/C TV TEL. Winter U.S.$330–$480 double; from U.S.$530 suite; from U.S.$1,650 villa. Off-season U.S.$220–$280 double; from U.S.$320 suite; from U.S.$1,320 villa. MAP U.S.$65 per person extra. AE, MC, V.

Located about 8 miles east of Montego Bay's city center and 6 miles from the international airport, this is a classic, and one of the 300

Montego Bay

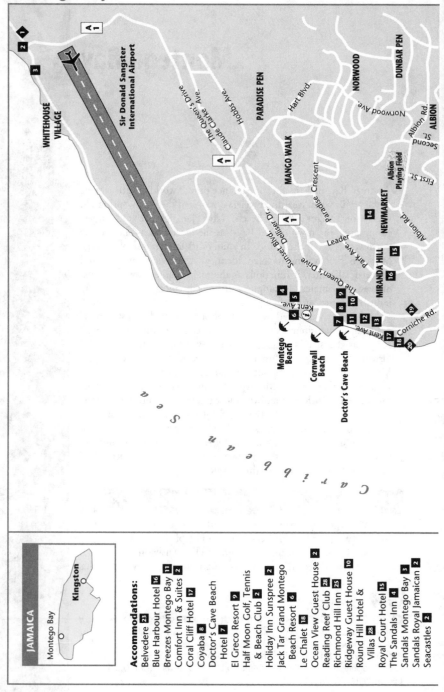

Accommodations:
Belvedere 23
Blue Harbour Hotel 16
Breezes Montego Bay 11
Comfort Inn & Suites 2
Coral Cliff Hotel 17
Coyaba 8
Doctor's Cave Beach Hotel 7
El Greco Resort 9
Half Moon Golf, Tennis & Beach Club 2
Holiday Inn Sunspree 2
Jack Tar Grand Montego Beach Resort 6
Le Chalet 18
Ocean View Guest House 2
Reading Reef Club 28
Richmond Hill Inn 25
Ridgeway Guest House 10
Round Hill Hotel & Villas 28
Royal Court Hotel 15
The Sandals Inn 4
Sandals Montego Bay 3
Sandals Royal Jamaican 2
Seacastles 2

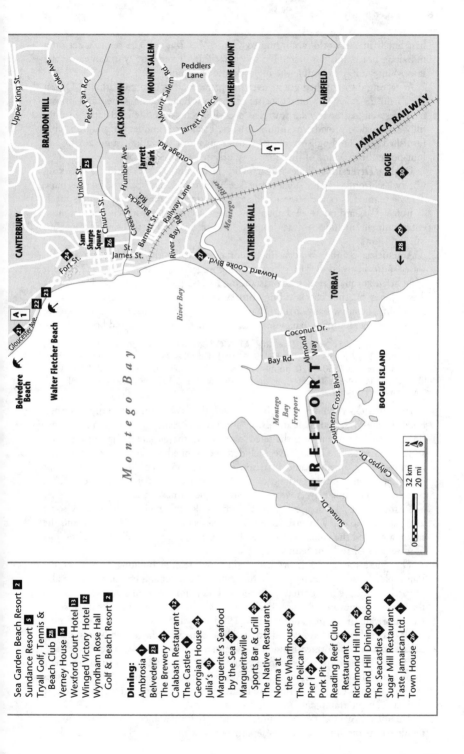

Sea Garden Beach Resort **2**
Sundance Resort **5**
Tryall Golf, Tennis &
  Beach Club **28**
Verney House **14**
Wexford Court Hotel **13**
Winged Victory Hotel **12**
Wyndham Rose Hall
  Golf & Beach Resort **2**

Dining:
Ambrosia **1**
Belvedere **23**
The Brewery **21**
Calabash Restaurant **42**
The Castles **1**
Georgian House **24**
Julia's **30**
Marguerite's Seafood
  by the Sea **20**
Margueriteville
  Sports Bar & Grill **20**
The Native Restaurant **22**
Norma at
  the Wharfhouse **29**
The Pelican **19**
Pier I **27**
Pork Pit **22**
Reading Reef Club
  Restaurant **29**
Richmond Hill Inn **23**
Round Hill Dining Room **29**
The Seacastles **4**
Sugar Mill Restaurant **1**
Taste Jamaican Ltd. **4**
Town House **26**

77

best hotels in the world, according to *Condé Nast Traveler*. The resort is set on a mile-long beach and has incredible sports facilities. From here, you can easily taxi into Montego Bay to sample the nightlife and shopping.

Attracting distinguished guests over the years, such as George Bush and Queen Elizabeth, the resort complex consists of spacious hotel rooms, suites, and private five- to seven-bedroom villas scattered over 400 acres of fertile landscape, all carefully arranged to provide maximum privacy. Each accommodation is comfortably furnished with an English colonial/Caribbean motif, including some mahogany four-poster beds. Many of the villas have private swimming pools.

Dining/Diversions: The Sugar Mill restaurant is set beside a working waterwheel from a bygone sugar estate (see "Where to Dine," below). The Seagrape Terrace (named after the 80-year-old sea grape trees on the property) offers meals al fresco. Il Giardino is an Italian restaurant serving a savory cuisine. Evening entertainment includes music from a resident band and nightly folklore and musical shows.

Amenities: Sailing, windsurfing, snorkeling, scuba diving, deep-sea fishing, water-sports instruction, 51 freshwater swimming pools, 13 tennis courts (7 floodlit at night), 4 lit squash courts, an outstanding 18-hole golf course designed by Robert Trent Jones Sr., horseback riding, fitness center, sauna, room service (7am to midnight), laundry, baby-sitting, massage, beauty salon. There's also a shopping village (with a pharmacy, Japanese restaurant, English-style pub, and boutiques).

✪ **Round Hill Hotel and Villas.** Rte. A1 (P.O. Box 64), Montego Bay, Jamaica, W.I. ☎ **800/972-2159** in the U.S., or 876/956-7050. Fax 876/956-7505. 36 units, 27 villas. A/C TEL. Winter U.S.$330–$420 double; U.S.$520–$730 villa. Off-season U.S.$220–$270 double; U.S.$310–$480 villa. Extra person U.S.$60. MAP U.S.$65 per person extra. AE, DC, MC, V.

Opened in 1953 and now a Caribbean legend, this is one of the most distinguished hotels in the West Indies. It stands on a lushly landscaped 98-acre peninsula that slopes gracefully down to a sheltered cove where the elegant reception area and social center stand. Guests have included the Kennedys, Cole Porter, and more recently, Steven Spielberg and Harrison Ford. Most evenings are informal, except Saturday, when a jacket and tie or black tie is required for men. Likewise, it's preferred that tennis players wear all white on the tennis courts.

Surrounded by landscaped tropical gardens, Round Hill accommodates some 200 guests, who enjoy its private beach, the views of Jamaica's north shore and the mountains, and the colonial elegance of the resort. There are full spa services, lots of water sports, and fine tennis facilities.

The guest rooms are in a richly appointed seaside building known as the Pineapple House, and each opens onto views of the water and beach. There are also privately owned villas dotted over the hillside, most available for rental when the owners are not in residence. Each contains two, three, or four individual suites with a private living area and/or patio; 19 of the villas have their own swimming pools. Each villa is individually decorated, sometimes lavishly so, and rates include the services of a uniformed maid, a cook, and a gardener.

Dining/Diversions: Guests congregate for informal luncheons in an intimate straw hut with an open terrace in a little sandy bay. Jamaican and continental dishes are served on a candlelit terrace or in the Georgian colonial room overlooking the sea. The entertainment is varied.

Amenities: Swimming pool, fitness center (with aerobics classes), top-quality tennis courts (lit at night), safety-deposit boxes, windsurfing, glass-bottomed-boat rides, scuba diving, horseback riding, sailing, paddleboats, rubber-sided inflatable boats, waterskiing, room service (7:30am to 9:30pm), concierge, laundry, baby-sitting, and valet service. You can have someone come and prepare your breakfast in your villa.

✪ **Tryall Golf, Tennis & Beach Club.** St. James (P.O. Box 1206), Montego Bay, Jamaica, W.I. ☎ **800/238-5290** in the U.S., or 876/956-5660. Fax 876/956-5673. 47 units, 48 villas. A/C TEL. Winter U.S.$500 double; from U.S.$750 villa. Off-season U.S.$350 double; from U.S.$420 villa. Extra person U.S.$70 in winter, U.S.$55 off-season. MAP U.S.$66 per person extra. AE, MC, V.

With more spacious grounds than almost any other hotel on Jamaica, this stylish and upscale resort sits 12 miles west of town on the site of a 2,200-acre former sugar plantation. It doesn't have the fine beach that Half Moon does, nor the house-party atmosphere of Trident at Port Antonio, but it's noteworthy, nevertheless. Known as one of the grandest resorts of Jamaica, the property lies along a 1½-mile seafront and is presided over by a 165-year-old Georgian-style Great House. It's a top choice for vacationers who are serious about their golf game.

The accommodations are in either modern wings or luxurious villas scattered throughout the surrounding acreage. The bedrooms are decorated in cool pastels with an English colonial decor. All contain ceiling fans, along with picture windows framing sea and mountain views. The resort's famous villas are set amid lush foliage and are designed for privacy. Each villa comes with a full-time staff, including a cook, maid, laundress, and gardener; all have private swimming pools.

Dining/Diversions: The most formal of the resort's dining areas is in the Great House, where antiques evoke the plantation era. More casual meals are served in a beachside cafe. A resident band plays everything from reggae to slow-dance music every night during dinner. Afternoon tea is served in the Great House.

Amenities: Championship 18-hole par-71 golf course (site of many world-class golf competitions and the pride of this elegant property), nine Laykold tennis courts, 2-mile jogging trail, swimming pool with a swim-up bar, windsurfing, snorkeling, deep-sea fishing, paddleboats, glass-bottom boats, room service, baby-sitting, laundry, and massage. You can book lessons in golf, tennis, and water sports.

EXPENSIVE

✪ **Coyaba.** Mahoe Bay, Little River, Montego Bay, Jamaica, W.I. ☎ **800/237-3237** or 876/953-9150. Fax 876/953-2244. 50 units. A/C TV TEL. Winter U.S.$240–$340 double; off-season U.S.$150–$210 double. Full meal plan U.S.$65 per person extra. Children 11 and under get a 50% discount. AE, MC, V.

With a graceful British colonial atmosphere, this is one of the smaller and more elegant all-inclusive resorts, an oceanfront retreat that is intimate and inviting, evoking a country inn. It was established in 1994 and built from scratch at a cost of $4 million. Set on a lovely strip of beachfront, a 15-minute drive east of the center of Montego Bay, it's centered around an adaptation of a 19th-century Great House. Coyaba is less rowdy and raucous than other Jamaican resorts geared to singles and young couples and prides itself on its peaceful and somewhat staid demeanor.

Accommodations in the main building overlook the garden; those in the pair of three-story outbuildings lie closer to the beach and are somewhat more expensive. The decor is British colonial, with traditional prints, fine chintz fabrics, French doors leading onto private patios or verandas, carved mahogany furniture, and other reminders of the plantation age. Children are welcome, but the hotel doesn't yet offer any special programs for them; however, you can arrange nanny service to help take care of your little ones. The owners are usually on hand to ensure that the operation runs smoothly.

Dining: The hotel's main and most formal restaurant, the Vineyard, is open only for dinner, serving first-rate Jamaican and continental cuisine. Less upscale is Docks Caribbean Bar & Grill, where there's a daily salad bar from which you can create a full meal. There are also three bars scattered amid the grounds. Afternoon teas keep up the British colonial theme.

Amenities: A tennis court that's lit at night, a rectangular swimming pool, exercise room, outdoor hot tub, water-sports center, gift shop, room service, massage, laundry.

✪ **Lethe Estate.** Lethe (P.O. Box 32), Montego Bay, Jamaica, W.I. ☎ **876/956-4920.** Fax 876/956-4927. 13 units. A/C TEL. Winter U.S.$190 double; off-season U.S.$150 double. Rates include breakfast. AE, DC, MC, V.

In 1996, the Tulloch family, owners of a 150-acre banana plantation, decided to diversify their holdings by building this riverfront hotel, which lies 10 miles inland from the sea. Fronted by a veranda, and set beneath a green roof that blends into the surrounding forest, the structure was inspired by the region's many antique plantation houses, and allows guests close exposure to the Great River's bird and animal life. It's definitely not a beach resort; all activities revolve around the river, such as rafting expeditions that carry participants from points 2 miles upriver back down to a point near the hotel. Bedrooms are airy, open to breezes, and equipped with comfortably formal furnishings that evoke Jamaica's English colonial age.

Amenities: The resort contains a swimming pool set into a verdant lawn, a restaurant, and easy access to the river and several hiking trails radiating out into the surrounding forest.

Wyndham Rose Hall Golf & Beach Resort. Rose Hall (P.O. Box 999), Montego Bay, Jamaica, W.I. ☎ **800/624-7326** in the U.S., or 876/953-2650. Fax 876/953-2617. 489 units. A/C TV TEL. Winter U.S.$185–$220 double, from U.S.$425 suite; off-season U.S.$130–$155 double, from U.S.$390 suite. MAP U.S.$50.60 per person extra. AE, DC, MC, V.

Wyndham Rose Hall sits at the bottom of a rolling 30-acre site along the north-coast highway 9 miles east of the airport. On a former sugar plantation that once covered 7,000 acres, the hotel abuts the 200-year-old home of the legendary "White Witch of Rose Hall," now a historic site, and has a thin strip of sandy beach. Although it's popular as a convention site, the hotel also caters to a family market (children are an important part of the clientele) and has serious golf and tennis facilities. The staff stays busy organizing games and social events. The seven-story H-shaped structure features a large and attractive lobby on the ground floor and, upstairs, guest rooms all have sea views and rather unremarkable furnishings. Most units have two queen-size beds, and each has a small private balcony. Although the rooms have paintings by local artists depicting typical Caribbean scenes, what's missing here is real Jamaican style and ambience.

Dining/Diversions: There are four restaurants, and it's never more than a short walk to one of the many bars scattered around the hotel property. Wednesday night in season features a poolside buffet and a Caribbean variety show with dancers, fire-eaters, and calypso and reggae performances.

Amenities: Three pools (one for wading that's suited to small children, two for swimming); complimentary sailboats; top-rated golf course meandering over part of the hotel grounds; tennis complex (with six lit all-weather Laykold courts) headed by pros who offer a complete tennis program; air-conditioned fitness center; room service (7am to 11pm); baby-sitting; laundry; massage. The "Kids Klub" has an array of supervised activities that's included in the rate.

MODERATE

Comfort Inn & Suites. Rte. A1, Rose Hall (P.O. Box 1), Montego Bay, St. James, Jamaica, W.I. ☎ **876/953-3250.** Fax 876/953-3062. 198 units. A/C MINIBAR TEL. Winter U.S.$156 suite for 2, U.S.$176 suite for 3, U.S.$256 suite for 4. Off-season U.S.$131.25 suite for 2, U.S.$151.25 suite for 3, U.S.$221.25 suite for 4. MAP U.S.$30 per person extra. AE, MC, V.

One of the most architecturally dramatic hotels in the region was built in 1991 along an isolated seafront 11 miles east of Montego Bay. Its development included at least a 50% participation by the Jamaican government, which helped to market many of the units as privately owned condominiums. The result is an airy, widely separated compound of postmodern buildings vaguely influenced by English colonial models. The resort contains only suites, each with kitchen or kitchenette, all scattered among a half dozen outbuildings ringed with greenery and capped with cedar-shingled roofs.

Lawns slope down to the beach, past arbors, gazebos, bars, and water-sports kiosks. The staff organizes activities like beer-drinking contests, volleyball on the beach, shows with staff and guests, bingo, and diving contests. The Castles restaurant (see "Where to Dine," below) overlooks the graceful freshwater swimming pool; less formal meals and drinks are offered in the Clifftop Bar. Other amenities include laundry, baby-sitting, water-sports facilities, and a tour desk for island tours.

✪ **Doctor's Cave Beach Hotel.** Gloucester Ave. (P.O. Box 94), Montego Bay, Jamaica, W.I. ☎ **876/952-4355.** Fax 876/952-5204. 90 units. A/C TEL. Winter U.S.$130–$140 double, U.S.$160 suite for 2; off-season U.S.$105–$115 double, U.S.$140 suite for 2. Extra person U.S.$30. MAP U.S.$35 per person extra. AE, DISC, MC, V.

Across the street from the well-known Doctor's Cave Beach in the bustle of the town's business district, this three-story hotel offers great value. It has its own gardens, a swimming pool, a Jacuzzi, and a small gymnasium, all set on 4 acres of tropical gardens. The rooms are simply but comfortably furnished, and suites have kitchenettes.

The two restaurants are the Coconut Grove, whose outdoor terrace is floodlit at night, and the less formal Greenhouse. In the Cascade Bar, where a waterfall tumbles down a stone wall, you can listen to a piano duo during cocktail hours.

Reading Reef Club. Rte. A1, on Bogue Lagoon, at the bottom of Long Hill (P.O. Box 225), Reading, Montego Bay, Jamaica, W.I. ☎ **800/315-0379** in the U.S., or 876/952-5909. Fax 876/952-7217. 34 units. A/C TEL. Winter U.S.$100–$165 double, U.S.$250 2-bedroom suite, U.S.$300 3-bedroom suite. Off-season U.S.$75–$125 double, U.S.$200 2-bedroom suite, U.S.$250 3-bedroom suite. AE, MC, V.

This pocket of posh was created by an American, JoAnne Rowe. A former fashion designer whose hobby is cooking, JoAnne has a sense of style and a flair for cuisine. Located on 2½ acres at the bottom of Long Hill Road, the hotel is a 15-minute drive west of Montego Bay, on a 350-foot sandy beach where people relax in comfort, unmolested by beach vendors. The complex of four buildings overlooks beautiful reefs once praised by Jacques Cousteau for their aquatic life.

The accommodations, which include two- and three-bedroom suites, open onto a sea view. All have air-conditioning and ceiling fans and a light Caribbean motif. The luxury rooms contain minibars, and the two- and three-bedroom suites offer kitchenettes.

See "Where to Dine," below, for details on the Reading Reef Club Restaurant. There's also a bar/lounge and a beachside luncheon barbecue specializing in Jamaican (jerk) sausages, English sausages, and Tex-Mex food. Services include laundry, valet, and drivers for island tours. Guests also enjoy the freshwater swimming pool and free water sports, including snorkeling, windsurfing, and sailing in a 12-foot sailboat; scuba diving costs extra.

Wexford Court Hotel. Gloucester Ave. (P.O. Box 108), Montego Bay, Jamaica, W.I. ☎ 876/952-2854. Fax 876/952-3637. 67 units. A/C TV TEL. Winter U.S.$137.50 double; U.S.$143 1-bedroom apt. Off-season U.S.$97.50 double; U.S.$115 1-bedroom apt. MAP U.S.$33 per person extra. AE, DC, MC, V.

Stay here for economy, not style. About 10 minutes from downtown Mo Bay, near Doctor's Cave Beach, this hotel has a small pool and a patio (where calypso is enjoyed in season). The apartments have living/dining areas and kitchenettes, so you can cook for yourself. All the very simple rooms contain patios shaded by gables and Swiss chalet-style roofs.

The Wexford Grill includes a good selection of Jamaican dishes, such as chicken deep fried with honey. Guests can enjoy drinks in a bar nearby.

INEXPENSIVE

The Belvedere. 33 Gloucester Ave., Montego Bay, Jamaica, W.I. ☎ **800/814-2237** in the U.S., or 876/952-0593. Fax 876/979-0498. 27 units. A/C TEL. Winter U.S.$65–$75 double; off-season U.S.$50–$60 double. DC, MC, V.

Simple and uncomplicated, this small hotel stands near Walter Fletcher Beach and offers a swimming pool. The beach is a 5-minute walk away, with shopping and restaurants nearby. Rooms are modestly furnished but incredibly cheap. On Tuesday evening, the hotel hosts a manager's cocktail party with live entertainment featuring calypso music. On the last Sunday of each month a jazz band plays.

☺ **Blue Harbour Hotel.** 6 Sewell Ave. (P.O. Box 212), Montego Bay, Jamaica, W.I. ☎ **876/952-5445.** Fax 876/952-8930. 24 units. A/C TV. Winter U.S.$80–$88 double, U.S.$98–$112 suite. Off-season U.S.$60 double, U.S.$80–$95 suite. Children 11 and under stay free in parents' room. AE, MC, V.

On a hillside overlooking the harbor, midway between the airport and town off Route A1, this small hotel offers basic service in a friendly atmosphere. The beach is a 5-minute walk from the hotel, which provides free transportation to and from the shore. The rooms are simple, while the suites offer kitchenettes to help you save even more money. For dinner, the hotel offers the option of a dine-around plan that includes 10 of Montego Bay's restaurants. (Transportation to and from the restaurants is provided.) The facilities include a swimming pool, an air-conditioned lounge, and a coffee shop serving breakfast and a light lunch. Tennis is nearby and arrangements can be made for golf, deep-sea fishing, scuba diving, and island tours.

☺ **Coral Cliff Hotel.** 165 Gloucester Ave. (P.O. Box 253), Montego Bay, Jamaica, W.I. ☎ **876/952-4130.** Fax 876/952-6532. 30 units. A/C TEL. Winter U.S.$85–$95 double; U.S.$97–$115 triple. Off-season U.S.$75–$85 double; U.S.$85–$95 triple. MC, V.

The Coral Cliff Hotel, a mile west of the center of town but only 2 minutes from Doctor's Cave Beach, is the best bargain in Montego Bay. The rates are extremely reasonable for what you get, including a luxurious swimming pool. The hotel grew from a colonial-style building that was once the private home of Harry M. Doubleday of the famous publishing family. Many of the light, airy, and spacious bedrooms open onto balconies with a view of the sea.

The hotel's breeze-swept restaurant, Coral Cliff Dining Room, overlooks the bay. The food is good, featuring local produce and fresh seafood whenever available.

El Greco Resort. 11 Queens Dr. (P.O. Box 1624), Montego Bay, Jamaica, W.I. ☎ **876/ 940-6116.** Fax 876/940-6115. 96 apts, all with kitchenette. A/C TV TEL. Year-round U.S.$104.62 1-bedroom apt for 2–4; U.S.$139.50 2-bedroom apt for 4–6. AE, MC, V.

This three-story, cream-colored hotel sits at the top of a rocky bluff, high above the surf, sand, and well-oiled bodies of Doctor's Cave Beach. A private elevator links the hotel's clifftop site to a point near the beachfront. Surrounded by a landscaped garden into which is nestled both a swimming pool and a pair of tennis courts that are lit for night play, the resort is well-maintained and well-priced. It's smack in the middle of Montego Bay's densest concentration of honky-tonk commercialism. But the location allows guests to rise above the congestion a bit; the hotel catches the trade winds, and most (but not all) of the rooms offer a sweeping view over the sea. Apartments contain full kitchenettes and have pure white ceramic floor tiles. The bedrooms are air-conditioned, but not the living rooms, which have ceiling fans instead. All of the two-bedroom units (32 in all) occupy the building's uppermost floor. There's both a bar and a restaurant on the premises, although many of the guests opt to cook at least some of their meals in-house.

Ocean View Guest House. 26 Sunset Blvd. (½ mile west of Sangster airport; P.O. Box 210), Montego Bay, Jamaica, W.I. ☎ **876/952-2662.** 12 units. A/C. Winter U.S.$38–$50 triple; off-season U.S.$29.50 double, U.S.$40.50 triple. No credit cards.

Stay here for a great deal; you won't get state-of-the-art maintenance or service, but the price is adjusted accordingly. Originally established in the 1960s, when the grandparents of the present owners began to rent extra rooms in their private home, this super bargain lies a half mile from the airport and the same distance from a public beach. The simple and uncomplicated bedrooms are supplemented with a small library and TV room (satellite reception is available). Six rooms are air-conditioned; the others are equipped with fans. Most open onto a veranda or the spacious front porch. It's quietest at the back.

Dinner is offered for guests only; reservations must be made by 2pm. The large and extremely reasonable menu features such fare as T-bone steak, pork chops, roast chicken, and fresh fish.

Richmond Hill Inn. Union St. (P.O. Box 362), Montego Bay, Jamaica, W.I. ☎ **876/ 952-3859.** Fax 876/952-6106. 20 units. A/C TV TEL. Winter U.S.$115 double, U.S.$120 1-bedroom suite for 2, U.S.$189 2-bedroom suite for 4, U.S.$256–$290 3-bedroom suite for up to 6. Off-season U.S.$90 double, U.S.$100 1-bedroom suite for 2, U.S.$168 2-bedroom suite for 4, U.S.$220 3-bedroom suite for up to 6. AE, MC, V.

If you're an avid beach lover, know in advance that the nearest beach (Doctor's Cave Beach) is a 15-minute drive away. Set high on a forested slope, 500 feet above sea level and the commercial center of Montego Bay, this place was originally built as the homestead of the Dewar family (the scions of scotch). Very little of the original villa remains, but what you'll find is a hilltop aerie ringed with urn-shaped concrete balustrades, a pool terrace suitable for sundowner cocktails, and comfortable, slightly fussy bedrooms with lace-trimmed curtains, homey bric-a-brac, and pastel colors. Maid and laundry service are included in the rates, and there's both a bar and a restaurant (featuring vistas over the blinking lights of Montego Bay).

Ridgeway Guest House. 34 Queen's Dr., Montego Bay, Jamaica, W.I. ☎ **876/952-2709.** 8 units. A/C TV TEL. Winter U.S.$60 double; off-season U.S.$55 double. Children 11 and under stay free in parents' room. DC, DISC, MC, V.

This warm and hospital B&B, far removed from the impersonal megaresorts (and their megaprices), is a great find. The helpful owners, Brenda and Bryan (Bryan is actually his last name as he doesn't like to divulge his first name), offer free pickup from the airport and transport to Doctor's Cave Beach, a 15-minute walk or 5 minutes by car. The Bryans are constantly improving their property, a two-story white-painted building set among flowers and fruit trees from which guests may help themselves, perhaps having an orange and grapefruit salad. Guests may partake of before-dinner drinks in the roof garden, enjoying a view of the airport and ocean. The large rooms are decorated in a tropical motif with two or three queen-size beds. The marble baths have modern fixtures, and TV is available in a public area. Next door is the Chatwick Garden Hotel, with a restaurant open to Ridgeway guests.

Royal Court Hotel. Sewell Ave. (P.O. Box 195), Montego Bay, Jamaica, W.I. ☎ **876/952-4531.** Fax 876/952-4532. 22 units. A/C TEL. Winter U.S.$80–$90 double; U.S.$150 suite. Off-season U.S.$60–$70 double; U.S.$100 suite. AE, MC, V.

This hotel is clean and attractive, has a charming atmosphere, and is a good value. It's located on the hillside overlooking Montego Bay, above Gloucester Avenue and off Park Avenue. The rooms are furnished with bright, tasteful colors, and all have patios; the larger ones contain fully equipped kitchenettes.

Meals are served in the Pool Bar and Eatery. Its restaurant, Leaf of Life, specializes in vegetarian food, among other selections. Free transportation is provided to the town, the beach, and the tennis club. Amenities and facilities include massage, gym, steam room, Jacuzzi, TV room, conference room, and a doctor on the premises.

Sundance Resort. 1 Kent Ave. (P.O. Box 467), Montego Bay, Jamaica, W.I. ☎ **876/952-4370.** Fax 876/952-6591. 72 units. A/C. Winter U.S.$75 double; off-season U.S.$60 double. Extra person U.S.$25–$30. AE, DISC, MC, V.

The Sundance Resort is a 5-minute walk from Doctor's Cave Beach. Its location beside the busy main thoroughfare of downtown Montego Bay is either an advantage or a disadvantage, depending on how much you value easy access to the resort's inexpensive bars and restaurants. Despite the traffic and crowds around it, the almond, mango, and grapefruit trees that surround the two-story main building, a series of individual cottages, and two swimming pools create a sense of rural isolation. You'll also find a restaurant serving Jamaican cuisine, a flower shop, a minigym, a bandstand for the rare concerts presented here, and a bar where a TV set provides at least some of the entertainment. The bedrooms have either a terrace or a balcony. The hotel is also a showcase for Jamaican and foreign art, featuring the works of Deborah Colvin, Song Jiang, and Sam Saki. A hall of fame row of cottages features the stunning black and white photography of Johnnie Black, whose work depicts Bob Marley, Third World, and Toots and the Maytals.

Verney House Resort. 3 Leader Ave. (P.O. Box 18), Montego Bay, Jamaica, W.I. ☎ **876/952-2875.** Fax 876/979-2944. 25 units. A/C. Winter U.S.$55 double, U.S.$75 triple, U.S.$95 quad. Off-season U.S.$50 double, U.S.$60 triple, U.S.$80 quad. MAP U.S.$18 per person extra. AE, MC, V.

In a verdant setting just far enough away from the urban congestion of Montego Bay, this hotel offers a feeling of remote calm. You can still get to where the action is by taking a short trek downhill, or head to one of several beaches, such as Cornwall Beach, that are only 5 minutes away on foot. The inn also provides transportation to and from the beach. The two-story structure was originally built on steeply sloping land in 1945. In 1995, the pastel-colored bedrooms were freshened up. Each accommodation has white walls and simple furnishings, and creates the sense that you're in a private home. The restaurant (the Kit-Kat) and bar overlook the swimming pool. The staff is usually gracious.

Winged Victory Hotel. 5 Queen's Dr., Montego Bay, Jamaica, W.I. ☎ **876/952-3892.** Fax 876/952-5986. 24 units. A/C TV TEL. Winter U.S.$90–$100 double; U.S.$175–$225 suite. Off-season U.S.$60–$80 double; U.S.$110–$150 suite. MAP U.S.$30 per person extra. AE, MC, V.

This tall and modern hotel on a hillside road in the Miranda Hill District of Montego Bay doesn't reveal its true beauty until you pass through its comfortable public rooms into a Mediterranean-style courtyard in back. Here, urn-shaped balustrades enclose a terraced garden, a pool, and a veranda looking over the faraway crescent of Montego Bay. The veranda's best feature is the Calabash Restaurant. Rooms are well-furnished and comfortably appointed. All but five have a private balcony or veranda, along with an attractively eclectic decor that's part Chinese, part colonial, and part Iberian.

ALL-INCLUSIVE RESORTS

Breezes Montego Bay. Gloucester Ave., Montego Bay, Jamaica, W.I. ☎ **800/859-SUPER** or 876/940-1150. Fax 876/940-1160. 124 units. A/C TV TEL. Winter U.S.$1,650–$2,158 double; U.S.$2,578 suite for 2. Off-season U.S.$1,378–$1,938 double; U.S.$2,338–$2,378 suite for 2. Rates are all-inclusive for 5 nights. AE, MC, V. No children under 16.

Built in 1995 as a boomerang-shaped five-story complex that encloses a swimming pool and a cluster of bars and boutiques, this is one of the newest members of Jamaica's SuperClub chain. Defined as "a sandbox for your inner child," it's the only major hotel set directly on the sands of Montego Bay's most popular public beach, Doctor's Cave. Guests here experience more of the street and beach life of Jamaica than those who stay at the more secluded resorts set off within compounds of their own. The resort is geared to adults (no children under 16 are admitted) and it has an indulgent atmosphere, but without the emphasis on raucous partying that's the norm at Negril's Hedonism II (a member of the same SuperClub chain). Bedrooms are simply furnished and breezy, and overlook either the beach or the garden that separates the hotel from the traffic of Montego Bay's main commercial boulevard, Gloucester Avenue. Nonresidents can buy a "Day Pay" for U.S.$45, allowing them the same unlimited access to the bars and buffets.

Dining/Diversions: Breakfast and informal lunches and dinners are served at Jimmy's Buffet, a dining terrace overlooking the swimming pool and the beach. A more formal, candlelit evening venue is available at Martino's, an Italian rooftop restaurant within the hotel. A poolside snack bar serves burgers and hot dogs throughout the day, and there are four bars (one with a live pianist) to quench your thirst. The staff works hard to provide group diversions, games, toga parties, mingle parties, "mixology" classes, steel bands, and reggae lessons.

Amenities: Freshwater swimming pool; rooftop Jacuzzi; a full range of water sports with instruction on how to use water skis, Hobie-Cats, and Windsurfers; a tennis court lit for night play; a fitness center with aerobics classes, water aerobics classes, and Nautilus equipment.

Holiday Inn SunSpree. 5 miles east of Montego Bay International Airport (P.O. Box 480), Rose Hall, Jamaica, W.I. ☎ **800/HOLIDAY** or 876/953-2485. Fax 876/953-2840. 523 units. A/C TV TEL. Winter U.S.$300–$490 double, U.S.$630 suite for 2. Off-season U.S.$240–$270 double, U.S.$340 suite. Children ages 13–19 U.S.$50 a night; 12 and under free when sharing parents' room. Rates are all-inclusive. AE, MC, V.

This is the only Holiday Inn resort in the world that can be booked on all-inclusive terms. It opened in 1995 following a $13 million renovation. It continues a tradition of catering to singles, couples, and honeymooners, but the resort has a new emphasis on programs for families with children. The 12-acre property fronts nearly half a mile of white-sand beach, lying on Jamaica's north shore.

The well-furnished, modern rooms and suites are for the most part spacious, housed in eight free-standing buildings, all with such amenities as hair dryers and a private balcony or patio. Of these, 76 are oceanfront, and 23 suites come complete with indoor Jacuzzis.

Dining/Diversions: A wide range of dining options is available even though the resort is all-inclusive. In the main building, the Mo Bay Festival offers views of the Caribbean and other specialties along with international menus, whereas Vista's, also with an ocean view, features a more formal setting and a continental cuisine. The Barefoot Bar & Grill at poolside is for heavy snacking, and the Beach Hut Bar is known for its Jamaican delicacies. Two nights a week are devoted to buffet theme nights, when guests dine on the beach and listen to live Jamaican music and dance. The Sports Bar with a large-size TV is a macho hangout, while the Witches Disco attracts a younger crowd.

Amenities: Spacious interlocking tropical-style freshwater swimming pools of varying depths, four night-lit tennis courts, water-sports center, basketball court, volleyball court, fitness center with Nautilus equipment, Kids Spree Vacation Club staffed by trained counselors, baby-sitting, shopping and sightseeing excursions.

Jack Tar Grand Montego Beach Resort. Gloucester Ave. (P.O. Box 144), Montego Bay, Jamaica, W.I. ☎ **800/999-9182** in the U.S., or 876/952-4340. Fax 876/952-6633. 131 units. A/C TV TEL. Winter U.S.$150–$180 double; U.S.$295–$365 triple. Off-season U.S.$130–$145 double; U.S.$255–$280 triple. Rates are all-inclusive. Children 2–12 in parents' room charged U.S.$85 extra in winter, U.S.$60 in summer. AE, MC, V.

Jack Tar isn't as upscale as many of the other all-inclusives on Jamaica, but it does offer an affordable, worry-free beach vacation for families on a budget. (The Sandals Inn next door is far superior, even though it's Sandals' budget property.) This 3¼-acre beachfront resort encompasses a pair of buildings set 2 miles north of the commercial core of Montego Bay. Noted for its cheap, all-inclusive format, this is one of the smaller members of a chain known for generous (if not blue-chip) food and drink policies.

In 1996, the resort underwent a $4 million renovation, in which each of the bedrooms was upgraded. The guest units are modern but bland, and they sit a few steps from the beach, with a view of the water. Private balconies open directly onto Montego Bay, and guests practically live in their bathing suits.

Dining/Diversions: Lunch is served at beachside or in the main dining room, and there is nightly entertainment. The international food isn't wildly creative or refined, but it's plentiful.

Amenities: Freshwater pool, tennis clinic and tennis courts (for daytime), sauna, windsurfing, waterskiing, snorkeling, sailing, reggae dance lessons, massage.

The Sandals Inn. Kent Ave. (P.O. Box 412), Montego Bay, Jamaica, W.I. ☎ **800/SANDALS** in the U.S. and Canada, or 876/952-4140. Fax 876/952-6913. 52 units. A/C TV TEL. Winter U.S.$1,335–$1,555 double; off-season U.S.$1,335–$1,495 double. Rates are all-inclusive for 4 days/3 nights. AE, MC, V.

The Sandals Inn is a couples-only (male and female) hotel built around a large pool and patio, with a beach a short walk across a busy highway. This is the least glamorous, spacious, and attractive of the Sandals all-inclusive resorts scattered across Jamaica. But it's a trade-off: You don't get luxury, but you do get reasonable rates, proximity to downtown Montego Bay, and free day passes (including free transportation) to both of the Sandals resorts of Montego Bay.

Thirty-eight rooms open onto the swimming pool; all units contain king-size beds, safes, and hair dryers. There is now "environmentally friendly" linen service, so that sheets and towels are not changed unless you request it.

Dining/Diversions: Food is served in bountiful portions in the resort's only dining room, and there's nightly entertainment. A specialty restaurant, Caryle, specializing in flambé dishes, breaks the routine of the main dining room.

Amenities: Recreational and sports program, exercise room, saunas, Jacuzzi, tennis courts, swimming pool, room service (9am to 10pm).

Sandals Montego Bay. Kent Ave. (P.O. Box 100), Montego Bay, Jamaica, W.I. ☎ **800/ SANDALS** in the U.S. and Canada, or 876/952-5510. Fax 876/952-0816. 243 units. A/C TV TEL. Winter U.S.\$1,660–\$1,980 double; U.S.\$2,140–\$3,780 suite for 2. Off-season U.S.\$1,310–\$1,560 double; U.S.\$2,070–\$3,610 suite for 2. Rates are all-inclusive for 4 days/ 3 nights. AE, MC, V.

Located 5 minutes northeast of the airport, this honeymoon haven next to Whitehouse Village is always booked solid (reserve as far ahead as possible). The 19-acre site is a couples-only (male and female), all-inclusive resort. Everything is covered in the price—that means all meals, snacks, nightly entertainment (including those notorious toga parties), unlimited drinks night or day at one of four bars, tips, and round-trip airport transfers and baggage handling from the Montego Bay airport. Lots of entertainment and sports facilities are available on the property, so many guests never leave.

In contrast to its somewhat more laid-back nearby counterpart (the Sandals Royal Jamaican), this resort offers many different activities for a clientele and staff who tend to be extroverted and gregarious. The Playmakers, as staff members are called, keep everybody amused and the joint jumping. If you want peace, quiet, and seclusion, it's not for you.

The accommodations are either in villas spread along 1,700 feet of white, sandy beach or in the main house where all bedrooms face the sea and contain private balconies. Try to avoid booking into a room over the dining room; these don't have balconies and may be noisy. All units are well furnished, with king-size beds and hair dryers.

Dining/Diversions: In addition to its main dining room, the resort has Tokyo Joe's, serving six-course Oriental meals; the Beach Grill; and the Oleander Deck, with "white-glove service," featuring Jamaican and Caribbean cuisine. The Oleander offers the finest dining in the Sandals chain. Those who haven't tired themselves out can head for the late-night disco, which often has rum and reggae nights.

Amenities: Waterskiing, snorkeling, sailing, scuba diving daily with a certification program (PADI or NAUI), windsurfing, paddleboats and a glass-bottom boat, two freshwater pools, three Jacuzzis, tennis (available day or night), fully equipped fitness center. There's also a free shuttle bus to the Sandals Royal Jamaican, whose facilities are open without charge to guests here.

Sandals Royal Jamaican. Mahoe Bay (P.O. Box 167), Montego Bay, Jamaica, W.I. ☎ **800/SANDALS** in the U.S. and Canada, or 876/953-2231. Fax 876/953-2788. 190 units. A/C TV TEL. Winter U.S.\$1,750–\$1,980 per couple; U.S.\$2,150–\$2,420 suite for 2. Off-season U.S.\$1,660–\$1,880 per couple; U.S.\$2,050–\$2,300 suite for 2. Rates are all-inclusive for 4 days/3 nights. AE, MC, V.

This all-inclusive, couples-only (male and female) resort is a reincarnation of a prestigious colonial-style Montego Bay hotel. The building lies on its own private beach (which, frankly, isn't as good as the one at the Sandals Montego Bay). Some of the British colonial atmosphere remains, as reflected by a formal tea in the afternoon, but there are modern touches as well, including a private island reached by boat where clothing is optional.

The spacious rooms range from standard to superior to deluxe. Even higher in price are the deluxe beachfront accommodations or a junior suite.

Dining/Diversions: The Regency Suite and Deck is the Jamaican-inspired main dining room. Specialty restaurants include Bali Hai, an Indonesian restaurant built on the previously mentioned offshore island, and the Courtyard Grill, with such offerings as grilled sirloin, grilled snapper, and smoked marlin. There are four bars, plus food and drink available throughout the day. There's often live music by a local reggae band.

Amenities: Scuba diving, windsurfing, sailing, three tennis courts, swimming pool, laundry, massage, free shuttle bus to the resort's twin Sandals (whose facilities are available without charge to any guests). Weddings can be arranged.

2 Where to Dine

The Montego Bay area offers some of the finest—and most expensive—dining on Jamaica. But if you're watching your wallet and don't have a delicate stomach, some intriguing food is sold right on the street. For example, on Kent Avenue, you might try jerk pork. Seasoned spareribs are also grilled over charcoal fires and sold with extra-hot sauce. Naturally, it goes down better with a Red Stripe beer. Cooked shrimp are also sold on the streets of Mo Bay; they don't look it, but they're very hotly spiced, so be warned. If you're cooking your own meals, you might also want to buy fresh lobster or the catch of the day from Mo Bay fishers.

VERY EXPENSIVE

✪ **Norma at the Wharfhouse.** Reading Rd. ☎ **876/979-2745.** Reservations recommended. Main courses U.S.$26–$32. AE, MC, V. Thurs–Sun noon–3:30pm; Tues–Sun 6:30–10pm. Drive 15 minutes west of the town center along Rte. A1. NOUVELLE JAMAICAN.

Set in a coral-stone warehouse whose 2-foot-thick walls are bound together with molasses and lime, this is the finest restaurant in Montego Bay. It's a favorite of many of Jamaica's visiting celebrities. Originally built in 1780, it was restored by Millicent Rogers, heiress of the Standard Oil fortune, and now serves as the north-shore domain of Norma Shirley, one of Jamaica's foremost restaurateurs. You can request a table either on the large pier built on stilts over the coral reef (where a view of Montego Bay glitters in the distance) or in an elegantly formal early-19th-century dining room illuminated only with flickering candles. Before or after dinner, drinks are served either in the restaurant or in an informal bar in a separate building, much favored by locals, the Wharf Rat.

Service in the restaurant is impeccable, and the food is praised throughout the island. Specialties include grilled deviled crab backs, smoked marlin with papaya sauce, chicken breast with callaloo, nuggets of lobster in a mild curry sauce, and chateaubriand larded with pâté in a peppercorn sauce. Many of the main dishes are served with a garlic sauce. Dessert might be a rum-and-raisin cheesecake or a piña-colada mousse. Each of these dishes is individually prepared and filled with flavor. This is the type of food you hope to find in Jamaica, but so rarely do.

EXPENSIVE

Ambrosia. Across from the Wyndham Rose Hall Resort, Rose Hall. ☎ **876/953-2650.** Reservations recommended. Main courses U.S.$15–$29. AE, MC, V. Daily 6:30–10pm. MEDITERRANEAN.

This restaurant sits across from one of the largest hotels in Montego Bay. With its cedar-shingled design and trio of steeply pointed roofs, it has the air of a country club. Once you enter the courtyard, complete with a set of cannons, you find yourself in one of the loveliest restaurants in the area. You'll enjoy a sweeping view over the rolling lawns leading past the hotel and down to the sea, interrupted only by Doric columns. Not everything is ambrosia on the menu, but the cooks turn out a predictable array of good pasta and seafood dishes. Many of the flavors are Mediterranean, especially the lobster tails and other seafood dishes. The chefs handle the Long Island duckling expertly, although it has been shipped in frozen.

The Castles. In the Comfort Inn & Suites, Rose Hall (along A1 east of Montego Bay, toward Falmouth). ☎ **876/953-3250.** Reservations recommended. Main courses U.S.$16.50–$26. AE, DC, MC, V. Daily 6:30–10pm. INTERNATIONAL.

One of the most elegant restaurants between Montego Bay and Falmouth is The Castles in the Comfort Inn & Suites (see "Where to Stay," earlier in this chapter). Its chefs range the globe in their search for dishes such as gazpacho from Spain and spicy spaghetti in meat sauce from Italy as an appetizer; beef consommé julienne is the chef's specialty appetizer. In a formal setting, open to the breezes, guests peruse a menu that is usually divided among seafood selections, such as a delicious lobster thermidor, or main dishes and roasts, perhaps tenderloin of pork with honey and thyme, or a savory roast prime rib of beef. Every night there is a selection of Italian dishes, ranging from veal parmigiana to chicken with peppers, although these tend to vary in quality. Carrot cake is the pastry chef's prized dessert.

Day-O Plantation Restaurant. Barnett Estate Plantation, Lot 1, Fairfield, Montego Bay. ☎ **876/952-1825.** Reservations required. Main courses U.S.$15–$28. AE, DC, DISC, MC, V. Tues–Sun 6:30–9:30pm (last order). Minivan service will pick up diners at any of the Montego Bay hotels and return them after their meal. INTERNATIONAL/JAMAICAN.

This place was originally built in the 1920s as the home of the overseer of one of the region's largest sugar producers, the Barnett Plantation. It opened as a restaurant in 1994, in a location an 8-minute drive west of town off the A-1 highway leading toward Negril. It occupies a long, indoor/outdoor dining room that's divided into two halves by a dance floor and a small stage. Here, the owner, Paul Hurlock, performs as a one-man band, singing and entertaining the crowd while his wife, Jennifer, and their three children manage the dining room and kitchen.

Every dish is permeated with Jamaican spices and a sense of tradition. Try the chicken made plantation-style, with dark red wine sauce and herbs; fillet of red snapper in Day-O style—with olives, white wine, tomatoes, and peppers—or, even better, there's one of the best versions of jerked snapper in Jamaica. We also like the grilled rock lobster with garlic butter sauce.

Georgian House. 2 Orange St. ☎ **876/952-0632.** Reservations recommended. Main courses U.S.$16–$33, lunch U.S.$6.50–$13. AE, DC, MC, V. Mon–Fri noon–3pm; daily 6–11pm. The restaurant runs a private van service running round-trip from most hotels; ask when you reserve. INTERNATIONAL/JAMAICAN.

The landmark Georgian House, which includes a restaurant and an art gallery, brings grand cuisine and an elegant setting to the heart of town. The 18th-century buildings were constructed by an English gentleman for his mistress, or so the story goes. You can select either the upstairs room, which is more formal, or the garden terrace, with its fountains, statues, lanterns, and cut-stone exterior.

You might begin with a traditional Jamaican appetizer such as ackee and bacon. Baked spiny lobster is another specialty, but ask that it not be overcooked. Continental dishes, such as tournedos Rossini, are prepared with flair. The lunch menu is primarily Jamaican, but dinner offerings are broader in scope, with a variety of fresh seafood pastas and vegetarian choices. There's a fine wine list.

Julia's. Julia's Estate, Bogue Hill. ☎ **876/952-1772.** Reservations required. Fixed-price dinner U.S.$35–$45. AE, MC, V. Daily 5:30–10:30pm. Private van transportation provided; ask when you reserve. ITALIAN.

The winding jungle road you take to reach this place is part of the before-dinner entertainment. After a jolting ride to a setting high above the city and its bay, you pass through a walled-in park that long ago was the site of a private home built in 1840 for the duke of Sutherland. Today, the focal point is a long, low-slung modern house with fresh decor and sweeping views. Raimondo and Julia Meglio, drawing on the cuisine of their native Italy, prepare chicken parmesan, breaded cutlet Milanese with tomato sauce and cheese, fillet of fresh fish with lime juice and butter, and 10 different kinds of pasta. Lobster, veal, and shrimp are also regularly featured. The food, although competently prepared with fresh ingredients whenever possible, can hardly compete with the view. The homemade breads and desserts, however, are always winning accompaniments.

Marguerite's Seafood by the Sea and Margueritaville Sports Bar & Grill. Gloucester Ave. ☎ **876/952-4777.** Reservations recommended only for Marguerite's Seafood by the Sea. Main courses (in restaurant) U.S.$18.75–$28; platters, sandwiches, and snacks (in sports bar) U.S.$5–$21. AE, DC, MC, V. Restaurant daily 6–11pm; sports bar daily 10am–3am. INTERNATIONAL/SEAFOOD.

This two-in-one restaurant across from the Coral Cliff Hotel specializes in seafood served on a breeze-swept terrace overlooking the sea. There's also an air-conditioned lounge with an adjoining "Secret Garden." The chef specializes in exhibition cookery at a flambé grill. The menu is mainly devoted to seafood, including fresh fish. The cooks also turn out a number of innovative pastas and rather standard meat dishes. The changing dessert list is homemade, and a reasonable selection of wines is served.

The sports bar and grill features a 110-foot Hydroslide, live music, satellite TV, water sports, a sundeck, a CD jukebox, and a display kitchen offering a straightforward menu of seafood, sandwiches, pasta, pizza, salads, and snacks—nothing fussy. Naturally, the bartenders specialize in margaritas.

Pier 1. Howard Cooke Blvd. ☎ **876/952-2452.** Reservations not required. Main courses U.S.$15–$28. AE, MC, V. Daily 11am–11pm (even later on Sat–Sun if business warrants it). A private minivan will pick you up and return you to your hotel. SEAFOOD.

Pier 1, one of the major dining and entertainment hubs of Mo Bay, was built on a landfill in the bay. Fisherfolk bring fresh lobster to the restaurant, which the chef prepares in a number of ways, including Créole style or curried. You might begin with one of the typically Jamaican soups such as conch chowder or red pea (which is actually red bean). At lunch, the hamburgers are the juiciest in town, or you might find the quarter-decker steak sandwich with mushrooms equally tempting. The chef also prepares such famous island dishes as jerk pork and chicken, and Jamaican red snapper. (The jerk dishes, however, are better at the Pork Pit, reviewed below.) Finish your meal with a slice of moist rum cake. You can drink or dine on the ground floor, open to the sea breezes, but most guests seem to prefer the more formal second floor. Although this place remains a local favorite and its waterfront setting is appealing, service is very laid-back.

Richmond Hill Inn. 45 Union St. ☎ **876/952-3859.** Reservations recommended. All main courses (including soup, salad, garlic bread, and dessert) U.S.$35. AE, MC, V. Daily 7:30am–9:30pm. Take a taxi (a 4-minute ride uphill, east of the town's main square), or ask the restaurant to have you picked up at your hotel. INTERNATIONAL/CONTINENTAL.

This plantation-style house was originally built in 1806 by owners of the Dewar's whisky distillery, who happened to be distantly related to Annie Palmer, the "White Witch of Rose Hall." Today, it's run by an Austrian family team, who prepare well-flavored food for an appreciative clientele. Dinners include a shrimp-and-lobster cocktail, an excellent house salad, different preparations of dolphin, breaded breast of chicken, surf and turf, Wiener schnitzel, filet mignon, and a choice of dessert cakes. Many of the dishes are of a relatively standard international style, but others, especially the lobster, are worth the trek up the hill.

Round Hill Dining Room. In the Round Hill Hotel and Villas, along Rte. A1, 8 miles west of the center of Montego Bay. ☎ **876/956-7050.** Reservations required for 10 or more. Main courses U.S.$18–$39. AE, DC, MC, V. Daily 12:30–2:30pm and 7:30–9:30pm. INTERNATIONAL.

One of the top dining rooms in Montego Bay, this place has attracted a smattering of celebrities with its sophisticated surroundings. To reach the dining room, you'll have to pass through the resort's open-air reception area and proceed through a garden. Many visitors opt for a drink in the large and high-ceilinged bar area, designed by Ralph Lauren, before moving on to their dinner, which is served either on a terrace perched above the surf or (during inclement weather) under an open-sided breezeway.

Although many dishes are classic, the same recipes fed to Noël Coward or Cole Porter, other more innovative dishes reflect a taste of Jamaica. The menu changes nightly, offering an array of well-prepared dishes, from Mediterranean to Jamaican, from American to Italian pastas. For example, shrimp and pasta Caribe is sautéed with chopped herbs, cream, and wine; and Rasta Pasta is tossed with vegetables and basil. Caribbean veal is stuffed with spicy crabmeat and seared, and the catch of the day is served jerked, broiled, or steamed with butter, herbs, and ginger. Of course, you can also order more classic dishes, including rack of lamb or a medallion of lobster sautéed with cream and served over fettuccine. Afternoon tea and sandwiches are served daily at 4pm in the English style.

✪ **Sugar Mill Restaurant.** At the Half Moon Club, Half Moon Golf Course, Rose Hall, along Rte. A1. ☎ **876/953-2314.** Reservations required. Main courses U.S.$18.50–$39.50. AE, MC, V. Daily noon–2:30pm and 7–10pm. A minivan can be sent to most hotels to pick you up. INTERNATIONAL/CARIBBEAN.

This restaurant, near a stone ruin of what used to be a waterwheel for a sugar plantation, is reached after a drive through rolling landscape. Guests dine by candlelight on an open terrace with a view of a pond, the waterwheel, and plenty of greenery. You can also dine inside.

Although he came from Switzerland, it was in the Caribbean that chef Hans Schenk blossomed as a culinary artist. He has entertained everyone from the British royal family to Farouk, the former king of Egypt. Lunch can be a relatively simple affair, perhaps an ackee burger with bacon, preceded by Mama's pumpkin soup and followed with a homemade rum-and-raisin ice cream. Smoked north-coast marlin is a specialty. The chef makes the most elegant Jamaican bouillabaisse on the island

and zesty jerk versions of pork, fish, or chicken. He also prepares the day's catch with considerable flair. On any given day you can ask the waiter what's cooking in the curry pot. Chances are, it will be a Jamaican specialty such as goat, full of flavor and served with island chutney. Top your meal with a cup of unbeatable Blue Mountain coffee.

Town House. 16 Church St. ☎ **876/952-2660.** Reservations recommended. Main courses U.S.$15–$30. AE, DC, MC, V. Mon–Sat 11:30am–3:30pm; daily 6–10:30pm. Free limousine service to and from many area hotels. JAMAICAN/INTERNATIONAL.

Housed in a redbrick building dating from 1765, the Town House is a tranquil luncheon choice. It offers sandwiches and salads, or more elaborate fare if your appetite demands it. At night, it's floodlit, with outdoor dining on a veranda over-looking an 18th-century parish church. You can also dine in what used to be the cellars, where old ship lanterns provide a warm light. Soups, which are increasingly ignored in many restaurants, are a specialty here. The pepperpot or pumpkin is a delectable opening to a meal. The chef offers a wide selection of main courses, including the local favorite, red snapper en papillote (wrapped in parchment paper). We're fond of the chef's large rack of barbecued spareribs, with the owners' special Tennessee sauce. Their pasta and steak dishes are also good, especially the home-made fettuccine with whole shrimp and the perfectly aged New York strip steak. The restaurant often attracts the rich and famous.

MODERATE

Also note that affordable meals are available at the **Margueritaville Sports Bar & Grill,** on Gloucester Avenue (☎ 876/952-4777). See the review above under "Expensive," for Marguerite's Seafood by the Sea.

Calabash Restaurant. In the Winged Victory Hotel, 5 Queen's Dr. ☎ **876/952-3892.** Reservations recommended. Main courses U.S.$12–$22. AE, MC, V. Daily noon–2:30pm and 6–10pm. INTERNATIONAL/JAMAICAN.

Perched on a hillside road in Montego Bay, 500 feet above the distant sea, this long-time favorite has amused and entertained Peter O'Toole and Roger Moore, among others. It was originally built as a private villa by a doctor in the 1920s. More than 25 years ago, owner Roma Chin Sue established the courtyard and elegantly simple eagle's-nest patio as a well-managed restaurant. The seafood, Jamaican clas-sics, and international favorites include curried goat, lobster dishes, the house spe-cialty of mixed seafood en coquille (served with a cheese-and-brandy sauce), and a year-round version of a Jamaican Christmas cake. Flavors are blended beautifully. Over the years the kitchen has been consistently good, and savvy locals keep returning.

✪ **The Native Restaurant.** Gloucester Ave. ☎ **876/979-2769.** Reservations recom-mended. Main courses U.S.$10–$35. AE, MC, V. Daily 7:30am–10pm. JAMAICAN.

This restaurant continues to win converts, turning out dishes that Jamaican foodies love. Visitors have also discovered it. You might start with a tropical drink while selecting one of the international wines to go with your dinner. You know you're getting island flavor when faced with such appetizers as jerk reggae chicken, ackee and saltfish (an acquired taste), or perhaps smoked marlin. These can be followed by our favorite dish here, steamed fish. The cook will also serve you jerk or fried chicken, each filled with flavor. Lobster with garlic butter, although more costly, actually pales next to the curried shrimp. A more recent specialty is Boonoonoonoos, billed as "A Taste of Jamaica," a big platter with a little bit of everything, meats and several kinds of fish and vegetables. Although fresh desserts are prepared daily, you may choose instead just to have a Jamaican Blue Mountain coffee, which rounds the meal off nicely.

✪ **Reading Reef Club Restaurant.** On Bogue Lagoon, on Rte. A1 at the bottom of Long Hill Rd. (4 miles west of the town center). ☎ **876/952-5909.** Reservations required. Pastas U.S.$8–$11; main courses U.S.$10–$22. AE, MC, V. Daily 6:30am–11pm. ITALIAN/CONTINENTAL/CARIBBEAN.

There are those who claim that the food served in this second-floor terrace overlooking Bogue Lagoon is the finest in Montego Bay. The menu is the creative statement of JoAnne Rowe, who has a passion for cooking and menu planning, a skill she perfected while entertaining prominent people in Montego Bay at her private dinner parties. Among her offerings are perfectly prepared scampi, imaginative pasta dishes, and a catch of the day, usually snapper, yellowtail, kingfish, or dolphin. She also imports quality New York sirloin steaks, but whenever possible likes to use local produce. Dinner might begin with Jamaican soup, such as pepperpot or pumpkin, and the restaurant is known for its lime pie. Lunches are low-profile, with a more limited menu.

INEXPENSIVE

The Brewery. In Miranda Ridge Plaza, Gloucester Ave. ☎ **876/940-2433.** Main courses J$180–J$590 (U.S.$5.15–$16.80). AE, MC, V. Daily 11am–2am. AMERICAN/JAMAICAN.

This is more a bar than a full-scale restaurant, but lunch and dinner are served. Basic hamburgers, salads, and sandwiches are available, and there's also a nightly Jamaican dinner special, a bargain at about U.S.$6. You can enjoy drinks and your meal on the outside patio overlooking the ocean. The best time to come for drinks is during happy hour, from 4 to 6pm daily. Drinks made with local liquor are all half price. If you're really daring, you might want to try the bartender's specialty "fire water"; he won't disclose the ingredients, but promises that it lives up to its name. On Saturday night, live entertainment is offered, and the bar has karaoke on Tuesday and Friday.

Le Chalet. 32 Gloucester Ave. ☎ **876/952-5240.** Main courses at lunch U.S.$2.25–$16; at dinner U.S.$4.50–$17. Mon–Sat noon–10pm, Sun 3:30–10pm. AE, MC, V. INTERNATIONAL/CHINESE/JAMAICAN.

Set in Montego Bay's tourist strip, this high-ceilinged restaurant lies across Gloucester Avenue from the sea. The decor has that Howard Johnson's look, but this place offers great value. Food is served in copious and well-prepared portions, including a lunchtime selection of burgers, sandwiches, platters of barbecued ribs, and salads, and a more substantial selection of evening platters. Dinner options might include chicken platters, steaks, fresh fish, and lobster, which seems to taste best here if prepared with Jamaican curry. The staff is articulate and helpful, and proud of their straightforward and surprisingly well-prepared cuisine.

The Pelican. At the Pelican, Gloucester Ave. ☎ **876/952-3171.** Reservations recommended. Main courses U.S.$5–$16.50. AE, DC, MC, V. Daily 7am–11pm. JAMAICAN.

A Montego Bay landmark, the Pelican has been serving good food at reasonable prices for more than a quarter of a century. It's ideal for families. Many diners come here at lunch for well-stuffed sandwiches, juicy burgers, and barbecued chicken. You can also select from a wide array of Jamaican dishes, including stew peas and rice, curried goat, Caribbean fish, fried chicken, and curried lobster. A "meatless menu," including such dishes as a vegetable plate or vegetable chili, is also featured. Sirloin and seafood are also available, and the soda fountain serves old-fashioned sundaes with real whipped cream, making it a kiddies' favorite.

✪ **The Pork Pit.** 27 Gloucester Ave., near Walter Fletcher Beach. ☎ **876/952-1046.** One pound of jerk pork U.S.$10. No credit cards. Daily 11am–11:30pm. JAMAICAN.

The Pork Pit, an open-air gazebo right in the heart of Montego Bay, is the best place to go for the famous Jamaican jerk pork and jerk chicken. Many beach buffs come over here for a big lunch. Picnic tables encircle the building, and everything is open-air and informal. Half a pound of jerk meat, served with a baked yam or baked potato and a bottle of Red Stripe, is usually sufficient for a meal. The menu also includes steamed roast fish. Prices are very reasonable.

3 Hitting the Beach, Hitting the Links & Other Outdoor Pursuits

BEACHES

Cornwall Beach (☎ 876/952-3463) is a long stretch of white-sand beach with dressing cabanas. Admission to the beach is U.S.$2 for adults and U.S.$1 for children, for the entire day. A bar and cafeteria offer refreshment daily from 9am to 5pm.

Across from the **Doctor's Cave Beach Hotel,** Doctor's Cave Beach, on Gloucester Avenue (☎ 876/952-2566), helped launch Mo Bay as a resort in the 1940s. Admission to the beach is U.S.$2 for adults, U.S.$1 for children up to 12. Dressing rooms, chairs, umbrellas, and rafts are available from 8:30am to 5:30pm daily.

One of the premier beaches of Jamaica, **Walter Fletcher Beach,** in the heart of Mo Bay (☎ 876/952-5783), is noted for its tranquil waters, which makes it a particular favorite for families with children. Changing rooms are available, as is lifeguard service. You can have lunch here in a restaurant. The beach is open daily from 9am to 10pm, with an admission charge of U.S.$1 for adults, 50¢ for children.

Frankly, you may want to skip all these public beaches entirely and head instead for the **Rose Hall Beach Club** (☎ 876/953-2323), lying on the main road 11 miles east of Montego Bay. It's set on half a mile of secure, secluded white-sand beach with crystal-clear water. The club offers a full restaurant, two beach bars, a covered pavilion, an open-air dance area, showers, rest rooms, and changing facilities, plus beach volleyball courts, various beach games, and a full water-sports activities program. There's also live entertainment. Admission fees are U.S.$8 for adults and U.S.$5 for children. This beach club is far better equipped than any of the beaches previously recommended. The club is open daily from 10am to 6pm.

DEEP-SEA FISHING

Seaworld Resorts, whose main office is at the Cariblue Hotel, Rose Hall Main Road (☎ 876/953-2180), operates flying-bridge cruisers, with deck lines and outriggers, for fishing expeditions. A half-day fishing trip costs U.S.$330 for up to four participants.

DIVING & OTHER WATER SPORTS

Seaworld Resorts (☎ 876/953-2180; see above for address), operates scuba-diving excursions, plus many other water sports, including sailing and windsurfing. Its scuba dives plunge to offshore coral reefs, among the most spectacular in the Caribbean. There are three certified dive guides, one dive boat, and all the necessary equipment for either inexperienced or already-certified divers. Most dives begin at U.S.$35, U.S.$50 for night dives.

If you would prefer to snorkel, the waters right on Montego Bay's beach are just fine. There are plenty of rental stores for snorkeling equipment, so gear is easy to find and very cheap to rent. The very best waters for seeing fish and other marine life, however, are across the channel. Cayaba Reef, Seaworld Reef, and Royal Reef are full of barjacks, blue and brown chromis, yellow-headed wrasses, and spotlight parrot fish. You must have a guide to visit these reefs because currents can get strong when the afternoon wind picks up. If you are not staying in a resort that offers snorkeling expeditions, we recommend visiting **Seaworld** (☎ **876/953-2180**), in the Trelawny Beach Hotel in Falmouth. They charge a bit more (U.S.$25 per person per hour) than some of the others, but the guides will swim along with you to point out the varieties of tropical fish, which is especially nice for the kids.

GOLF

With four championship courses, Montego Bay makes Jamaica the best place to play in the West Indies.

Wyndham Rose Hall Golf & Beach Resort, Rose Hall (☎ **876/953-2650**), has a noted course with an unusual and challenging seaside and mountain layout, built on the shores of the Caribbean. Its eighth hole skirts the water, then doglegs onto a promontory and a green thrusting 200 yards into the sea. The back nine are the most scenic and interesting, rising up steep slopes and falling into deep ravines on Mount Zion. The 10th fairway abuts the family burial grounds of the Barretts of Wimpole Street, and the 14th passes the vacation home of singer Johnny Cash. The 300-foot-high 13th tee offers a rare panoramic view of the sea and the roof of the hotel, and the 15th green is next to a 40-foot waterfall, once featured in a James Bond movie. A fully stocked pro shop, a clubhouse, and a professional staff are among the amenities. Nonresidents of the Wyndham pay U.S.$60 for 18 holes and U.S.$40 for 9 holes. Guests at the Wyndham are charged U.S.$50 for 18 holes, U.S.$30 for 9 holes. Mandatory cart rental costs U.S.$33 for 18 holes, and the use of a caddy (also mandatory) is another U.S.$12 for 18 holes.

The excellent course at the **Tryall** (☎ **876/956-5660**), 12 miles from Montego Bay, is so regal it's often been the site of major golf tournaments, including the Jamaica Classic Annual and the Johnnie Walker Tournament. For 18 holes, guests of Tryall are charged U.S.$40 in spring, summer, and fall, U.S.$60 in winter. Nonresidents of Tryall pay U.S.$75 from mid-April to mid-December and U.S.$150 in winter.

Half Moon, at Rose Hall (☎ **876/953-2560**), features a championship course designed by Robert Trent Jones Sr. The course has manicured and diversely shaped greens. For 18 holes, nonresidents pay U.S.$110 year-round. Half Moon hotel guests receive a 50% discount. Carts in any season cost U.S.$30 for 18 holes, and caddies (mandatory in any season) are hired for U.S.$15 in any season.

Ironshore Golf & Country Club, Ironshore, St. James, Montego Bay (☎ **876/953-2800**), another well-known 18-hole golf course with a 72 par, is privately owned. It is, however, open to all golfers who show up. Greens fees for 18 holes are U.S.$57.50.

HORSEBACK RIDING

A good program for equestrians is offered at the **Rocky Point Riding Stables,** at the Half Moon Club, Rose Hall, Montego Bay (☎ **876/953-2286**). Housed in the most beautiful barn and stables in Jamaica, built in the colonial Caribbean style, it offers around 30 horses and a helpful staff. A 90-minute beach or mountain ride costs U.S.$50, whereas a 2½-hour combination ride (including treks along hillsides, forest trails, and beaches, and ending with a salt-water swim) goes for U.S.$70.

RIVER RAFTING

Mountain Valley Rafting, 31 Gloucester Ave. (☎ 876/956-0020), offers rafting excursions on the Great River, which depart from the Lethe Plantation, about 10 miles south of Montego Bay. Rafts are available for U.S.$36 for up to two participants. Trips last about an hour and operate daily from 8:30am to 4:30pm. The rafts are composed of bamboo trunks with a raised dais to sit on. In some cases, a small child can accompany two adults on the same raft, although due caution should be exercised if you choose to do this. Ask about pickup by taxi at the end of the rafting run to return you to your rented car. For U.S.$45 per person, a half-day experience will include transportation to and from your hotel, an hour's rafting, lunch, a garden tour of the Lethe property, and a taste of Jamaican liqueur.

TENNIS

Half Moon Golf, Tennis, and Beach Club, outside Montego Bay (☎ 876/953-2211), has the finest tennis courts in the area, even outclassing Tryall (see below). Its 13 state-of-the-art courts, seven of which are lit for night games, attract tennis players from around the world. Guests play free anytime. Lessons cost U.S.$25 per half hour, U.S.$45 per hour. The pro shop, which accepts reservations for court times, is open daily from 7am to 8pm. If you want to play after those hours, you switch on the lights yourself. If you're not a guest of the hotel, you must purchase a day pass (U.S.$50 per person) at the front desk. It will allow you access to the resort's tennis courts, gym, sauna, Jacuzzi, pools, and beach facilities.

  Tryall Golf, Tennis, & Beach Club, St. James (☎ 876/956-5660), offers nine hard-surface courts, three lit for night play, near its Great House. Day games are free for guests; nonguests pay U.S.$25 per hour. All players are assessed U.S.$12 per hour to have a court lit for night play. Four on-site pros provide lessons, costing U.S.$17 to U.S.$25 per half hour, or U.S.$25 to U.S.$40 per hour, depending on the rank of the pro.

  Outside Montego Bay, **Wyndham Rose Hall Golf & Beach Resort,** Rose Hall (☎ 876/953-2650), is an outstanding tennis resort, although it's not the equal of Half Moon or Tryall. Wyndham offers six hard-surface courts, each lighted for night play. As a courtesy, nonguests are sometimes invited to play for free, but permission has to be obtained from the manager. The resident pro charges U.S.$50 per hour for lessons, or U.S.$30 for 30 minutes.

4 Seeing the Sights

If you ever feel like deserting Montego Bay's sandy beaches, there are several notable sights and activities in the area.

THE GREAT HOUSES

Occupied by plantation owners, the Great Houses of Jamaica were always built on high ground so that they overlooked the plantation itself and could see the next house in the distance. It was the custom for the owners to offer hospitality to travelers crossing the island by road; travelers were spotted by the lookout, and bed and food were given freely.

Barnett Estates and Bellfield Great House. Barnett Estates. ☎ **876/952-2382.** Admission U.S.$10. Daily 9:30am–5pm.

Once a totally private estate sprawled across 50,000 acres, this Great House has hosted everybody from President Kennedy to Churchill and even Queen Elizabeth II over the years. Now anybody who pays the entrance fee can come in and take a

The White Witch of Rose Hall

Annie Mary Paterson, a beautiful bride of only 17, arrived at the Rose Hall Great House near Montego Bay on March 28, 1820, to take up residence with her new husband, John Palmer. The house was said to affect her badly from the moment she entered it.

When John Palmer found out she was having an affair with a young slave, he is said to have beaten her with a riding whip. John Palmer died that night, and before long, rumors were swirling that his young wife had poisoned his wine.

With her husband buried, Annie Palmer began a reign of terror at Rose Hall. Fearing her slave lover might blackmail her, she watched from the back of a black horse while he was securely tied, gagged, and flogged to death. Legend says that she then began to drift into liaison after liaison with one slave after another. But she was fickle: When her lovers bored her, she had them killed.

Her servants called her the "*Obeah* (voodoo) woman," the daughter of the devil, and "the White Witch of Rose Hall."

Although some scholars claim that they can produce no evidence of this legendary figure's cruelty or even of her debauchery, her story has been the subject of countless paperback Gothic novels.

When Ms. Palmer was found strangled in her bed in 1833, few speculated who her murderer might have been. Her household servants just wanted her buried as soon as possible in the deepest hole they could dig.

look. The domain of the Kerr-Jarret family during 300 years of high society, this was once the seat of a massive sugar plantation. At its center is the 18th-century Bellfield Great House (not as ornate as Rose Hall; see below). Restored in 1994, it is a grand example of Georgian architecture. Guides in costumes offer narrated tours of the property. After the tour, drop into the old Sugar Mill Bar for a tall rum punch.

Greenwood Great House. On Rte. A1, 14 miles east of Montego Bay. ☎ **876/953-1077.** Admission U.S.$10 adults, U.S.$5 children under 12. Daily 9am–6pm.

Some people find the 15-room Greenwood even more interesting than Rose Hall (see below). Erected on its hillside perch between 1780 and 1800, the Georgian-style building was the residence of Richard Barrett (cousin of poet Elizabeth Barrett Browning). Elizabeth Barrett Browning herself never visited Jamaica, but her family used to be one of the largest landholders here. An absentee planter who lived in England, her father once owned 84,000 acres and some 3,000 slaves. On display is the original library of the Barrett family, with rare books dating from 1697, along with oil paintings of the family, Wedgwood china, rare musical instruments, and a fine collection of antique furniture. The house today is privately owned but open to the public.

✪ **Rose Hall Great House.** Rose Hall Hwy., 9 miles east of Montego Bay. ☎ **876/ 953-2323.** Admission U.S.$15 adults, U.S.$10 children. Daily 9am–5:15pm.

The legendary Rose Hall is the most famous Great House on Jamaica and charges a steep admission fee. The subject of at least a dozen Gothic novels, Rose Hall was immortalized in the H. G. deLisser book *White Witch of Rosehall*. The house was built from 1778 to 1790 by John Palmer, a wealthy British planter. At its peak, this was a 6,600-acre plantation, with more than 2,000 slaves. However, it was Annie Palmer, wife of the builder's grandnephew, who became the focal point of fiction and fact. Called "Infamous Annie," she was said to have dabbled in witchcraft. She took slaves as lovers and then killed them off when they bored her. Servants called her "the Obeah woman" (*Obeah* is Jamaican for "voodoo"). Annie was said to have murdered several of her husbands while they slept and eventually suffered the same fate herself in a kind of poetic justice. Long in ruins, the house has now been restored and can be visited by the public. Annie's Pub is on the ground floor.

VISITING WITH SOME FEATHERED FRIENDS

Rocklands Wildlife Station. Anchovy, St. James. ☎ **876/952-2009.** Admission J$300 (U.S.$8.55). Daily 2:30–5pm.

It's a unique experience to have a Jamaican doctor bird perch on your finger to drink syrup, to feed small doves and finches millet from your hand, and to watch dozens of other birds flying in for their evening meal. Don't take children 5 and under to this sanctuary, as they tend to bother the birds. Rocklands is about a mile outside Anchovy on the road from Montego Bay.

ORGANIZED TOURS & CRUISES

The **Croydon Plantation,** P.O. Box 1348, Catadupa, St. James (☎ **876/ 979-8267**), is a 25-mile ride from Montego Bay. It can be visited on a half-day tour from Montego Bay (or Negril) on Tuesday, Wednesday, and Friday. Included in the U.S.$55 price are round-trip transportation from your hotel, a tour of the plantation, a taste of tropical fruits in season, and a barbecued-chicken lunch. Most hotel desks can arrange this tour.

For a plantation tour, go on a **Hilton High Day Tour,** through Beach View Plaza (☎ **876/952-3343**). The tour includes round-trip transportation on a scenic drive through historic plantation areas. Your day starts at an old plantation house with a continental breakfast. You can roam the 100 acres of the plantation and visit the German village of Seaford town or St. Leonards village nearby. Calypso music is played throughout the day, and a Jamaican lunch is served at 1pm. The charge for the day is U.S.$50 per person for the plantation tour, breakfast, lunch, and transportation. Tour days are Tuesday, Wednesday, Friday, and Sunday.

Day and evening cruises are offered aboard the *Calico,* a 55-foot gaff-rigged wooden ketch that sails from the Montego Bay waterfront. An additional vessel, *Calico B,* also carries another 40 passengers per boat ride. You can be transported to and from your hotel for either cruise. The day voyage, which departs at 10am and returns at 1pm, provides a day of sailing, sunning, and snorkeling (with equipment supplied). The cruise costs U.S.$50 per person and is offered daily. On the *Calico's* evening voyage, which goes for U.S.$25 per person and is offered Wednesday to Saturday from 5 to 7pm, cocktails and wine are served as you sail through sunset. For information and reservations, call Capt. Bryan Langford, North Coast Cruises (☎ **876/952-5860**). A 3-day notice is recommended.

A picnic to Miskito Cove Beach could be the highlight of your visit here. Hotel tour desks book the **Miskito Cove Beach Picnic (☎ 876/952-5164**), which leaves at 10am, returning at 4pm, with pickups at Tryall and Round Hill. For U.S.$55 per person, you can enjoy an open Jamaican bar, buffet lunch, calypso band, a glass-bottom-boat ride, a raft ride with a calypso singer on board, and water sports including snorkeling with a guide and equipment provided. Sunfish sailing with trained captains, jetskiing, waterskiing, and windsurfing. The picnics are offered on Sunday, Tuesday, and Thursday.

5 Shopping

For many visitors, Montego Bay is their introduction to shopping Jamaica-style. After surviving the ordeal, some visitors may vow never to go shopping again. Literally hundreds of Jamaicans pour into town hoping to peddle something, often something they made, to hordes of cruise-ship passengers.

Since their selling a craft may determine whether they can feed their family that night, there is often a feverish attempt to peddle goods to overseas visitors, all of whom are viewed as rich. Therefore, prepare yourself for some aggressive selling when you venture into the shopping centers.

Pandemonium greets many an unwary shopper, who must also be prepared for some fierce haggling. Every vendor asks too much for an item at first, which gives them the leeway to "negotiate" until the price reaches a more realistic level.

The main shopping areas are at **Montego Freeport,** within easy walking distance of the pier, **City Centre** (where most of the nonhotel in-bond shops are), and **Holiday Village Shopping Centre.**

ARTS & CRAFTS

The **Old Fort Craft Park,** a shopping complex with 180 vendors (all licensed by the Jamaica Tourist Board), fronts Howard Cooke Boulevard up from Gloucester Avenue in the heart of Montego Bay on the site of Fort Montego. A market with a varied assortment of handcrafts, it is ideal browsing not only for that little souvenir of Jamaica but for some more serious purchases as well. You'll see a selection of wall hangings, handwoven straw items, and hand-carved wood sculpture, and you can even get your hair braided if that's your desire. Vendors can be powerfully aggressive trying to get you to buy something, so be prepared for major hassle. If you want some item, also be prepared for some serious negotiation. Persistent bargaining on your part will lead to substantial discounts. Fort Montego, now long gone, was constructed by the British in the mid-18th century as part of their defense of "fortress Jamaica." But it never saw much action, except for firing its cannons every year to salute the monarch's birthday.

At the **Crafts Market** near Harbour Street in downtown Montego Bay, you can find the best selection of handmade souvenirs of Jamaica, including straw hats and bags, wooden platters, straw baskets, musical instruments, beads, carved objects, and toys. That jipijapa hat is important if you're going to be out in the island sun.

Ambiente Art Gallery. 9 Fort St. ☎ **876/952-7919.**

A 100-year-old clapboard-sided cottage set close to the road houses this gallery. Austrian-born owner Maria Hitchins is one of the doyennes of the Montego Bay art scene. She has personally encouraged and developed scores of local artists toward prominence, yet many of her good paintings sell for under U.S.$300.

Blue Mountain Gems Workshop. At the Holiday Village Shopping Centre. ☎ **876/953-2338.**

Here you can take a tour of the workshops to see the process from raw stone to the finished product you can buy later. Wooden jewelry, local carvings, and one-of-a-kind ceramic figurines are also sold.

Neville Budhai Paintings. Budhai's Art Gallery, Reading Main Rd. (5 miles east of Montego Bay), Reading. ☎ **876/979-2568.** Take bus no. 11 from Mo Bay.

This is the art center of a distinguished artist, Neville Budhai, president and cofounder of the Western Jamaica Society of Fine Arts. He has a distinct style, and captures the special flavor of the island and its people in his works. The artist may sometimes be seen sketching or painting in Montego Bay or along the highways of rural Jamaica.

Things Jamaican Ltd. 44 Fort St. ☎ **876/952-5605.**

Affiliated with the government and set up to encourage the development of Jamaican arts and crafts, Things Jamaican is a showcase for the talents of the artisans of this island nation. There's a wealth of Jamaican products on display, even food and drink, including rums and liqueurs, along with jerk seasoning and such jellies as orange pepper. Look for Busha Browne's fine Jamaican sauces, especially their spicy chutneys such as banana or their planters spicy piquant sauce or their spicy tomato (called love apple) sauce, which is not to be confused with catsup. These recipes are prepared and bottled by the Busha Browne Company in Jamaica just as they were 100 years ago. Many items for sale are carved from wood, including not only sculpture but salad bowls and trays. You'll also find large hand-woven Jamaican baskets and women's handbags made of bark (in Jamaica, these are known unflatteringly as "old lady bags").

Look also for reproductions of the Port Royal collection, named for the wicked city buried by an earthquake and tidal wave in 1692 (see chapter 7). After resting in a sleepy underwater grave for 275 years, beautiful pewter items were recovered and are living again in reproductions (except the new items are leadless). Impressions were made, and molds were created to reproduce them. They include rat-tail spoons, a spoon with the heads of the monarchs William and Mary, Splay-footed Lion Rampant spoons, and spoons with Pied-de-Biche handles. Many items were reproduced faithfully, right down to the pit marks and scratches. To complement this pewter assortment, Things Jamaican created the Port Royal Bristol-Delft Ceramic Collection, based on original pieces of ceramics found in the underwater digs.

DUTY-FREE SHOPPING

In Montego Bay, you can purchase good duty-free items, including Swiss watches, Irish crystal, French perfumes, English china, Danish silverware, Portuguese linens, Italian handbags, Scottish cashmeres, Indian silks, and liquors and liqueurs. Appleton's overproof, special, and punch rums are an excellent value. The best liqueurs are Tía Maria (coffee flavored) and Rumona (rum flavored). Khus Khus is the local perfume. Jamaican arts and crafts are available throughout the resort and at the Crafts Market (see above).

Golden Nugget. 8 St. James Shopping Centre, Gloucester Ave. ☎ **876/952-7707.**

Golden Nugget is a duty-free shop with an impressive collection of watches for both women and men, and a fine assortment of jewelry, especially gold chains. Set within the manicured confines of one of Montego Bay's most modern shopping compounds, it is run by India-born Sheila Mulchandani.

FASHION

Jolie Madame Fashions. 30 City Centre Building. ☎ **876/952-3126.**

Its racks of clothing for women and girls might contain an appropriately cool garment for a romantic dinner or a lunch beside the swimming pool, or something to wear as a cover-up at the beach. Many garments range from U.S.$25 to U.S.$200.

Norma McLeod, the establishment's overseer, designer, coordinator, and founder, is always on hand to arrange custom-made garments.

Klass Kraft Leather Sandals. 44 Fort St. ☎ **876/952-5782.**

Next door to Things Jamaican, this store offers sandals and leather accessories made on location by a team of Jamaican craftspeople. All sandals cost less than U.S.$35.

6 Montego Bay After Dark

There's a lot more to Montego Bay evenings than just discos. But most of the entertainment is based at the various hotels, which has spelled doom for local nightclubs trying to attract tourists.

Pier 1, Howard Cooke Boulevard (☎ 876/952-2452), already previewed as a dining option, might also be your choice for a night on the town. On Friday night there's disco action from 10pm to 5am, with a J$200 (U.S.$5.70) cover charge, and cheap Red Stripe beer.

Cricket Club, at the Wyndham Rose Hall (☎ 876/953-2650), is more than just a sports bar. It's a place where people go to meet and mingle with an international crowd. Televised sports, karaoke sing-alongs, tournament darts, and backgammon are all part of the fun. The club is open daily from 7pm to 1am. There's no cover charge.

We've enjoyed the atmosphere of **Walter's,** 39 Gloucester Ave. (☎ 876/952-9391), which has an authentic Jamaican laid-back feel—complete with a constant flow of calypso and reggae music from as early as 9am daily (for the diehards) until 2am. There is never a cover, and they have live bands on the weekends.

If you want to stick to a more familiar kind of setting, try the **Witches Nightclub,** in the Holiday Inn SunSpree Resort (☎ 876/953-2485). Non-guests of the hotel can pick up a pass at the front desk for U.S.$50, which allows them all-inclusive privileges of the nightclub. The pass is good from 6pm to 2am. We found their policy to be a bit restrictive but the house/disco/jazz music selection is as imaginative as what you'll find at a club in the U.S.

Walter's is definitely a Jamaican experience, and Witches is definitely an American experience in Jamaica. But **Margueritaville,** Gloucester Avenue (☎ 876/952-4777), is a hybrid of the two. This place is entirely Jamaican in its feel—but you're as likely to hear country and western here as you are reggae. The crowd, music, and fun run the gamut. In addition to the U.S.$3 nightly entrance charge and U.S.$10 Saturday night cover, there is only one other requirement: "Just have a good time, mon."

Although a bit pricey, an interesting Jamaican experience is **Combo at Lollypop on the Beach** at Sandy Bay, Hanover, half a mile west of Tryall, held every Wednesday from 7:30 to 11pm (also on Sunday if the demand is heavy). Your U.S.$65 includes round-trip transport to the beach from Mo Bay hotels, a dinner of seafood and jerk meats, traditional dance groups performing Kumina, reggae, the basket dance, the bamboo dance, and the limbo, plus dancing on the beach. Children go for half price. For more information, call **Lollypop on the Beach** at ☎ 876/953-5314.

7 A Side Trip to Falmouth

A port on the north coast about 23 miles east of Montego Bay, Falmouth is an interesting but ramshackle town. There is talk about fixing it up for visitors, but no one seems to have gotten around to it yet. If you leave your car at Water Square, you can explore the town in about an hour or so.

The present Courthouse was reconstructed from the early 19th-century building, and fishers still congregate on Seaboard Street. You'll pass the Customs Office and a parish church dating from the closing years of the 18th century. Later, you can go on a shopping expedition outside of town to Caribatik Island Fabrics (see below).

RIVER RAFTING NEAR FALMOUTH

Rafting on the Martha Brae is an adventure. To reach the starting point from Falmouth, drive approximately 3 miles inland to **Martha Brae's Rafters Village** (☎ 876/952-0889). The rafts are similar to those on the Rio Grande, near Port Antonio, and cost U.S.$40 per raft, with two riders allowed on a raft, plus a small child if accompanied by an adult (but use precaution). The trips last 1¼ hours and operate daily from 9am to 4pm. You sit on a raised dais on bamboo logs. Along the way you can stop and order cool drinks or beer along the banks of the river. There's a bar, a restaurant, and two souvenir shops in the village.

A SPECIAL SHOPPING EXPEDITION FOR BATIKS

Two miles east of Falmouth on the north-coast road is **Caribatik Island Fabrics,** at Rock Wharf on the Luminous Lagoon (☎ 876/954-3314). This is the private living and work domain of Keith Chandler, who established the place with his late wife, Muriel, in 1970. Today, the batiks whose forerunners were created by Muriel Chandler are viewed as stylish garments by chic boutiques in the States.

In the shop there is a full range of fabrics, scarves, garments, and wall hangings, some patterned after such themes as Jamaica's "doctor bird" and various endangered animal species of the world. Muriel's Gallery continues to sell a selection of her original batik paintings. Either Keith or a member of the staff will be glad to describe the intricate process of batiking during their open hours: 9am to 4pm Tuesday through Saturday. They are closed in September.

WHERE TO STAY

✪ **Good Hope.** 5 miles south of Falmouth (P.O. Box 50), Falmouth, Jamaica, W.I. ☎ **800/ OUTPOST** or 876/954-3289. Fax 876/954-3289. 10 units. Winter U.S.$150–$250 double; off-season U.S.$100–$175 double. AE, MC, V.

Set on 2,000 acres, this estate was first granted to a Col. Thomas Williams in 1742, and the Great House was built in 1755. It was the center for growing sugarcane and coconuts, and crops are still grown here, the land irrigated by the Martha Brae River, which meanders through the property. Renovated to its original Georgian style, Good Hope offers four bedrooms in the great house, one in the "Counting House," and five in the "Coach House." The Coach House can be rented as a self-contained villa for a family or group of friends, as it has a full kitchen, living and dining room, and balcony. Staff will be provided to prepare meals at the Coach House, if guests prefer to dine in rather than at the hotel's restaurant. The Great House has been extensively restored and refurbished. Bedrooms have elegant furnishings and four-poster beds.

Dining: The formal dining room offers very Jamaican, plantation-style cooking, yet with a continental flair. Another more informal dining area is on the large terrace behind the pool. Outside guests who call for a reservation can also dine here. Lunch is served daily from noon to 3pm and dinner from 6:30 to 9:30pm.

Amenities: Swimming pool, tennis courts, bird sanctuary, riding stables; guests can also enjoy facilities of the Half Moon Club.

WHERE TO DINE

Glistening Waters Inn and Marina. Rock Falmouth. ☎ **876/954-3229.** Reservations not required. Main courses U.S.$8.50–$22. AE, MC, V. Daily 7am–9:30pm. SEAFOOD.

Residents of Montego Bay often make the 28-mile drive out here, along Route A1, just to sample the ambience of old Jamaica. This well-recommended restaurant, with a veranda overlooking a lagoon, is housed in what was originally a private clubhouse of the aristocrats of nearby Trelawny. The furniture here may remind you of a stage set for *Night of the Iguana.* Menu items usually include local fish dishes, such as snapper or kingfish, served with bammy (a form of cassava bread). Other specialties include three different lobster dishes, three different preparations of shrimp, three different conch viands, fried rice, and pork served as chops or in a stew. The food is just what your mama would make (if she came from Jamaica).

The waters of the lagoon contain a rare form of phosphorescent microbe which, when the waters are agitated, glows in the dark. Ask about evening booze cruises; departures are nightly at about 6:30pm.

5

Negril, the South Coast & Mandeville

Situated on the arid western tip of Jamaica, **Negril** has had a reputation for bacchanalia, hedonism, marijuana smoking, and nude bathing since hippies discovered its sunny shores during the late 1960s. The resort became more mainstream in the early 1990s as the big-money capitalists of Kingston and North America built several new megaresorts, most of them managed by Jamaica's Super-Clubs. Not all of the old reputation has disappeared, however, for some resorts here reserve stretches of their beach for nude bathers, and illegal ganja is peddled openly.

Whether clothed or unclothed, visitors are drawn here to Negril's 7-mile stretch of white sand and some of the best snorkeling and scuba diving in Jamaica. Opening onto a tranquil lagoon protected from the Caribbean by a coral reef, this great beach is set against a backdrop of sea grapes and coconut palms. Local authorities mandate that no building can be taller than the highest palm tree, resulting in an ecologically conscious setting, with the resorts blending gracefully into the flat and sandy landscape.

While Negril gets the crowds, the **South Coast** of Jamaica has only recently begun to attract large numbers of tourists. The Arawak once lived in sylvan simplicity along these shores before their civilization was destroyed. Early Spanish settlers came here searching for gold. Today's traveler comes looking for the untrammeled sands of its secluded beaches. Fishers still sell their catch at colorful local markets, and the prices, as they say here, are "the way they used to be" in Jamaica.

Most visitors to the south head east from Negril through Savanna-La-Mar to the high-country, English-style town of **Mandeville,** then on to a boat tour up the Black River, home of freshwater crocodiles. Those with more time continue southeast along the coast to Treasure Beach before heading up to Mandeville. On the South Coast, the best center for overnighting is either the town of Black River or the village of Treasure Beach.

Mandeville, about midway between Negril and Kingston, lies in the interior of the island at 2,000 feet above sea level. A large North American contingent employed in the bauxite industry lives here. Although dating from 1814, Mandeville was developed in the late 19th century as a retreat for English visitors attracted to the town's pleasant climate. The temperature in summer averages 70°F, and in

Negril

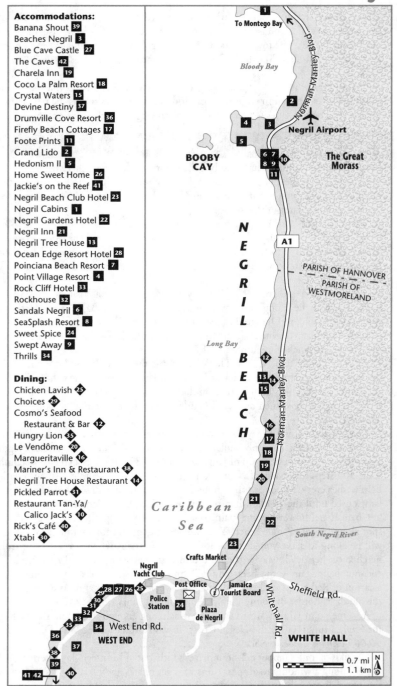

Accommodations:
Banana Shout 39
Beaches Negril 3
Blue Cave Castle 27
The Caves 42
Charela Inn 19
Coco La Palm Resort 18
Crystal Waters 15
Devine Destiny 37
Drumville Cove Resort 36
Firefly Beach Cottages 17
Foote Prints 11
Grand Lido 2
Hedonism II 5
Home Sweet Home 26
Jackie's on the Reef 41
Negril Beach Club Hotel 23
Negril Cabins 1
Negril Gardens Hotel 22
Negril Inn 21
Negril Tree House 13
Ocean Edge Resort Hotel 28
Poinciana Beach Resort 7
Point Village Resort 4
Rock Cliff Hotel 33
Rockhouse 32
Sandals Negril 6
SeaSplash Resort 8
Sweet Spice 24
Swept Away 9
Thrills 34

Dining:
Chicken Lavish 25
Choices 29
Cosmo's Seafood
   Restaurant & Bar 12
Hungry Lion 35
Le Vendôme 20
Margueritaville 16
Mariner's Inn & Restaurant 38
Negril Tree House Restaurant 14
Pickled Parrot 31
Restaurant Tan-Ya/
   Calico Jack's 10
Rick's Café 40
Xtabi 30

To Montego Bay

Bloody Bay

Negril Airport

BOOBY CAY

The Great Morass

N E G R I L   B E A C H

A1

PARISH OF HANNOVER
PARISH OF WESTMORELAND

Long Bay

Norman-Manley-Blvd.

Caribbean Sea

South Negril River

Crafts Market

Negril Yacht Club

Post Office

Jamaica Tourist Board

Police Station

Plaza de Negril

West End Rd.

WEST END

Sheffield Rd.

Whitehall Rd.

WHITE HALL

0   0.7 mi
    1.1 km

N

winter, a comfortably cool 60°F, which also helped make Mandeville the center of the Jamaican coffee industry during an earlier era. Fortunes were also made in pimento (allspice). The town contains the oldest golf course on Jamaica, and one of its major attractions is Marshall's Pen, an 18th-century Great House on a 300-acre cattle farm.

Partly because of its Victorian gingerbread architecture, Mandeville has been called the most English town in Jamaica. Today, it accepts its role as the sleepiest of the larger Jamaican cities—a fact that contributes significantly to its charm.

1 Introducing Negril

Long before the hippies established Negril's reputation for debauchery in the 1960s, it was noted for the buccaneer Calico Jack, famous for his carousings with the infamous women pirates Ann Bonney and Mary Read (see the box "Ann Bonney & Her Dirty Dog," later in this section).

When the laid-back young Americans and Canadians arrived in the late '60s, Negril was a sleepy village with no electricity or telephones. The young people rented modest digs in little houses on the West End, where the locals extended their hospitality. The sunsets were beautiful and free, and the ganja was cheap and readily available.

But those days are gone. Negril today is a tourist mecca. Visitors flock to its beaches, which lie along three well-protected bays: Long Bay, Negril Harbour (or Bloody Bay), and Orange Bay. This new Negril, lined with all-inclusive resorts such as Hedonism II and Sandals, draws a better-heeled—if not necessarily less rowdy—crowd, including hundreds of European visitors.

There are really two Negrils. The West End is the site of many little authentic restaurants with names like Chicken Lavish, and of modest cottages that still take in paying guests. The other Negril is on the east end, along the road from Montego Bay. The best hotels, such as Negril Gardens, line the panoramic beachfront one after the other.

The actual town itself may have power and phones these days, but it has little of interest to travelers. The only building of any historical note in the area is Negril Lighthouse, at the westerly tip of Jamaica. Built in 1894, it offers a chance to climb some 100 steps for a view of Negril Point, the bay, and the sea inlet. An automatic light flashes every 2 seconds throughout the night. You can still see the old kerosene lamps used until the 1940s, when they were replaced by gas lamps.

Chances are, however, your main concern will be staking out your own favorite spot along Negril's 7-mile beach. You don't need to get up for anything; somebody will be along to serve you. Perhaps it'll be the banana lady, with a basket of fruit perched on her head. Maybe the ice-cream man will set up a stand right under a coconut palm. Surely the beer lady will find you as she strolls along the beach, a carton of Red Stripe on her head and a bucket of ice in her hand. And just like in the old days, hordes of young men peddling illegal ganja will seek you out.

At some point you'll want to leave the beach long enough to explore Booby Key (or Cay), a tiny islet off the Negril Coast. It was featured in the Walt Disney film *20,000 Leagues Under the Sea.*

Negril is 50 miles (about a 2-hour drive) southwest of Montego Bay international airport along a winding road, past ruins of sugar estates and great houses. (Most of the resorts here will arrange to pick you up and provide your transfer from the Montego Bay airport.) It's 150 miles (about a 4-hour drive) west of Kingston.

2 Getting There

If you are going to Negril, you will fly into **Donald Sangster Airport** in Montego Bay. Most hotels, particularly the all-inclusive resorts, will pick you up and drive you directly to your hotel. Be sure to ask when you book.

If your hotel does not provide transfers, you have a few options. You can fly on from Montego Bay to Negril's small airport aboard the independent carrier, **Air Jamaica Express,** booking your connection through the Air Jamaica reservations network (☎ **800/523-5585** in the U.S.). The airfare is U.S.$45 one way.

If you don't want to deal with another flight, public and private bus companies have desks in the Montego Bay airport, all offering a U.S.$20 one-way fare to get you to Negril. The public bus is not a comfortable way to go for the 2-hour trip. Two private companies making the run are **Tour Wise** (☎ **876/979-1027** in Montego Bay, or 876/957-4223 in Negril) and **Caribic Vacations** (☎ **876/953-9874** in Montego Bay, or 876/957-3309 in Negril). All buses make one refreshment stop at a halfway point during the trip. Buses depart as flights arrive and will drop you off at your hotel once you reach Negril.

Yet another option is renting a car. Information on car rentals is given in the "Getting Around" section in chapter 3. From Montego Bay, drive 52 miles west along Highway A1. Because of conditions, plan for a 90-minute drive.

A final option is to take a taxi; dozens are available at the airport. A typical one-way fare from Montego Bay to Negril is U.S.$40 to U.S.$50. Always negotiate and agree upon the fare before getting into the taxi.

3 Where to Stay

Refer to the end of this section for a complete rundown on all of the all-inclusive resorts.

EXPENSIVE

The Caves. P.O. Box 15, Lighthouse Station, Negril, Jamaica, W.I. ☎ **800/OUT-POST** in the U.S., or 876/957-0270. Fax 876/957-4930. 8 units. Winter U.S.$400 double; U.S.$460 1-bedroom apt for 2; U.S.$580–$600 2-bedroom apt for 2; U.S.$725 2-bedroom apt for 4. Off-season U.S.$325 double; U.S.$400 1-bedroom apt for 2; U.S.$500–$525 2-bedroom apt for 2; U.S.$625 2-bedroom apt for 4. Rates are nightly and include all meals and domestic Jamaican drinks. AE, MC, V.

This place might be well suited for groups of friends traveling together or for a family reunion. This small-scale hotel was established in 1990 on 2 acres of land that's perched above a honeycombed network of cliffs, 32 feet above the surf on a point near Negril's lighthouse, close to Jamaica's westernmost tip. Accommodations are summer-style units within five cement and wood-sided cottages, each with a thatch roof and sturdy furniture. Matisse could have designed them. None has air-conditioning, and the windows are without screens. A TV and VCR can be brought in if you request them. Suites contain some limited cooking equipment. There's a saltwater pool and a Jacuzzi on the premises, but unless you're interested in snorkeling in the rocky waters offshore, you'll have to drive to Negril to reach a sandy beachfront. Meals are prepared only for residents, not for outsiders, and are included, along with domestic Jamaican drinks from the bar, as part of the all-inclusive price.

Seasplash Resort. Norman Manley Blvd. (P.O. Box 123), Negril, Jamaica, W.I. ☎ **800/ 254-2786** in the U.S., or 876/957-4041. Fax 876/957-4049. 15 units. A/C TV TEL. Winter U.S.$199 suite for 2; U.S.$219 suite for 3; U.S.$239 suite for 4. Off-season U.S.$135 suite for 2; U.S.$155 suite for 3; U.S.$175 suite for 4. Full board U.S.$33 per person extra. AE, CB, DC, MC, V.

Partly because of its small size, this beachfront resort often has a friendly, personable feeling. In deliberate contrast to the megaresorts nearby, it lies on a small but carefully landscaped sliver of beachfront land planted with tropical vegetation. The suites are spacious and stylishly decorated with wicker furniture and fresh pastel colors. All are the same size and contain the same amenities (a kitchenette, a balcony or patio, large closets, and either a king-size bed or twin beds), although those on the upper floor have higher ceilings and feel more spacious.

Dining: The resort contains two different restaurants, Calico Jack's (a simple lunchtime *bohio*) and the more elaborate Tan-Ya's (see "Where to Dine," below). There's also a poolside bar.

Amenities: Guests have use of a small gym, a Jacuzzi, and a swimming pool. Baby-sitting, laundry, and room service are also offered.

MODERATE

✪ **Charela Inn.** Norman Manley Blvd. (P.O. Box 33), Negril, Jamaica, W.I. ☎ **876/957-4648.** Fax 876/957-4414. 49 units. A/C TEL. Winter U.S.$154–$200 double; off-season U.S.$105–$135 double. MAP U.S.$38 per person extra. 5-night minimum stay in winter. MC, V.

Simplicity, a quiet kind of elegance, and excellent value for the money are the hallmarks here. A seafront inn reminiscent of a Spanish hacienda, this place sits on the main beach strip on 3 acres of landscaped grounds. The building has an inner courtyard with a tropical garden and a round freshwater swimming pool opening onto one of the widest (250 feet) sandy beaches in Negril. The inn attracts a loyal following of visitors seeking a home away from home.

Its dining room faces both the sea and the garden and offers both an à la carte menu and a five-course fixed-price meal that's changed daily. Sunsets are toasted on open terraces facing the sea. Sunset cruises, lasting 3½ hours, are offered, along with Sunfish sailing, windsurfing, and kayaking. On Thursday and Saturday nights there's live entertainment.

Coco La Palm Resort. Norman Manley Blvd., Negril, Jamaica, W.I. ☎ **800/896-0987** or 876/957-4227. Fax 876/957-3460. 41 units. A/C MINIBAR TV TEL. Winter U.S.$140–$160 double; U.S.$160–$180 suite. Off-season U.S.$120–$140 double; U.S.$140–$150 suite. MC, V.

This is a well-conceived hotel with very little plastic or glitter, and lots of opportunity for relaxation and rest. Wedged between another hotel and a vacant lot, behind a screen of sea grapes, directly at the edge of Negril's long and sandy beach, this is one of Negril's newest resorts, the brainchild of a Minnesota-based real estate developer who fell in love with Jamaica during his many vacations here. It consists of a pair of long and narrow two-story buildings whose slender ends face the beach, and whose long sides form the edges of a carefully landscaped garden containing a Jacuzzi and a kidney-shaped swimming pool. Rooms are shaped like an octagon, and each has its own patio or balcony, a safety deposit box, white-painted furniture, and a coffeemaker. On the premises is a bar and a restaurant (The Seaside).

Coconuts. Little Bay, Jamaica, W.I. ☎ **800/962-5548** in the U.S., or 876/997-5013. Fax 715/686-7143. 10 cottages. Winter U.S.$695 per person per week, cottage for 2. Off-season U.S.$645 per person per week, cottage for 2. Children 14–17 U.S.$395 extra; ages 6–13 U.S.$295 extra; ages 5 and under U.S.$195 extra. Rates include all meals. MC, V.

In a fishing village on a quiet country road on the South Coast, 8 miles east of Negril on the way to Savanna-La-Mar, this getaway offers a respite from the hustle and bustle of life. Guests stay in cedar-and-stone cottages that have their own private garden patios surrounded by flowers. Only two units have full baths; the rest contain half baths. The philosophy here is, in a climate as beautiful as Jamaica's, why lather up in an indoor cubicle when you can enjoy the garden and ocean views offered by the four totally private coral-stone showers located in the terraced gardens?

Your stay includes the use of the saltwater pool and sporting equipment, including snorkeling and fishing gear. Island tours and excursions into Negril or Savanna-La-Mar can be arranged. Your meals consist of freshly caught fish and lobster, chicken, fresh local vegetables, and local fruits and juices that you can enjoy at the seaside restaurant or on your private patio served by the staff.

Crystal Waters. Norman Manley Blvd. (P.O. Box 18), Negril Beach, Negril, Jamaica, W.I. ☎ **876/957-4284.** Fax 876/957-4889. 10 villas. A/C TEL. Winter U.S.$130 1-bedroom villa; U.S.$215–$260 2-bedroom villa; U.S.$355 3-bedroom villa. Off-season U.S.$95 1-bedroom villa; U.S.$130–$190 2-bedroom villa; U.S.$260 3-bedroom villa. Maximum of 2 people per room. MC, V.

Located on Negril Beach, a 1½-hour drive from the international airport in Montego Bay, this hotel offers simple accommodations at reasonable prices. Nehru Caolsingh owns and operates these villas, which were opened in the mid-1960s. The accommodations are tropically decorated, furnished with a mixture of hardwoods and wicker. The villas include ceiling fans (plus air-conditioning) and full kitchens, and each is staffed with a housekeeper who will cook breakfast, lunch, and dinner for you. There's also a freshwater pool.

Jackie's on the Reef. West End Rd., Negril, Jamaica, W.I. ☎ **876/957-4997,** or 718/ 783-6763 in New York state. 3 units, 1 cottage. Winter U.S.$150 per person; off-season U.S.$115 per person. Rates include breakfast, dinner, and yoga class. No credit cards. Drive 2½ miles past the oldest lighthouse in Negril; just keep heading out the West End until you come to the sign. No children accepted.

This is one of the most offbeat places to stay in all of Jamaica. It's like a counterculture "spa"—actually a holistic health retreat housed in a one-story gray-stone building called "the temple." The hotel lies 7 miles from the nearest beach, but there's a small seawater pool and a ladder down to the reef for swimming.

The bedrooms are generous in size, with mosquito netting draped over the beds in the old plantation style. However, there are no TVs, phones, or air-conditioning (or even fans). But you'll find simple furnishings, such as twin beds and small tables. The yoga classes are conducted on a large porch; other services offered include massage, "scrubs," facials, and something known as "past-life regression and energy balancing." The food is Jamaican style and generous in quality. If nothing at the juice bar turns you on, you can always order a Red Stripe.

Negril Beach Club Hotel. Norman Manley Blvd. (P.O. Box 7), Negril, Jamaica, W.I. ☎ **800/526-2422** in the U.S. and Canada, or 876/957-4220. Fax 876/957-4364. 53 units. A/C. Winter U.S.$100–$135 double; U.S.$175 suite for 2. Off-season U.S.$68–$108 double; U.S.$138 suite for 2. MAP U.S.$30 per person extra. AE, MC, V.

This casual, informal resort, where topless bathing is the norm, has many fans, though it's too laid-back and too basically furnished and maintained to appeal to those of you who want some comfort and pampering on your vacation. The resort is designed around a series of white stucco cottages with exterior stairways and terraces. The entire complex is clustered like a horseshoe around a rectangular garden that abuts a sandy beach. The accommodations range from simply furnished rooms, rented either as singles or doubles, to one- and two-bedroom suites, each with a kitchenette. The well-appointed rooms each have a private bath with either a shower or a tub with a showerhead; the less expensive units don't have balconies. Because some of the units are time-shares, not all of the accommodations are available.

There's easy access to a full range of sports facilities, including snorkeling, a pool, volleyball, table tennis, and windsurfing. Other activities can be organized nearby, and beach barbecues and buffet breakfasts are ample and frequent. The Seething Cauldron Restaurant on the beach serves barbecues and seafood.

✪ **Negril Cabins.** Rutland Point, Negril, Jamaica, W.I. ☎ **876/957-5350.** Fax 876/ 957-5381. 70 cabins. Winter U.S.$150–$176 cabin for 2; U.S.$192 cabin for 3. Off-season $130–U.S.$154 cabin for 2; $162 cabin for 3. Children 12 and under stay free in parents' rm. AE, MC, V.

In many ways, this is the best bargain in Negril, suitable for the budget-conscious traveler eager to get away from it all. Except for the palm trees and the sandy beach, you might imagine yourself at a log-cabin complex in the Maine woods. The cabins are in a forest, across the road from a beach called Bloody Bay (where the infamous 18th-century pirate, Calico Jack, was captured by the British). The 9 acres of gardens are planted with royal palms, bull thatch, and a rare variety of mango tree.

The unadorned cabins are really small cottages, none more than two stories high, rising on stilts. Each timber cottage includes a balcony and some are air-conditioned. The bar and restaurant serve tropical punch, a medley of fresh Jamaican fruits, and flavorful but unpretentious Jamaican meals. A children's program is also available, and live entertainment is offered on some nights.

Negril Gardens Hotel. Norman Manley Blvd. (P.O. Box 58), Negril, Jamaica, W.I. ☎ **800/752-6824** in the U.S., 800/567-5327 in Canada, or 876/957-4408. Fax 876/ 957-4374. 66 units. A/C TV TEL. Winter U.S.$165–$225 double; U.S.$280 1-bedroom suite; U.S.$350 2-bedroom suite. Off-season U.S.$145 double; U.S.$175 1-bedroom suite; U.S.$275 2-bedroom suite. Additional person U.S.$40 extra; 2 children under 12 stay free in parents' rm. MAP U.S.$40 per person extra. AE, MC, V.

Attracting a young, international clientele, Negril Gardens rests amid tropical greenery on the famous 7-mile stretch of beach. The two-story villas are well furnished, and rooms open onto a front veranda or a balcony with either a beach or a garden view. The units on the garden side are cheaper and face the swimming pool with a pool bar and a tennis court.

Directly on the beach is a Tahitian-style bar, and right behind it stands an alfresco restaurant, the Orchid Terrace, serving some of the best food in Negril, including international and authentically Jamaican dishes. Recently the hotel has introduced a number of Chinese dishes to reflect the Asian influence on Jamaica's culture. Nonguests are also welcome to dine here.

Negril Tree House. Norman Manley Blvd. (P.O. Box 29), Negril, Jamaica, W.I. ☎ **800/NEGRIL-1** in the U.S. and Canada, or 876/957-4287. Fax 876/957-4386. 67 units. A/C TV TEL. Winter U.S.$139.50–$175 double; U.S.$290–$383 family suite for up to 4. Off-season U.S.$85–$115 double; U.S.$145–$185 family suite. AE, MC, V.

The Negril Tree House is a desirable little hideaway with an ideal beachfront location. Simply furnished units, including 12 suites, each with very small tile baths, are scattered across the property in 11 octagonal buildings. Suites also have kitchenettes. This rather rustic resort features a number of water sports, including parasailing, snorkeling, and jet-skiing. The Tree House also has a swimming pool and Jacuzzi and offers beach volleyball.

Point Village Resort. Rutland Point, P.O. Box 105, Negril, Jamaica, W.I. ☎ **800/752-6824** or 876/957-5170. Fax 876/752-6824. 256 units, 177 of which are available for rentals. A/C MINIBAR TV TEL. Winter (with no meals included) U.S.$125 suite for 2; U.S.$180 1-bedroom apt for 2; U.S.$280 2-bedroom apt for 4. Winter (all-inclusive) U.S.$346 suite for 2; U.S.$366 1-bedroom apt for 2; U.S.$546 2-bedroom apt for 4. Off-season (with no meals included) U.S.$100 suite for 2; U.S.$155 1-bedroom apt for 2; U.S.$255 2-bedroom apt for 4. Off-season (all-inclusive) U.S.$276 suite for 2, U.S.$296 1-bedroom apt for 2, U.S.$398 2-bedroom apt for 4. 1 child under 13 stays in parents' room free whether or not you take the meal plan. AE, MC, V.

This condo complex is especially family-friendly, so couples with children make up a large part of the clientele. It's a cluster of three-story, tile-roofed buildings nestled within the edges of a 14-acre sandy peninsula dotted with sea grapes and salt-resistant shrubs. The only drawback of the beach here is that it's relatively narrow, and separated from the broader, longer sands of Seven-Mile Beach by a rocky barrier. You can opt for all-inclusive rates or, if you want to cook some of your meals yourself (all units contain a kitchenette), you can arrange a stay here without the meal plan.

Amenities: Baby-sitting services and child care are provided without charge every day from 9am to 5pm, after which "childminders" can be arranged for U.S.$5 per child per hour. There's a curve-sided swimming pool on the premises, plus a tennis court, an arts and crafts pavilion, a "kiddie" restaurant, a self-service soda fountain, and a billiards room.

INEXPENSIVE

Banana Shout. 4 West End Rd. (P.O. Box 4), Negril, Jamaica, W.I. ☎ and fax **876/967-0384.** 7 cottages. Winter U.S.$50–$100 cottage for 1 or 2; U.S.$85–$120 cottage for 4; U.S.$200 cottage for 8. Off-season U.S.$35–$60 cottage for 1 or 2; U.S.$60–$70 cottage for 4; U.S.$160 cottage for 8. MC, V.

Set on 2½ acres of landscaped grounds with waterfalls, lily ponds, tropical flowers, and fruit trees, this property comprises seven cottages with three units poised on a cliff overlooking the sea. A series of tiered decks with concrete steps leads down the rocks to water. The garden cottages are located across the road with private access to the beach. Each of the secluded units contains a kitchenette and ceiling fan. The rooms are furnished with locally crafted pieces and artwork from Indonesia and Bali. The best deal at this hideaway is the cottage with the patio barbecue. For a group of eight, each person would spend only U.S.$20 to U.S.$25, depending on the time of year for your visit. Rick's Café is across the street.

✪ **Blue Cave Castle.** Lighthouse Rd., Negril, Jamaica, W.I. ☎ and fax **876/957-4845.** 10 units. Winter U.S.$65 double; off-season U.S.$45 double. Extra person U.S.$10. No credit cards.

Filled with a sense of whimsy and fun, this little mock castle is a terrific deal. It's been featured by the Jamaica Tourist Board in its TV ads, and the Dallas Cowboy cheerleaders calendar for 1997 was shot here. Battlements and turrets re-create medieval days, and the resort, covering an acre, is built over a cave. There are steps down to the cave from the garden, where local wedding receptions are held regularly. The guest rooms are decorated with handmade mahogany furniture and antique Turkish carpets covering the walls. Many of the objects decorating the "castle" were collected by the owner Susan Evanko during her globetrotting days. Three rooms are air-conditioned, although there are no room phones or TVs. There's no pool either, although you can swim off the cliffs in lieu of a beach. All rooms have sea views, refrigerators, ceiling fans, and balconies. A good restaurant in

Ann Bonney & Her Dirty Dog

It was at Bloody Bay, off the coast of Negril, that one of the most notorious pirates of all time, Calico Jack Rackham, was finally captured in 1720. His is a name that will live in infamy, along with Blackbeard's. He was captured with his lover Ann (also Anne) Bonney, the most notorious female pirate of all time. (The bay isn't called bloody, however, because of these pirates. Whalers used to disembowel their catch here, turning the waters red with blood.)

After tracking her husband, a penniless ne'er-do-well sailor named James Bonney, to a brothel in the Virgin Islands, Ann slit his throat. However, she soon fell for Captain Jack Rackham, who was known as "Calico Jack." Some say he came by his nickname because of the colorful shirts he wore; others claim it was because of his undershorts.

Until he met this lady pirate, Calico Jack hadn't done so well as a pirate, but she inspired him to greatness. In a short time, they became the scourge of the West Indies. No vessel sailing the Caribbean Sea was too large or too small for them to attack and rob. Ann is said to have fought alongside the men, and, according to reports, was a much tougher customer than Calico Jack himself. With her cutlass and marlinespike, she was usually the first to board a captured vessel.

It was late in October, off the Negril coast, when Calico Jack and all the pirates were getting drunk on rum, that a British Navy sloop attacked. Calico Jack ran and hid, but Ann fought bravely, according to reports. She flailed away with battle-ax and cutlass.

Calico Jack and the other captured pirates were sentenced to be hanged. Ann, however, pleaded with "Milord" that she was pregnant. Since British law did not allow the killing of unborn children, she got off though her comrades were sentenced to death. Her final advice to Calico Jack: "If you'd fought like a man, you wouldn't be hanged like the dirty dog you are." So much for a lover's parting words. Ann's father in Ireland purchased her release and she opened a gaming house in St. Thomas and prospered until the end.

front is open to the public, but the dining area oceanside is reserved for guests only. You can take breakfast and lunch by the sea and enjoy a daily sunset barbecue.

Devine Destiny. Summerset Rd., West End (P.O. Box 117), Negril, Jamaica, W.I. ☎ **876/957-9184.** Fax 876/957-3846. 44 units. Winter U.S.$77–$130 double, U.S.$180 suite; off-season U.S.$58–$88 double, U.S.$125 suite. Children 11 and under stay free in parents' rm. AE, DC, MC, V.

Lying about 550 yards from the West End cliffs, this funky retreat is about a 20-minute walk from the beach. There's a shuttle to Seven-Mile Beach if you don't want to walk. The resort is a two-story structure with a terra-cotta roof surrounded by gardens where wedding receptions are often staged. The rooms are furnished in a standard style, and although some are small, all are quite comfortable and contain refrigerators. The suites are the best deal, with ceiling fans, kitchens, and living rooms with pull-out beds, TVs, and patios. An on-site restaurant serves simple fare three times a day, and there's both a pool bar and a gazebo bar. Room service and baby-sitting are available, and the hotel has a TV room, sundeck, games room, gift shop, and tour desk.

Drumville Cove Resort. West End Rd. (P.O. Box 72), Negril, Jamaica, W.I. ☎ **876/957-4369.** Fax 876/978-4971. 15 units, 5 cottages. Winter U.S.$55–$60 double, U.S.$55–$70 cottage; off-season U.S.$45–$50 double, U.S.$45–$60 cottage. AE, MC, V.

The rooms here are housed in cream-colored structures trimmed in brown overlooking the sea near the lighthouse, whereas the cottages are scattered throughout the property. All the rooms and cottages have ceiling fans, but only seven of the rooms and none of the cottages are air-conditioned; five rooms offer TVs. Included on the property is a restaurant serving Jamaican specialties with a few American dishes. The nearest beach is a 5-minute drive away (the hotel provides transportation), and there's a freshwater swimming pool for guest use.

Firefly Beach Cottages. Norman Manley Blvd. (P.O. Box 54), Negril, Jamaica, W.I. ☎ **800/477-9530** in the U.S., or 876/957-4358. Fax 876/957-3447. 19 units. Winter U.S.$104–$160 double; U.S.$136 2-bedroom apt for 4; U.S.$140 1-bedroom apt with 3 double beds for 4; U.S.$170 2-bedroom apt for 8. Off-season U.S.$75–$110 double; U.S.$91 2-bedroom apt for 4; U.S.$92 1-bedroom apt with 3 double beds for 6; U.S.$115 2-bedroom apt for 8. AE, MC, V.

With a lot of Jamaican flair, this laid-back hodgepodge of several white concrete and wooden buildings opens directly onto the beach. There's even a so-called penthouse in the garden with sleeping lofts. In addition to these, there are various studios and cottages, including one large two-bedroom unit that can sleep up to eight in cramped conditions. Most of the units are cooled by air-conditioning and ceiling fans, and many beds are canopied. When they rent "rooms with a view" here, they mean it: The hotel opens onto a stretch of clothing-optional beach. All rooms have verandas and kitchens as well, but there's no restaurant, although many little local spots are within walking distance. There' no pool, but the beach is close at hand (and you don't even have to put on your bathing suit to enjoy it).

Foote Prints. Norman Manley Blvd. (P.O. Box 100), Negril, Jamaica, W.I. ☎ **876/957-4300.** Fax 876/957-4301. 31 units. A/C TV TEL. Winter U.S.$135–$145 double, U.S.$165 double with kitchenette; U.S.$255 apt. Off-season U.S.$85–$95 double, U.S.$115 double with kitchenette; U.S.$185 apt. Extra person U.S.$30 in winter, U.S.$20 off-season. AE, MC, V.

Dane and Audrey Foote started this enterprise with one building in the mid-1980s; it has since expanded to three. Located on Seven-Mile Beach next door to the Swept Away resort, this place offers its best deals during the off-season (mid-April to mid-December). The rooms, four of which contain kitchenettes, are tropically decorated with hardwood furnishings, air-conditioning, and private baths. The hotel's restaurant, Robinson Crusoe's, serves breakfast, lunch, and dinner, specializing in a mix of Jamaican and American dishes. On Friday nights, a barbecue with local bands livens up the place.

Home Sweet Home. West End Rd., Negril, Jamaica, W.I. ☎ and fax **800/925-7418** in the U.S., or 876/957-4478. 16 units. Winter U.S.$100 double; U.S.$180 penthouse; U.S.$210 2-bedroom town house. Off-season U.S.$80 double; U.S.$150 penthouse; U.S.$175 2-bedroom town house. Extra person U.S.$15. Children 11 and under stay free in parents' rm. AE, DC, DISC, MC, V.

On the cliff side, this is a cozy, down-home place. At times it seems to re-create Negril's hippie heyday of the swinging '60s. You may find your groove here, as the writer Terry McMillan did when she visited many little inns while doing research for her hot seller, *How Stella Got Her Groove Back.* "Home" is a single pink concrete building with a garden with lots of greenery and flowering plants. There's also a pool and a Jacuzzi. When you see the bedrooms, you'll know that many visitors have slept here before you. All accommodations have ceiling fans, a radio and cassette player, and a balcony or veranda, but no TV or phone. There's a sundeck on the cliffs, and you can swim, dive, or snorkel. A simple restaurant serves three inexpensive Jamaican-style meals a day.

Ocean Edge Resort Hotel. West End Rd. (P.O. Box 71), Negril, Jamaica, W.I. ☎ **876/ 957-4362.** Fax 876/957-4842. 25 units. TV TEL. Winter U.S.$65–$75 double; U.S.$80 penthouse; U.S.$130 suite. Off-season U.S.$45–$55 double; U.S.$60 penthouse; U.S.$110 suite. Children 11 and under stay free in parents' rm. AE, MC, V.

Located on a cliff on West End Road across from Kaiser's Café, the Ocean Edge offers simple accommodations in a friendly atmosphere. The hotel provides transportation to and from the beach, a 5-minute drive away. The lodgings are modestly decorated in a tropical motif with hardwood furnishings and a few pictures on the walls. Accommodations with garden views are air-conditioned, whereas others are cooled by ceiling fans. Ocean-view rooms also contain kitchenettes. Facilities include a swimming pool, Jacuzzi, and the Seven Seas restaurant, which specializes in fresh seafood.

Rock Cliff Hotel. West End Rd. (P.O. Box 67), Negril, Jamaica, W.I. ☎ **876/957-4331** or 876/957-4108. 33 units. A/C. Winter U.S.$115–$140 double; U.S.$290 suite for 2. Off-season U.S.$80–$100 double; U.S.$170–$190 suite for 2. AE, MC, V.

This hotel is one of the better of the dozens of raffish guest houses that lie among the palms and sea grapes west of Negril's center. Set atop a low cliff overlooking the sea, and popular with divers, it features a restaurant, two bars, and a Sunday-night all-you-can-eat lobster buffet. There's a pool on the premises, and you can inch your way down the cliff for sea dips offshore from the rocks, though most people trek 2 miles to the nearest beach. The suites (but not the conventional bedrooms) contain kitchenettes. The bedrooms have mahogany furniture, pastel-colored draperies, and off-white walls. Maid service is included, and baby-sitting and laundry can be arranged. There's a Jacuzzi, volleyball and basketball courts, a kiosk for sundries and souvenirs, and a well-recommended PADI-affiliated dive shop.

✪ **Rockhouse.** West End Rd. (P.O. Box 24), Negril, Jamaica, W.I. ☎ and fax **876/ 957-4373.** 14 units. MINIBAR. Winter U.S.$100 studio; U.S.$130–$165 villa for up to 4. Off-season U.S.$85 studio; U.S.$100–$120 villa for up to 4. Extra person U.S.$25. Children 12 and under stay free in parents' rm. AE, MC, V.

One of the special accommodations in Negril, this little secluded and tranquil inn stands in stark contrast to the hedonistic all-inclusive resorts. A team of young Australians recently restored and expanded this retreat, with thatched roofs capping stone-and-pine huts. The rooms have minibars, ceiling fans, and refrigerators, but no TVs or phones. You'll really feel you're in Jamaica when you go to bed in a mosquito-draped four-poster bed or take a shower in the open air (mercifully, the toilet facilities are inside, however).

A quarter mile from the beach, Rockhouse has a ladder down to a cove where you can swim and snorkel; equipment is available for rent. After a refreshing dip in the pool, you can dine in the open-sided restaurant pavilion that serves spicy local fare three times a day. The restaurant and bar are quite fashionable.

Thrills. West End (P.O. Box 99, Negril Post Office), Westmoreland, Jamaica, W.I. ☎ **876/957-4390.** Fax 876/957-4153. 25 units. Winter U.S.$65 double, U.S.$75 triple; off-season U.S.$50 double, U.S.$65 triple. MAP U.S.$21 per person extra. MC, V.

Southwest of the center of Negril, on sloping, palm-dotted land that descends toward a rocky beach, this is a simple but well-managed resort. Its centerpiece is a hexagonal tower set adjacent to a low-slung motel-like complex containing the bedrooms. Each room is simply decorated with white walls, island-made mahogany furniture and louvered doors, and tiled floors. An in-house restaurant serves international cuisine.

Beach lovers negotiate a 10-minute drive (or a 20-minute walk) eastward to the famous sands of Negril's legendary beach, and Thrills also provides shuttle service. Snorkelers, however, find ample opportunities for pursuing their favorite sport off the low cliffs and caves along the coast. The resort has its own tennis courts and swimming pool, and a wide choice of dive shops and water-sports facilities are nearby.

ALL-INCLUSIVE RESORTS

Beaches Negril. Norman Manley Blvd., Negril, Jamaica, W.I. ☎ **800/BEACHES** or 876/ 957-9274. Fax 876/957-9269. 215 units. A/C TV TEL. Winter U.S.$880 per person double; U.S.$1,120–$1,350 per person, double occupancy, in a suite. Off-season U.S.$840 per person double; U.S.$1,080–$1,260 per person, double occupancy, in a suite. Rates are all-inclusive for a 3-day stay. AE, MC, V.

One of the newest resorts in Negril was established in 1997 as the family-oriented wing of the Sandals chain, an all-inclusive outfit that remains stoically opposed to allowing children in its other resorts. The resort occupies a highly desirable 20-acre lot studded with palms and sea grapes adjacent to a sandy beach. At Beaches Negril, you can either spend time with your kids or relax on the beach in the knowledge that they're entertained and supervised elsewhere, thanks to a roster of child and teen activities in segregated areas (where adults enter only at their children's specific invitation!). Accommodations are clustered into three individual villages (Savannah, Montpellier, and Santa Cruz), which are each subdivided into a cluster of cement and wood buildings accented with cedar shingles.

Dining/Diversions: The resort's five separate restaurants include a completely unpretentious Beach Grill, which is reserved only for children between 5 and 9pm every night, and the most formal of the five, the Seville Room, where the international cuisine and the decor evoke Andalusia. There's live entertainment nightly (usually music from a local reggae band).

Amenities: Services include concierge laundry, a tour desk that will arrange visits to other parts of the island, as well as lessons in tennis, sailing, and scuba diving. Facilities include two tennis courts, two freshwater swimming pools with swim-up bars, three Jacuzzis, a gym/sauna/steam room/health club, and a fine beach. Most water sports (including scuba and sailing) are included in the resort's all-inclusive price.

✪ Grand Lido. Negril Bloody Bay (P.O. Box 88), Negril, Jamaica, W.I. ☎ **800/859-7873** in the U.S., 800/553-4320 in Canada, or 876/957-5010. Fax 876/957-5517. 200 units. A/C MINIBAR TV TEL. Winter U.S.$2,360–$3,140 suite for 2. Off-season U.S.$1,700–$2,580 suite for 2. Rates are all-inclusive for the minimum stay of 4 days/3 nights. AE, MC, V. No children accepted.

The grandest and most architecturally stylish hotel in Negril, the Grand Lido sits on a flat and lushly landscaped stretch of beachfront adjacent to Hedonism II. Much more subdued than its neighbor, this is the most upscale and deliciously luxurious of the string of resorts known as Jamaica's SuperClubs, boasting two fine beaches lined with lounge chairs. Each suite contains a stereo system, lots of space, and either a patio or a balcony that (except for a few) overlooks the beach. The smaller of the resort's two beaches is reserved for nudists. Only adults are welcome, but unlike many other all-inclusive resorts, especially Club Med, there's no resistance here to giving a room to a single occupant.

Dining/Diversions: In addition to the cavernous and airy main dining room, there's a trio of restaurants, including one devoted to nouvelle cuisine, another to continental food, and a third to Italian pasta. Guests also enjoy an all-night disco, a piano bar, pool tables, and nine bars. Even after the four restaurants close, there are three different dining enclaves that remain open throughout the night, each with a bubbling Jacuzzi nearby.

Amenities: Four tennis courts, two swimming pools, four Jacuzzis, gym/sauna/health club, and one of the most glamorous yachts in the West Indies, the *M-Y Zein*, given by Aristotle Onassis to Prince Rainier and Grace of Monaco as a wedding present. Services include 24-hour room service, concierge, laundry, a tour desk that arranges visits to other parts of Jamaica, and instructors to teach tennis and sailing.

Hedonism II. Negril Beach Rd. (P.O. Box 25), Negril, Jamaica, W.I. ☎ **800/859-7873** in the U.S., or 876/957-5200. Fax 876/957-4289. 280 units. A/C. Winter U.S.$1,478–$1,658 double. Off-season U.S.$1,118–$1,378 double. Rates are all-inclusive for 4 days/3 nights. AE, MC, V. No children under 18.

Devoted to the pursuit of pleasure, Hedonism II packs the works into a one-package deal, including all the drinks and partying anyone could want. There's no cash accepted for anything, and tipping is not permitted. Of all the members of its chain, this is the most raucous. It's a meat market, deliberately inviting its mainly single guests to go wild for a week. (To provide a sense of the ambience, we'll tell you that one manager boasted that the resort holds the record for packing the most people into a single Jacuzzi at once.) The rooms are stacked in two-story clusters dotted around a sloping 22-acre site about 2 miles east of the town center. Most of the guests are Americans. Closed to the general public, this is not a couples-only resort; singles are both accepted and encouraged. The hotel will find you a roommate if you'd like to book in on the double-occupancy rate.

On one section of this resort's beach, clothing is optional. It's called the "Nude" section; the other is known as "the Prude." The resort also has a secluded beach on nearby Booby Cay, where guests are taken twice a week for picnics.

Dining/Diversions: Nightly entertainment is presented, along with a live band, a high-energy disco, and a piano bar. International cuisine is served in daily buffets. There's also a clothing-optional bar, a prude bar, and a grill.

Amenities: Sailing, snorkeling, waterskiing, scuba diving, windsurfing, glass-bottom boat, clothing-optional Jacuzzi, swimming pool, six tournament-class tennis courts (lit at night), two badminton courts, basketball court, two indoor squash courts, volleyball, table tennis, Nautilus and free-weight gyms, aerobics, indoor games room, massage.

Negril Inn. Norman Manley Blvd. (P.O. Box 59), Negril, Jamaica, W.I. ☎ **876/957-4209.** Fax 876/957-4365. 46 units. A/C. Winter U.S.$280 double; U.S.$390 triple. Off-season U.S.$220 double; U.S.$270 triple. Rates are all-inclusive. AE, MC, V. No children accepted in winter.

Located about 3 miles east of the town center in the heart of the 7-mile beach stretch, this is one of the smallest all-inclusive resorts in Negril. Because of its size, the atmosphere is much more low-key than what you'll find at its larger competitors, such as Hedonism II, and it doesn't have the host of facilities the others do. The resort, which is not confined to couples only, offers very simple but comfortably furnished guest rooms with private balconies, in a series of two-story structures in a garden setting. The helpful staff sponsors a host of activities, day and night.

Dining/Diversions: Included in the package are all meals, all alcoholic drinks (except champagne), and nightly entertainment (including a disco). Meals are served in the resort's only restaurant, although there are bars in the disco and beside the pool, and the food is pretty good.

Amenities: Windsurfing, waterskiing, scuba diving, snorkeling, hydrosliding, aqua bikes, two floodlit tennis courts, Jacuzzi, piano room, Universal weight room, freshwater pool, room service (for breakfast only), laundry.

Poinciana Beach Resort. Norman Manley Blvd. (P.O. Box 44), Negril, Jamaica, W.I. ☎ **800/468-6728** in the U.S., or 876/957-5100. Fax 876/957-4229. 108 units, 22 villas. A/C TV. Winter U.S.$456 double; U.S.$494 studio for 2; U.S.$662 suite for 2; U.S.$668 villa for 2. Off-season U.S.$310–$330 double; U.S.$394–$424 studio for 2; U.S.$420–$454 suite for 2; U.S.$336–$344 villa for 2. Rates are per person and include all meals. AE, MC, V.

Set on 6 acres of land right on Seven-Mile Beach, this hotel and villa vacation resort attracts couples, singles, and families with a variety of accommodations and an extensive sports program. It's a mixture of both contemporary and colonial design, with tile floors, rattan and wood furnishings, and private balconies and ocean views. Superior rooms consist of one bedroom and a private balcony or patio; suites have a kitchenette and a large wraparound balcony. Some suites offer Jacuzzi-type tubs, and villas consist of one or two bedrooms, a living/dining area with kitchenette, and a private balcony or patio.

Dining/Diversions: A poolside restaurant, the Captain's Table, serves three meals daily, with both Jamaican dishes and international specialties. Other dining choices include the Paradise Plum, with many innovative recipes, and the Starlight Terrace, offering fresh pastas and grilled selections under the stars. The Upper Deck Café serves after-dinner snacks, and at the Beach Bar a lively native band entertains 5 evenings a week during happy hour. Other evening entertainment is often staged, including a reggae/soca barbecue night on Saturday.

Amenities: Two freshwater swimming pools, heated Jacuzzi, children's program, lawn and table tennis, 24-hour gyms, water sports (including windsurfing, snorkeling, kayaks, glass-bottom-boat rides, Sunfish and Hobie Cat sailing), beauty salon. Scuba diving and waterskiing cost extra. Baby-sitting and massage are available.

Sandals Negril. Rutland Point, Negril, Jamaica, W.I. ☎ **800/SANDALS** in the U.S. and Canada, or 876/957-5216. Fax 876/957-5338. 215 units. A/C TV TEL. Winter U.S.$1,720–$2,080 double; U.S.$2,180–$2,540 suite. Off-season U.S.$1,640–$2,000 double; U.S.$2,100–$2,420 suite. Rates are all-inclusive for 4 days/3 nights. AE, MC, V.

Sandals Negril is an all-inclusive, couples-only (male-female) resort, part of the expanding empire of the enterprising local businessman Gordon "Butch" Stewart, who pioneered similar operations in Montego Bay. If you're the wildest of raunchy party types, you'd be better off at Hedonism II—life isn't exactly subdued at Sandals, but it's tamer. The resort occupies some 13 acres of prime beachfront land a short drive east of Negril's center, on the main highway leading in from Montego Bay. It's about a 1½-hour drive (maybe more) from the Montego Bay airport.

The developers linked two older hotels into a unified whole, and most guests never leave the property. The crowd is usually convivial, informal, and young. There are five divisions of accommodations, rated standard, superior, deluxe, deluxe beachfront, and one-bedroom suite. The casually well-furnished rooms have a tropical motif, and hair dryers and radios. For a balcony and sea view, you have to pay the top rates.

Dining/Diversions: Rates include all meals, even snacks, and unlimited drinks day and night at one of four bars (two of which are swim-up pool bars). Coconut Cove is the main dining room, but guests can also elect to eat at one of the specialty rooms, including the Sundowner, offering white-glove service and a Jamaican cuisine, with low-calorie health food served beside the beach. Kimono features a Japanese cuisine; nightly entertainment, including theme parties, is also included.

Amenities: Three freshwater swimming pools, tennis courts for day or night play, scuba diving, snorkeling, Sunfish sailing, windsurfing, canoeing, aerobics classes, glass-bottom boat, fitness center with saunas and Universal exercise equipment, laundry service, massage.

✪ **Swept Away.** Norman Manley Blvd. (P.O. Box 77), Negril, Jamaica, W.I. ☎ **800/ 545-7937** in the U.S. and Canada, or 876/957-4061. Fax 876/957-4060. 134 units. A/C TEL. Winter U.S.$1,500–$1,875 per couple. Off-season U.S.$1,380–$1,710 per couple. Rates are all-inclusive for 3 nights. AE, DC, MC, V.

This is one of the best-equipped hotels in Negril—it's certainly the one most conscious of both sports and relaxation. All-inclusive, it caters to male-female couples who are eager to have all possible diversions available but don't want an organized schedule or pressure to participate if they just want to relax. The resort occupies 20 flat and sandy acres of prime beachfront, which straddle both sides of the highway leading in from Montego Bay.

The accommodations (the hotel calls them "veranda suites" because of their large balconies) are in 26 two-story villas clustered together and accented with flowering shrubs and vines, a few steps from the 7-mile beachfront. Each accommodation contains a ceiling fan, a king-size bed, and (unless the vegetation obscures it) sea views. They're lovely, airy, and spacious.

Dining/Diversions: The resort's social center is its international restaurant, Feathers, which lies inland, across the road from the sea. There's also an informal beachfront restaurant and bar, and four bars scattered throughout the property, including a "veggie bar."

Amenities: Racquetball, squash, and 10 lighted tennis courts; fully equipped gym; aerobics; yoga; massage; steam; sauna; whirlpool; billiards; bicycles; beachside swimming pool; scuba diving; windsurfing; reef snorkeling; room service (for continental breakfast only); laundry; tour desk for arranging sightseeing excursions.

4 Where to Dine

Although many visitors in Negril dine at their hotels, there are several other atmospheric and intriguing dining possibilities around.

EXPENSIVE TO MODERATE

Le Vendôme. In the Charela Inn, Negril Beach. ☎ **876/957-4648.** Reservations recommended for Sat dinner. Main courses U.S.$20–$30; fixed-price meal U.S.$23–$31.50; continental breakfast U.S.$4.60; English breakfast U.S.$10. MC, V. Daily 7:30am–10pm. JAMAICAN/FRENCH.

This place, some 3½ miles from the town center, enjoys a good reputation. You don't have to be a hotel guest to sample the cuisine, which is, in the words of owners Daniel and Sylvia Grizzle, a "dash of Jamaican spices" with a "pinch of French flair." Their wine and champagne are imported from France. You dine on a terra-cotta terrace, where you can enjoy a view of the palm-studded beach. You may want to order a homemade pâté, or perhaps a vegetable salad to begin with, and then follow with baked snapper, duckling à l'orange, or a seafood platter. You may have eaten

In case you want to see the world.

At American Express, we're here to make your journey a smooth one. So we have over 1,700 travel service locations in over 120 countries ready to help. What else would you expect from the world's largest travel agency?

do more

AMERICAN EXPRESS

Travel

http://www.americanexpress.com/travel

In case you want to be welcomed there.

We're here to see that you're always welcomed at establishments everywhere. That's why millions of people carry the American Express® Card—for peace of mind, confidence, and security, around the world or just around the corner.

do more®

AMERICAN EXPRESS

Cards

And just in case.

We're here with American Express® Travelers Cheques and Cheques *for Two.*® They're the safest way to carry money on your vacation and the surest way to get a refund, practically anywhere, anytime.

Another way we help you...

do more

AMERICAN EXPRESS

Travelers Cheques

better versions of these dishes at many other places, of course, yet the food is quite satisfying here, and there's rarely an unhappy customer.

Rick's Café. Lighthouse Rd. ☎ **876/957-0380.** Reservations accepted only for parties of 6 or more. Main courses U.S.$12–$28. MC, V. Daily 2–10pm. SEAFOOD/STEAK.

At sundown, everybody in Negril heads toward the lighthouse along the West End strip to Rick's Café, whether or not they want a meal. This laid-back cafe was made famous in the '70s as a hippie hangout, and ever since it's attracted the bronzed and the beautiful (and some who want to be), the best sunset-watching crowd this side of Key West. Here the sunset is said to be the most glorious in Negril, and after a few fresh-fruit daiquiris (pineapple, banana, or papaya), you'll give no argument. Casual dress is the order of the day, and reggae and rock comprise the background music.

There are several stateside specialties, including imported steaks along with a complete menu of blackened dishes (Cajun style). The fish is always fresh, including red snapper, fresh lobster, or grouper, and you might begin with the smoked marlin platter. The food is rather standard fare, and expensive for what you get, but that hardly keeps the crowds away. You can also buy plastic bar tokens at the door, which you can use instead of money, à la Club Med.

INEXPENSIVE

✪ **Chicken Lavish.** West End Rd. ☎ **876/957-4410.** Main courses U.S.$5–$13. AE, DISC, MC, V. Daily 10am–10pm. JAMAICAN.

Chicken Lavish, whose name we love, is the best of the cheap restaurants lining this West End beach strip. Just show up on the doorstep and see what's cooking. Curried goat is a specialty, as is fresh fried fish. The red snapper is caught in local waters. But the main reason we've recommended the place is because of its name-sake dish. Ask the chef to make his special Jamaican chicken lavish. He'll tell you, and you may agree, that it's the best on the island. What to wear here? Dress as you would to clean up your backyard on a hot August day.

Choices. West End Rd. El. ☎ **876/957-4841.** Main courses U.S.$4.20–$18. No credit cards. Daily 7am–11pm. JAMAICAN.

This no-frills open-air restaurant offers local food in a bustling atmosphere. The food is simple and the portions are hearty. You'll pay about U.S.$5 to U.S.$6 for breakfast, which includes ackee and salt codfish prepared with Jamaican spices, onions, green peppers, and tomatoes. Daily soup specials may include pumpkin or red pea. For a real island experience, try the spicy jerk chicken, fish, or pork. Other dishes might include stewed beef, curried goat, or a dish of oxtail. Most dishes come with salad and your choice of vegetable.

✪ **Cosmo's Seafood Restaurant & Bar.** Norman Manley Blvd. ☎ **876/957-4330.** Main courses J$200–J$620 (U.S.$5.70–$17.65). AE, MC, V. Daily 9am–10pm. SEAFOOD.

One of the best places to go for local seafood is centered around a Polynesian thatched *bohio* open to the sea and bordering the main beachfront. This is the dining spot of Cosmo Brown, who entertains locals as well as visitors. You can order his famous conch soup, or conch in a number of other ways, including steamed or curried. He's also known for his savory kettle of curried goat, or you might select freshly caught seafood or fish, depending on what the catch turned up. It's a rustic joint, and the prices are among the most reasonable in town. Cosmo's cooking is right on target, and he doesn't charge a lot for it, either.

Hungry Lion. West End Rd. ☎ **876/957-4486.** Main courses U.S.$7.50–$24. AE, MC, V. Daily 5:30–10:30pm. JAMAICAN/INTERNATIONAL.

Some of the best seafood and vegetarian dishes are found at this laid-back alfresco hangout on the cliffs. Instead of the usual Red Stripe beer, you can visit the juice bar and sample the tropical punches with or without rum. This is a cozy, two-story, green-painted concrete and wood building. The first floor has an open-air section with booths inside, but on the second floor it's all windows. Menus change daily, depending on what's available in the local markets. About seven main courses are offered nightly, not only seafood and vegetarian platters, but many tasty chicken dishes as well, even shepherd's pie, pasta primavera, grilled kingfish steak, and panfried snapper. Lobster is prepared in many different ways, and everything is accompanied by rice and peas along with steamed vegetables. The homemade desserts are luscious, especially the pineapple-carrot cake, our favorite.

Margueritaville. Norman Manley Blvd. ☎ **876/957-4467.** Reservations not necessary. Burgers and sandwiches U.S.$5.75–$7.75; main courses U.S.$7.75–$25.95. AE, MC, V. Daily 9am–11pm. AMERICAN/INTERNATIONAL.

From its open, breeze-filled windows and veranda, it's only a short walk across the sand, past hundreds of sunbathing bodies, to the sea. Set in the center of Negril, adjacent to the Beachcomber Hotel, this restaurant combines a gift shop, an art gallery, and a bar into one high-energy, well-managed, and sometimes very crowded place. Look for at least 50 variations of margaritas (for prices beginning at U.S.$5.15 each). Menu items include burgers, sandwiches, lobster, grilled chicken and fish, and conch. Most of the paintings in the on-site art gallery, incidentally, were executed by a longtime resident of Negril, American-born Geraldine Robbins. Every evening, beginning around 9pm, there's live music performed, usually loudly, on the site. Artists include local reggae stars Cowboys on Pebbles, Fathers & Sons, and on Saturday night, old-timey Jamaican music known as *mentho*, whose style most locals remember from their childhoods. Sunday and Wednesday, everyone can be a star, thanks to a karaoke setup.

Mariners Inn & Restaurant. West End Rd. ☎ **876/957-0392.** Pizzas U.S.$6.60–$10.20; main courses U.S.$9.50–$20. AE, MC, V. Daily 8am–3pm and 6–10pm. JAMAICAN/AMERICAN/CONTINENTAL.

Many guests escaping from their all-inclusive dining rooms head here, looking for some authentic Jamaican flavor. The bar is shaped like a boat, and there's an adjoining restaurant, entered through a tropical garden. As you drink or dine, the sea breezes waft in, adding to the relaxed experience. The one appetizer is a bacon-wrapped banana, not everybody's favorite way to begin a meal, but the food picks up considerably after that. The chef knows how to use curry effectively in the lobster and chicken dishes, and even the goat. The coq au vin (chicken in wine) has never been to France, so you're better off sticking to such dishes as panfried snapper or fried chicken.

Negril Tree House. Norman Manley Blvd. ☎ **876/957-4287.** Main courses U.S.$7–$26. AE, MC, V. Daily 7am–11pm. JAMAICAN.

This informal beachfront place takes its name from a mamee tree that grows through the main building of this resort hotel. Dining is on the second floor, but guests can come early and have a drink in the beachfront bar. This is a lively place both day and night. At lunch, you can have a homemade soup, perhaps pepperpot, a sandwich, or else more elaborate fare, such as a typically Jamaican dish of escovitched fish (raw fish in a spicy marinade). Some of the produce comes from the owner's own farm in the country.

At night, Gail Y. Jackson, your hostess, offers her full repertoire of dishes, including a great lobster spaghetti. You might begin with a callaloo quiche and later follow with roast chicken (a specialty) or conch steak. Try the Tia Maria parfait for dessert. You can dine both inside and out.

The Pickled Parrot. West End Rd. ☎ **876/957-4864.** Main courses U.S.$5.95–$22.95. AE, MC, V. Daily 9am–midnight. MEXICAN/JAMAICAN/AMERICAN.

With a name like The Pickled Parrot, you know you're heading for a night of fun here. It doesn't live up to the riotous times at Rick's, but it's a serious rival for the sundowner market. The restaurant stands at the edge of a cliff and is open to the trade winds. There's a rope swing and a water slide outside to indulge your inner child. Slot machines inside add to the funky ambience. The cook claims he serves the best lobster fajitas in town. You can also order the usual array of stateside burgers, sandwiches, and freshly made salads at lunch. Actually, you can order the full dinner menu at lunch if you so desire. They prepare a predictable array of burritos, nachos, and even Mexican pizza (we prefer Italian). But you might also be tempted by the fresh fish, lobster Jamaican style (also shrimp in the same method), and the famous jerk chicken.

Restaurant Tan-Ya's/Calico Jack's. In the Sea Splash Resort, Norman Manley Blvd. ☎ **876/957-4041.** Reservations recommended. Main courses U.S.$10–$19; Breakfast from U.S.$6, lunch from U.S.$6. AE, MC, V. Daily 11am–3pm and 6:30–10pm. JAMAICAN/INTERNATIONAL.

Set within the thick white walls of a previously recommended resort, these two restaurants provide well-prepared food and the charm of a small, family-run resort. Informal and very affordable lunchtime food is served at Calico Jack's, whose tables are in an enlarged gazebo, near a bar and the resort's swimming pool. The resort's gastronomic showcase, however, is Tan-Ya's. Here, specialties include lemon-flavored shrimp, Tan-Ya's snapper with herb butter, three different preparations of lobster, smoked Jamaican lobster with a fruit salsa, and deviled crab backs sautéed in butter. On many nights, these dishes are filled with flavor and well prepared; on some occasions, they're slightly off the mark.

Sweet Spice. 1 White Hall Rd. ☎ **876/957-4621.** Reservations not accepted. Main courses U.S.$4.50–$14. MC, V. Daily 8:30am–11pm. JAMAICAN.

This is everybody's favorite mom-and-pop eatery, a real local hangout beloved by locals as well as scantily clad visitors to Negril. It serves good food and plenty of it. The Whytes welcome guests warmly and serve them in an alfresco setting. The portions are large and most satisfying, and the cookery is home-style. Bring grandmother, mom and dad, and all the kids, as many Jamaican families do. You get what's on the stove that night or in the kettle, perhaps the fresh catch of the day or a conch steak. The grilled chicken is done to perfection, and shrimp is steamed and served with garlic butter or cooked in coconut cream. A number of curry dishes tempt, including concoctions made with goat, lobster, and chicken. Meals come with freshly cooked Jamaica-grown vegetables. The fruit juices served here (in lieu of alcoholic beverages) are truly refreshing, and the menu is the same at lunch or dinner.

Xtabi. West End Rd. ☎ **876/957-4336.** Main courses U.S.$10–$26; lunch U.S.$4.50–$15. AE, MC, V. Daily 7am–11pm. JAMAICAN/INTERNATIONAL.

The setting is formal and upscale for laid-back Negril, although prices are most affordable—if you read from the right-hand side of the menu. Sitting on a cliff, near a series of caves where you can snorkel during daylight hours, the octagonal Xtabi has a patio facing the ocean where you can dine under the stars. The walls are painted aquamarine, a theme carried out in the matching cloths on the tables. Lunch is acceptable, if you're in the area. You get the usual grill items, an assortment of burgers, grilled cheese, steak or club sandwiches, and a series of salads ranging from fresh greens to avocado. But at night, the chefs try harder and the setting is more dramatic. The lobster thermidor is a sumptuous choice, as are the scampi grilled Jamaican style and the batter-fried shrimp. The catch of the day can be steamed, fried, or grilled as you wish, and steak and chicken are also prepared in a number of delectable ways. For dessert, opt for the fruit salad or—even better—one of the homemade cakes, perhaps chocolate, lemon, or marble.

5 Scuba Diving & Snorkeling

You're likely to spend most of your time on Negril's beach, and most resorts provide plenty of water-sports toys to keep their guests busy. Offshore, the reefs protecting Negril offer some of Jamaica's top scuba diving.

If your resort doesn't have its own diving operation, the most modern, best-equipped diving facility here is **Negril Scuba Centre,** in the Negril Beach Club Hotel, Norman Manley Boulevard (☎ **800/818-2963** or 876/957-9641). A professional staff of internationally certified scuba instructors and divemasters teach and guide divers to several of Negril's colorful and exciting coral reefs. Beginners' dive lessons are offered daily as well as multiple-dive packages for certified divers. Full scuba certifications and specialty courses are also available. A resort course, designed for first-time divers with basic swimming abilities, includes all instruction, equipment, a lecture on water and diving safety, and one open-water dive. It begins at 10am daily and ends at 2pm; its price is U.S.$75. A one-tank dive costs U.S.$30 per dive plus U.S.$20 for equipment rental (not necessary if you bring your own gear). More economical is a two-tank dive that includes lunch. It costs U.S.$55, plus U.S.$20 for the optional rental of equipment. The organization is PADI-registered, and accepts all recognized certification cards.

One of the best-recommended dive facilities in Negril is **Scuba World,** a PADI-approved five-star dive shop located at Orange Bay (☎ **876/957-6290**). It's open daily from 8am to 5pm and offers a 4-day certification course for U.S.$350. A resort course for beginners costs U.S.$70, and a one-tank dive for already-certified divers costs U.S.$30, plus U.S.$20 for the rental of the necessary equipment. A two-tank dive goes for U.S.$55, plus only U.S.$10 for equipment rental. More than 20 dive sites, including coral reefs and caves, are located at Poinciana.

You will find Negril's best area for snorkeling off the cliffs in the West End. The coral reef here is extremely lively with a depth of about 10 to 15 feet. The waters are so clear and sparkling that just by wading in and looking down you will see lots of marine life. For the most part, the fish here are very small, but extremely colorful. Unfortunately, the larger fish have all but disappeared from shallower waters due to the local trade. The Negril Coral Reef Preservation Society has taken charge to make sure this does not continue, enforcing regulations and forbidding fishing boats to dock near the live coral reefs. Along the West End Road are tons of shops where snorkeling equipment can be rented for just a few dollars a day. There is no snorkeling on the beachfront.

6 Negril After Dark

Evenings in Negril really begin before dark, when everyone heads to Rick's Café for sundowner cocktails or a few Red Stripes (see "Where to Dine," above).

All the resorts have bars. Most offer evening entertainment for their guests, and some welcome nonguests as well.

Although smaller than Mo Bay, Negril is not without spots to have a good time. Fun places are easy to find, since nearly *everything* is on Norman Manley Boulevard, the only major road in Negril. We found **Alfred's** (☎ **876/957-4735**) a neat Jamaican experience with enough American fabric to make travelers feel welcome. There is no cover, and in addition to grabbing a drink, you can also order a bite to eat until 1am, which is late for a kitchen to be open in these parts. Particularly interesting is their beach party area. Not only do they have a bar on the beach, but they offer a stage for live acts. Live reggae is presented on Tuesday, Wednesday, and weekends, and live jazz on Monday and Thursday. Of course, you can boogie on the dance floor inside, shaking to hits you'll hear at clubs stateside.

For more Jamaican/American nightclub experiences, try **De Buss** (☎ **876/957-4405**). Cover depends on special events or live acts, so call ahead to see what's planned.

Action is also lively at the **Seasplash Resort,** on Norman Manley Boulevard (☎ **876/957-4041**), whose bar is located amid allamander vines, midway between a swimming pool and the edge of the sea. Sheltered from the sun with a teepee-shaped roof of palm leaves and thatch, it offers a tempting array of tropical drinks. These include such foamy concoctions as Calico Jack's rum punch or a white sands, either of which sells from U.S.$3. The bar is open daily from 8am to 11pm.

7 A Side Trip to the South Coast

Think of this as undiscovered Jamaica. The arid South Coast is just beginning to attract more foreign visitors every year; they're drawn by Jamaica's sunniest climate.

Columbus discovered the Arawak living here when he circumnavigated Jamaica in 1494. When not repelling French pirates, five generations of Spaniards raised cattle on ranches on the broad savannas of St. Elizabeth.

Local adventures are plentiful on the South Coast. Among the most popular is South Coast Safaris' boat tour up the Black River, once a major logging conduit and still home to freshwater crocodiles. Another favorite is the trip to the Y. S. Falls, where seven spectacular cascades tumble over rocks in the foothills of the Santa Cruz Mountains, just north of the town of Middle Quarters, famed for its spicy, freshwater shrimp.

EXPLORING THE SOUTH COAST

To reach the South Coast, head east from Negril, following the signposts to Savanna-La-Mar. This is known as Sheffield Road, and the highway isn't particularly good until it broadens into the A2 at Savanna. After passing through the village of **Bluefields,** continue southeast to the small town of **Black River,** which opens onto Black River Bay.

After leaving Black River, where you can find hotels and restaurants (see "Where to Stay," below), you can continue north along A2 to Mandeville or else go directly southeast to Treasure Beach.

The A2 north takes you to **Middle Quarters,** a village on the plains of the Great Morass, through which the Black River runs. Day visitors often stop here and order a local delicacy, pepper shrimp.

Just north of the town of Middle Quarters is **Y. S. Falls,** where seven waterfalls form crystal pools. Guests take a jitney and go through grazing lands and a horse paddock on the way to the falls, where they cool off in the waters and often enjoy a picnic lunch.

After Middle Quarters, the road cuts east toward Mandeville along **Bamboo Avenue,** a scenic drive along 2 miles of highway covered with bamboo. Here you will see a working plantation, the **Holland Estate,** growing sugarcane, citrus, papaya, and mango.

If you've decided to take the southern coast route to **Treasure Beach,** follow the signs to Treasure Beach directly southeast of Black River. The treasures here are seashells in many shapes and sizes, making for a beachcomber's paradise. Swimming here is tricky because of the undertow, and the sand is gray, but it's secluded and comfortable, and dramatic waves crash onto the shore. This is the site of the Treasure Beach Hotel (see "Where to Stay," below).

To the east of Treasure Beach is **Lovers' Leap** in Southfield, a cliff plunging hundreds of feet into the sea. Two slave lovers reportedly jumped to their deaths here rather than be sold off to different masters.

THE BLACK RIVER

The longest stream in Jamaica, the Black River has mangrove trees, crocodiles, and the insectivorous bladderwort, plus hundreds of different species of bird. You can indeed go on a safari to this wilderness. The best tours are operated by **South Coast Safaris** in Mandeville (☎ **876/965-2513** for reservations). The cost is U.S.$15, and children under 12 go for half price. Tours last 1½ hours and cover 12 miles (6 miles upstream, 5 miles back). Daily tours are at 9am, 11am, 12:30pm, 2pm, and 4pm. Children under 3 go free.

WHERE TO STAY

Invercauld Great House & Hotel. High St. (on the harborfront, a few blocks west of Black River's commercial center), Black River, St. Elizabeth, Jamaica, W.I. ☎ **876/965-2750.** Fax 876/965-2751. 48 units. A/C TV TEL. Year-round U.S.$68–$74 double, U.S.$82–$97 suite. AE, MC, V.

In 1889, when Black River's port was one of the most important in Jamaica, a Scottish merchant imported most of the materials for the construction of this white-sided manor house. Today, the renovated and much-enlarged house functions as a hotel. Only a handful of rooms are within the original high-ceilinged house; most lie within a cement outbuilding that was added in 1991. Rooms are clean, stripped down, and simple, usually with mahogany furniture made by local crafts-people. Gradually the hotel has added five small houses filled with suites; these come either with a king-size bed or twin beds, and the units also have a fold-out couch, are air-conditioned, with cable TV and phone, plus either a patio or veranda. On the premises is a cement patio and a swimming pool, Jacuzzi, a tennis court, and a conservative restaurant with white tiles and white walls. It's open daily for breakfast, lunch, and dinner.

Irie Sandz Hotel. 67 Crane Rd., Black River, St. Elizabeth, Jamaica, W.I. ☎ **876/965-2756.** Fax 876/965-2466. 10 units. TV. Year-round U.S.$40–$50 double. MC, V.

Owned by a local doctor, Oliver Myers, and operated by a well-intentioned resident staff, this simple hotel lies on its own beachfront about 1¼ miles south of Black River's commercial core, and about a mile from the banks of the town's namesake, the Black River. Originally built in the late 1980s, and under present management since 1997, the accommodations are simple and completely unpretentious, with views overlooking the sands. Each has either ceiling or standing fans (or both), and about half contain air conditioners. You shouldn't expect luxury—but at these prices, it's still a bargain. There's a bar and a low-key restaurant on the premises. Service is slow, but the staff can arrange 2-hour boat tours (through Jacana Aqua-Tours, the hotel's sibling company) on the nearby river for a fee of U.S.$20 per person.

✪ **Jake's.** Calabash Bay, Treasure Beach, St. Elizabeth, Jamaica, W.I. ☎ **800/OUTPOST** in the U.S., or 876/965-0552. Fax 876/965-0552. 8 units. Year-round U.S.$75–$95 double; U.S.$150–$180 suite. AE, MC, V.

In a setting of cactus-studded hills in the arid southwest (in total contrast to the rest of tropically lush Jamaica), this is a special haven, an ideal place to get away from it all. Perched on a cliff side overlooking the ocean, this complex of cottages is an explosion of colors, everything from funky purple to "toreador red." Each room is individually decorated, everything inspired by Sally Henzell, a Jamaican of British ancestry who is married to Perry Henzell, art director on *The Harder They Come*, that classic reggae film. Sally cites the controversial Catalán architect, Gaudí, as her mentor in the creation of Jake's—especially in the generous use of cracked mosaic. The bedrooms could contain anything that Sally might have picked up at the flea market, or wherever. If it appealed to her, it's likely to be used to decorate one of the rooms. But be warned: There's no air-conditioning and days are hot here in the "desert." The fare is simple Jamaican, but it's tasty and good, made with fresh ingredients. Begin with the pepperpot soup and go on to the catch of the day, perfectly prepared.

Treasure Beach Hotel. Treasure Beach (on the coast, midway between Black River and Pedro Cross; P.O. Box 5), Black River, St. Elizabeth, Jamaica, W.I. ☎ **876/965-2305.** Fax 876/965-2544. 36 units. A/C TEL. Winter U.S.$90–$100 double, U.S.$130 suite; off-season U.S.$80–$90 double, U.S.$103 suite. MAP U.S.$25 per person extra. AE, MC, V.

Set on a steep but lushly landscaped hillside above a sandy beach with an active surf, this white-sided hotel was built in the mid-1970s. Although its staff is young and inexperienced, this is the largest and most elaborate hotel on Jamaica's South Coast. Its centerpiece is a long and airy rattan-furnished bar whose windows look down the hillside to the beach and the hotel's 11 acres that flank it. Bedrooms lie within a series of outlying cottages, each of which contains between two and six accommodations. Each unit has a ceiling fan and veranda or patio, and—in some cases—a TV.

Amenities include two freshwater pools, a loosely organized array of such activities as volleyball and horseshoes, and a simple restaurant with slow and casual service that's open for lunch and dinner.

WHERE TO DINE

Bridge House Inn. 14 Crane Rd. (on the eastern outskirts of Black River, on the opposite side of the town's only bridge from the commercial center), Black River. ☎ **876/965-2361.** Full meals U.S.$15–$30. MC, V. Daily 6am–11:30pm. JAMAICAN.

This is the simple and very Jamaican restaurant that is contained within one of the town's two hotels. The cement-sided structure that houses it was built in the early 1980s; it's done with a beachfront motif and set within a grove of coconut palms and sea grapes.

On the premises are 13 bedrooms, each with air-conditioning, ceiling fan, and simple furniture, but no TV and no telephone. Most clients appreciate this place, however, for its restaurant. Patrons include a cross-section of the region, including the occasional conference of librarians or nurses. Menu items—everything is home style—include complete dinners (fish, chicken, curried goat, oxtail, stewed beef, or lobster) with soup and vegetables, served politely and efficiently by a staff of hardworking waiters. A separate bar area off to the side dispenses drinks.

8 Mandeville

The "English Town" of Mandeville lies on a plateau more than 2,000 feet above sea level in the tropical highlands. The commercial part of town is small, surrounded by a sprawling residential area that has a large North American expatriate population, mostly involved with the bauxite-mining industry.

Mandeville is the sort of place where you can become well-acquainted with the people and feel like part of the community in very short order. Much cooler than the coastal resorts, it's a comfortable base from which to explore the entire country.

Shopping here is a pleasure, whether in the old center or in one of the modern complexes, such as Grove Court. The central market teems with life, particularly on weekends when country folk bus into town for a visit. The town has several interesting old buildings. The square-towered church built in 1820 has fine stained glass, and gravestones in the little churchyard tell an interesting story of past inhabitants of Mandeville. The Court House was built in 1816, a fine old Georgian stone-and-wood building with a pillared portico reached by a steep, sweeping double staircase. Another key attraction is Marshall's Pen, one of Mandeville's Great Houses.

WHAT TO SEE & DO

The Manchester Country Club, Brumalia Road (☎ **876/962-2403**), is Jamaica's oldest golf course, but has only nine holes. Beautiful vistas unfold from 2,201 feet above sea level. Greens fees are U.S.$12.50, with caddy fees running U.S.$4. The course also has a clubhouse. The club is also one of the best venues in central Jamaica for tennis.

One of the largest and driest caves on the island is at Oxford, about 9 miles northwest of Mandeville. Signs direct you to it after you leave Mile Gully, a village dominated by St. George's Church, which is some 175 years old.

Among the interesting attractions, **Marshall's Pen** is one of the Great Houses. A coffee plantation home some 200 years old, it has been restored and furnished in traditional style. In 1795, it was owned by one of the governors of Jamaica, the earl of Balcarres. It has been in the hands of the Sutton family since 1939; they farm the 300 acres and breed Jamaican Red Poll cattle. This is very much a private home and should be treated as such, although guided tours can be arranged. A contribution of U.S.$10 per person is requested. For information or an appointment to see the house, contact Ann or Robert Sutton, Marshall's Pen, Great House, P.O. Box 58, Mandeville, Jamaica, W.I. (☎ **876/904-5454**).

At **Marshall's Pen cattle estate and private nature reserve,** near Mandeville, guided birding tours of the scenic property and other outstanding birding spots on Jamaica may be arranged in advance for groups of bird-watchers. Self-catering accommodation is sometimes available for bird-watchers only, but arrangements must be made in advance. For further information, contact Ann or Robert Sutton, Marshall's Pen, P.O. Box 58, Mandeville, Jamaica, W.I. (☎ **876/904-5454**).

Robert Sutton is coauthor of *Birds of Jamaica,* a photographic field guide published by Cambridge University Press.

Milk River Mineral Bath, Milk River, Clarendon (☎ 876/924-9544; fax 876/986-4962), lies 9 miles south of the Kingston–Mandeville highway. It boasts the world's most radioactive mineral waters, recommended for the treatment of arthritis, rheumatism, lumbago, neuralgia, sciatica, and liver disorders. These mineral-laden waters are available to guests of the Milk River Mineral Spa & Hotel, Milk River, Clarendon, Jamaica, W.I., as well as to casual visitors to the enclosed baths or mineral swimming pool. The baths contain water at approximate body temperature (90°F) and are channeled into small tubs 6 feet square by 3 feet deep, each enclosed in a cubicle where participants undress. The cost of a bath is J$50 ($1.45) for adults and J$25 (70¢) for children. Baths usually last about 15 minutes (it isn't good to remain too long in the waters).

The restaurant offers fine Jamaican cuisine and health drinks in a relaxed old-world atmosphere. Some guests check into the adjacent hotel, where there are 25 rooms (17 with bath), many with air-conditioning, TV, and phone. Six of the rooms are in the main body of the hotel (a century-old Great House that was converted into a hotel in the 1930s). With MAP included, rates for rooms with bath are U.S.$102 double. Rates for rooms without bath are U.S.$96 double. American Express, MasterCard, and Visa are accepted.

WHERE TO STAY

Hotel Astra. 62 Ward Ave., Mandeville, Jamaica, W.I. ☎ **876/962-3265.** 22 units. TV TEL. U.S.$65 double; U.S.$150 suite. Rates include continental breakfast. AE, MC, V.

Our top choice for a stay in this area is the family-run Hotel Astra, operated by Diana McIntyre-Pike, known to her family and friends as Thunderbird. She's always coming to the rescue of guests, happily picking them up in her car and taking them around to see the sights. The rather spartan accommodations are mainly in two buildings. There's a pool and a sauna, and the inn offers therapeutic massages. You can also spend the afternoon at the Manchester Country Club, where tennis and golf are available. Horses can be provided for cross-country treks; the stable lies a 45-minute drive away.

The Country Fresh Restaurant offers excellent meals. Lunch or dinner is a choice of a homemade soup such as red pea or pumpkin, followed by local fish and chicken specialties. The kitchen is under the personal control of Diana, who is always collecting awards in Jamaican culinary competitions. A complete meal costs U.S.$10 to U.S.$15. Dinner is served from 6 to 9:30pm every day of the week.

Mandeville Hotel. 4 Hotel St. (a short walk from the police station; P.O. Box 78), Mandeville, Jamaica, W.I. ☎ **876/962-2138.** Fax 876/962-0700. 56 units. TV TEL. Year-round U.S.$65–$125 double; from U.S.$95 suite. AE, MC, V.

This richly ornate hotel in the heart of Mandeville was first established around the turn of the century, and for a while housed part of the British military garrison. In the 1970s, the original structure was replaced with this modern peach-colored substitute, containing plain and simple but clean bedrooms. Today, you'll find a large outdoor bar and spacious lounge. There are attractive gardens with many fine old trees and beautiful plants.

Popular with local businesspeople, the coffee shop by the pool is a quick, appetizing luncheon stop offering a wide selection of sandwiches, plus milk shakes, tea, and coffee. For the restaurant, see below. Golf and tennis can be played at the nearby Manchester Country Club. Horseback riding can also be arranged.

WHERE TO DINE

Mandeville Hotel. 4 Hotel St. ☎ **876/962-2460.** Reservations recommended. Main courses J$275–J$395 (U.S.$7.85–$11.25). AE, MC, V. Daily 6:30am–9:30pm. JAMAICAN.

Close to the city center, near the police station, and popular with local business-people, the Mandeville Hotel offers a wide selection of sandwiches, plus milk shakes, tea, and coffee. In the restaurant, the à la carte menu features Jamaican pepperpot soup, lobster thermidor, fresh snapper, and kingfish. Potatoes and vegetables are included in the main-dish prices. There is no pretension to the food at all. It's homemade and basic, almost like that served in the house of a typical Jamaican family. From the restaurant's dining room, you'll have a view of the hotel's pool and the green hills of central Jamaica.

The North Coast Resorts: Runaway Bay, Ocho Rios & Port Antonio

6

Situated on Jamaica's northeast coast, the resort areas of Runaway Bay, Ocho Rios, and Port Antonio helped to launch large-scale tourism in Jamaica. Known for its abundant rainfall, verdant landscapes, rolling hills, and jagged estuaries, this region was once the preferred hangout for Noël Coward, Errol Flynn, and a host of British and American literati. Ian Fleming, creator of the James Bond spy thrillers, lived at Goldeneye, near Ocho Rios.

Starting from Montego Bay and heading east, you first reach **Discovery Bay,** whose name refers to the belief that Columbus first landed here in 1494. Finding no water, Columbus is said to have named it Puerto Seco (Dry Harbor). Puerto Seco Beach today is a popular stretch of sand, with a few places where you can get lunch or a drink.

Just beyond Discovery Bay is **Runaway Bay,** with some of the best-known resort hotels along the North Coast. There is no real town of Runaway Bay; it is mainly a beachfront strip of hotels and sandy shores. Much of the resort area takes up space once occupied by Cardiff Hall, a sprawling plantation owned by one of Jamaica's first English settlers.

From Runaway Bay, continue east along the A3, bypassing the sleepy hamlet of St. Anne's Bay, and you'll reach **Ocho Rios.** Today, this is the North Coast's major tourist destination, although it's not up there with Montego Bay.

Although Ocho Rios is the cruise-ship capital of Jamaica, with as many as a half-dozen major vessels anchored offshore at any one time, it is not a port at the mouth of eight rivers, as its Spanish name ("Eight Rivers") might suggest. It was once the lair of pirate John Davis, who remains famous for his plundering of French and Spanish vessels on the nearby seas. One of his best-known exploits was the sacking and burning of St. Augustine, Florida.

The sleepy village of long ago has been enveloped by massive resort hotels (many all-inclusive). Ocho Rios is fine for a lazy beach vacation, but it's definitely not for anyone seeking a remote hideaway. You might see calypso and reggae bands greeting cruise-ship passengers, who are then herded onto buses and shuttled off to Dunn's River Falls. Here, they take a sometimes precarious trek across wooded limestone cliffs whose broad waterfalls are among the most frequently photographed sights in Jamaica. To the discomfiture of many visitors, souvenir vendors assail you at almost every point.

From Ocho Rios, drive east along Highway A4/A3, which will take you through some sleepy fishing villages, including Port Maria, until you reach **Port Antonio.** Since it's situated on the coast just north of the Blue Mountains, Port Antonio is surrounded by some of the most rugged and beautiful scenery in Jamaica. Many visitors prefer to visit the mountains and highlands from a base here, rather than starting out in Kingston, thus avoiding the capital's crime and urban sprawl.

Although Port Antonio was the cradle of Jamaican tourist development, it has been eclipsed by other areas such as Montego Bay, Ocho Rios, and Negril. It remains a preferred hideaway, however, for a chic and elegant crowd that still vacations in its handful of posh hotels. The tourist flow to Port Antonio began in the 1890s, when cruise-ship passengers started to arrive for rest and relaxation. Perched above twin harbors, the estuary was pronounced by the poet Ella Wheeler as "the most exquisite harbor on earth."

1 Runaway Bay

Runaway Bay used to be just a western satellite of Ocho Rios. However, with the opening of some large resorts, plus a colony of smaller hotels, it's now become a destination in its own right.

This part of Jamaica's North Coast has several distinctions: It was the first part of the island seen by Columbus, the site of the first Spanish settlement on the island, and the point of departure of the last Spaniards to leave Jamaica following their defeat by the British. Columbus landed at Discovery Bay on his second voyage of exploration in 1494, and in 1509 Spaniards established a settlement called Sevilla Nueva (New Seville) near what is now St. Anne's Bay, about 10 miles east of the present Runaway Bay village. Sevilla Nueva was later abandoned, the inhabitants moving to the southern part of the island.

In 1655, an English fleet sailed into Kingston Harbour and defeated the Spanish garrison there. However, a guerrilla war broke out on the island between the Spanish and English in which the English prevailed. The remnants of the Spanish army embarked for Cuba in 1660 from a small fishing village on the North Coast. Some believe that this "running away" from Jamaica gave the name Runaway Bay to the village. However, later historians believe that the name possibly came from the traffic in runaway slaves from the north-coast plantations to Cuba.

WHERE TO STAY & DINE

Runaway Bay offers several unusual accommodations as well as all-inclusive resorts and notable bargains.

VERY EXPENSIVE

Breezes Golf and Beach Resort. P.O. Box 58 (6 miles west of Ocho Rios), Runaway Bay, Jamaica, W.I. ☎ **800/GO-SUPER** or 876/973-2436. Fax 876/973-2352. 238 units. A/C TEL. Winter U.S.$1,618–$1,778 double; from U.S.$1,900 suite for 2. Off-season U.S.$1,258–$1,518 double; from U.S.$1,500 suite for 2. Rates are all-inclusive for 3 nights. AE, DC, MC, V. No children under 15.

This stylish resort has had several identities since it was built. It operates on a price plan that includes three meals a day, all free drinks, and lots of other freebies. Its long, low-lying clubhouse is approached by passing through a park filled with tropical trees and shrubbery. Near the wide, sandy beach is a mini-jungle with dangling hammocks and a swimming pool, and there's even a nearby nude beach. Inside the lobby is the best re-creation of the South Seas on Jamaica, with hanging wicker chairs and totemic columns. Each of the rooms has a view of a well-landscaped courtyard, with a private balcony overlooking the sea.

Dining/Diversions: Live music emanates from the stylish Terrace every evening at 7pm, and a nightclub offers live shows 6 nights a week at 10pm. You dine either in the beachside restaurant or in the more formal Italian restaurant, Martino's.

Amenities: Gym filled with Nautilus equipment, swimming pool, sports activities center (featuring scuba diving, windsurfing, and a golf school), 18-hole championship golf course, reggae exercise classes held twice daily.

Chukka Cove Farm and Resort. 4 miles east of Runaway Bay off A1 (P.O. Box 177), Richmond Llandovery, St. Ann's Bay, Jamaica, W.I. ☎ **876/972-2771.** Fax 876/972-0814. 6 villas. A/C MINIBAR TEL. Winter U.S.$2,000 villa per week; off-season U.S.$1,500 villa per week. Rates can be prorated for shorter stays. No credit cards.

Known for its equestrian tours (see "Golf & Horseback Riding," below), Chukka Cove is also an ideal center for horse lovers who'd like to live on the grounds. Located 4 miles east of Runaway Bay, it is frequented by Capt. Mark Phillips, former husband of Britain's Princess Anne. On the estate's acreage lie six two-bedroom villas, each suitable for four guests, with a veranda, plank floors, and an architectural plan vaguely reminiscent of 18th-century models. A pampering staff will prepare meals in your villa. Snorkeling is also included.

FDR (Franklyn D. Resort). Main St. (P.O. Box 201), Runaway Bay, St. Ann, Jamaica, W.I. ☎ **800/654-1FDR** in the U.S., or 876/973-4591. Fax 876/973-3071. 76 units. A/C TV TEL. Winter U.S.$300 per person; off-season U.S.$265 per person. Rates are all-inclusive. Children 15 and under stay free in parents' suite. AE, MC, V.

An all-inclusive resort on Route A1, 17 miles west of Ocho Rios, FDR is geared to families with children. The resort, named after its Jamaican-born owner and developer (Franklyn David Rance), is on 6 acres of flat, sandy beachfront dotted with flowering shrubs and trees, on the main seaside highway. Each of the Mediterranean-inspired buildings has a terra-cotta roof, a loggia or outdoor terrace, Spanish marble in the bathroom, and a personal attendant (a "vacation nanny") whose cooking, cleaning, child-care, and miscellaneous services come with each of the units. Although neither its narrow beach nor its modest swimming pools are the most desirable on the island, many visitors appreciate the spacious units and the resort's wholehearted concern for visiting children. Each unit contains a kitchenette where, if you want, meals can be prepared by the personal attendant.

Dining/Diversions: Two restaurants on the property serve free wine with lunch and dinner (and offer special children's meals), a piano bar provides music every evening, and a handful of bars keeps the drinks flowing whenever you're ready for them. Live music is provided nightly.

Amenities: An attendant baby-sits for free every day between 9:30am and 4:45pm, after which she can be hired privately for U.S.$3 an hour. There's a children's supervisor in attendance at "Kiddies' Centre" (where a computer center, a kiddies' disco, and even kiddies' dinners are regular features). Adults appreciate the scuba lessons, picnics, photography lessons, arts and crafts lessons, and donkey rides that keep the kids entertained. Also offered are water sports, illuminated tennis courts, a satellite TV room, a whirlpool area with some spa facilities, a gym, free use of bicycles, free tours to Dunn's River Falls and Ocho Rios for shopping.

MODERATE

Club Ambiance Jamaica. Runaway Bay, Jamaica, W.I. ☎ **800/523-6504** or 876/973-4606. Fax 876/973-2067. 82 units. A/C TV TEL. Winter U.S.$105–$120 per person double or triple; U.S.$130 per person suite. Off-season U.S.$90–$120 per person double or triple; U.S.$110 per person suite. Rates are all-inclusive. AE, MC, V. No children under 18.

Last refurbished in 1995, this is one of the most basic of the all-inclusives, catering mainly to European travelers on a budget. The hotel is laid-back and casual. Lying at the west end of Runaway Bay, we recommended it primarily for its reasonable rates—not for its somewhat bleak two-story appearance (instead of gardens in front, you get a sprawling parking lot). The shoreline near the hotel is rocky, and a small crescent of sand won't win the beach sweepstakes. Units are reasonably comfortable and clean, if not very stylish. Regional art decorates the walls, and the furniture is often upholstered wicker. Accommodations come with either double or king-size beds, with balconies opening onto views of the water.

Dining/Diversions: A standard Jamaican cuisine is served in the Coconut Terrace Dining Room and in Café Calypso. Later, you can work off the calories in the Safari Disco. Sometimes this sleepy place wakes up with theme nights and cultural shows including beach parties and a live band.

Amenities: Exercise room, swimming pool. For scuba divers, the hotel recently added an accredited PADI center.

✪ **Runaway H.E.A.R.T. Country Club.** Ricketts Ave. (off Main St.; P.O. Box 98), Runaway Bay, St. Ann, Jamaica, W.I. ☎ **876/973-2671.** Fax 876/973-2693. 20 units. A/C TV TEL. Winter U.S.$138 double; off-season U.S.$122 double. Rates include MAP (breakfast and dinner). AE, MC, V.

The best-kept secret in Jamaica, this place is located on the main road, and it practically wins hands down as the bargain of the North Coast. One of Jamaica's few training and service institutions, the club and its adjacent academy are operated by the government to provide a high level of training for young Jamaicans interested in the hotel trade. The hotel is well run; its professional staff includes trainees who are helpful and eager to please and offer perhaps the finest service of any hotel in the area.

The rooms are bright and airy and have either a king-size bed, a double bed, or twins. The accommodations open onto private balconies with views of well-manicured tropical gardens or vistas of the bay and golf course. By the time of your visit, another three dozen accommodations may have been added.

Runaway H.E.A.R.T. shares a private beach called Breezes Runaway Beach with Breezes Gold & Beach Resort. They offer free shuttle service to and from the beach (the ride takes about 5 minutes) several times a day. Comfortable sunning chairs and umbrellas are also provided for clients.

Dining/Diversions: Guests enjoy having a drink in the piano bar (ever had a cucumber daiquiri?) before heading for the dining room, the Cardiff Hall Restaurant, which has a combination of Jamaican and continental dishes. Nonresidents can also enjoy dinner, served nightly from 7 to 10pm. The academy has won awards for some of its dishes, including "go-go banana chicken" and curried codfish.

Amenities: Swimming pool, golf course, laundry service.

INEXPENSIVE

Caribbean Isle Hotel. P.O. Box 119, Runaway Bay, St. Ann, Jamaica, W.I. ☎ **876/973-2364.** Fax 876/973-4835. 23 units. A/C. Winter U.S.$75 double, U.S.$85 triple; off-season U.S.$65 double, U.S.$75 triple. AE, MC, V.

This small hotel, located directly on the beach a mile west of Runaway Bay, offers personalized service in an informal atmosphere. Stay here only for the affordable rates; we find the rooms somewhat tattered. But they do all have ocean views, and the superior units all have private balconies. The hotel has a TV in the bar-lounge and a dining room leading onto a sea-view patio. Meals are served from 7:30am to 11pm daily. Dinner includes lobster, fish, shrimp, pork chops, chicken, and local dishes prepared on request.

NEARBY PLACES TO STAY & DINE

Grand Lido Braco. Rio Bueno P.O., Trelawny, Jamaica. ☎ **800/859-7873** or 876/954-0000. Fax 876/954-0020. 178 units. A/C TV TEL. Winter U.S.$760–$1,160 double; U.S.$1,220 suite for 2. Off-season U.S.$730–$910 double; U.S.$900–$960 suite for 2. Rates are all-inclusive. AE, DC, DISC, MC, V. No children under 16.

This is one of the most historically evocative all-inclusive resorts in Jamaica. Set on 85 acres of land near Buena Vista, a 15-minute drive west of Runaway Bay, it was designed as a re-creation of a 19th-century Jamaican Victorian village set adjacent to an impressive stretch of prime beachfront. Meetings and entertainment are presented in a stately duplication of a courthouse, benches and flowering trees line the symmetrical borders of a town square, and meals are served within four separate venues inspired by an idealized version of Jamaica of long ago. Employees, most of whom come from the nearby hamlet of Rio Bueno, are encouraged to mingle with guests and share their personal and community stories. Here, you get a more vivid insight into Jamaican life than would be possible at more cloistered and remote all-inclusive resorts. It's a relaxed and reasonably permissive place.

Accommodations lie within 12 independent blocks of three-story buildings, each trimmed in colonial-style gingerbread and filled with wicker furniture. Each unit has a private patio or veranda and faces the ocean, although blocks 1 through 6 are closer to the beachfront and blocks 5 and 6 face a strip of sand designated as a "clothing optional" area.

Dining/Diversions: Four separate dining areas include a venue devoted to Jamaican cuisine, pizza and pasta, an international emporium called the Victorian Market, and a dinner-only upscale affair, the Piacere Restaurant, the only one to impose a dress code. Four bars make getting a drink relatively easy.

Amenities: A soccer field where a local Jamaican team sometimes volunteers to play with (or against) aficionados from the village; a fitness center, a nine-hole golf course, disco, three fishing ponds, bike and jogging trails, four tennis courts, use of a glass-bottom boat for snorkeling tours, and one of the largest swimming pools in Jamaica. Above all, there's a staff who keeps conversations and good times rolling along.

Hotel and Gallery Joe James. Rio Bueno, Trelawny, Jamaica, W.I. ☎ **876/954-0048.** Fax 876/952-5911. 22 units. Winter U.S.$125 double; U.S.$235 suite for 1; U.S.$250 suite for 2. Off-season U.S.$120 double; U.S.$200 suite for 1; U.S.$225 suite for 2. Rates include breakfast. AE, DC, MC, V.

For a 4- or 5-year period in the 1970s, Joe James was a bright flame on the arts scene of Jamaica, with exhibitions of his works in New York, Philadelphia, and Washington, D.C. Although his fame and press coverage have greatly diminished in recent years, the artist continues his endeavors in a concrete-sided compound of buildings set close to the shore of the sheltered harbor of Rio Bueno. Many visitors are fascinated by the showroom, which is loaded with large-scale paintings and wood carvings with Jamaican and African themes. All the objects are for sale, and Mr. James is usually on the premises to explain his artistic theories.

Mr. James has within a few steps of his showroom and the beach an angular two-story concrete building containing 32 simple and functional accommodations. All have ceiling fans; most have views over the bay and the massive industrial plant whose cranes and smokestacks rise on the opposite side of the harbor. Don't expect luxury here: The primary allure lies in the low cost, the proximity to the studio of one of Jamaica's better-known artists, and the complete lack of pretensions.

Dining: The place gets most of its business from the Lobster Bowl Restaurant, serving breakfast, lunch, and dinner daily. There's an outdoor terrace whose foundations were sunk into the waters of the harbor. The view encompasses the sea, the shore, and one of the neighborhood's largest industrial entities. Lunchtime platters include burgers, salads, sandwiches, and grilled fish. Evening meals are more copious and feature a choice of set menus comprised of grilled fish, broiled lobster, sirloin steak, or chicken, served with soup, salad, dessert, coffee, and Tía María as part of the all-inclusive price.

BEACHES & SNORKELING

The two preferred beaches in Runaway Bay are Paradise Beach and Cardiffall Lot Public Beach. Both beaches have great sand and are terrific spots. Runaway Bay has some of the nicest areas for snorkeling on the island. The reefs are very close to shore and extremely lively. You are likely to see enormous schools of tropical fish: mostly blue chromis, trigger fish, small skate rays, and snapper. Unfortunately, the fishing industry is active here, so the fish are likely to be a bit small in shallower waters. Also, snorkeling on your own can be a bit dangerous here if you're not careful. The boats and fishing canoes will run you right over. Your best bet is to go on a snorkeling excursion with a diving facility. We recommend **Resort Divers** in Runaway Bay (☎ 876/973-5761). This five-star PADI facility will take you to one of several protected reefs where the water currents are very small and the fishing boats are obliged to stay at least 200 yards away from the snorkelers. Resort Divers also provides sport-fishing jaunts as well scuba diving certification and equipment, and sailing lessons and equipment.

GOLF & HORSEBACK RIDING

SuperClub's Runaway Golf Club (☎ 876/973-2561) charges no admission for guests staying at any of Jamaica's affiliated SuperClubs. For nonguests, the price is U.S.$58 year-round.

Jamaica's most complete equestrian center is **Chukka Cove Farm and Resort,** St. Ann's Bay (☎ 876/972-2771), at Richmond Llandovery, less than 4 miles east of Runaway Bay (see "Where to Stay & Dine," above). The best ride here is a 3-hour jaunt to the sea, where you can unpack your horse and swim in the surf. Refreshments are served as part of the U.S.$55 charge. A 6-hour beach ride, complete with picnic lunch, goes for U.S.$130. Polo lessons are also available, costing U.S.$50 for 30 minutes.

SEEING THE SIGHTS

Columbus Park Museum. Queens Hwy., Discovery Bay. ☎ 876/973-2135. Admission free. Daily 9am–5pm.

This is a large, open area between the main coast road and the sea at Discovery Bay. You just pull off the road and then walk among the fantastic collection of exhibits. There's everything from a canoe made of a solid piece of cottonwood (the way Arawaks did it more than 5 centuries ago), to a stone cross that was originally placed on the Barrett estate at Retreat (9 miles east of Montego Bay) by Edward Barrett, brother of poet Elizabeth Barrett Browning. You'll see a tally, used to count bananas carried on men's heads from plantation to ship, as well as a planter's strongbox with a weighted lead base to prevent its theft. Other items are 18th-century cannons, a Spanish water cooler and calcifier, a fish pot made from bamboo, a corn husker, and a waterwheel. Pimento trees, from which allspice is produced, dominate the park.

Seville Great House. Heritage Park. ☎ **876/972-2191.** Admission U.S.$4. Daily 9am–5pm.

Built in 1745 by the English, the house contains a collection of artifacts once used by everybody from the Amerindians to African slaves. In all, you're treated to an exhibit of 5 centuries worth of Jamaican history. Modest for a Great House, it has a wattle and daub construction. A small theater presents a 15-minute historical film about the house.

2 Ocho Rios

A 2-hour drive east of Montego Bay or west of Port Antonio, Ocho Rios was once a small banana and fishing port, but tourism long ago became its leading industry. Now Jamaica's cruise-ship capital, the bay is dominated on one side by a bauxite-loading terminal and on the other by a range of hotels with sandy beaches fringed by palm trees.

Ocho Rios and neighboring Port Antonio have long been associated with celebrities, the two most famous writers being Sir Noël Coward, who invited the world to his Jamaican doorstep, and Ian Fleming, who created James Bond while writing here.

It is commonly assumed among Spanish-speakers that Ocho Rios was named for eight rivers, its Spanish meaning, but the islanders disagree. In 1657, British troops chased off a Spanish expeditionary force that had launched a raid from Cuba. The battle was near Dunn's River Falls, now the resort's most important attraction. Seeing the rapids, the Spanish called the district los chorreros. That battle between the Spanish and the British forces was so named. The British and the Jamaicans weren't too good with Spanish names back then, so los chorreros was corrupted into "ocho rios."

Ocho Rios has its own unique flavor, offering the usual range of sports and a major fishing tournament every fall in addition to a wide variety of accommodations, including all-inclusive resorts, couples-only complexes, elegant retreats (some with spas), and inns of character holding to what is left of the area's former colonial culture.

But frankly, unless you're a passenger, you may want to stay away from the major attractions on cruise-ship days. Even the duty-free shopping markets are overrun then, and the street hustlers become more strident in trying to sell their souvenirs. Dunn's River Falls becomes almost impossible to visit at these times.

GETTING THERE

You'll likely fly into **Donald Sangster Airport** in Montego Bay. Many hotels, particularly the larger resorts, will arrange to pick you up at the airport and transfer you to your hotel at that point. Be sure to ask when you book.

If your hotel does not provide transfers, your options are limited to a bus, rental car, or taxi. Public and private bus companies operate desks in the Montego Bay airport, all offering a U.S.$20 one-way fare to Ocho Rios. The public bus isn't very comfortable, so try two private companies we recommend: **Tour Wise**

(☎ **876/979-1027** in Montego Bay, or 876/974-2323 in Ocho Rios) or **Caribic Vacations** (☎ **876/953-9874** in Montego Bay, or 876/974-9106 in Ocho Rios). All buses make one refreshment stop at a halfway point during the trip. Buses depart as flights arrive and will drop you off at your final destination once you reach Ocho Rios.

Yet another option is renting a car. Information on car rentals is given in the "Getting Around" section in chapter 3. From Montego Bay, drive 67 miles east along Highway A1. Because of the travel conditions, plan for a 2-hour drive.

A final option is taking a taxi. A typical one-way fare from Montego Bay to Ocho Rios is U.S.$50 to U.S.$60. Always negotiate and agree upon the fare before getting into the taxi.

WHERE TO STAY

Some of the accommodations in and around Ocho Rios include the best in all Jamaica. See also "Seeing the Sights," later in this section, for details on Prospect Plantation, which rents several luxurious villas.

VERY EXPENSIVE

✪ **Jamaica Inn.** Main St. (P.O. Box 1), Ocho Rios, Jamaica, W.I. ☎ **800/837-4608** in the U.S., or 876/974-2514. Fax 876/974-2449. 45 units. A/C TEL. Winter (including all meals) U.S.$475–$525 double; from U.S.$600 suite for 2. Off-season (including breakfast and dinner) U.S.$275–$375 double; from U.S.$345 suite for 2. AE, MC, V. No children under 13.

Built in 1950, this gracious, family-run inn, long a Jamaican landmark, is a series of long, low, buildings set in a U shape on a wide champagne-colored sand beach, 1½ miles east of town. It's an elegant anachronism, a true retro hotel, and has remained little changed in 4 decades, avoiding the brass and glitter of all-inclusives like Sandals. Close to the shore, the sea is almost too clear to make snorkeling an adventure, but farther out it's rewarding.

Lovely patios open onto the lawns, and the bedrooms are reached along garden paths. The old charm, including the antique furniture, remains. The rooms open onto balconies, and the White Suite here was a favorite of Winston Churchill. Over the years, many other celebrities have favored the inn with their patronage. Noël Coward, arriving with Katharine Hepburn or Claudette Colbert, was a regular, and Errol Flynn and Ian Fleming used to drop in from time to time.

Dining: The European-trained chef prepares both international and Jamaican dishes. The emphasis is on cuisine that uses fresh local produce. Men must wear a jacket and tie at night in winter.

Amenities: Swimming pool, tennis, comfortable lounge with books, games room with cards and jigsaw puzzles, room service, laundry service; golf close by at the Upton Golf Course.

EXPENSIVE

High Hope Estate. Box 11, St. Ann's Bay, near Ocho Rios. ☎ **876/972-2277.** Fax 876/972-1607. 6 units. TEL. Year-round U.S.$174–$270 double. Rates include breakfast. MC, V.

Because of the small size of this upscale hotel, your happiness here will depend a lot on whether your chemistry is right with the owner and the other guests (or you could rent the entire villa with a group of friends). It's conceived as a tranquil private home that accepts paying guests, in the style of the British colonial world at its most rarefied. It was built for a socially prominent heiress, Kitty Spence, granddaughter of prairie-state populist William Jennings Bryan, and later served as the home and laboratory of a horticulturist who successfully bred 560 varieties of

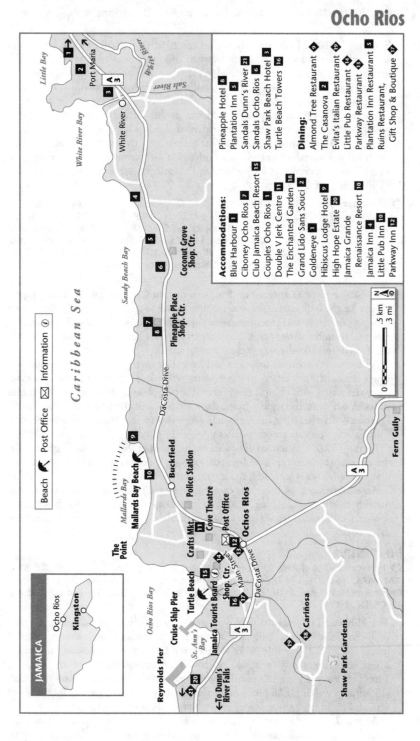

Ocho Rios

Accommodations:
Blue Harbour **1**
Ciboney Ocho Rios **7**
Club Jamaica Beach Resort **15**
Couples Ocho Rios **1**
Double V Jerk Centre **11**
The Enchanted Garden **18**
Grand Lido Sans Souci **2**
Goldeneye **1**
Hibiscus Lodge Hotel **9**
High Hope Estate **20**
Jamaica Grande
Renaissance Resort **10**
Jamaica Inn **4**
Little Pub Inn **10**
Parkway Inn **12**

Pineapple Hotel **8**
Plantation Inn **5**
Sandals Dunn's River **21**
Sandals Ocho Rios **6**
Shaw Park Beach Hotel **3**
Turtle Beach Towers **16**

Dining:
Almond Tree Restaurant **9**
The Casanova **2**
Evita's Italian Restaurant **11**
Little Pub Restaurant **13**
Parkway Restaurant **10**
Plantation Inn Restaurant **5**
Ruins Restaurant,
   Gift Shop & Boutique **17**

Beach ✦   Post Office ✉   Information ⓘ

Caribbean Sea

JAMAICA

Ocho Rios

Kingston

N

0   .5 km

0   .3 mi

flowering hibiscus. Consequently, the estate's 40 acres, set 550 feet above the coast and 7 miles west of Ocho Rios, thrive with flowering plants and memories of such luminaries as Noël Coward, who used to play the grand piano that graces one of the public areas. There are sweeping views out over the Jamaican coastline; the nearest beach is a 10-minute drive away.

There are absolutely no planned activities at this place. Basically, it's an upscale private home, the domain of U.S. entrepreneur Dennis Rapaport, whose staff is on hand to help with supervising children, maintaining the property, and preparing meals for anyone who gives advance notice. On the premises is a swimming pool, a tennis court, a communal TV room, and a semienclosed courtyard modeled on a 15th-century villa.

✪ **Plantation Inn.** Main St. (P.O. Box 2), Ocho Rios, Jamaica, W.I. ☎ **800/752-6824** in the U.S., or 876/974-5601. Fax 876/974-5912. 76 units, 2 villas. A/C TEL. Winter U.S.$225–$335 double; U.S.$270–$400 triple; U.S.$385–$870 suite for 2. Off-season U.S.$150–$210 double; U.S.$200–$260 triple; U.S.$230–$550 suite for 2. Villas (7-night minimum): winter U.S.$4,375–$5,800 up to 4; off-season U.S.$3,800–$5,100 up to 4. Children under 14 stay free in parents' rm. MAP (breakfast and dinner) U.S.$55 per person extra. AE, MC, V.

This hotel evokes an antebellum Southern mansion. At any moment, you expect Vivien Leigh as Scarlett to come rushing down to greet you. You'll drive up a sweeping driveway and enter through a colonnaded portico, set above the beach in gardens, 1½ miles east of town. There are two private beaches (36 steps down from the garden; seats on the way provide resting spots).

All bedrooms open off balconies and have their own patios overlooking the sea, where the hotel has a variety of water sports available. The double rooms are attractively decorated with chintz and comfortable furnishings, and there are also junior suites. Apart from the regular hotel, there are two units that provide lodgings: the Plantana Villa above the eastern beach sleeps two to six people; the Blue Shadow Villa on the west side accommodates up to eight guests.

Dining: There's an indoor dining room, but most of the action takes place under the tropical sky. You can have breakfast on your balcony and lunch is served outdoors. English tea is served on the terrace every afternoon.

Amenities: Gym with exercise equipment, sauna, two tennis courts, snorkeling, Sunfish sailing, windsurfing, scuba diving, kayaking, glass-bottom boat, room service, facials, massages, waxing. Golf is available at an 18-hole course a 15-minute drive away.

INEXPENSIVE

✪ **Hibiscus Lodge Hotel.** 87 Main St. (P.O. Box 52), Ocho Rios, Jamaica, W.I. ☎ **876/ 974-2676.** Fax 876/974-1874. 27 units. Winter U.S.$105 double; U.S.$150 triple. Off-season U.S.$93 double; U.S.$129 triple. Rates include breakfast. Tax and service extra. AE, CB, DC, MC, V.

The Hibiscus Lodge Hotel gives you more bang for your buck than any resort in Ocho Rios. It's an intimate little inn with character and charm, perched precariously on a cliff side 3 blocks from the Ocho Rios Mall, along the shore. There are two sandy beaches nearby—Fisherman's Point, which is about 5 minutes away driving (20 minutes walking), and the beach at Inn on the Beach (15 minutes walking). All bedrooms, either doubles or triples, have ceiling fans and verandas opening to the sea. Singles can be rented for the double rate.

After a day spent swimming in a pool with a large sundeck suspended over the cliffs, guests can enjoy a drink in the unique swinging bar, which features swinging chairs. The 3-acre site also contains a Jacuzzi, a tennis court, and conference facilities. Dining at the Almond Tree (see "Where to Dine," below) is among the best at the resort, and the Grotto is a piano bar open daily from 5pm to 2am.

Little Pub Inn. 59 Main St. (P.O. Box 256), Ocho Rios, St. Ann, Jamaica, W.I. ☎ **876/974-2324.** Fax 876/974-5825. 22 units. A/C TEL. Winter U.S.$70 double; off-season U.S.$66 double. Extra person U.S.$20 in winter, U.S.$15 off-season. Children 11 and under stay free in parents' rm. Higher rates include full American breakfast. AE, MC, V.

If you don't mind a little noise, this place offers simple accommodations at sensible prices. Although this is not the perfect place for peace and quiet, the hotel is located in the heart of Ocho Rios, offering easy access to Turtle Beach, shopping, restaurants, evening entertainment, and a variety of other activities. This hotel is in the Little Pub Complex containing a small nightclub, slot machines, and a restaurant that offers indoor and outdoor dining. The Little Pub Inn pays a small fee to keep a small parcel of the Ocho Rios Beach (which is just below the inn). However, we recommend making the 5-minute walk to Turtle Beach, where the sand is a little nicer.

The air-conditioned rooms have a tropical decor; some contain small lofts that can be reached by ladder for extra bed space. The restaurant serves international cuisine and a few local specialties. Hotel guests receive a VIP card good for a 15% discount at the restaurant and nightclub.

Parkway Inn. Main St., Ocho Rios, St. Ann, Jamaica, W.I. ☎ **876/974-2667.** 21 units. A/C. Year-round U.S.$60–$67 double. AE, MC, V.

Its setting in the commercial heart of Ocho Rios appeals to any budget traveler who wants easy access to the town's inexpensive restaurants, shops, and bars. Built in the early 1990s, the hotel sports a bar on its third floor where patrons can enjoy a grand view over the lights of Ocho Rios. Although there aren't any resort-style facilities on site, guests are invited to use the pool, tennis courts, and water-sports facilities at the Jamaica Grand Hotel, next door. The closest beach is a 10-minute walk away. There's a Chinese/Jamaican restaurant on the premises serving simple meals. This hotel attracts a strong repeat business of business travelers hailing from other regions of Jamaica.

Pineapple Hotel. Pineapple Place (P.O. Box 263), Ocho Rios, St. Ann, Jamaica, W.I. ☎ **876/974-2727.** Fax 876/974-1706. 20 units. A/C. Year-round U.S.$60 double; U.S.$85 triple. Children 11 and under stay free in parents' rm. AE, MC, V.

Next door to the Pineapple Place Shopping Centre, this hotel offers basic accommodations at bargain prices. Expect no frills here. The tropically decorated quarters include private baths, tile floors, and air-conditioning, but if you want to make a phone call, you must do it from the front desk. TVs are available in some accommodations. The Pineapple Pizza Pub is on the property, serving a combination of cuisines that include Italian, American, and Jamaican influences. Water sports can be arranged at the front desk, and there's a swimming pool on the premises. For a seaside romp, try Turtle Beach, a short walk away.

Tamarind Tree Hotel. P.O. Box 235, Runaway Bay, St. Ann, Jamaica, W.I. ☎ **876/973-4819.** Fax 876/973-5013. 16 units, 3 3-bedroom cottages with kitchenettes. A/C TV TEL. Winter U.S.$73–$90 double; off-season U.S.$62–$85 double. Year-round U.S.$188 cottage for up to 4. MC, V.

This small family-style hotel was named after a lavishly blossoming tamarind tree (which has since been cut down) that grew near its entrance. Stucco, red-roofed buildings with awnings and pastel-trimmed balconies house cream-colored and carpeted bedrooms. There's a pool terrace and the nearest beach (Cardiff Hall) is within a 5-minute walk. Although the occupants of the cottages usually cook their own meals in their lodgings, there's a simple restaurant (The Bird Wing), which serves three meals a day, and a disco (The Stinger) whose drinks and recorded music create some fun at this otherwise quiet, out-of-the-way hotel. The more appealing bedrooms are on the second floor, partly because they catch more cooling breezes.

Turtle Beach Towers. Main St. (P.O. Box 73), Ocho Rios, St. Ann, Jamaica, W.I. ☎ **876/974-2801.** 116 apts. A/C TEL. Winter U.S.$110–$125 studio; U.S.$126–$155 1-bedroom apt; U.S.$198–$212 2-bedroom apt. Off-season U.S.$86–$94 studio; U.S.$106–$112 1-bedroom apt; U.S.$132–$152 2-bedroom apt. Children 11 and under stay free in parents' apt (no children allowed in studios). AE, MC, V.

Located in a commercial district opposite the cruise-ship pier, these accommodations are housed in four high-rise towers offering apartment living with the added bonus of daily maid service. These air-conditioned lodgings contain fully equipped kitchenettes. The property has a swimming pool and tennis courts lit for night play, in addition to the beach. Water sports can also be arranged. Also on the premises is a restaurant serving both Jamaican and international specialties for breakfast, lunch, and dinner. On Tuesday evening, there's a manager's complimentary rum-punch party.

Nearby Places to Stay

Blue Harbour. On the North Coast road (A4) 80 miles west of Montego Bay and 60 miles north of Kingston (P.O. Box 50), Port Maria, St. Mary's, Jamaica, W.I. ☎ **876/994-0289,** or 505/586-1244 in Questa, New Mexico. Fax 876/586-1087. 3 villas. U.S.$170 double, or U.S.$4,000 weekly in winter; U.S.$3,000 weekly in summer for entire complex (all-inclusive). No credit cards.

This retreat was once owned by Sir Noël Coward, who entertained the rich and famous of his day here. Coward dubbed Blue Harbour, his first Jamaica retreat, "Coward's Folly." Eventually the place became so popular that Coward built Firefly, a "retreat from his retreat," and stopped staying at Blue Harbour (see the box called "Noël's Folly," later in this chapter).

Today, the compound is rented in whole or part to paying guests. The compound can accommodate 10 to a dozen guests comfortably, although the actual bed count is 18. The main house is the Villa Grande, with two bedrooms and two baths, along with a kitchen, dining room, and terrace. Villa Rose, a guest house, contains two large bedrooms, and the smaller Villa Chica is a one-bedroom, one-bath cottage once favored by Marlene Dietrich. Meals, both Jamaican and international, are cooked by a friendly, helpful staff who run the place and see to the needs of guests, some of whom book in here like a house party, renting the entire compound. At other times, individual units are rented separately.

Jamel Jamaica Hotel. 2 Richmond Estate, Priory P.A., St. Ann, Jamaica, W.I. ☎ **876/ 972-1031.** Fax 876/972-0714. 24 units. A/C TV TEL. Year-round U.S.$80 double, U.S.$105 triple, U.S.$105 suite for 2, U.S.$125 suite for 3, U.S.$145 master suite, double or triple. AE, DISC, MC, V.

Some 7 miles west of Ocho Rios, this property lies on a windswept stretch of coastline. From Ocho Rios, take the N. Coastal Highway until you see signs for the hotel, which will be on the right. Despite the hotel's isolated locale, its designers managed to infuse the grounds with some degree of drama, using hundreds of gallons of white paint, erecting urn-shaped balustrades separating pool terraces from the wild waterfront nearby, and landscaping with flowering shrubs and trees.

Each accommodation features a balcony with a sea view, lots of pastel colors, and floral fabrics. Although there's a restaurant and bar on the premises, many guests cook in their own kitchens or kitchenettes. (Cooking areas in the suites are larger and a bit better equipped than those in the conventional rooms.) The entertainment provided includes disco evenings and calypso parties with live musicians. Overall, the place is well managed and might be a good bet for families or couples.

Shaw Park Beach Hotel. Cutlass Bay, P.O Box 17, Ocho Rios, St. Ann, Jamaica, W.I. ☎ **800/377-1126** or 876/974-5042. 130 units. All-inclusive rates for 3-day package: winter U.S.\$406 per person double, U.S.\$517 per person for 4 in a 2-bedroom suite; off-season U.S.\$339 per person double, U.S.\$419 per person for 4 in a 2-bedroom suite. Daily rates including breakfast only: winter U.S.\$182–\$200 double, U.S.\$453 2-bedroom suite; off-season U.S.\$144–\$163 double, U.S.\$376 2-bedroom suite. Half-board U.S.\$33 extra per person per day. AE, DC, MC, V.

Set about 1½ miles east of the congested town center, near the edge of the White River, within a garden studded with almond and palm trees, this is one of the oldest hotels in the area, though it's well maintained. Divided into a pair of pink-walled, cement-sided, two-story buildings adjacent to the beach, it evokes something of the early 1960s in its design. The staff is usually helpful, and many visitors overlook its shortcomings because of its (relatively) low costs. Most guests book the all-inclusive plans, wherein all drinks, meals, entertainment, and most water sports are included in one net price. But if you're interested in hopping off to other nightspots in Ocho Rios, you might prefer the B&B rate, which is also quoted above. On the premises is an oval-shaped swimming pool, a bar and restaurant, a tennis court, and a sandy beachfront. All rooms have views overlooking the sea.

ALL-INCLUSIVE RESORTS

✪ **Ciboney Ocho Rios.** Main St. (P.O. Box 728), Ocho Rios, St. Ann, Jamaica, W.I. ☎ **800/333-3333** in the U.S. and Canada, or 876/974-1027. Fax 876/974-7148. 254 units. A/C MINIBAR TV TEL. Winter U.S.\$424–\$440 double; U.S.\$480 junior villa suite; U.S.\$580 1-bedroom villa suite; U.S.\$1,104 honeymoon villa; U.S.\$800 2-bedroom villa for 4. Off-season U.S.\$400–\$420 double; U.S.\$460 junior suite; U.S.\$540 1-bedroom villa suite; U.S.\$1,106 honeymoon villa; U.S.\$760 2-bedroom villa for 4. Rates are per couple for all-inclusive 3-night package. AE, DC, MC, V. No children under 15.

This all-inclusive Radisson Hotel franchise lies a 1½-mile drive southeast of town. It's set on 45 acres of a private estate dotted with red-tile villas. A Great House in the hills overlooks the Caribbean. Across from the imposing gate near the entrance to the resort are the white sands of a private beach.

All but a handful of the accommodations are in one-, two-, or three-bedroom villas, each of which offers a pool, fully equipped kitchen, and shaded terrace. Honeymoon villas have their own whirlpools. Thirty-six of the accommodations are traditional single or double rooms on the third floor of the Great House. Regardless of their location, the airy accommodations have high ceilings and are decorated in Caribbean colors. Throughout the property, a series of stone retaining walls frames the sloping grounds, which include carefully landscaped beds of flowering trees and vines.

Dining/Diversions: The Manor Restaurant & Bar offers both indoor and outdoor patio dining for dinner and entertainment, with classic Jamaican food. The Marketplace Restaurant has a contemporary menu of both American and Jamaican foods, and Alfresco Casa Nina, in a seaside setting, highlights Italian cuisine. Orchids is a restaurant developed in collaboration with the Culinary Institute of America, with a menu based on haute cuisine, as well as healthy food. Late-night entertainment and dancing are featured at Nicole.

Amenities: European-style beauty spa with its own health-and-fitness center (guests receive complimentary manicure and pedicure, and a choice of 25-minute massages is available—one massage is complimentary), six tennis courts (lit for night play), beach club offering an array of water sports, two main swimming pools with swim-up bars (plus 90 other semiprivate swimming pools on the grounds), 20 Jacuzzis; golf nearby.

Club Jamaica Beach Resort. P.O. Box 343, Turtle Beach, Ocho Rios, Jamaica, W.I. ☎ **800/818-2964** or 876/974-6632. Fax 876/974-6644. 95 units. TEL. Winter U.S.$290 double; off-season U.S.$240 double. Rates are all-inclusive. AE, DC, MC, V.

The newest resort in Ocho Rios, and one of its least expensive all-inclusives, results from the 1993 takeover of what was originally built in the mid-1980s as the Inn on the Beach. It lies near the geographical heart of Ocho Rios, adjacent to its crafts market, and it's easy to see more of local life here than in many of the island's more secluded resorts. The setting is a compound of cement-sided, completely unpretentious motel-style bedrooms adjacent to Turtle Beach.

Don't expect a particularly pulled-together staff, as the ambience here is very laid-back, and at least from the outside, not overwhelmingly organized. Bedrooms are accessorized with white tiles, contemporary furniture, and bright colors.

Dining/Diversions: There's lots of emphasis on local color and live music that emanates, beginning at the cocktail hour, from the compound out into the surrounding neighborhood. The resort has three bars and a restaurant, serving local/international cuisine. The food is nothing special, but perfectly fine if you stick to basics. Breakfast and lunch are always served buffet-style. Dinner is all a buffet, except for Tuesday and Sunday nights when there is an à la carte menu. From 2:30 to 5pm, you may also get hamburgers, hot dogs, and other American-style snacks and sandwiches at the snack bar.

Amenities: Swimming pool, glass-bottom boat, snorkeling equipment that's dispensed from a kiosk on the sands of the public beach.

Couples Ocho Rios. Tower Isle, along Rte. A3 (P.O. Box 330), Ocho Rios, Jamaica, W.I. ☎ **800/268-7537** in the U.S., or 876/975-4271. Fax 876/975-4439. 213 units. A/C TEL. Winter U.S.$1,350–$1,980 per couple; off-season U.S.$1,230–$1,770 per couple. Rates are all-inclusive for 3 nights. AE, MC, V. No children under 17.

Don't come here alone—you won't get in! The management defines couples as "any *man and woman* in love," and this is a couples-only resort. Most visiting couples are married, and many are on their honeymoon. Everything is in pairs, even the chairs by the beach. Some couples slip away from the resort, which is an 18-minute drive (5 miles) east of town, to Couples' private island to bask in the buff. In general, this is a classier operation than the more mass-market Sandals branches in Dunn's River and Ocho Rios.

The bedrooms have either a king-size bed or two doubles and pleasantly traditional furnishings. Each has a patio, fronting either the sea or the mountains. The hotel usually accepts bookings for a minimum of any 3 nights of the week, but most guests book in here on weekly terms. A 4-day stay is sometimes required at certain peak periods, such as over the Christmas holidays.

Dining/Diversions: You get three meals a day, including all the wine you want; breakfast is bountiful. Dinners are five courses, and afterward there's dancing on the terrace every evening, with entertainment. Guests have a choice of six restaurants, including the most recent one to open, Calabash Café, featuring a refined Jamaican cuisine.

Amenities: Five tennis courts (three lit at night), Nautilus gym, scuba diving, snorkeling, windsurfing, sailing, waterskiing, room service (breakfast only), laundry.

✪ **The Enchanted Garden.** Eden Bower Rd. (P.O. Box 284), Ocho Rios, Jamaica, W.I. ☎ **800/847-2535** in the U.S. and Canada, or 876/974-1400. Fax 876/974-5823. 113 units. A/C TV TEL. Winter U.S.$330–$370 double; from U.S.$440 suite for 2. Off-season U.S.$270–$310 double; from U.S.$370 suite for 2. Rates are all-inclusive. AE, DC, MC, V.

This most verdant of Jamaican resorts sits on a secluded hilltop high above the commercial center of town. Owned and developed by Edward Seaga, former Jamaican prime minister, the land includes 20 acres of rare botanical specimens and nature trails. The resort's lobby is housed in a pink tower accented with white gingerbread; the interior sports marble floors, big windows, and enormous potted palms. Bisected by the Turtle River, whose 14 cascading waterfalls are highlighted with garden paths and spotlights, the place is of particular interest to botanists and bird-watchers, though it's also hosted the occasional visiting celeb, such as Mick Jagger.

The bedrooms have sturdy rattan furniture and are contained in eight different low-rise buildings set amid the resort's carefully conceived landscaping. Each has a private patio or balcony, and some contain kitchens.

Dining/Diversions: The resort's restaurants serve continental food, plus Thai, Japanese, Indonesian, and regional Chinese cuisines. A Pasta Bar is designed like a tree house amid a tropical forest. Guests may also dine at the Seaquarium, offering a cold buffet in a setting surrounded by tropical fish. A Beach Club is a minivan ride from the hotel. Annabella's nightclub provides a variety of after-dinner entertainment amid a decor like something out of the *Arabian Nights.*

Amenities: Spa, beauty salon, swimming pool, two lighted tennis courts, walk-in aviary featuring hundreds of exotic birds (feeding time is every afternoon around 4pm), fitness center, daily transportation to the Beach Club, shuttle for shopping. There's also a Seaquarium with 15 aquariums for marine-life exotica.

✪ **Goldeneye.** Oracabessa, St. Mary's, Jamaica, W.I. ☎ **800/688-7678** or 876/974-3354. Fax 876/975-3679. 11 bungalows and villas. Winter U.S.$650 bungalow for 2, U.S.$1,000 1-bedroom villa for 2, U.S.$1,650 2-bedroom villa for up to 4; U.S.$2,000 3-bedroom villa for up to 6; U.S.$5,000 Ian Fleming's 3-bedroom original house for up to 8. Discounts of up to 20% in off-season. Rates are all-inclusive. AE, MC, V.

It was here that the most famous secret agent in the world, James Bond (007) was created in 1952 by then-owner Ian Fleming. Fleming built the imposing but simple house in 1946, and within its solid masonry walls wrote each of the 13 original James Bond books. During its heyday, Noël Coward was a frequent guest, along with Graham Greene, Truman Capote, and Evelyn Waugh. In the early 1990s, music impresario Chris Blackwell bought and restored the by-then dilapidated property to its original, somewhat spartan-looking dignity, retaining the large bronze pineapples on its entrance gates. Fleming's original desk remains, and the overall decorative theme of oversized Indonesian furniture is enhanced, Hollywood-style, with memorabilia from what later became the most famous spy movies in the world.

Unless you opt to rent the main house, which the occasional wealthy mogul does for a private beach holiday, you'll have to settle for any of the relatively simple bungalows set adjacent to the beach. With appealing but undistinguished furniture, they're cozy, comfortable, idiosyncratic, and rather glamorous. The layout of the place lends itself well to booking a cluster of units for a group of friends or family members vacationing together.

There's no swimming pool on the premises, but considering the splendors of the nearby beach, no one seems to mind. The nearest town, Oracabessa, doesn't have all the tourist amenities that abound in nearby Ocho Rios, but that fact adds considerably to its somewhat seedy charm.

✪ **Grand Lido Sans Souci.** On Rte. A3 (P.O. Box 103), Ocho Rios, Jamaica, W.I. ☎ **800/859-7873** in the U.S., or 876/974-2353. Fax 876/974-2544. 111 units. A/C MINIBAR TV TEL. Winter U.S.$2,260 double; from U.S.$2,580 suite for 2; U.S.$3,660 penthouse for 2. Off-season U.S.$1,740–$1,760 double; U.S.$1,880–$1,980 suite for 2; U.S.$2,780–$2,900 penthouse for 2. Rates are all-inclusive for a 3-night package. AE, DC, MC, V.

This is one of the finest spas in the Caribbean and has fabulous sports facilities. If a cookie-cutter resort is the last thing you want in Jamaica, don your best resort wear and head for a classier joint: this one. Sans Souci is a pink cliff-side fantasy that recently completed a $7 million renovation, turning it into an all-inclusive Jamaica SuperClub. It's located 3 miles east of town on a forested plot of land whose rocky border abuts a good beach. A cliff-side elevator brings guests to an outdoor bar. A labyrinth of catwalks and bridges stretches over rocky chasms filled with surging water.

Each accommodation features a veranda or patio, copies of Chippendale furniture, plush upholstery, and subdued colonial elegance. Some contain Jacuzzis.

Dining/Diversions: The resort offers guests The Casanova restaurant (see "Where to Dine," below). In addition, there's the Ristorante Palazzina by the beach. The Balloon Bar tries to bring back some 1920s style, and there are also several terraces for drinks.

Amenities: Charlie's Spa grew out of the hotel's mineral springs, which have been frequented for their medicinal benefits since the 1700s (they were considered effective for treating certain skin disorders, arthritis, and rheumatism). The mineral bath is big enough for an elephant. The spa is one of the finest places in the Caribbean for a health-and-fitness vacation, offering treatments and massages. Sports lovers appreciate the hotel's three Laykold tennis courts (two lighted), the freshwater pool, and the nearby croquet lawn. Scuba diving, snorkeling, windsurfing, deep-sea fishing, and Sunfish and catamaran sailing are available at the beach. Guests can golf on an 18-hole course and watch polo matches while they take afternoon tea at the St. Ann Polo Club, Drax Hall. Also offered are 24-hour room service and laundry/valet service.

Jamaica Grande Renaissance Resort. Main St. (P.O. Box 100), Ocho Rios, St. Ann, Jamaica. ☎ **800/HOTELS-1** in the U.S. and Canada, or 876/974-2201. Fax 876/974-2162. 720 units. A/C TV TEL. Winter U.S.$450–$475 double; U.S.$680–$920 suite. Off-season U.S.$320–$340 double; U.S.$680 suite. Rates include meals, drinks, tax, and water sports. AE, DC, MC, V.

This is the largest hotel on Jamaica, a combination of two high-rise beachfront properties constructed in 1975 and 1976. In 1993, an elaborate cluster of waterfalls and swimming pools were inserted into what had been parking lots between the towers, and the entire complex was unified into a coherent whole. The place is pure theatrics and special effects, like a Hollywood production, but is short on true Jamaican style. It seems to be meant to overwhelm guests. Today, the end result boasts more beachfront than any other hotel in Ocho Rios and a comfortable array of public rooms (often filled with members of tour or conference groups). The standard bedrooms are tile-floored and furnished with Caribbean furniture; each opens onto a private balcony.

Dining/Diversions: The restaurants include the Dragon (Chinese) and L'Allegro (Italian), and the less formal Café Jamique and Mallard's Court (international). The newest restaurant is called Cool Runnings, named for the Disney movie about the first Jamaican bobsled team. There's also a beachfront grill and a total of eight bars scattered throughout the premises. The hotel operates the Jamaic'N Me Crazy Disco and a casino, with only slot machines. Every Thursday, the Jamaica Grande is transformed into a village for Jump Up Carnival, with Jamaican food, a live band, and shopping.

Amenities: Tennis courts lit for nighttime play, year-round children's program, a full range of water sports, daily activities program.

Sandals Dunn's River. Along Rte. A3 (P.O. Box 51), Ocho Rios, Jamaica, W.I. ☎ **800/ SANDALS** in the U.S. and Canada, or 876/972-1610. Fax 876/972-1611. 266 units. TV TEL. Winter U.S.$1,720–$1,340 double; U.S.$2,580–$3,880 suite for 2. Off-season U.S.$1,640–$2,010 double; U.S.$2,460–$2,680 suite for 2. Rates are all-inclusive for 4 days/ 3 nights (the minimum stay). AE, MC, V.

Having been through various incarnations as the Jamaica Hilton and Eden II, this luxury, all-inclusive resort has now found its latest identity as a member of Jamaican entrepreneur Butch Stewart's rapidly expanding Sandals empire. Located on a wide, sugary beach, this is the finest of the Sandals resorts, at least in the opinion of some guests who have sampled them all. Only male-female couples are allowed.

Set on the beachfront between Ocho Rios and St. Ann's Bay, the resort is very sports-oriented. It occupies 25 well-landscaped acres, offering attractively furnished and often quite spacious accommodations. All the rooms were reconstructed after the Sandals takeover and given an Italianate/Mediterranean motif. The guest rooms are scattered among the six-story main building, two lanai buildings, and a five-story west wing.

Dining/Diversions: Before retreating to the disco, guests choose among several dining options. The International Room is elegant, with fabric-covered walls and rosewood furniture. West Indian Windies serves Caribbean specialties. D'Amore offers Italian cuisine, and Restaurant Teppanyaki features Chinese, Polynesian, and Japanese dishes. There's also a beach bar and one of the most spectacular swim-up bars on Jamaica.

Amenities: Three Jacuzzis, two whirlpool baths, fitness center, jogging course, pitch-and-putt golf course, lagoon-shaped pool, transport to the Sandals Golf and Country Club. Tours to Dunn's River Falls, shuttles to Sandals Ocho Rios, and massages are all complimentary.

Sandals Ocho Rios Resort & Golf Club. Main St. (P.O. Box 771), Ocho Rios, Jamaica, W.I. ☎ **800/SANDALS** in the U.S. and Canada, or 876/974-5691. Fax 876/974-5700. 237 units. TV TEL. Winter U.S.$1,540–$2,160 double; off-season U.S.$1,460–$2,060 double. Rates are all-inclusive for 4 days/3 nights. AE, MC, V.

Another Jamaican addition to the ever-expanding couples-only empire of Gordon "Butch" Stewart, who pioneered similar properties in Montego Bay and Negril, Sandals Ocho Rios attracts a mix of coupled singles and married folk, including honeymooners. At times, the place seems like a summer camp for grown-ups (or others who didn't quite grow up). The resort uses the same formula: one price per male-female couple, including everything.

This is the most low-key of the Sandals resorts. Is it romantic? Most guests think so, although we've encountered other couples here whose relationship didn't survive the 3-night minimum stay.

On 13 well-landscaped acres a mile west of the town center, it offers comfortably furnished but uninspired rooms with either ocean or garden views, and there are some cottage units, too. All rooms are reasonably large, with king-size beds and hair dryers.

Dining/Diversions: You can sip free drinks at an oceanside swim-up bar. Nightly theme parties and live entertainment take place in a modern amphitheater. A unique feature of the resort is an open-air disco. The resort's main dining room is St. Anne's, whereas Michelle's serves Italian food, and the Reef Terrace Grill does gourmet Jamaican cuisine and fresh seafood. If you want more man-sized grub and drinks, head for a new addition, the Arizona Steak House.

Amenities: Three freshwater pools, private artificial beach, sporting equipment and instruction (including waterskiing, windsurfing, sailing, snorkeling, and scuba diving), paddleboats, kayaks, glass-bottom boat, Jacuzzi, saunas, fully equipped fitness center, two tennis courts, tours to Dunn's River Falls, massages, laundry.

WHERE TO DINE

Since nearly all the major hotels in Ocho Rios have gone all-inclusive, smaller independent restaurants are being smothered. There are some, however, struggling to survive.

VERY EXPENSIVE

The Casanova. In the Grand Lido Sans Souci, along Rte. A3, 3 miles east of Ocho Rios. ☎ **876/974-2353.** Reservations required except Tues and Fri. Nonresident evening pass of U.S.$75 per person includes dinner (Tues and Fri a beach buffet), entertainment, and drinks. AE, DC, MC, V. Daily 6:30–9:30pm. INTERNATIONAL.

The suave Casanova is one of the most elegant enclaves along the North Coast, a super choice when you feel like dressing up and hitting the high spots. Meals are included for guests of the hotel, of course, but nonguests who purchase a pass can also dine here and be entertained as well. All drinks are included. Jazz wafting in from a lattice-roofed gazebo might accompany your meal.

In the late 1960s, Harry Cipriani (of Harry's Bar fame in Venice) taught the staff some of his culinary techniques, and a little more care seems to go into the cuisine here, as opposed to the mass-market chow-downs at some of the other all-inclusives. Salads, vegetarian dishes, and soups are made fresh daily, along with many of the other staples. Typical dishes include smoked chicken breast in a continental berry sauce as an appetizer, or a small vegetable mousse with a fontina cheese sauce. For your main course, you might prefer osso buco (braised veal shanks) or roast Cornish hen with citrus and mild spice. Desserts are sumptuous and might be followed by one of the house's four special coffees.

EXPENSIVE

✪ **Plantation Inn Restaurant.** In the Plantation Inn, Main St. ☎ **876/974-5601.** Reservations required. Main courses U.S.$20–$35; 3-course fixed-price U.S.$35. AE, DC, MC, V. Daily 7:30–10am, 1–1:30pm, 4:30–5:30pm (afternoon tea), and 7–10pm. JAMAICAN/CONTINENTAL.

You'll think you've arrived at Tara in *Gone With the Wind*. An evening here offers one of the most romantic experiences in Ocho Rios as you dine and dance by candlelight. The continental cuisine is spiced up a bit by Jamaican specialties. You're seated at beautifully laid tables with crisp linen, and after the dinner plates are cleared, a band plays for dancing. It's definitely the pampered life. The restaurant is divided into the indoor part (The Dining Room) and an outdoor section (Bougainvillea Terrace), with an annex, the Peacock Pavilion, a few steps away. Here, afternoon tea is served daily.

Appetizers are always spicy and tangy, our favorite being "Fire & Spice," which is a chicken and beef kebab with a ginger-pimiento sauce. For the main course, we always ask the chef to prepare a whole roast fish from the catch of the day. The always perfectly cooked fish is served boneless and seasoned with island herbs and spices. It's slowly roasted in the oven and presented with fresh country vegetables. Since the place attracts a lot of meat eaters, the chefs always prepare the classics, lamb chops Provençale and the like. The fixed-price menu featured every evening is also a good value. Opt for the banana cream pie for dessert, if featured—it's creamy and tasty.

Ruins Restaurant, Gift Shop, and Boutique. Turtle River, DaCosta Dr. ☎ **876/ 974-2442.** Reservations recommended. Main courses U.S.$13–$37. AE, DC, MC, V. Mon–Sat noon–2:30pm; daily 6–9:30pm. CHINESE/INTERNATIONAL/JAMAICAN.

Here, you dine at the foot of waterfalls in the center of town. The falls are so inviting that they're a tourist attraction in their own right. In 1831, a British entre-preneur constructed a sugar mill on the site, using the powerful stream to drive his waterwheels. Today, all that remains is a jumble of ruins, hence the restaurant's name. After you cross a covered bridge, perhaps stopping off for a drink at the bar in the outbuilding first, you find yourself in a fairyland where the only sounds come from the tree frogs, the falling water from about a dozen cascades, and the discreet clink of silver and china. Tables are set on a wooden deck leading all the way up to the pool at the foot of the falls, where moss and other vegetation line the stones at the base. At some point you may want to climb a flight of stairs to the top of the falls, where bobbing lanterns and the illuminated waters below afford one of the most delightful experiences on the island.

The only problem is that the setting is more dramatic than the cuisine. It's more Chinese-American than authentic regional Chinese—witness the several kinds of chow mein or chop suey and the sweet-and-sour pork. Lobster in a stir-fry is the house specialty. Dishes such as chicken Kiev try to justify the restaurant's "inter-national" label, but we wouldn't recommend it. Your best bet is to stick with the vegetarian dishes, which aren't bad.

MODERATE

✪ **Almond Tree Restaurant.** In the Hibiscus Lodge Hotel, 87 Main St. ☎ **876/ 974-2813.** Reservations recommended. Main courses U.S.$15.50–$37. AE, DC, MC, V. Daily 7am–2:30pm and 6–9:30pm. INTERNATIONAL.

The food, drink, reasonable prices, and casual cool keep them coming back night after night. Aptly, the Almond Tree is a two-tiered patio restaurant with a tree growing through its roof. It overlooks the Caribbean at the previously recommended resort (3 blocks from the Ocho Rios Mall). Lobster thermidor is the most delectable item on the menu and lobster Almond Tree is a specialty, but we prefer the bouillabaisse (made with conch and lobster). Also excellent are the roast suckling pig, medallions of beef Anne Palmer, and a fondue bourguignonne. Jamaican plantation rice is a local specialty. The wine list offers a variety of vintages, including Spanish and Jamaican. Have an apéritif in the unique "swinging bar" (with swinging chairs, that is).

✪ **Evita's Italian Restaurant.** Eden Bower Rd. (a few steps from the Enchanted Garden resort). ☎ **876/974-2333.** Reservations recommended. Main courses U.S.$7–$24. AE, MC, V. Daily 11am–11pm. ITALIAN.

Located a 5-minute drive south of Ocho Rios, this restaurant in a white, ginger-bread-trimmed house is set in a hillside residential neighborhood with a panoramic view of the city's harbor. The premier Italian restaurant of Ocho Rios, this is also one of the most fun restaurants along the North Coast of Jamaica. Its soul and artistic flair come from Eva Myers, the convivial former owner of some of the most legendary bars of Montego Bay. An outdoor terrace offers additional seating and enhanced views. Even if the cuisine isn't as extraordinary as Evita claims, it's still pretty good. More than half the menu is devoted to pastas, and the selection includes almost every variety known in northern and southern Italy. The fish dishes are excellent, especially the snapper stuffed with crabmeat and the lobster and scampi in a buttery white cream sauce. Italian (or other) wines by the bottle might accompany your menu choice.

Little Pub Restaurant. 59 Main St. ☎ **876/974-2324.** Reservations recommended. Main courses U.S.$13.50–$28.50. AE, MC, V. Daily 7am–1am. JAMAICAN/INTERNATIONAL/ITALIAN.

It's a little too touristy for our tastes, but yet has undeniable appeal both for visitors and locals. Located in a redbrick courtyard with a fountain and a waterfall, this spot is surrounded by souvenir shops in the center of town. The indoor-outdoor pub's centerpiece is a restaurant in the dinner-theater style. Top local and international artists are featured, as are Jamaican musical plays. No one will mind if you just enjoy a drink while seated on one of the pub's barrel chairs. But if you want dinner, proceed to one of the linen-covered tables topped with fresh-cut flowers and candles. Menu items include very familiar fare, and that means grilled kingfish, stewed snapper, barbecued chicken, and the inevitable and overpriced lobster. The cookery is competent, but it's all very casual here. Come for the convivial atmosphere rather than for the food.

INEXPENSIVE

Double V Jerk Centre. 109 Main St. ☎ **876/974-5998.** Jerk pork or chicken J$360–J$460 ($10.25–$13.10) per pound. AE, MC, V. Mon–Sat 8:30am–1:30am. JERK/JAMAICAN.

When the moon is full and only the fiery taste of Jamaican jerk seasonings can ease your stomach growls, head here, and don't dress up. Set on Ocho Rios' main commercial boulevard, about a 3-minute drive east of the town center, this place serves up the best jerked pork and chicken in town. Don't expect anything fancy. Just come for platters of meat that can be sold in quarter-pound or half-pound portions, depending on your appetite. Vegetables, salad, and fried breadfruit come with your main course, and everyone's preferred lubricant seems to be a frosty Red Stripe. Although lots of local office workers and shopkeepers come here at lunch, the place is especially lively after 10pm, when live music transforms it into the closest approximation of a singles bar in town.

Parkway Restaurant. 60 DaCosta Dr. ☎ **876/974-2667.** Main courses U.S.$8–$20. AE, MC, V. Daily 8am–11:30pm. JAMAICAN.

Come here to eat as Jamaicans eat. This popular spot in the commercial center of town couldn't be plainer or more unpretentious, but it's always packed. Local families and businessmen know they can get some of Ocho Rios's best-tasting and least expensive regional dishes here. It's a drinking joint and is a bit disdainful of all those Sandals and Couples resorts with their contrived international food. Hungry diners are fed Jamaican-style chicken, curried goat, sirloin steak, and fillet of red snapper, and to top it off, banana cream pie. Lobster and fresh fish are usually featured. The food is straightforward, honest, and affordable. The restaurant recently renovated its third floor to offer entertainment and dancing. Tuesday night is the highlight, with local bands showing up for Reggae Night.

BEACHES, GOLF, FISHING & TENNIS

BEACHES   In Ocho Rios, waters are clear and visibility good, and the North Coast teems with marine life. Most visitors to Ocho Rios head straight for a beach.

The most visited is the often overcrowded **Mallards Beach,** shared by hotel guests and cruise-ship passengers. Locals may also steer you to **Turtle Beach** in the south. The best place for snorkeling is the **Resort Divers Shop** (☎ 876/974-6632) at the Club Jamaica Resort. Regardless of whether or not you are a guest here, these guys will be happy to take you snorkeling. Unfortunately, the best spot requires a short boat trip that will transport you just 200 yards away from the shore, where the depth is between 8 and 10 feet. The boat leaves every day at 1pm for Paradise Reef where the tropical fish are truly in abundance.

DEEP-SEA FISHING   The **Grand Lido Sans Souci** (☎ 876/974-2353) offers deep-sea fishing for U.S.$430 for a half day for one to six people. See "All-Inclusive Resorts," above. The trip lasts 3 hours, and lunch, sodas, and bottled water are provided as well as fishing equipment. Your captain will take you out to fish mainly for tuna, bonita, or marlin.

GOLF   **Sandals Golf & Country Club** (☎ 876/975-0119), lying a 10-minute ride from the center of the resort, is a 6,500-yard course, known for its panoramic scenery some 700 feet above sea level. The 18-hole, par-71 course was designed by P. K. Saunders and opened in 1951 as the Upton Golf Club. Rolling terrain, lush vegetation, and flowers and fruit trees dominate the 120-acre course. A putting green and driving range are available for those who wish to hone their skills before challenging the course. Sandals guests play free; otherwise, the cost is U.S.$50 for 9 holes or U.S.$70 for 18 holes. To reach the course from the center of Ocho Rios, travel along the main bypass for 2 miles until you reach Mile End Road. A Texaco gas station is located at the corner of Mile End Road. Turn right and drive for 5 miles until you come to the Sandals golf course on the right.

TENNIS   **Ciboney Ocho Rios,** Main Street, Ocho Rios (☎ 876/974-1027), focuses more on tennis than any other resort in the area. It offers three clay-surface and three hard-surface courts, all lit for nighttime play. Residents play free either day or night, but nonresidents must call and make arrangements with the manager. An on-site pro offers lessons for U.S.$15 an hour. Ciboney also sponsors twice-a-day clinics for both beginners and advanced players. Frequent guest tournaments are also staged, including handicapped doubles and mixed doubles.

SEEING THE SIGHTS

A scenic drive south of Ocho Rios along Route A3 will take you inland through **Fern Gully.** This was originally a riverbed, but now the main road winds up some 700 feet among a profusion of wild ferns, a tall rain forest, hardwood trees, and lianas. There are hundreds of varieties of ferns, and roadside stands offer fruit and vegetables, carved-wood souvenirs, and basketwork. The road runs for about 4 miles, and then at the top of the hill you come to a right-hand turn onto a narrow road leading to Golden Grove, a small Jamaican community with a bauxite mine. It is of no touristic interest.

Head west when you see the signs pointing to Lydford, lying southwest of Ocho Rios. To reach the community, take A3 (also called Fern Gully Road) south from the center of Ocho Rios. When you come to a small intersection directly north of Walkers Wood, follow the signpost west to Lydford. You'll pass the remains of **Edinburgh Castle,** built in 1763, the lair of one of Jamaica's most infamous murderers, a Scot named Lewis Hutchinson, who used to shoot passersby and toss their bodies into a deep pit. The authorities got wind of his activities, and although he tried to escape by canoe, he was captured by the navy under the command of Admiral Rodney and was hanged. Rather proud of his achievements (evidence of at

Noël's Folly

Arriving in Jamaica in 1944, the gay English playwright, songwriter, raconteur, and actor Noël Coward discovered his dream island.

He returned in 1948 and rented Goldeneye from his friend Ian Fleming, the real-life spy who later created the James Bond character at this estate. During this stopover, Coward found a magical spot 10 miles down the coast at St. Mary's. The land was once owned by Sir Henry Morgan, the notorious buccaneer who had built a small fortress on the property so he could spy on any stray galleon entering local waters. It was here that Coward began construction on what he called his "folly"—Blue Harbour, which can be rented today (see "Nearby Places to Stay," earlier in this section).

Once settled in, Coward sent out invitations to his "bloody loved ones." They included Laurence Olivier, Vivien Leigh, Alfred Lunt, Lynn Fontane, Errol Flynn, Katharine Hepburn, Mary Martin, Claudette Colbert, and John Gielgud, among others. Some stayed an entire month.

Blue Harbour became so popular on the North Coast cocktail circuit that in 1956 Coward fled it and built Firefly on a panoramic nearby hilltop. It still stands today much as he left it. Coward lived at Firefly with his longtime companion, Graham Payn.

In 1965, the Queen Mother came to visit Coward, who prepared a lobster mousse for her only to have it melt in the hot sun. He quickly rushed to the kitchen and opened a can of split-pea soup. She found it "divine"—perhaps because Coward had hastily laced it with sherry.

Sir Winston Churchill, who also loved Jamaica, visited Coward several times at Firefly. He told the playwright: "An Englishman has an inalienable right to live wherever he chooses."

Coward died at Firefly and is buried on the grounds. You can still see his plain, flat white marble gravestone, which is inscribed simply: "Sir Noël Coward, born December 16, 1899, died March 26, 1973."

least 43 murders was found), he left £100 and instructions for a memorial to be built. It never was, but the castle ruins remain.

Continue north on Route A1 to **St. Ann's Bay,** the site of the first Spanish settlement on the island, where you can see the **statue of Christopher Columbus,** cast in his hometown of Genoa and erected near St. Ann's Hospital on the west side of town, close to the coast road. There are a number of Georgian buildings in the town—the **Court House** near the parish church, built in 1866, is the most interesting.

EAST OF OCHO RIOS

Brimmer Hall Estate. Port Maria, St. Mary's. ☎ **876/974-2244.** Tours U.S.$15. Tours given Thurs at 2pm.

Some 21 miles east of Ocho Rios, in the hills 2 miles from Port Maria, this 1817 estate is an ideal place to spend a day. You can relax beside the pool and sample a wide variety of brews and concoctions. The Plantation Tour Eating House offers typical Jamaican dishes for lunch, and there's a souvenir shop with a good selection of ceramics, art, straw goods, wood carvings, rums, liqueurs, and cigars. All this is on a working plantation where you're driven around in a tractor-drawn jitney to see the tropical fruit trees and coffee plants and learn from the

AT&T

AT&T Direct℠ Service

Steps to follow for easy calling worldwide:

1. Just dial the AT&T Access Number for the country you are calling from.
2. Dial the phone number you're calling.
3. Dial your card number.

AT&T Access Numbers

Anguilla ✦	1-800-872-2881	Brit. Vir. Isl ✦	1-800-872-2881
Antigua ✦	1-800-872-2881	Canada	1 800 CALL ATT
Argentina	0-800-54-288	Cayman Isl ✦	1-800-872-2881
Aruba	800-8000	Chile	800-800-311
Bahamas	1-800-872-2881	Colombia	980-11-0010
Barbados ✦	1-800-872-2881	Costa Rica	0-800-0-114-114
Belize ▲	811	Dominica ✦	1-800-872-2881
Belize †	555	Dom. Rep. ★ □	1-800-872-2881
Bermuda ✦	1-800-872-2881	Ecuador ▲	999-119
Bolivia ●	0-800-1112	El Salvador○	800-1785
Brazil	000-8010	Grenada ✦	1-800-872-2881

AT&T

AT&T Direct℠ Service

Steps to follow for easy calling worldwide:

1. Just dial the AT&T Access Number for the country you are calling from.
2. Dial the phone number you're calling.
3. Dial your card number.

AT&T Access Numbers

Anguilla ✦	1-800-872-2881	Brit. Vir. Isl ✦	1-800-872-2881
Antigua ✦	1-800-872-2881	Canada	1 800 CALL ATT
Argentina	0-800-54-288	Cayman Isl ✦	1-800-872-2881
Aruba	800-8000	Chile	800-800-311
Bahamas	1-800-872-2881	Colombia	980-11-0010
Barbados ✦	1-800-872-2881	Costa Rica	0-800-0-114-114
Belize ▲	811	Dominica ✦	1-800-872-2881
Belize †	555	Dom. Rep. ★ □	1-800-872-2881
Bermuda ✦	1-800-872-2881	Ecuador ▲	999-119
Bolivia ●	0-800-1112	El Salvador○	800-1785
Brazil	000-8010	Grenada ✦	1-800-872-2881

AT&T Access Numbers

Guatemala ○×	99-99-190		Paraguay ▲2	008-11-800
Guyana*	165		Peru ▲	0-800-50000
Haiti	183		Puerto Rico	1 800 CALL ATT
Honduras	800-0-123		St. Kitts/Nevis+	1-800-872-2881
Jamaica □	872		St. Vincent △	1-800-872-2881
Mexico ✓1	01-800-288-2872		Suriname △	156
Montserrat	1-800-872-2881		Turks & Caicos △	01-800-872-2881
Neth. Ant. ⊙	001-800-872-2881		Uruguay	000-410
Nicaragua	174		U.S. Virgin Isl.	1 800 CALL ATT
Panama	109		Venezuela	800-11-120

For access numbers not listed ask any operator for **AT&T Direct**℠ Service.
In the U.S., call 1-800-331-1140 for a wallet card listing all worldwide AT&T Access Numbers.

Visit our Web site at: www.att.com/traveler
Bold-faced countries permit country-to-country calling outside the U.S.

+ Public phones and select hotels.
● Public phones require coin or card deposit.
◆ May not be available from every phone/public phone.
✓ Collect calling only.
✦ Available from hotels only.
× Available from select hotels.
○ From St. Maarten at Bobby's Marina, use 1-800-872-2881.
⊙ Public phones require local coin payment during call.
△ When calling from public phones, use phones marked "Ladatel."
▽ Available from public phones only.
□ Calling card calls available from select hotels.
1 If call does not complete, use 001-800-462-4240.
2 From Asunción only.

When placing an international call *from* the U.S.,
dial 1 800 CALL ATT.

© 5/98 AT&T

AT&T Access Numbers

Guatemala ○×	99-99-190		Paraguay ▲2	008-11-800
Guyana*	165		Peru ▲	0-800-50000
Haiti	183		Puerto Rico	1 800 CALL ATT
Honduras	800-0-123		St. Kitts/Nevis+	1-800-872-2881
Jamaica □	872		St. Vincent △	1-800-872-2881
Mexico ✓1	01-800-288-2872		Suriname △	156
Montserrat	1-800-872-2881		Turks & Caicos △	01-800-872-2881
Neth. Ant. ⊙	001-800-872-2881		Uruguay	000-410
Nicaragua	174		U.S. Virgin Isl.	1 800 CALL ATT
Panama	109		Venezuela	800-11-120

For access numbers not listed ask any operator for **AT&T Direct**℠ Service.
In the U.S., call 1-800-331-1140 for a wallet card listing all worldwide AT&T Access Numbers.

Visit our Web site at: www.att.com/traveler
Bold-faced countries permit country-to-country calling outside the U.S.

+ Public phones and select hotels.
● Public phones require coin or card deposit.
◆ May not be available from every phone/public phone.
✓ Collect calling only.
✦ Available from hotels only.
× Available from select hotels.
○ From St. Maarten at Bobby's Marina, use 1-800-872-2881.
⊙ Public phones require local coin payment during call.
△ When calling from public phones, use phones marked "Ladatel."
▽ Available from public phones only.
□ Calling card calls available from select hotels.
1 If call does not complete, use 001-800-462-4240.
2 From Asunción only.

When placing an international call *from* the U.S.,
dial 1 800 CALL ATT.

© 5/98 AT&T

(put on a happy face)

Going someplace festive? Bring along an **AT&T Direct**® Service wallet guide. It's a list of access numbers you need to call

home fast and clear from around the world, using an AT&T Calling Card or credit card. And that's something to smile about.

For a list of **AT&T Access Numbers,** take the attached wallet guide.

I t ' s   a l l   w i t h i n   y o u r   r e a c h .   **AT&T**

For
Travelers
who want more than
the Official Line

Macmillan Publishing USA

Also Available:

- The Unofficial Guide to Branson
- The Unofficial Guide to Chicago
- The Unofficial Guide to Cruises
- The Unofficial Disney Companion
- The Unofficial Guide to Disneyland
- The Unofficial Guide to the Great Smoky & Blue Ridge Mountains
- The Unofficial Guide to Miami & the Keys
- Mini-Mickey: The Pocket-Sized Unofficial Guide to Walt Disney World
- The Unofficial Guide to New York City
- The Unofficial Guide to San Francisco
- The Unofficial Guide to Skiing in the West
- The Unofficial Guide to Washington, D.C.

knowledgeable guides about the various processes necessary to produce the fine fruits of the island.

Coyaba River Garden and Museum. Shaw Park Rd. ☎ **876/974-6235.** Admission U.S.$4.50 ages 13 and up, free for children 12 and under. Daily 8:30am–5pm. Take the Fern Gully–Kingston road, turn left at St. John's Anglican Church, and follow the signs to Coyaba, just half a mile farther.

A mile from the center of Ocho Rios, at an elevation of 420 feet, this park and museum were built on the grounds of the former Shaw Park plantation. The word *coyaba* comes from the Arawak name for paradise. Coyaba is a Spanish-style museum with a river and gardens filled with native flora, a cut-stone courtyard, fountains, and a crafts shop and bar. The museum boasts a collection of artifacts from the Arawak, Spanish, and English settlements in the area.

Firefly. Grants Pen, in St. Mary, 20 miles east of Ocho Rios above Oracabessa. ☎ **876/997-7201.** Admission U.S.$10. Daily 8:30am–5:30pm.

Firefly was the home of Sir Noël Coward and his longtime companion, Graham Payn, who, as executor of Coward's estate, donated it to the Jamaica National Heritage Trust. The recently restored house is more or less as it was on the day Sir Noël died in 1973. His Hawaiian-print shirts still hang in the closet of his austere bedroom, with its mahogany four-poster. The library contains a collection of his books, and the living room is warm and comfortable, with big armchairs and two grand pianos (where he composed several famous tunes). Coward's guests were housed at Blue Harbour, a villa closer to Port Maria, and included Evelyn Waugh, Sir Winston Churchill, Errol Flynn, Laurence Olivier, Vivien Leigh, Claudette Colbert, Katharine Hepburn, and Mary Martin. Paintings by the noted playwright, actor, author, and composer adorn the walls. An open patio looks out over the pool and the sea, and across the lawn, on his plain, flat white marble gravestone is inscribed simply: "Sir Noël Coward, born December 16, 1899, died March 26, 1973."

Harmony Hall/The Garden Café. Tower Isles on Rte A3, 4 miles east of Ocho Rios. ☎ **876/975-4222.** Free admission. Gallery Mon–Sat 10am–6pm, restaurant and café daily 10am–10pm.

Harmony Hall was built near the end of the 19th century as the centerpiece of a sugar plantation. Today, it has been restored and is now the focal point of an art gallery and restaurant that showcases the painting and sculpture of Jamaican artists as well as a tasteful array of arts and crafts. Among the featured gift items are Sharon McConnell's Starfish Oils, which contain natural additives harvested in Jamaica. The gallery shop also carries the "Reggae to Wear" line of sportswear, designed and made on Jamaica.

The Garden Café, which is also known as Alexander's after its co-owner, serves Jamaican cuisine as part of full evening meals priced at J$550 to J$900 (U.S.$15.70 to U.S.$25.65). The food is full of flavor with an authentic taste that may not be to everybody's liking. If you prefer to stop just for a cup of tea and a slice of homemade cake, it will cost about J$100 (U.S.$2.85).

Prospect Plantation. On Rte. A3, 3 miles east of Ocho Rios, in St. Ann, Jamaica, W.I. ☎ **800/733-5077** or 876/994-1058. Fax 876/974-2468. Tours U.S.$12 adults, free for children 12 and under; 1-hour horseback ride U.S.$20. Tours given Mon–Sat at 10:30am, 2pm, and 3:30pm; Sun at 11am, 1:30pm, and 3pm.

This working plantation adjoins the 18-hole Prospect Mini Golf Course. A visit to this property is an educational, relaxing, and enjoyable experience. On your leisurely ride by covered jitney through the scenic beauty of Prospect, you'll readily see why this section of Jamaica is called "the garden parish of the island." You can view the many trees planted by such visitors as Sir Winston Churchill, Dr. Henry Kissinger, Charlie Chaplin, Pierre Trudeau, Sir Noël Coward, and many others. You'll learn about and observe pimento (allspice), bananas, cassava, sugarcane, coffee, cocoa, coconut, pineapple, and the famous leucaena "Tree of Life." You'll see Jamaica's first hydroelectric plant and sample some of the exotic fruit and drinks.

Horseback riding is available on three scenic trails at Prospect. The rides vary from 1 to 2¼ hours. Advance booking of 1 hour is necessary to reserve horses.

The plantation also rents five luxuriously furnished villas. Each villa, set on its own 1½ acre plot, has a private pool, sundeck, and sea access (the most expensive villa has its own private white sandy beach). All are air-conditioned with cable TV, phone, and private security guards. Villas are fully staffed with cook, housekeeper, butler, and gardener. Weekly rates in winter range from U.S.$3,000 for the cheapest villa up to U.S.$10,000 for the most expensive. In off-season, the weekly rates go from U.S.$2,000 to U.S.$8,000. A tennis court is located within walking distance of all villas. Guests can also enjoy the beaches, spas, and sporting facilities of Sans Souci Lido and Shaw Park Hotel for free. MasterCard and Visa are accepted.

WEST OF OCHO RIOS

✪ **Dunn's River Falls.** On Rte. A3. ☎ **876/974-2857.** Admission U.S.$6 adults, U.S.$3 children 2–12; free for children under 2. Daily 9am–5pm (8am–5pm on cruise-ship arrival days). From St. Ann's Bay, follow Rte. A3 east back to Ocho Rios and you'll pass Dunn's River Falls; there's plenty of parking.

For a charge, you can relax on the beach or climb with a guide to the top of the 600-foot falls. You can splash in the waters at the bottom of the falls or drop into the cool pools higher up between the cascades of water. The beach restaurant provides snacks and drinks, and dressing rooms are available. If you're planning to climb the falls, wear old tennis shoes to protect your feet from the sharp rocks and to prevent slipping.

SHOPPING

Prepare yourself for some aggressive selling when you venture into the shopping centers mentioned below. We don't recommend these centers; we mention them because they are there. Is shopping fun in Ocho Rios? A resounding no. Do cruise ship passengers indulge in it anyway? A decided yes.

Warning: Some so-called "duty-free" prices are actually lower than stateside prices, but then the government hits you with a 10% General Consumption Tax on all items purchased.

THE CENTERS & MALLS

There are seven main shopping plazas. We can't heartily recommend them because of all the hassles you'll encounter, but cruise-ship passengers usually go anyway, or maybe you'll have a rainy day to kill or just need something. The originals are Ocean Village, Pineapple Place, and Coconut Grove. Newer ones include the New Ocho Rios Plaza, in the center of town, with some 60 shops. Island Plaza is another major shopping complex, as is the Mutual Security Plaza with some 30 shops. Opposite the New Ocho Rios Plaza is the Taj Mahal, with 26 duty-free stores.

Ocean Village Shopping Centre (☎ 876/974-2683) contains numerous boutiques, food stores, a bank, sundries purveyors, travel agencies, service facilities, and what have you. The **Ocho Rios Pharmacy** (☎ 876/974-2398) sells most proprietary brands, perfumes, and suntan lotions, among its many wares.

Just east of Ocho Rios, the **Pineapple Place Shopping Centre** is a collection of shops in cedar-shingle-roofed cottages set amid tropical flowers.

Ocho Rios Craft Park is a complex of some 150 stalls through which to browse. An eager seller will weave you a hat or a basket while you wait, or you can buy from the mixture of ready-made hats, hampers, handbags, place mats, and lampshades. Other stands stock hand-embroidered goods and will make small items while you wait. Wood carvers work on bowls, ashtrays, wooden-head carvings, and statues chipped from lignum vitae, and make cups from local bamboo.

The **Coconut Grove Shopping Plaza** is a low-rise collection of shops linked by walkways and shrubs. The merchandise consists mainly of local craft items. Many of your fellow shoppers may be cruise-ship passengers.

Right in the heart of Ocho Rios, **Island Plaza** has some of the best Jamaican art, all paintings by local artists. You can also purchase local handmade crafts (be prepared to do some haggling over price and quality), carvings, ceramics, even kitchenware, and most definitely the inevitable T-shirts.

SPECIALTY SHOPS

In general, the shopping is better in Montego Bay if you're going there. If not, wander the Ocho Rios crafts markets, although much of the merchandise is the same old stuff. Among the places that deserve special mention, **Casa dé Oro,** Soni's Mall, 19 Soni's Plaza (☎ 876/974-5392), specializes in selling duty-free watches, fine jewelry, and the classic perfumes. **Swiss Stores,** in the Ocean Village Shopping Centre (☎ 876/974-2519), sells all the big names in Swiss watches, including Juvenia, Tissot, Omega, Rolex, Patek Philippe, and Piaget. And here the Rolex watches are real, not those fakes touted by hustlers on the streets of Ocho Rios. The Swiss outlet also sells duty-free handcrafted jewelry, some of dubious taste but some really exquisite jewelry as well.

If you'd like to avoid the hassle of the markets but still find some local handcrafts or art, head for **Beautiful Memories,** 9 Island Plaza (☎ 876/974-2374), which has a limited but representative sampling of Jamaican art, as well as an exhibit of local crafts, pottery, woodwork, and hand-embroidered items.

We generally ignore hotel gift shops, but the **Jamaica Inn Gift Shop** in the Jamaica Inn, Main Street (☎ 876/974-2514), is better than most, selling everything from Blue Mountain coffee to Walkers Wood products, even guava jelly and jerk seasoning. If you're lucky, you'll find marmalade from an old family recipe, plus Upton Pimento Dram, a unique liqueur flavored with Jamaican allspice. Local handcrafts include musical instruments for kids, brightly painted country cottages of tin, and intricate jigsaw puzzles of local scenes. The store also sells antiques, a constantly replenished collection ranging from sterling silver collectibles to 18th-century teaspoons and serving pieces. The antique maps of the West Indies are among the finest in Jamaica. We recently purchased a 1576 map of Jamaica for a surprisingly reasonable price. You may even find a novel by Daphne DuMarier called *Jamaica Inn*, although it's set in Cornwall.

One of the best bets for shopping is **Soni's Plaza,** 50 Main St., the address of all the shops recommended below.

Bollomongo (☎ 876/974-7318) has one of the island's widest selections of T-shirts, often in screen-printed designs. Bob Marley appears on many of them, and you can even get Bob Marley beach towels. Swimwear such as "Sharkbite" is also sold.

Chulani's (☎ 876/974-2421) sells a goodly assortment of quality watches and brand-name perfumes, although some of the leather bags might tempt you as well.

Jewelry is set in a wide variety of 14-karat and 18-karat settings with diamonds, emeralds, rubies, and sapphires.

Gem Palace (☎ 876/974-2850) is the place to go for diamond-ring solitaires and tennis bracelets. The shop specializes in 14-karat gold chains and bracelets.

Taj Gift Centre (☎ 876/974-9268) has a little bit of everything: Blue Mountain coffee, film, Jamaican cigars, and hand-embroidered linen tablecloths. For something different, look for Jamaican jewelry made from hematite, a mountain stone.

Mohan's (☎ 876/974-9270) offers one of the best selections of 14-karat and 18-karat gold chains, rings, bracelets, and earrings in Ocho Rios. Jewelry studded with precious gems such as diamonds and rubies are peddled here as well.

Soni's (☎ 876/974-2303) dazzles here with gold, but also cameras, French perfumes, watches, china and crystal, linen tablecloths, and even the standard Jamaican souvenirs.

Tajmahal (☎ 876/974-6455) beats most competition with its name-brand watches, jewelry, and fragrances. It also has Paloma Picasso leather wear and porcelain by Lladró.

OCHO RIOS AFTER DARK

Hotels often provide live entertainment that nonguests can sample as well. Ask at your hotel desk where the action is on any given night.

Otherwise, you may want to look in on **Silks Discothèque,** in the Shaw Park Hotel, Cutlass Bay (☎ 876/974-2552), which has a smallish dance floor and a sometimes-animated crowd of drinkers and dancers. If you're not a guest of the hotel, you can enter for an all-inclusive price of J$200 (U.S.$5.70).

The name may elicit groans, but if you want to put on your dancing shoes, you might try **Jamaic'N Me Crazy,** at the Jamaican Grande Hotel (☎ 876/974-2201), which resembles a stateside dance club rather than anything authentically Jamaican. If you're not a guest of the hotel, there's a charge of U.S.$30 to cover everything you can shake or drink daily from 10pm to 3am. They have the best lighting and sound system in Ocho Rios (and perhaps Jamaica), and the crowd can include anyone from the passing yachter to the curious tourist.

For more of the same without an overbearing Americanized atmosphere, try the **Acropolis,** 70 Main St. (☎ 876/974-2633). Cover is required only on nights they have a live band, and it rarely is any higher than U.S.$10.

3 Port Antonio

Port Antonio is a verdant and sleepy seaport 63 miles northeast of Kingston (you may have seen it as the setting for Tom Cruise's film *Cocktail*). Here you can still catch a glimpse of the Jamaica of 100 years ago. The titled and the wealthy have come here before you—European duchesses and barons, along with film stars like Linda Evans, Raquel Welch, and Peter O'Toole. Whoopi Goldberg came here to film *Clara's Heart.*

The small, bustling town itself is like many on Jamaica: clean but ramshackle, with sidewalks around a market filled with vendors; tin-roofed shacks competing with old Georgian and modern brick and concrete buildings; lots of people busily shopping, talking, and laughing, others sitting and playing dominoes (loudly banging the pieces on the table, which is very much part of the game). The colorful market is a place to browse for local craftwork, spices, and fruits.

Port Antonio

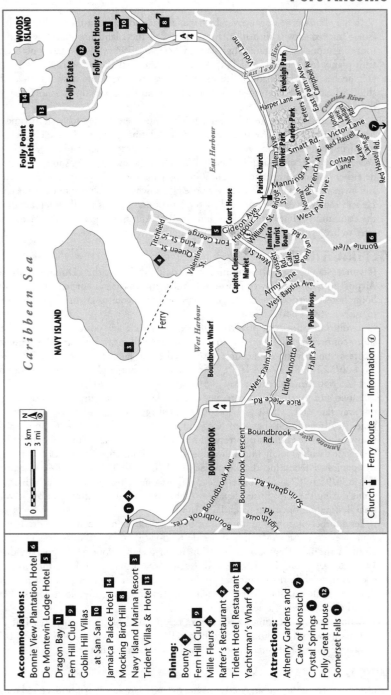

Accommodations:
Bonnie View Plantation Hotel 6
De Montevin Lodge Hotel 5
Dragon Bay 11
Fern Hill Club 9
Goblin Hill Villas
    at San San 10
Jamaica Palace Hotel 14
Mocking Bird Hill 8
Navy Island Marina Resort 3
Trident Villas & Hotel 13

Dining:
Bounty 3
Fern Hill Club 9
Mille Fleurs 8
Rafter's Restaurant 2
Trident Hotel Restaurant 13
Yachtsman's Wharf 4

Attractions:
Athenry Gardens and
    Cave of Nonsuch 7
Crystal Springs 1
Folly Great House 12
Somerset Falls 1

In the old days, visitors arrived by banana boat and stayed at the Titchfield Hotel (since burned down) in a lush, tropical part of the island unspoiled by modern tourist gimmicks. Captain Bligh landed here in 1793 with his cargo of bread-fruit plants from Tahiti, and Port Antonio claims that the breadfruit grown here are the best on the island. Visitors still arrive by water, but now it's on cruise ships, which moor close to Navy Island and send their passengers ashore just for the day.

Navy Island and the long-gone Titchfield Hotel were owned for a short time by film star Errol Flynn. The story is that after suffering damage to his yacht, he put into Kingston for repairs, visited Port Antonio by motorbike, fell in love with the area, and in due course acquired Navy Island (in a gambling game, some say). Later, he either lost or sold it and bought a nearby plantation, Comfort Castle, which is still owned by his widow, Patrice Wymore Flynn, who spends most of her time here. He was much loved and admired by the Jamaicans and was totally integrated into the community. They still talk of him in Port Antonio, especially the men, who refer to his legendary womanizing and drinking in reverent tones.

GETTING THERE

If you're staying in Port Antonio, you could fly into either **Donald Sangster Airport** in Montego Bay or **Norman Manley International Airport** in Kingston. Some hotels, particularly the large resorts, will pick you up at the airport; be sure to ask when you book.

If your hotel does not provide transfers, you have a few options. You can take a short connecting flight on to Port Antonio's small airport aboard **Air Jamaica Express** (book your connection through the Air Jamaica reservations number, ☎ 800/523-5585 in the U.S.). The one-way airfare is U.S.$37 from Kingston and U.S.$50 from Montego Bay.

Public and private bus companies operate desks in both airports, all offering a one-way fare of U.S.$40 to U.S.$50, or even higher, depending on your arrival time. Road conditions between Kingston and Port Antonio are quite poor, so we really only advise taking a bus from Montego Bay. In any case, don't take the public bus, which will be really uncomfortable for the 4-hour trip. Try one of two private companies we recommend: **Tour Wise** (☎ 876/979-1027) or **Caribic Vacations** (☎ 876/953-9874). All buses make at least one refreshment stop at a halfway point during the trip. Buses depart as flights arrive and will drop you off at your final destination once you reach Port Antonio.

Yet another option is renting a car, but we really don't recommend driving on your own on these roads. If you decide to anyway, information on car rentals is given in the "Getting Around" section in chapter 3. From Montego Bay, drive 133 miles east along Highway A1. To reach Port Antonio from Kingston, you can take A4 through Port Morant and up the east coast. You can also drive north on A3 through Castleton, and then approach Port Antonio along the North Coast. Plan on either drive taking at least 4 hours.

A final option is taking a taxi; they're readily available at the airports. But the typical one-way fare from Montego Bay to Port Antonio is a whopping U.S.$100. Always negotiate and agree upon the fare before getting into the taxi.

WHERE TO STAY

Despite its reputation as an enclave of the rich and famous, you'll find a good range of accommodations in Port Antonio.

VERY EXPENSIVE

✪ **Trident Villas & Hotel.** Rte. A4 (P.O. Box 119), Port Antonio, Jamaica, W.I. ☎ **876/ 993-2602.** Fax 876/993-2960. 22 units. A/C TV TEL. Winter U.S.$385 double; U.S.$620 suite. Off-season U.S.$220 double; U.S.$340 suite. Rates include MAP (breakfast and dinner). AE, MC, V.

This elegant rendezvous of the rich and famous is about 2½ miles east of Port Antonio along Allan Avenue, on the coast toward Frenchman's Cove. It's one of the most tasteful and refined hotels on the north shore. Sitting regally above jagged coral cliffs with a seaside panorama, it's the personal and creative statement of Earl Levy, scion of a prominent Kingston family. Nearby he has erected a multimillion-dollar replica of a European château, known as Trident Castle, which can be rented as one unit. Here, guests are grandly housed in eight large bedrooms beautifully furnished in plantation style.

The hotel's main building is furnished with antiques, and flowers decorate the lobby, which is cooled by sea breezes. Your accommodations will be a studio cottage or tower, reached by a pathway through the gardens. In a cottage, a large bedroom with ample sitting area opens onto a private patio with a view of the sea. All cottages and tower rooms have ceiling fans and plenty of storage space. Jugs of ice and water are constantly replenished. Solo travelers are accommodated in either junior or deluxe villa suites, whereas two or three guests are lodged in junior, deluxe villa, prime minister's, or imperial suites. There's a small private sand beach, and the gardens surround a pool and a gingerbread gazebo. Lounges, tables, chairs, and bar service add to your pleasure.

Dining: The main building has two patios, one covered, where breakfast and lunch are served. You can also have breakfast on your private patio, served by your own butler. At dinner, when men are required to wear jackets and ties, silver service, crystal, and Port Royal pewter sparkle on the tables. Dinner is a multicourse fixed-price meal, so if you have dietary restrictions, make your requirements known early.

Amenities: Swimming pool, tennis, water sports such as sailing and snorkeling, room service, laundry, baby-sitting.

EXPENSIVE

Fern Hill Club Hotel. Mile Gully Rd., San San (P.O. Box 100), Port Antonio, Jamaica, W.I. ☎ **876/993-7374.** Fax 876/993-7373. 31 units. A/C TV. Winter U.S.$300 double; U.S.$310–$390 suite for 2. Off-season U.S.$209–$220 double; U.S.$231–$253 suite for 2. Rates are all-inclusive. AE, MC, V. Drive east along Allan Ave. and watch for the signs.

Attractive, airy, and panoramic, Fern Hill occupies 20 forested acres high above the coastline, attracting primarily a British and Canadian clientele. A shuttle bus makes daily trips down the steep hillside to the beach. The accommodations come in a wide range of configurations, including standard rooms, junior suites, spa suites, and villas with cooking facilities. This is a far less elegant choice than its main competitor, Goblin Hill (see below). Technically classified as a private club, the establishment is comprised of a colonial-style clubhouse and three outlying villas, plus a comfortable annex at the bottom of the hill. The accommodations are highly private and attract many honeymooners. Many of the rooms are rather bland, and there is no air-conditioning.

Dining: There is the Blue Mahoe Bar and a patio for dining. The hotel restaurant offers an international menu (see "Where to Dine," below).

Amenities: Three swimming pools, tennis court.

Goblin Hill Villas at San San. San San (P.O. Box 26), Port Antonio, Jamaica, W.I. ☎ **876/993-7331.** Fax 876/993-9616. 28 villas. Winter U.S.$110–$195 1-bedroom villa; U.S.$185–$245 2-bedroom villa. Off-season U.S.$90–$165 1-bedroom villa; U.S.$145–$195 2-bedroom villa. Rates include transfers and rental car. AE, MC, V.

This green and sun-washed hillside—once said to shelter goblins—is now filled with Georgian-style vacation homes on San San Estate. The swimming pool is surrounded by a vine-laced arbor, which lies just a stone's throw from an almost-impenetrable forest. A long flight of steps leads down to the crescent-shaped sands of San San beach. This beach is now private, but guests of the hotel receive a pass. The accommodations are town-house style, and some units have ceiling fans and king-size beds, but no phones or TVs. Housekeepers prepare and serve meals and attend to chores in the villas. There is also a restaurant and bar on the premises, serving a rather good international/Jamaican menu.

Amenities: Two Laykold tennis courts, beach, swimming pool. Dragon Bay, about a 5- to 10-minute drive away, offers a variety of water sports, including snorkeling, windsurfing, and scuba diving.

MODERATE

Dragon Bay. P.O. Box 176, Port Antonio, Jamaica, W.I. ☎ **876/993-8751.** Fax 876/993-3284. 33 bungalows, divisible into a maximum of up to 97 units. A/C TEL. Winter U.S.$145 double; U.S.$211–$290 1-bedroom suite; U.S.$310 2-bedroom suite; U.S.$383–$429 3-bedroom suite. Off-season U.S.$106 double; U.S.$145–$205 1-bedroom suite; U.S.$210 2-bedroom suite; U.S.$271–$304 3-bedroom suite. AE, MC, V.

Set on 55 acres of forested land that slopes down to a sandy beach, this resort has changed hands frequently during its lifetime, and gone through a series of up and down swings. Today, it's a well-managed, carefully designed compound of bungalows and villas that caters to a mostly European clientele, most of whom check in for relatively long stays of 2 weeks or more. All but the smallest units contain kitchens, so you can do at least some of your own cooking by stocking up at neighborhood grocery stores. Accommodations lie within about 30 pink-and-white, two-story bungalows, some built on flatlands beside the beach, others on the steeply sloping terrain leading uphill to the resort's "clubhouse." Doors open and close into a flexible configuration of space that can include everything from a simple and conventional bedroom to a four-bedroom fully detached villa. Furnishings are durable and uncontroversial, but comfortable.

Dining/Diversions: Two restaurants, one of which lies beside the beach; the other is the more substantial Pavilion Restaurant. There are three bars, our favorite of which is the "Cruise Bar," which was used as a set for Tom Cruise in *Cocktail.*

Amenities: On-site dive shop with instruction, a swimming pool adjacent to the beach, two tennis courts, hiking paths through the forest, aerobics classes.

Jamaica Palace. Williamsfield (5 miles east of Port Antonio; P.O. Box 277), Port Antonio, Jamaica, W.I. ☎ **800/472-1149** in the U.S., or 876/993-7720. Fax 876/993-7759. 80 units. A/C TEL. Winter U.S.$160 double; U.S.$200–$325 suite. Off-season U.S.$145 double; U.S.$180–$290 suite. MAP (breakfast and dinner) U.S.$60 per person extra in winter, U.S.$50 off-season. AE, MC, V.

This hotel rises like a stately mansion from a hillock surrounded by five tropically landscaped acres. Its owner, German-born Siglinde von Stephani-Fahmi, set out to combine the elegance of a European hotel with the relaxed atmosphere of a Jamaican resort. The public rooms are filled with furnishings and art from Europe, including a 6-foot Baccarat crystal candelabrum and a pair of Italian ebony-and-ivory chairs from the 15th century. Outside, the Palace offers white marble columns, sun-filled patios and balconies, and an unusual 114-foot swimming pool shaped like the island of Jamaica.

Most accommodations are large, with 12½-foot ceilings and oversize marble bathrooms. Some, however, are rather small but still elegantly furnished. Suites are individually furnished with crystal chandeliers, Persian rugs, and original works of art. TV is available upon request.

Dining/Diversions: Both continental and Jamaican food are served in the main dining room with its lighted "waterwall" sculpted from Jamaican cave stones. Men are requested to wear jackets and ties. There's also a poolside cafe with a barbecue area, and live dance music and calypso bands are featured.

Amenities: Swimming pool, room service, laundry, baby-sitting, massage facilities, fashion boutique (operated by Patrice Wymore Flynn, widow of Errol Flynn), complimentary shuttle service to private San San Beach, to which hotel guests are admitted.

Navy Island Marina Resort. Navy Island (P.O. Box 188), Port Antonio, Jamaica, W.I. ☎ 876/993-2667. 7 villas. Year-round U.S.$120 for 2 in 1-bedroom villa, U.S.$180 for 3 in 1-bedroom villa; U.S.$250 for 3 in 2-bedroom villa, U.S.$275 for 4 in 2-bedroom villa. Children under 12 stay free in parents' rm. MC, V.

Jamaica's only private island getaway, this resort and marina is on that "bit of paradise" once owned by actor Errol Flynn. Today, this cottage colony and yacht club is one of the best-kept travel secrets in the Caribbean. To reach the resort, you'll have to take a ferry from the dockyards of Port Antonio on West Street for a short ride across one of the most beautiful and convoluted harbors of Jamaica.

Each accommodation is designed as a villa branching out from the main club. Ceiling fans and trade winds keep the cottages cool, and mosquito netting over the beds adds a plantation touch.

One of the resort's beaches is a secluded clothing-optional stretch of sand known as Trembly Knee Cove. You can also explore the island, whose grounds are dotted with hybrid hibiscus, bougainvillea, and palms (many of which were originally ordered planted by Flynn himself).

Dining: At night, after enjoying drinks in the HMS Bounty Bar, guests can dine in the Navy Island Restaurant. A five-course dinner is served nightly.

Amenities: Swimming pool, water sports (including windsurfing), free ferry service.

INEXPENSIVE

Bonnie View Plantation Hotel. Richmond Hill (P.O. Box 82), Port Antonio, Jamaica, W.I. ☎ 876/993-2752. Fax 876/993-2862. 20 units. Winter U.S.$98–$102 double; off-season U.S.$82–$98 double. MAP (breakfast and dinner) U.S.$24 per person extra. AE, MC, V.

The two-story house that contains this hotel is the subject of several local legends. Some claim that it was built by an expatriate Englishman as a holiday home around 1900; others maintain that it was the center of a large plantation and built around 1850. Other stories claim that Errol Flynn himself owned it briefly and used it as a place to carouse. Regardless of the details, it's obvious that this high-ceilinged, wood-framed building once boasted pretentions of grandeur and many of the grace notes of the Old World.

Today, it's a rather battered shell of its original self, with a white-painted exterior, a much-renovated dining room, and 15 rooms in the main house (another five bedrooms are in cabaña-style outbuildings in the garden). The accommodations contain Jamaican-made furniture and not many extras, although a very limited number offer views of the sea. There's a smallish swimming pool in back and a bar.

The nearest beach (Frenchman's Cove) is about a 20-minute drive away. You'll get a sense of small-town Jamaican life here.

De Montevin Lodge Hotel. 21 Fort George St. (in the town center on Titchfield Hill), Port Antonio, Jamaica, W.I. ☎ **246/993-2604.** 13 units (3 with bathroom). U.S.$39 double without bathroom; U.S.$52 double with bathroom. Rates include breakfast. AE.

De Montevin, the most ornate and best-maintained gingerbread house in town, stands on a narrow back street whose edges are lined with architectural reminders (some not well-preserved) of colonial days. Built as a sea captain's house in 1881, the hotel is really worth a photograph. Cast-iron accents and elongated red-and-white balconies set a tone for the charm you find inside: cedar doors, art deco cupboards, a ceiling embellished with lacy plaster designs, and the most elaborate cove moldings in town. Don't expect modern amenities here; your old-fashioned room might be a study of another, not-yet-renovated era.

A NEARBY PLACE TO STAY

✪ **Hotel Mocking Bird Hill.** Mocking Bird Hill (P.O. Box 254), Port Antonio, Jamaica, W.I. ☎ **876/993-7267.** Fax 876/993-7133. 10 units. Winter U.S.$140–$160 double; off-season U.S.$100–$120 double. MC, V.

A 6-mile drive east of Port Antonio, this hotel occupies the much-renovated premises of what was originally built in 1971 as the holiday home of an American family. In 1993, two imaginative women transformed the place into a blue-and-white enclave of good taste, reasonable prices, and ecological consciousness. Set about 600 feet above the coastline, on a hillside laden with tropical plants, the place attracts a clientele of mostly German and Dutch visitors, who seem to revel in the artsy and ecologically conscious setting. The accommodations are simple but tasteful, and other than their ceiling fans, they're utterly devoid of the electronic gadgets that prevail in the urban world.

Much of the establishment's interior, including its restaurant (Mille Fleurs; see "A Nearby Place to Dine," below), is decorated with Ms. Walker's artworks, and as this hotel grows, the gallery aspect will probably be expanded. On the premises is a bar, a lounge with TV, and a public telephone. You can participate in rafting tours, day hikes, or classes in painting and papermaking, or you could just relax and enjoy an herbal massage or the sweeping views out over the Blue Mountains and the Jamaican coastline. Your consciousness just might be raised in this healthful and highly palatable setting.

WHERE TO DINE

An array of atmospheric choices awaits you in Port Antonio. All hotels welcome outside guests for dinner, but reservations are required.

EXPENSIVE

✪ **Trident Hotel Restaurant.** On Rte. A4. ☎ **876/993-2602.** Reservations required. Jackets and ties required for men. Fixed-price dinner U.S.$44. AE, MC, V. Daily 8am–4pm and 8–10pm. Head east on Allan Ave. INTERNATIONAL.

The Trident Hotel Restaurant has long been sought out by travelers in search of fine cuisine. Part of the main hotel building, the restaurant has an air of elegance. The high-pitched wooden roof set on white stone walls holds several ceiling fans that gently stir the air. The antique tables are set with old china, English silver, and Port Royal pewter. The formally dressed waiters will help you choose your wine and whisper the name of each course as they serve it: Jamaican salad, dolphin (fish) with mayonnaise-and-mustard sauce, steak with broccoli and sautéed potatoes, and peach Melba and Blue Mountain coffee with Tía María, a Jamaican liqueur. The six-course dinner menu is changed everyday. The cuisine is always fresh and prepared with first-class ingredients, though the setting and the white-gloved service are generally more memorable than the food.

MODERATE

Bounty. In the Navy Island Marina Resort, Navy Island. ☎ **876/993-2667.** Reservations recommended for dinner. Lunch or dinner U.S.$12–$20. MC, V. Daily 7am–10pm. JAMAICAN.

In Errol Flynn's former retreat, the Bounty, reached by ferry across the Port Antonio harbor, is the perfect place for a romantic tryst—all at surprisingly moderate prices. There's a convivial nautical atmosphere. The kitchen here is known for its fresh fish and its down-home Jamaican cookery often appearing on the menu as daily specials. Come here early so you can enjoy a drink, taking in the view from the bar. (Flynn used to have quite a few, all recorded in *My Wicked, Wicked Ways*, his auto-biography.) The lunch and dinner menus are the same. Steak is prepared delectably in a variety of ways, as are lobster, shrimp, chicken, and crayfish.

Fern Hill Club Hotel. Mile Gully Rd. ☎ **876/993-7374.** Reservations recommended. Lunch main courses U.S.$3–$10; dinner main courses U.S.$11–$18. AE, MC, V. Daily 7:30am–9:30pm. Head east on Allan Ave. INTERNATIONAL/JAMAICAN.

One of the finest dining spots in Port Antonio, this restaurant has a sweeping view of the rugged coastline. Sunset watching here is the best in the area. Well-prepared specialties are served: jerk chicken, jerk pork, grilled lobster, and Créole fish. Depending on who's in the kitchen at night, the food here can be quite satisfactory, though once in a while, especially off-season, the cuisine might be a bit of a letdown. The club also offers entertainment: a calypso band and piano music during the week, and disco music on weekends.

INEXPENSIVE

De Montevin Lodge Restaurant. 21 Fort George St. ☎ **876/993-2604.** Reservations recommended a day in advance. Fixed-price meal U.S.$11–$19.50. AE. Daily noon–2pm and 7–9:30pm. JAMAICAN/AMERICAN.

At the previously recommended lodge, start with pepperpot or pumpkin soup, follow with curried lobster or chicken Jamaican style with local vegetables, and finish with coconut or banana-cream pie, or perhaps bread pudding, washed down with coffee. We suggest an ice-cold Red Stripe beer with the meal, too. The menu changes according to the availability of fresh supplies, but the standard of cooking and the full Jamaican character of the meal are constant. Always call the day before to let them know you're coming or to request a special dish, or just show up and take potluck.

Yachtsman's Wharf. 16 West St. ☎ **876/993-3053.** Reservations not required. Main courses U.S.$7–$15. No credit cards. Daily 7:30am–10pm. INTERNATIONAL.

This restaurant beneath a thatch-covered roof is at the end of an industrial pier, near the departure point for ferries to Navy Island. The rustic bar and restaurant is a favorite of the expatriate yachting set. Crews from many of the ultraexpensive yachts have dined here and have pinned their ensigns on the roughly textured planks and posts. It opens for breakfast and stays open all day. Menu items include the usual array of tropical drinks, burgers, seafood ceviche, curried chicken, and ackee with saltfish. Main dishes include vegetables. Come here for the setting, the camaraderie, and the good times; the food is only secondary.

A NEARBY PLACE TO DINE

Mille Fleurs. In the Hotel Mocking Bird Hill, Port Antonio. ☎ **876/993-7267.** Reservations recommended. Fixed-price dinner U.S.$40; lunch platters U.S.$6.20–$17.90. AE, MC, V. Daily 8:30am–10am, noon–3pm, and 7–9:30pm. INTERNATIONAL.

This restaurant is terraced into a verdant hillside about 600 feet above sea level with sweeping views over the Jamaican coastline and the faraway harbor of Port Antonio. Sheltered from the frequent rains, but open on the side for maximum access to cooling breezes, it features candlelit dinners, well-prepared food, and lots of New Age charm. Menu items at lunch include sandwiches, salads, grilled fish platters, and soups. Evening meals are fixed-price three-course affairs featuring wholesome, healthful, and stylish dishes derived from around the world. The restaurant has been acclaimed by *Gourmet* magazine for its dishes. You may want to try the coconut-and-garlic soup, and the fish with spicy mango-shrimp sauce is a specialty. Breads and most jams are made on the premises. Some (but not all) of the dishes are designed for vegetarians.

BEACHES & OUTDOOR PURSUITS

BEACHES   Port Antonio has several white-sand beaches, including the famous **San San Beach,** which has recently gone private, although guests of certain hotels can be admitted with a pass. Some beaches are free and others charge for the use of facilities. **Boston Beach** is free and often has light surfing; there are picnic tables as well as a restaurant and snack bar. Before heading to this beach, stop nearby and get the makings for a picnic lunch at the most famous center for peppery jerk pork and chicken in Jamaica, the **Boston Jerk Centre,** in rustic shacks east of Port Antonio and the Blue Lagoon.

Also free is **Fairy Hill Beach** (Winnifred), with no changing rooms or showers. **Frenchman's Cove Beach** attracts a chic crowd to its white-sand beach with its freshwater stream. Nonhotel guests are charged a fee.

Navy Island, once Errol Flynn's personal hideaway, is a fine choice for swimming (one beach is clothing-optional) and snorkeling (at **Crusoe's Beach**). Take the boat from the Navy Island dock on West Street, across from the Exxon station. It's a 7-minute ride to the island, a one-way fare costing 30¢. The ferry runs 24 hours a day. The island is the setting for the Navy Island Marina Resort (see "Where to Stay," above).

SNORKELING   The place to go for snorkel gear around Port Antonio is **Lady Godiva's Dive Shop** (☎ 876/993-8988), in Dragon Bay, 7 miles from Port Antonio. Technically, you can snorkel off most of the beaches in Port Antonio, but you are not likely to see much unless you move a little farther offshore. The very best spot is off San San Bay by Monkey Island. The reef here is extremely active and full of a lot of exciting marine life. Lady Godiva offers two excursions daily to this spot for U.S.$10 per person. Equipment rents for U.S.$9 for the whole day.

DEEP-SEA FISHING   Northern Jamaican waters are world renowned for their game fish, including dolphin, wahoo, blue and white marlin, sailfish, tarpon, Allison tuna, barracuda, and bonito. The Jamaica International Fishing Tournament and Jamaica International Blue Marlin Team Tournaments run concurrently at Port Antonio every September or October. Most major hotels from Port Antonio to Montego Bay have deep-sea-fishing facilities, and there are many charter boats.

A 30-foot-long **sport-fishing boat** (☎ 876/993-3209) with a tournament rig is available for charter rental. Taking out up to six passengers at a time, it charges

U.S.$250 per half day or U.S.$450 per day, with crew, bait, tackle, and soft drinks included. It docks at Port Antonio's Marina, off West Palm Avenue, in the center of town. Call for bookings.

RAFTING   Rafting started on the Rio Grande as a means of transporting bananas from the plantations to the waiting freighters. In 1871, a Yankee skipper, Lorenzo Dow Baker, decided that a seat on one of the rafts was better than walking, but it was not until Errol Flynn arrived that the rafts became popular as a tourist attraction. Flynn used to hire the craft for his friends, and he encouraged the rafters to race down the Rio Grande. Bets were placed on the winner. Now that bananas are transported by road, the raft skipper makes one or maybe two trips a day down the waterway. If you want to take a raft trip, **Rio Grande Attractions Limited,** % Rafter's Restaurant, St. Margaret's Bay (☎ **876/993-5778**), can arrange it for you.

The rafts, some 33 feet long and only 4 feet wide, are propelled by stout bamboo poles. There's a raised double seat about two-thirds of the way back for the two passengers. The skipper stands in the front, trousers rolled up to his knees, the water washing his feet, and guides the craft down the lively river, about 8 miles between steep hills covered with coconut palms, banana plantations, and flowers, through limestone cliffs pitted with caves, through the "Tunnel of Love," a narrow cleft in the rocks, then on to wider, gentler water.

The day starts at the Rafter's Restaurant, west of Port Antonio, at Burlington on St. Margaret's Bay. Trips last 2 to 2½ hours and are offered from 8am to 4pm daily at a cost of U.S.$40 per raft, which is suitable for two people. From the Rafter's Restaurant, a fully insured driver will take you in your rented car to the starting point at Grants Level or Berrydale, where you board your raft. The trip ends at the Rafter's Restaurant, where you collect your car, which has been returned by the driver. If you feel like it, take a picnic lunch, but bring enough for the skipper, too, who will regale you with lively stories of life on the river.

SEEING THE SIGHTS

Athenry Gardens and Cave of Nonsuch. Portland. ☎ **876/993-3740.** Admission (including guide for gardens and cave) U.S.$5 adults, U.S.$2.50 children 11 and under. Daily 9am–5pm (last tour at 4:30pm). From Harbour St. in Port Antonio, turn south in front of the Anglican church onto Red Hassel Rd. and proceed approximately a mile to Breastworks community (fork in road); take the left fork, cross a narrow bridge, go immediately left after the bridge, and proceed approximately 3½ miles to the village of Nonsuch.

Twenty minutes from Port Antonio, it's an easy drive and an easy walk to see the stalagmites, stalactites, fossilized marine life, and evidence of Arawak civilization in Nonsuch. The cave is 1.5 million years old. From the Athenry Gardens, there are panoramic views over the island and the sea. The gardens are filled with coconut palms, flowers, and trees, and complete guided tours are given.

Crystal Springs. Buff Bay, Portland. ☎ **876/929-6280.** Admission J$100 (U.S.$2.85) adults, J$50 (U.S.$1.45) children. Daily 9am–5pm.

Crystal Springs is a tract of forested land whose borders were originally specified in 1655. Then it was attached to a nearby plantation whose Great House is now under separate (and private) ownership. Visitors, however, can trek through the organization's 156 acres of forest whose shelter is much beloved by birds and wildlife. A simple restaurant is on the premises, as well as a series of cottages erected in the early 1990s. These are usually rented to visiting ornithologists who don't care for the amenities or distractions of a traditional resort.

Folly Great House. On the outskirts of Port Antonio on the way to Trident Village, going east along Rte. A4. Free admission.

This house was reputedly built in 1905 by Arthur Mitchell, an American millionaire, for his wife, Annie, daughter of Charles Tiffany, founder of the famous New York store. Seawater was used in the concrete mixtures of its foundations and mortar, and the house began to collapse only 11 years after they moved in. Because of the beautiful location, it's easy to see what a fine Great House it must have been.

Somerset Falls. 8 miles west of Port Antonio, just past Hope Bay on Rte. A4. ☎ **876/ 913-0108.** Tour U.S.$3. Daily 9am–5pm.

Here, the waters of the Daniels River pour down a deep gorge through a rain forest, with waterfalls and foaming cascades. You can take a short ride in an electric gondola to the hidden falls. A stop on the daily Grand Jamaica Tour from Ocho Rios, this is one of Jamaica's most historic sites; the falls were used by the Spanish before the English captured the island. At the falls, you can swim in the deep rock pools and buy sandwiches, light meals, soft drinks, beer, and liquor at the snack bar. The guided tour includes the gondola ride and a visit to both a cave and a freshwater fish farm.

Kingston & the Blue Mountains

With 660,000 inhabitants, Jamaica's capital of Kingston is the largest English-speaking community in the Caribbean. This busy city occupies some 40 square miles on the South Coast plains between the Blue Mountains and the sea. With the world's seventh-largest harbor, it is the country's hub of transportation, industry, finance, and public administration. It's also Jamaica's main cultural center, with a campus of the University of the West Indies at its edge. The buildings here are a mixture of very modern, graceful old, and plain ramshackle.

Unfortunately, squalid living conditions in parts of the city have helped foster crime and political violence, and visitors should be cautious. All of the city's leading hotels employ guards to help ensure your safety.

Nearby Port Royal and Spanish Town are well worth a visit; Kingston's history is linked to both of these historic towns. It was founded by survivors of the great 1692 earthquake that destroyed Port Royal. In 1872 it replaced Spanish Town as Jamaica's capital.

1 Where to Stay

When you inquire about a reservation, ask whether the room tax is included in the rate quoted. The following rates are year-round, unless noted otherwise. Prices are quoted in U.S. dollars.

EXPENSIVE

Crowne Plaza Kingston. 211A Constant Spring Rd., Jamaica, W.I. ☎ **800/618-6534** or 876/925-7676. Fax 876/925-5757. 150 units. A/C MINIBAR TV TEL. Year-round U.S.$199–$235 double, U.S.$250–$449 suite. Rates include round-trip transfer from airport. AE, DC, MC, V.

This glorified Holiday Inn, in an ochre-colored high-rise, stands in an relatively prosperous suburb about 15 minutes by taxi from the center of Kingston. Opened in December of 1997, it's aiming primarily for business travelers and diplomats, although it welcomes vacationers with equal enthusiasm.

The hotel opens onto panoramic views of Kingston and the surrounding Blue Mountains, but is convenient for banking, business, and financial centers. This is the first major new hotel development in the island capital in 2 decades, and its high-tech facilities are the best on the island. Each room and suite is equipped with a desk,

Kingston Area

JAMAICA

○Negril   **Kingston** ○

Accommodations:
Courtleigh Hotel **14**
Hotel Four Seasons **10**
Indies Hotel **9**
Le Meridien Jamaica Pegasus **15**
Terra Nova Hotel **5**
Wyndham Kingston Hotel **13**

Dining:
Blue Mountain Inn ◆27
Chelsea Jerk Centre ◆12
Devonshire Restaurant/
   The Grogg Shoppe ◆6
El Dorado Room ◆5
The Hot Pot ◆16
Indies Pub and Grill ◆11
Jade Garden ◆1
Peppers ◆8
The Port Royal Restaurant ◆15
Queen of Sheba ◆4

Attractions:
Coke Church ●22
Devon House ●7
Hope Botanical Gardens ●26
Institute of Jamaica ●21
Jamaica House ●3
King's House ●2
Kingston Crafts Market ●19
Kingston Mall ●20
Mico College ●17
National Arena ●24
National Heroes Park ●18
National Library
   of Jamaica ●21
National Stadium ●23
University of
   West Indies ●25

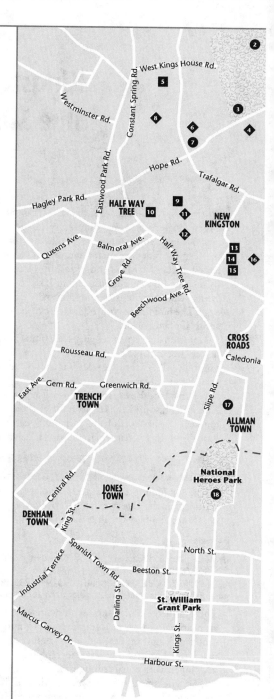

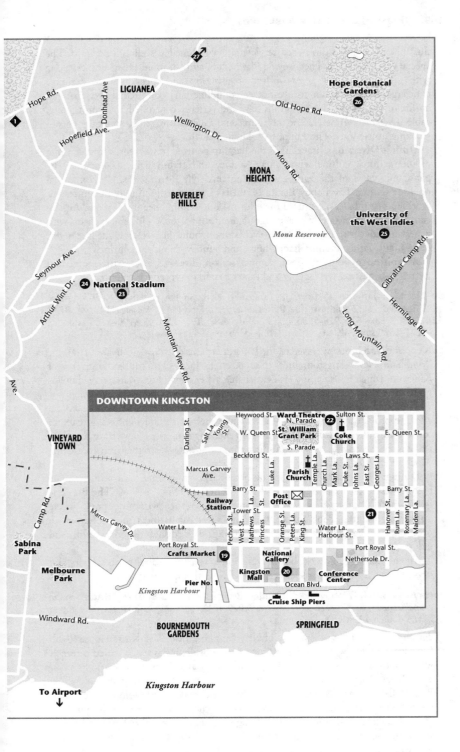

DOWNTOWN KINGSTON

dual-line phone, and direct-dial service, plus voice mail as well as a dataport. The special executive floor, The Crowne Plaza Club, adds in-room fax machines, along with private floor key access, private registration and checkout, and exclusive concierge. In addition, it also features a complimentary continental breakfast and an honor bar. All accommodations have individually controlled air-conditioning, cable TV, in-room safes, and coffeemakers. Guests can select smoking or no-smoking units. Some suites even have kitchen facilities.

Dining/Diversions: Isabella's is the flagship gourmet restaurant, offering a mix of international cuisine with Jamaica's spicy and stylish flair, accompanied by panoramic views of the harbor and mountains. The Bistro serves in an informal poolside setting. The Lobby Bar and Isabella's Lounge (adjoining the main restaurant) are piano bars, often used for informal one-on-one meetings by day. An elegant cigar bar with state-of-the-art ventilation features the world's finest cigars, with wines and liquors to match. Theme events throughout the week include jazz night, Latin night, Friday evening happy hour, and Sunday champagne brunch.

Amenities: Swimming pool, tennis, squash, fitness center with sauna and Jacuzzi, business center, jogging and exercise trail, room service, laundry.

Le Meridien Jamaica Pegasus. 81 Knutsford Blvd. (in the center of New Kingston, off Oxford Rd.; a 12-mile taxi ride from the airport), Kingston 5, Jamaica, W.I. ☎ **876/ 926-3690.** Fax 876/929-5855. 343 units. A/C TV TEL U.S.$190–$205 double; U.S.$275–$570 suite. AE, DC, MC, V. Free parking.

A favorite with business travelers, the Jamaica Pegasus outclasses its nearest rival, the Wyndham New Kingston, in a close race. It's located in the banking area of Kingston, which is also a fine residential area. After a major renovation, the hotel is now better than ever, and is the site of many conventions and social events.

The hotel combines English style with Jamaican warmth. The staff makes an effort to provide activities, such as arranging water sports and sightseeing. Each of the well-furnished bedrooms contains coffeemaking equipment, a satellite color TV, and a radio. Several floors of luxuriously appointed suites form the Knutsford Club, which offers special executive services.

Dining: The 4pm tea service is a bit of a social event among some residents. The premier restaurant is The Port Royal (see "Where to Dine," below). The Brasserie is the hotel's informal restaurant that opens to the swimming pool, where a splashing fountain cools the air. It adjoins a circular bar near the pool at which occasional barbecues are prepared, featuring such dishes as grilled fish and jerk pork.

Amenities: Jogging track, health club, tennis courts, outdoor pool, laundry and dry-cleaning, 24-hour room service, baby-sitting, therapeutic massage.

Terra Nova Hotel. 17 Waterloo Rd., Kingston 10, Jamaica, W.I. ☎ **800/74-CHARMS** in the U.S. and Canada, or 876/926-2211. Fax 876/929-4933. 35 units. A/C TV TEL. Year-round U.S.$165 double. AE, MC, V.

This house is on the western edge of New Kingston, near West Kings House Road. Built in 1924 as a wedding present for a young bride, it has had a varied career. It was once the family seat of the Myers rum dynasty and the birthplace and home of Chris Blackwell, promoter of many Jamaican singers and musical groups, including Bob Marley and the Wailers. In 1959, the house was converted into a hotel, and, set in 2½ acres of gardens with a backdrop of greenery and mountains, it's now one of the best small Jamaican hotels, although the rooms are rather basic and not at all suited for those who want a resort ambience. Most of the bedrooms are in a new wing.

Dining/Diversions: The Spanish-style El Dorado Room, with a marble floor, wide windows, and spotless linen, offers local and international food. Your à la carte breakfast is served on the coffee terrace, and there's a swimming pool at the front of the hotel, with a pool bar and grill.

Wyndham Kingston Hotel. 77 Knutsford Blvd. (in the center of New Kingston, near Oxford Rd.; P.O. Box 112), Kingston 5, Jamaica, W.I. ☎ **800/822-4200** in the U.S., or 876/ 926-5430. Fax 876/929-7439. 303 units. A/C TV TEL. U.S.$195–$210 double; U.S.$320–$575 suite. Children under 12 stay free in parents' room. AE, DC, MC, V. Free parking.

The Wyndham Kingston rises as an imposing mass of pink-colored stucco pierced with oversized sheets of tinted glass. The main core of the hotel is a 17-floor tower, containing 220 guest rooms. In addition, poolside units add to the diversity of the hotel's accommodations. Completely refurbished, bedrooms feature up-to-date amenities, including coffeemakers and remote-control satellite TV.

Dining/Diversions: Fine cuisine is offered at the Terrace Café, providing à la carte Jamaican and international food. The health-conscious appreciate the fare served from the café's popular salad and pasta bars. The Rendezvous Bar and Palm Court Restaurant offer more elegant dining and fine wines. For details on the hotel's nightclub, refer to the Jonkanoo Lounge, below.

Amenities: Olympic-size swimming pool, floodlit tennis courts, health club, tour desk, laundry, valet, baby-sitting, massage.

MODERATE

The Courtleigh. 85 Knutsford Blvd., Kingston 5, Jamaica, W.I. ☎ **876/968-6339.** Fax 876/926-7744. 134 units. A/C MINIBAR TV TEL. Year-round U.S.$125 double, U.S.$190 suite. AE, MC, V.

In 1997, the Courtleigh abandoned its somewhat rundown premises in another neighborhood of Kingston and moved into a 10-story beige-and-green tower that had originally been built as the site of another hotel, the Skyline. As part of the process, they radically renovated their new home, bringing the bedrooms up to the standards of its nearby competitors, the Pegasus and the Wyndham, which lie on either side. Today, you'll find a hard-working, business-oriented hotel with better prices than its neighbors. There's a rectangular swimming pool on the premises, a bar/lounge, and a restaurant (Alexander's), which is separately recommended in "Where to Dine." All rooms contain a safety-deposit box.

INEXPENSIVE

Hotel Four Seasons. 18 Ruthven Rd. (near Halfway Tree Rd.), Kingston 10, Jamaica, W.I. ☎ **800/742-4276** in the U.S., or 876/929-7655. Fax 876/929-5964. 76 units. A/C TV TEL. U.S.$78–$100 double. AE, DC, MC, V. Free parking.

Small and respectable, this hotel (not affiliated with the famous Four Seasons chain) is an old house on the western outskirts of New Kingston with a colonial-style veranda along the front, with a view of mango trees and a garden through which you drive. Old mahogany woodwork enhances the appearance of the reception area, the bar, and the formal dining room. Guest rooms are decorated in wicker or plantation-style furniture, although they are more likely to remind you of a motel. The new building is simple and white, containing 40 deluxe bedrooms, each furnished with two queen-size beds and decorated with wicker furniture. All the rooms have French doors that open onto private balconies overlooking the newly installed swimming pool. Meals are served to both guests and nonresidents, either on the terrace or in the formal dining room; a buffet lunch Monday through Friday attracts the city's business leaders. The hotel also has two bars (one inside, the other outside).

Indies Hotel. 5 Holborn Rd. (near the intersection of Trafalgar Rd.), Kingston 10, Jamaica, W.I. ☎ **876/926-2952.** Fax 876/926-2879. 15 units. A/C TV TEL. U.S.$58–$62 double; U.S.$77 triple. AE, MC, V. Free parking.

On one of the small side streets in the heart of New Kingston, opening onto a flower garden, this half-timbered building with double gables features a small reception area decorated with potted plants, a lounge, and a TV lounge. The barely adequate bedrooms, restaurant, and bar are grouped around a cool patio.

Indies has a reputation among the locals for friendly atmosphere and good-quality budget meals. Their fish-and-chips are good, and they specialize in pizza. They also serve steak with all the trimmings, and when they get fancy, lobster thermidor.

NEARBY PLACES TO STAY

Pine Grove Mountain Chalets. Content Gap P.A., St. Andrew (for information, write Pine Grove Mountain Chalets, 62 Duke St., Kingston, Jamaica, W.I.). ☎ **876/977-8009.** Fax 876/977-8001. 17 units. Year-round U.S.$80 double. MAP (breakfast and dinner) U.S.$20 per person extra. MC, V.

This simple inn occupies a site originally developed in the 1930s as a coffee plantation, lying a 1-hour drive from the center of Kingston. The setting includes a view over misty hills and the lights of faraway Kingston, landscaped brick walkways, topiary trees, and bedrooms that, although basic, are clean and quiet. You'll depend on catching a breeze, since there's no air-conditioning. The accommodations are in low-slung, one-story motel-like units, each with basic amenities. There's a restaurant on-site, and hiking trips into the nearby mountains can be arranged. Three of the rooms contain slightly battered kitchenettes, for which there's no additional charge.

2 Where to Dine

Kingston has a good range of places to eat, whether you're seeking stately meals in plantation houses, hotel buffets, or fast-food shops.

EXPENSIVE

The Port Royal Restaurant. In Le Meridien Jamaica Pegasus Hotel, 81 Knutsford Blvd. (in New Kingston, off Oxford Rd.). ☎ **876/926-3690.** Main courses U.S.$16–$30. AE, DC, MC, V. Mon–Sat 7–11pm. SEAFOOD/CONTINENTAL.

This elegantly furnished restaurant is your best bet if you're looking for upmarket seafood. It's a favorite place for local businesspeople hoping to impress out-of-town clients. We prefer to begin with the Jamaican baby lobster as an appetizer. It's served in a shell with a salad. If you want something hot for a starter, make it the baked stuffed Jamaican crab back presented on vermicelli. Doubloon is one of the chef's better specialties—a medley of chicken suprême and veal presented on a layer of pasta. Many of the main meat and poultry dishes are quite ordinary, although the seafood specialties are more radiant, especially the snapper fillet filled with crab mousse and baked in Parmesan and fresh herbs. The Créole shrimp is also good—simmered in beer and flavored with Cajun spices. Service is first class. You might also visit "The Pizza Cellar," the hotel's pizza parlor and wine cellar offering a wide selection of succulent pies and exclusive wines from around the world.

MODERATE

Alexander's. In the Courtleigh Hotel, 85 Knutsford Blvd. ☎ **876/968-6339.** Reservations recommended. Main courses U.S.$9–$20. AE, MC, V. Daily noon–3pm and 6–10:30pm. INTERNATIONAL.

This is the showplace dining room of one of Kingston's best-respected hotels, and as such, it often attracts business meetings, government delegations, and international travelers who appreciate its good service and culinary savvy. Within a setting inspired by the Jamaican sugar plantations of the 1800s, with muted tropical colors and a view that overlooks the hotel's swimming pool, you can order such starters as smoked marlin or Caribbean crab backs, then move to sirloin steaks, medallions of beef with grilled tomatoes, and fillets of pork with brandy, mustard, and cream sauce. After your dinner, consider a drink within the hotel's bar/lounge, Mingles.

Devonshire Restaurant/The Grogg Shoppe. 26 Hope Rd., in Devon House (near Trafalgar Park). ☎ **876/929-7046** or 876/929-7027. Reservations recommended in the Devonshire, not necessary in the Grogg Shoppe. Devonshire main courses U.S.$6–$24 at lunch, U.S.$8–$28 at dinner. Grogg Shoppe main courses U.S.$6–$24 at lunch, U.S.$6–$28 at dinner. AE, MC, V. Mon–Sat noon–midnight. JAMAICAN.

These two restaurants are in the brick-sided former servant's quarters of Kingston's most-visited mansion, Devon House. The more formal of the two is the Devonshire, where you can eat on patios under trees, in view of the royal palms and the fountain in front of the historic great house. For true Jamaican flavor, head here, as the kitchen turns out the most authentic dishes in Kingston. Appetizers include a "tidbit" of jerk pork or a bowl of soup (perhaps Jamaican red pea—really bean—or pumpkin). Zesty main dishes feature Jamaican ackee and saltfish, barbecued chicken, and curried seafood. Also tasty are unusual homemade ice creams flavored with local fruits, such as soursop. Blue Mountain tea or coffee is also served. The bars for both restaurants serve 11 different rum punches and 10 fruit punches, such as a tamarind fizz or a papaya (pawpaw) punch. Many aficionados opt for these drinks on one of the Grogg Shoppe's two different terraces, labeled "mango" or "mahogany" after nearby trees. Especially popular is the "Devon Duppy," combining into one pastel-colored glass virtually every variety of rum in the bartender's inventory.

Jade Garden. 106 Hope Rd., in Sovereign Centre (north of the town center, west of National Stadium). ☎ **876/978-3476.** Reservations recommended. Main courses U.S.$9.70–$34. AE, MC, V. Daily noon–10pm. CHINESE.

The best Chinese restaurant in Kingston, Jade Garden serves well-prepared food in an elegant, formal setting. The menu is so large we wonder how they manage. The typical chow mein and chop suey dishes are here, but we'd ignore them to concentrate on the more challenging offers from the chefs. The beef with oyster sauce is delectable, as is the pork with ham choy. For unusual flavors, go shopping in the "China Gems" section of the menu, where you'll find some really savory offerings, including Pi Paw bean curd with chopped Chinese sausage, shrimp, black mushrooms, and water chestnuts. Also excellent is Subgum War Bar, a combination of meats sautéed with Chinese vegetables and served on a sizzling-hot platter. Count on several good seafood specialties always being featured, especially deep-fried prawns stuffed with prawn mousse and served in a garlic-butter sauce.

INEXPENSIVE

Chelsea Jerk Centre. 7 Chelsea Ave. (between the New Kingston Shopping Centre and the Wyndham New Kingston Hotel). ☎ **876/926-6322.** Reservations not accepted. Jerk half-chicken U.S.$5.70; pound of jerk pork U.S.$8.50. AE, MC, V. Mon–Thurs 10am–10pm, Fri–Sun 10am–1pm. JAMAICAN.

Chelsea Jerk Centre is the city's most popular seller of the Jamaican delicacies jerk pork and jerk chicken. Set in a low-slung angular concrete building, it offers food to take out or to eat in the comfortably battered dining room. Although no formal appetizers are served, you might order a side portion of what the scrawled black-board refers to as "Festival," which is fried cornmeal dumplings. The best bargain is Chelsea's Special, which is like an old-fashioned blue plate special at a U.S. road-side diner. It consists of rice, peas, and vegetables, along with jerked pork or chicken.

El Dorado Room. In the Terra Nova Hotel, 17 Waterloo Rd. (on the western edge of New Kingston, near West Kings House Rd.). ☎ **876/926-9334.** Reservations recommended. Main courses U.S.$9–$38 at lunch, U.S.$14–$38 at dinner. AE, MC, V. Daily noon–3pm and 6:30–10:30pm. INTERNATIONAL/JAMAICAN.

Situated in one of the small, respectable hotels of Kingston, this restaurant hosts a crowd of local businesspeople and dignitaries. The grandeur of the portico, the elaborate moldings of the hotel reception area, and the formal dining room are vestiges of the wealthy former owners.

The restaurant emphasizes fish and shellfish dishes, and the chef is noted for flambé and fondues. We've found smoked marlin and Jamaican pepperpot soup to be the most tasty starters, followed by one of the specialties such as a blackened snapper, which is evocative of New Orleans. The best items emerge from the grill, including grilled lobster or a jerk pork loin. The latter is a real taste of Jamaica, having been marinated with herbs, then "jerked," and served with yams and honey-baked plantain. Among the seafood selections, we gravitate to the steamed ginger snapper with onions and garlic, plus a garnish of okra.

The Hot Pot. 2 Altamont Terrace. ☎ **876/929-3906.** Main courses U.S.$5–$14. MC, V. Daily 7am–10pm. JAMAICAN.

Set within a short walk of both the Pegasus and Wyndham hotels, this is a simple local restaurant with an animated crowd of regulars and straightforward, unfussy cuisine. Within a green-and-white interior, near a view of a modest garden, you can drink Red Stripe beer or rum drinks. Menu items include red pea soup, beef stew, roast chicken, steaks, mutton, and fish. The place stays open throughout the day, serving breakfast, lunch, and dinner without interruption. The food is what you'd be served in a typical Jamaican home—nothing fancy, but satisfying and filling—and the prices are astonishingly low.

Indies Pub and Grill. 8 Holborn Rd. (in New Kingston, off Hope Rd.). ☎ **876/920-5913.** Main courses U.S.$9–$26.20; pizzas U.S.$9–$16.50. AE, V. Sun–Thurs 10am–midnight, Fri–Sat 10am–2am. JAMAICAN.

Indies, an informal neighborhood restaurant across the street from the Indies Hotel, was designed around a garden terrace, which on hot nights provides the best (and coolest) place to sit. You can also dine in the inner rooms, which are haphazardly but pleasantly decorated with caribou horn, tortoiseshell, half-timber walls, an aquarium sometimes stocked with baby sharks, and even a Canadian moose head.

There's a full sandwich menu at lunchtime. In the evening, you can enjoy grilled lobster, fish-and-chips, barbecued chicken or pork, chicken Kiev, or roast beef. It's a little better than standard pub grub. Pizza is a specialty. A bottle of Red Stripe, the Jamaican national beer, is the beverage of choice here.

Peppers. 31 Upper Waterloo Rd. ☎ **876/925-2219.** Main courses U.S.$10–$26. MC, V. Daily noon until ? (varies night to night). JAMAICAN.

The current hot spot for dining is this open-air spot near a shopping mall. It's especially popular on Wednesday and Friday nights, when half of Kingston seems to show up for dancing—and are these dancers ever hot! The food isn't neglected either. It's good and reasonable in price, specializing in jerk pork and chicken with French fries. The most elegant dish is grilled lobster, although more burgers and salads are sold instead. That's it—no vegetables, no other dishes. The Red Stripe flows like a river here.

Queen of Sheba. 56 Hope Rd. ☎ **876/978-0510.** Main courses U.S.$6–$7.80. No credit cards. Daily 9am–5:30pm. JAMAICAN/ETHIOPIAN.

On the grounds of the Bob Marley Museum (see below) is this Ethiopian restaurant honoring the late emperor Haile Selassie, whom the Rastas view as their Messiah, a descendant of King Solomon and the Queen of Sheba (hence, the restaurant's name). On the grounds where the famous reggae star once walked (keep your eye out for his son, Ziggy) you can enjoy an exotic cuisine served with equally exotic natural juices. The Jamaican dishes include beef, chicken, or fish, although most of the Ethiopian cuisine is vegetarian. Steamed fish with Ethiopian sauces is a regular feature, but it might be more appetizing to order any number of the vegetarian plates, ranging from lentils with garlic and herbs to steamed callaloo with herbs and sesame. Excellent cakes are served for dessert.

Service is slow and the staff is blasé, but as a cultural experience it's unmatched anywhere else in Kingston. Amid posters of Selassie, African art, and homages to Bob Marley, you sit on a carpeted floor, cross-legged, beneath low Ethiopian-style wooden tables.

3 Exploring Kingston

Even if you're staying in one of Jamaica's resort towns, such as Montego Bay or Ocho Rios, you may want to sightsee in Kingston and visit nearby Spanish Town and Port Royal. Following are notable places of interest in Kingston; Spanish Town and Port Royal are described in "Side Trips to Spanish Town & Port Royal," later in this chapter.

The **Bob Marley Museum** (formerly Tuff Gong Studio), 56 Hope Rd. (☎ **876/927-9152**), is the most-visited sight in Kingston. The clapboard house, painted in Rastafarian green, yellow, and red, with its garden and high surrounding wall, was the famous reggae singer's home and recording studio until his death. The museum is open on Monday, Tuesday, Thursday, and Friday from 9:30am to 4:30pm and on Wednesday and Saturday from noon to 5:30pm. Admission is J$180 (U.S.$5.15) for adults, J$25 (70¢) for children 4 to 12, free for children 3 and under. It's reached by bus no. 70 or 75 from Halfway Tree, but take a cab to save yourself the hassle of dealing with Kingston public transportation.

✪ **Devon House,** 26 Hope Rd. (☎ **876/929-7029**), was built in 1881 by George Stiebel, a Jamaican who, after mining in South America, became one of the first black millionaires in the Caribbean. A striking classical building in the Georgian style, the house has been restored to its original beauty by the Jamaican National Trust. The grounds contain craft shops (see "Shopping," below), boutiques, restaurants (see "Where to Dine," above), shops that sell the best ice cream in Jamaica in exotic fruit flavors, and a bakery and pastry shop with Jamaican puddings and desserts. The main house also displays furniture of various periods and styles. Admission to Devon House is U.S.$3. The house is open Tuesday through Saturday from 9:30am to 5pm.

Almost next door to Devon House are the sentried gates of **Jamaica House,** residence of the country's prime minister. It is a fine, white-columned building set well back from the road.

Cays & Mangroves

Although you may be close to the urban sprawl of Kingston, you can return to nature by taking a boat tour leaving from **Morgan's Harbour Hotel Marina** in Port Royal (call ☎ **876/967-8061** to reserve). The nearby mangroves are a natural habitat for Jamaica's bird life, especially pelicans and frigates, which use the area as a breeding ground. Entirely surrounded by water, it is also an important haven for other water-loving birds and wildlife.

Close to Morgan's Harbour and the Kingston airport, the mangroves have survived hurricanes and earthquakes. Jamaican officials created a waterway, allowing small boats to enter. During this trip you can see oyster beds, fish-breeding grounds, and a wide assortment of mangroves, along with wrecks never removed from Hurricane Gilbert's visit in 1988. If you're lucky, you may even spot a pod of dolphins.

After the mangroves, you're taken on a tour of some of Jamaica's most famous cays, including Lime Cay and Maiden Cay. Close to them is Gun Cay, so aptly named for the remains of cannons and large guns. Many a "bloody war" among notorious pirates was fought here.

The cost of this tour is U.S.$10, lasting 45 minutes. Departures can usually be arranged at your convenience.

Continuing along Hope Road, at the crossroads of Lady Musgrave Road and King's House Road, turn left and you'll see a gate on the left with its own personal traffic light. This leads to **King's House,** the official residence of the governor-general of Jamaica, the British monarch's representative on the island. The outside and front lawn of the gracious residence, set on 200 acres of well-tended parkland, is sometimes open to view Monday through Friday from 10am to 5pm. The secretarial offices are housed next door in an old wooden building set on brick arches. In front of the house is a gigantic banyan tree in whose roots, legend says, duppies (as ghosts are called in Jamaica) take refuge when they're not living in the cotton trees.

Between Old Hope Road and Mona Road, a short distance from the Botanical Gardens, is the **University of the West Indies** (☎ **876/927-1660**), built in 1948 on the Mona Sugar Estate, the third of the large estates in this area. Ruins of old mills, storehouses, and aqueducts are juxtaposed with modern buildings on what may be the most beautifully situated college campus in the world. The chapel, an old sugar-factory building, was transported stone by stone from Trelawny and rebuilt on the campus close to another old sugar factory, the remains of which are well-preserved and give a good idea of how sugar was once made.

The entrance to **National Stadium,** Briggs Park, of which Jamaica is justly proud, features an aluminum statue of Arthur Wint, a national athlete. The stadium is used for soccer, field sports, and cycling. Beside the stadium is the **National Arena,** used for indoor sports, exhibitions, and concerts, and there is an Olympic-size pool. Admission prices vary according to activities.

A mile above Kingston, if you go north on Duke Street, lies **National Heroes Park,** formerly known as George VI Memorial Park. This was the old Kingston racecourse. An assortment of large office blocks, including the Ministries of Finance and Education, overlooks the park. There are statues of Simón Bolívar, of Nanny of the Maroons, and of George Gordon and Paul Bogle, martyrs of the Morant Bay revolt. Norman Manley and Alexander Bustamante, national heroes of Jamaica, are buried here, as is Sir Donald Sangster, a former prime minister.

Just north of Heroes Park, at 1A Marescaux Rd., is **Mico College** (☎ 876/ 929-5260), a coeducational post-secondary teacher-training institution. Lacy Mico, a rich London widow, left her fortune to a favorite nephew on the condition that he marry one of her six nieces. He did not, and the inheritance was invested, the interest being used to ransom victims of the Barbary pirates. With the end of piracy in the early 19th century, it was decided to devote the capital to founding schools for newly emancipated enslaved persons, and Mico College was established.

The central administrative offices of the **Institute of Jamaica,** founded in 1879, are between 12 and 16 East St. (☎ 876/922-0620), close to the harbor. Open from 8:30am to 5pm Monday through Thursday, until 4pm on Friday, the institute fosters and encourages the development of culture, science, and history in the national interest. The institute has responsibility for several divisions and organizations, of which Junior Centre, the Natural History Division (repository of the national collection of flora and fauna), and the National Library are at the East Street headquarters. Those located elsewhere are the Cultural Training Centre, 1 Arthur Wint Dr., with schools of music, dance, art, and drama; the African-Caribbean Institute, 12 Ocean Blvd., which conducts research on cultural heritage; the Museums Division, with sites in Port Royal and Spanish Town, which has responsibility for the display of artifacts relevant to the history of Jamaica; the National Gallery, 12 Ocean Blvd.; and the Institute of Jamaica Publications Ltd., 4B Camp Rd., which publishes a quarterly, the *Jamaica Journal,* as well as other works of educational and cultural merit.

The **National Library of Jamaica** (formerly West India Reference Library), Institute of Jamaica, 12 East St. (☎ 876/922-0620), a storehouse of the history, culture, and traditions of Jamaica and the Caribbean, is the world's finest working library for West Indian studies. It holds the most comprehensive, up-to-date, and balanced collection of materials—including books, newspapers, photographs, maps, and prints— to be found anywhere in the Caribbean. Of special interest to visitors are regular exhibitions that attractively and professionally highlight different aspects of Jamaican and West Indian life. It is open Monday through Thursday from 9am to 5pm and Friday from 9am to 4pm.

4 Shopping

Downtown Kingston, the old part of the town, is centered around Sir William Grant Park, formerly Victoria Park, a showpiece of lawns, lights, and fountains. North of the park is Ward Theatre, the oldest theater in the New World, where traditional Jamaican pantomime is staged from December 26 to early April. To the east is Coke Methodist Church, and to the south is the equally historic Kingston Parish Church.

Cool arcades lead off King Street, but everywhere are many people going about their business. There are some beggars and the inevitable peddlers who sidle up and offer "hot stuff, mon"—which frequently means highly polished brass lightly dipped in gold and fraudulently offered at high prices as real gold. The hucksters accept a polite but firm "no," but if you let them keep you talking, you may end up buying. They're very persuasive!

On King Street are the imposing General Post Office and the Supreme Court buildings.

ART

For many years the richly evocative paintings of Haiti were viewed as the most valuable contribution to the arts in the Caribbean basin. But there's a rapidly growing perception that Jamaica is one of the artistic leaders of the developing nations. An articulate group of Caribbean critics is focusing the attention of the art world on the unusual, eclectic, and sometimes politically motivated painting produced in Jamaica.

Frame Centre Gallery. 10 Tangerine Place. ☎ **876/926-4644.**

Frame Centre is one of the most important galleries in Jamaica. The founder and guiding force, Guy McIntosh, is widely respected today as a patron of Jamaican arts. Committed to presenting quality Jamaican works, the gallery has three viewing areas and carries a varied collection of more than 300 pieces. It represents both pioneer and contemporary artists, some of whom are internationally known. Younger, newer talents are always on display.

Mutual Life Gallery. Mutual Life Centre, 2 Oxford Rd. ☎ **876/929-4302.**

One of Jamaica's most prominent art galleries is in the corporate headquarters of this major insurance company. This center offers an insight into the changing face of Jamaican art. The gallery's exhibitions are organized by Gilou Bauer, who encourages unknowns and showcases established artists with flair. Exhibitions change once a month, but there are usually long-term exhibits as well. The Mutual Life Insurance Company donates the space as part of its effort to improve the status of Caribbean arts. The gallery is a not-for-profit institution.

HANDCRAFTS

Kingston Crafts Market. At the west end of Harbour St., downtown.

A large, covered area of individually owned small stalls, Kingston Crafts Market is reached through thoroughfares like Straw Avenue, Drummer's Lane, and Cheapside. All kinds of Jamaican crafts are on sale—wooden plates and bowls, trays, ashtrays, and pepperpots made of mahoe, the national wood. Straw hats, mats, and baskets are on display, as are batik shirts and cotton shirts with gaudy designs. Banners for wall decoration are inscribed with the Jamaican coat of arms, and wood masks often have elaborately carved faces. Apart from being a good place to buy worthwhile souvenirs, the market is where you can learn the art of bargaining and ask for a brawta, a free bonus.

The Shops at Devon House. 26 Hope Rd. (at Devon House). ☎ **876/929-7029.**

Associated with one of the most beautiful and historic mansions in Jamaica, a building operated by the Jamaican National Trust, these shops ring the borders of a 200-year-old courtyard once used by slaves and servants. Although about 10 shops operate from these premises, four of the largest are operated by Things Jamaican, a nationwide emporium dedicated to the enhancement of the country's handcrafts. Shops include the Cookery, selling island-made sauces and spices; the Pottery, offering crockery; and Elaine Elegance, which sells handcrafts.

LIQUOR

Sangster's Old Jamaica Spirits. 17 Holborn Rd. ☎ **876/926-8888.**

Sangster's has a full array of unusual rum-based liqueurs available in this well-scrubbed factory outlet on a side street off the modern uptown New Kingston business area. The entrance isn't well-marked, but once you're in the showroom, the hundreds of bottles tell you that you're in a rum-lover's mecca. The prices vary, based on the quality and size of the container. You can purchase such tempting flavors as coconut, coffee-orange, coffee cream, and coconut cream rums, plus

Blue Mountain coffee liqueurs. There's a large trolley filled with samples of rums and liqueurs, and you can sample from small cups before buying.

A SHOPPING CENTER

New Kingston Shopping Centre. 30 Dominica Dr., New Kingston.

One of the most modern shopping centers in Jamaica, New Kingston is known for its overall merchandise rather than for a particular merchant. It is sleek and contemporary, and stores are centered around a Maya-style pyramid, down the sides of which cascades of water irrigate trailing bougainvillea. Fast-food outlets, fashion boutiques, and shops selling many other items are here. Free concerts are often presented in the open-air theater.

5 Kingston After Dark

Kingston offers a variety of nighttime entertainment. Most entertainment is listed in the daily press, along with a host of other attractions, including colorful carnivals and festivals held islandwide throughout the year. *Caution:* The city is unsafe at night. Be careful!

THE PERFORMING ARTS

Kingston is a leading cultural center of the West Indies. Notable theaters include **Ward Theatre,** on North Parade Road (☎ 876/922-0453), and the **Little Theatre,** on Tom Redcam Drive near the National Stadium (☎ 876/926-6129). Both stage local or imported plays and musicals, light opera, revues, and internationally acclaimed Jamaican dance and choral groups and pop concerts. Ticket prices vary. From downtown Kingston (Parade and Cross roads), buses nos. 90A and 90B run here to the Creative Arts Centre.

THE CLUB & BAR SCENE

Red Hills Strip, a suburban area of Kingston, has a number of nightclubs, but we avoid them all like the plague.

On the other hand, the Wyndham Kingston Hotel's **Jonkanoo,** 77 Knutsford Blvd. (☎ 876/926-5430), is a contemporary and elegant venue offering entertainment that changes according to the night of the week, ranging from sports events shown on a big-screen TV to live reggae bands. There's a U.S.$3 cover charge, and beers cost U.S.$2.50. It's open Wednesday through Saturday from 7pm to 2am.

6 Side Trips to Spanish Town & Port Royal

Historic Spanish Town and Port Royal can both be reached easily from Kingston, and are well worth a visit.

SPANISH TOWN

Spanish Town, some 10 miles west of Kingston, was the capital of Jamaica from 1662 to 1872, and was founded by the Spanish as Villa de la Vega. But all traces of Roman Catholicism were obliterated by Cromwell's men in 1655.

The English cathedral, surprisingly retaining a Spanish name, **St. Jago de la Vega,** was founded in 1666 and rebuilt shortly after being destroyed by a hurricane in 1712. As you drive into the town from Kingston, the ancient cathedral catches your eye, with its brick tower and two-tiered wooden steeple, added in 1831. Because the cathedral was built on the foundation and remains of the old Spanish church, it is half English, half Spanish, showing two definite styles—one Romanesque, the other Gothic.

Of cruciform design and built mostly of brick, St. Jago (Spanish for St. James) de la Vega is one of the most interesting historic buildings in Jamaica. The black-and-white marble stones of the aisles are interspersed with ancient tombstones, and the walls are heavy with marble memorials that almost form a chronicle of Jamaica's history, dating back as far as 1662. Episcopalian services, held regularly on Sundays at 7 and 10:30am and at 6:30pm, are sometimes conducted by the bishop of Jamaica, whose see this is.

Beyond the cathedral, turn right and go 2 blocks to Constitution Street and the **Town Square.** Graceful royal palms surround this little square. On the west side is **Old King's House,** residence of Jamaica's British governors until 1872, when the capital was transferred to Kingston. It hosted many celebrated guests—among them Lord Nelson, Admiral Rodney, Captain Bligh of HMS *Bounty* fame, and King William IV—stayed here. Gutted by fire in 1925, its facade has been restored.

Beyond the house is the **Jamaica People's Museum of Craft & Technology,** Old King's House, Constitution Square (☎ 876/922-0620), open Monday to Friday from 10am to 1pm. Admission is J$35 (U.S.$1) for adults and J$15 (45¢) for children. The garden contains examples of old farm machinery, an old water-mill wheel, a hand-turned sugar mill, a fire engine, and other items. An outbuilding displays a museum of crafts and technology, together with a number of smaller agricultural implements. In the small archaeological museum are old prints, models, and maps of the town's grid layout from the 1700s.

The streets around the old Town Square contain many fine Georgian town houses intermixed with tin-roofed shacks. Nearby is the **market,** so busy in the morning that you'll find it difficult, almost dangerous, to drive through. It provides, however, a bustling scene of Jamaican life.

On the north side of the square is the **Rodney Memorial,** the most dramatic building on the square, commissioned by a grateful assembly to commemorate the victory in 1782 of British admiral Baron George Rodney over a French fleet, which saved the island from invasion.

The remaining side of the square, the east, contains the most attractive building, the **House of Assembly,** with a shady brick colonnade running the length of the ground floor, above which is a wooden-pillared balcony. This was the stormy center of the bitter debates for Jamaica's governing body. Now the ground floor is the parish library. Council officers occupy the upper floor, along with the Mayor's Parlour, all closed to the public.

PORT ROYAL

From West Beach Dock, Kingston, a ferry ride of 20 to 30 minutes takes you across the harbor to Port Royal, which conjures up images of swashbuckling pirates, led by Henry Morgan, swilling grog in harbor taverns. Blackbeard stopped here regularly on his Caribbean trips.

The town was once one of the largest trading centers of the New World, but the whole thing came to an end at 11:43am on June 7, 1692, when a devastating earthquake shoved one-third of the town underwater. With its rich heritage, Port Royal has been designated by the government for redevelopment as a tourist attraction.

At Morgan's Harbour in Port Royal, **Buccaneer Scuba Club** (☎ 876/924-8148) is one of Jamaica's leading dive and water-sports operators. It offers a wide range of dive sites to accommodate various divers' tastes—from the incredible *Texas* wreck to the unspoiled beauty of the Turtle Reef. PADI courses are also

The Wickedest City on Earth

As the notorious pirate Henry Morgan made his way through the streets in the late 17th century, the prostitutes hustled customers, the rum flowed, and buccaneers were growing rich and sassy. The town was Port Royal, at the entrance to the world's seventh-largest natural harbor. It was filled with drinking parlors, gambling dens, billiard rooms, brothels, and joints offering entertainment such as cock fights, target shoots, and bear baiting. Buccaneers not only got drunk— they fought duels and pursued "foul vices" after long months at sea. All this earned for Port Royal the title of "The Wickedest City on Earth."

All this came to a thundering end on the hot morning of June 7, 1692. Without warning, a severe earthquake sunk most of the town, killing some 2,000 people. The skies turned copper over this once-vibrant pirate city. To this day, it is known as the famous "Sunken City" of Port Royal.

Today, Port Royal is a small fishing village at the end of the Palisades strip. Some 2,000 residents—and a lot of ghosts—live here. Its seafaring traditions continue, and the town is famous for both its fresh seafood and quaint architecture of old days. Once there were six forts here with a total of 145 guns; some of the guns remain today, but only Fort Charles still stands.

Actually, the 1692 earthquake was only one of nine that descended upon Port Royal. And that's not all: 16 of the worst hurricanes to hit the Caribbean and three devastating fires ravaged the town. It's a wonder anything is still standing today.

Norman Manley International Airport shares the same thin peninsula with Port Royal, but otherwise, all is quiet in the town today. It's easy to conjure up images not only of Morgan but of another buccaneer, Roche Brasiliano, who liked to roast Spaniards alive. To celebrate he'd break out a keg of wine on the streets of Port Royal; whether they wanted to or not, he forced passersby to have a drink with him at gunpoint.

What happened to Henry Morgan after piracy was outlawed here in 1681? He was knighted in England and sent back to arrest his old hell-raising mateys.

available. There's also a wide array of water sports offered, including waterskiing, body-boarding, ring-skiing, and even a banana-boat ride. One-tank dives cost from U.S.$35, and the other sports mentioned are U.S.$15 per person for 15 minutes.

As you drive along the Palisades, you arrive first at **St. Peter's Church.** It's usually closed, but you may persuade the caretaker, who lives opposite, to open it if you want to see the silver plate, said to be a spoil captured by Henry Morgan from the cathedral in Panama. In the ill-kept graveyard is the tomb of one Lewis Galdy, a Frenchman swallowed up and subsequently regurgitated by the 1692 earthquake.

Fort Charles, the only one of Port Royal's six forts still standing, has withstood attack, earthquake, fire, and hurricane. Built in 1656 and later strengthened by Morgan for his own purposes, the fort was expanded and further armed in the 1700s, until its firepower boasted more than 100 cannons, covering both land and sea approaches. After subsequent earthquakes and tremors, the fort ceased to be at the water's edge and is now well inland. In 1779, Britain's naval hero, Lord Horatio Nelson, commanded the fort and trod the wooden walkway inside the western parapet as he kept watch for the French invasion fleet. It is administered by the **Institute of Jamaica** (☎ 876/922-0620).

Giddy House, once the Royal Artillery storehouse and part of the Fort Charles complex, is another example of what earthquakes can do. Walking across its tilted floor is an eerie and strangely disorienting experience.

WHERE TO STAY

Morgan's Harbour Hotel & Beach Club. Port Royal, Kingston 1, Jamaica, W.I. ☎ **800/ 44-UTELL** in the U.S., or 876/967-8030. Fax 876/967-8073. 51 units. A/C MINIBAR TV TEL. Year-round U.S.$150 double; U.S.$170–$200 suite. AE, DC, MC, V. Take the public ferryboat that departs every 2 hours from near Victoria Pier on Ocean Blvd.; many visitors drive or take a taxi.

The yachtie favorite, since it has the largest marina facility near Kingston, this hotel is in Port Royal, once believed to be the wickedest city on earth. Rebuilt after 1988's Hurricane Gilbert, Morgan's lies near the end of a long sandspit whose rocky and scrub-covered length shelters Kingston's harbor. On the premises is a 200-year-old redbrick building once used to melt pitch for His Majesty's navy, a swimming area defined by docks and buoys, and a series of wings whose eaves are accented with hints of gingerbread. Set on 22 acres of flat and rock-studded seashore, the resort contains a breezy waterfront restaurant called Henry Morgan's and a popular bar (where ghost stories about the old Port Royal seem especially lurid as the liquor flows on Friday night). Longtime residents claim that the ghosts of soldiers killed by a long-ago earthquake are especially visible on hot and very calm days, when British formations seem to march out of the sea.

The hotel rents well-furnished bedrooms, each laid out in an 18th-century Chippendale-Jamaican motif. The Buccaneer Scuba Club is on-site, organizing dives to some of the 170-odd wrecks lying close to shore. Deep-sea-fishing charters and trips to outlying cays can also be arranged.

WHERE TO DINE

Sir Henry Morgan's Restaurant. In Morgan's Harbour Hotel & Beach Club, Port Royal. ☎ **876/967-8075.** Main courses U.S.$9–$34 at lunch, U.S.$10.70–$34 at dinner. AE, DC, MC, V. Daily 7am–10:30pm. INTERNATIONAL/JAMAICAN.

The bar and restaurant offer guests panoramic views over Kingston Bay and the Blue Mountains. Except for the elegant lobster or seafood salad, lunch is a relatively simple affair. You can order various sandwiches and desserts, along with a daily luncheon special, a traditional Jamaican dish. The catch of the day is steamed or fried. You get more of a choice at dinner; your best bet is either the fresh Jamaican lobster, which can be prepared in a number of ways—everything from thermidor to grilled with garlic butter. The traditional Jamaican pepper steak, with hot and sweet peppers, is excellent, as is the selection of homemade ice creams to finish your meal.

7 Exploring the Blue Mountains

Jamaica has some of the most varied and unusual topography of any island in the Caribbean. It first began to appeal to 18th-century mariners because it has so much fresh water, which pours in the form of rivers, streams, and waterfalls, from the heights of a mountain ridge appropriately named the Blue Mountains. These lie within the 192-acre Blue Mountain–John Crow Mountain National Park, which is maintained by the Jamaican government.

You can explore the Blue Mountains by heading in from the south, near Kingston, but it's also possible to enjoy this area by using Port Antonio, on the north coast, as your gateway. See chapter 6 for more information about where to stay in Port Antonio. The Blue Mountains provide a rich environment for coffee production, producing a blended version that is among Jamaica's leading and most expensive exports. But for the nature enthusiast, the mountains reveal an astonishingly complex series of ecosystems that change radically as you climb from sea level to the mountain's misty peaks.

The most popular climb begins at **Whitfield Hall,** a high-altitude hostel and coffee estate about 6 miles from the hamlet of Mavis Bank. Reaching the summit of **Blue Mountain Peak** (3,000 feet above sea level) requires between 5 and 6 hours each way. En route, hikers pass through acres of coffee plantations and forest, where temperatures are cooler (sometimes much cooler) than you might expect, and where high humidity encourages thick vegetation. Along the way, watch for an amazing array of bird life, including hummingbirds, many species of warblers, rufous-throated solitaires, yellow-bellied sapsuckers, and Greater Antillean pewees.

The best preparation against the wide ranges of temperature you'll encounter is to dress in layers and bring bottled water. If you opt for a 2am departure in antici-pation of watching the sunrise from atop the peak, carry a flashlight as well. Sneakers are usually adequate, although many climbers bring their hiking boots to Jamaica just for this trek up Blue Mountain. Be aware that even during the "dry" season (from December to March), rainfall is common. During the "rainy" season (the rest of the year), these peaks can get up to 150 inches of rainfall a year, and fogs and mists are frequent.

You can always opt to head out alone into the Jamaican wilderness for hiking expeditions on your own, but considering the dangers of such an undertaking, and the crime you might encounter en route, we don't advise it. A better bet involves engaging one of Kingston's best-known specialists in ecosensitive tours, **Sunventure Tours,** 30 Balmoral Ave., Kingston 10, Jamaica, W.I. (☎ **876/960-6685**). The staff here can always arrange an individualized tour for you and/or your party, but their regular roster of offerings includes the following two options: Their **Blue Mountain Sunrise Tour** involves a camp-style overnight in one of the most remote and inaccessible areas of Jamaica. For a fee ranging from U.S.$80 to U.S.$115 per person, participants are retrieved at their Kingston hotels, driven to an isolated ranger station, Wildflower Lodge, that's accessible only via four-wheel drive vehicle, in anticipation of a two-stage hike that begins at 4:30pm. A simple mountaineer's supper is served at 6pm around a campfire at a ranger station near Portland Gap. At 3am, climbers hike by moonlight and flashlight to a mountaintop aerie that's selected because of its view of the sunrise over the Blue Mountains. Climbers stay aloft until around noon that day, before heading back down the mountain for an eventual return to their hotels in Kingston by 4pm.

A second popular offering involves an excursion from Kingston "Y's Waterfall" on the Black River, in southern Jamaica's Elizabeth Parish. Participants congregate in Kingston at 6:30am for a transfer to a raft and boating party near the hamlet of Lacovia, and an all-day waterborne excursion to a region of unusual ecological interest. Depending on the number of participants, fees range from U.S.$80 to U.S.$100 per person, a price that includes lunch.

WHERE TO STAY

Forres Park Guest House. 2 miles east of Mavis Bank (17 miles due north of Kingston center; mailing address: 23 Liguanea Ave., Kingston 6), Jamaica, W.I. ☎ **876/927-5957.** Fax 876/978-6942. 7 units, 3 bungalows. Year-round U.S.$60 double, U.S.$45 bungalow for 2. Rates include breakfast. MC, V.

Consider a sojourn at this isolated hotel, due north of Kingston's commercial core, only if you're really serious about climbing and hiking in the Blue Mountains. Built on the verdant grounds of a 20-year-old coffee plantation in the mid-1990s, it was designed like a Caribbean version of a Swiss chalet, with natural wood, dark-stained planks sheathing the building's exterior. It stands on sloping land that offers partial views over the nearby hills. Three of the accommodations lie within fully detached and very basic bungalows, which are more raw-boned than rooms within the main house. There's a communal kitchen where you can prepare a basic meal, and someone from the staff can arrange a guide, priced at about U.S.$30, for a ¾-day tour up a meandering route through the Blue Mountains.

✪**Strawberry Hill.** Irish Town, Blue Mountains, Jamaica, W.I. ☎ **800/OUTPOST** or 876/944-8400. Fax 876/944-8408. 16 rms in 1-, 2-, and 3-bedroom units. TV TEL. Winter U.S.$306–$950 double; off-season U.S.$313–$490 double. AE, DC, MC, V. Guests are personally escorted to the hotel in a customized van or via a 7-minute helicopter ride. It's a 50-minute drive from the Kingston airport or 30 minutes via mountain roads from the center of the city.

The best place to stay in the Kingston area is well outside of Kingston. Strawberry Hill, in the Blue Mountains, lies 3,100 feet above the sea, overlooking this turbulent city, which seems far removed in this lush setting. A self-contained facility with its own power and water-purification system, Strawberry Hill has elaborate botanical gardens.

This cottage complex was built on the site of a Great House from the 1600s, which Hurricane Gilbert disposed of in 1988. The property was conceived by multimillionaire Chris Blackwell, the impresario who launched Bob Marley into reggae fame through Island Records. One former guest described this exclusive resort as a "home away from home for five-star Robinson Crusoes."

Local craftspeople fashioned the cottages and furnished them in a classic plantation style, with canopied four-poster beds and louvered windows. In one case, a doorway was carved with figures inspired by Madonna's book *Sex.*

Dining: The food is better than you'll find in Kingston, with such Jamaican dishes as grilled shrimp with fresh cilantro, or fresh grilled fish with jerk mango and sweet-pepper salsa. It's called "new Jamaican cuisine," and so it is.

Amenities: Activities include coffee-plantation tours, and hiking and mountain biking through the Blue Mountains. The hotel also offers a gym/spa/steam room/sauna, and there is 24-hour room service and a laundry.

Whitfield Hall. [c/o] John Allgrove, 8 Armon Jones Crescent, Kingston 6, Jamaica, W.I. ☎ **876/927-0986.** 7 units (none with bathroom), 1 2-bedroom cottage. U.S.$14 per person; U.S.$50 cottage for up to 4. No credit cards. See below for directions.

One of the most isolated places in Jamaica, this hostel is located more than halfway up Blue Mountain at some 4,000 feet above sea level. The main draw here is the opportunity to see the Blue Mountains from a hillclimber's point of view. Whitfield Hall is a coffee plantation dating from 1776, and it is the last inhabited house from that period. It provides basic accommodation for 30 guests in rooms containing two or more beds. Blankets and linen are provided, but personal items, such as towels, soap, and food, are not. There is no restaurant, but there's a deep freeze, a refrigerator, and good cooking facilities including crockery and cutlery. All water comes from a spring, and lighting is by kerosene pressure lamps called Tilleys. A wood fire warms the hostel and its guests, as it gets cold in the mountains at night. You bring your own food and share the kitchen.

To get here, you can drive to Mavis Bank, about 20 miles from Kingston. Head northeast along Old Hope Road to the suburb of Papine, then proceed to Gordon Town. At Gordon Town, turn right over the bridge near the police station and drive into the hills for some 10 miles until you reach Mavis Bank. You can also reach Mavis Bank by bus from the Kingston suburb of Papine. The bus departs from the northeast edge of town, at the end of Old Hope Road. Mavis Bank is the terminus of this bus line. Transportation from Mavis Bank to Whitfield costs U.S.$20 each way. Most guests simplify matters by requesting pickup in Kingston by the hostel's Land Rover, which costs U.S.$40 each way for up to six passengers.

WHERE TO DINE

✪**Blue Mountain Inn**. Gordon Town Rd. ☎ **876/927-1700.** Reservations required. Jackets required for men (ties optional). Dinner main courses J$450–J$1,200 (U.S.$12.85–$34.20); lunch main courses J$400–J$1,000 (U.S.$11.40–$28.50). AE, DC, MC, V. Mon–Fri noon–2pm; Mon–Sat 7–9:30pm. Head north on Old Hope Rd. into the mountains. CARIBBEAN/INTERNATIONAL.

About a 20-minute drive north from downtown Kingston is an 18th-century coffee plantation house set high on the slopes of Blue Mountain. Surrounded by trees and flowers, it rests on the bank of the Mammee River. On cold nights, log fires blaze, and the dining room gleams with silver and sparkling glass. The inn is one of Jamaica's most famous restaurants, not only for food but also for atmosphere and service. The effort of dressing up is worth it, and the cool night air justifies it; women are advised to take a wrap.

Olivia della Costa offers fine cuisine, especially the fresh seafood and vegetables from the gardens of Jamaica, prepared with a contemporary touch. Menus change monthly. Top off your meal with one of the fresh-fruit desserts or homemade ice creams.

8 | Getting to Know Barbados

In 1751, a young American major named George Washington visited Barbados with his half-brother, Lawrence, who had developed tuberculosis. Regrettably, the future American president contracted smallpox here, and it left him marked for life. Barbados is said to have been the only place outside the United States that George Washington ever visited.

In the 19th century Barbados became famous as the sanatorium of the West Indies. Mainly British guests suffering from "the vapors" came here for the perfect climate and the relaxed, unhurried life.

The smallpox danger long gone, Barbados remains salubrious to the spirit, with its lush vegetation, its coral reefs, and its seemingly endless miles of pink-and-white sandy beaches. The most easterly of the long chain of Caribbean islands, it retains old-world charm, an imprint of grace and courtesy left from 300 years of British tradition.

Barbados is renowned for its hospitable people. In a way, Barbados is like an England in the tropics, with bandbox cottages set in neat little gardens, centuries-old parish churches, and a scenic, hilly area in the northeast known as the Scotland District, where a mist rises in the morning. Narrow roads ramble through the sugarcane fields trimmed with hedgerows. In Barbados, sugar is king and rum is queen.

1 The Regions in Brief

An uplifted coral island, Barbados is flat, especially when compared to the wild, volcanic terrain of the Antilles. It is about 21 miles long and 14 miles wide, with an area of 166 square miles. Barbados lies 200 miles from Trinidad, 1,610 miles southeast of Miami, 575 miles southeast of Puerto Rico, and 600 miles northeast of Caracas, Venezuela. Most hotels are on the western side, a sandy shoreline. The eastern side, fronting the Atlantic, is a breezy coastline lapped by whitecapped rollers. Experienced surfers like it, but it's not safe for amateur swimmers.

The beaches of Barbados are among the most beautiful in the Caribbean, and all are open to the public. White, sandy beaches start in the north at Hey at the Almond Beach Club—about a mile of sand—and continue almost unbroken to Brighton Beach, a local

<table>
<tr><td>

❷ **Did You Know?**

</td></tr>
</table>

- There is nothing but ocean between Barbados and Africa.
- Fine, red sand from the Sahara can tint Bajan sunsets.
- The Arawak established villages on Barbados 400 years before the birth of Christ.
- Ninety-four percent of the original immigrants from England were male—mostly in their teens and twenties.
- In the 1640s, 23,000 British colonials and 20,000 slaves from Africa lived on Barbados.
- Barbados is governed by the third-oldest parliament in the Commonwealth of Nations. Only those of Great Britain and Bermuda are older.
- Rachel Pringle, a Bajan, once operated the most successful house of prostitution in the Caribbean, catering at times to royalty.
- Barbados is the only place outside the United States visited by George Washington. He contracted smallpox here.
- Church and state at one point tried to ban calypso music in Barbados because of its political content.
- Barbados is the most densely populated island in the West Indies.
- About 38% of tourists to Barbados come from the United States, about 22% from Great Britain, and about 14% from Canada.

favorite, in the south. Needham's Point, with a lighthouse, is the one of the most typical beaches on the heavily built-up South Coast. Local beach lovers flock here on weekends, although we have other favorites.

The island is divided, for administrative purposes, into several parishes. The most interesting for visitors include the following:

Bridgetown & St. Michael   On the southwestern corner of the island, the capital, **Bridgetown,** is small but pulsating with life—in fact, it's one of the liveliest capitals in the Caribbean, although there's nowhere near the activity (or danger) of bustling Kingston, Jamaica. Colonial buildings and contemporary office blocks go hand in hand—for some, mere backdrops to the vendors hawking their wares. The city is reached by two bridges, both in the east, including one spanning the Constitution River (it's not actually a river) and Chamberlin Bridge, which will take you to the waterfront, called the Careenage.

The surrounding parish of **St. Michael** traditionally has been the hub of Bajan business activity and culture. Although Barbados has far more interesting parishes from a traveler's point of view, St. Michael is visited for shopping in Bridgetown and for its **Barbados Museum,** directly south of Bridgetown. Standing across the street from the museum is **Garrison Savannah,** one of the finest parade grounds in the Caribbean.

St. James (The Gold Coast)   This is the heart of the West Coast tourist district, sometimes referred to as the Gold Coast or the Platinum Coast. Most of its posh hotels and restaurants stretch along Highway 1, which runs up the West Coast from Bridgetown. Nearly all the deluxe resorts are found here, including the Colony Club; the rich and famous have hung out at Sandy Lane. Over the years everyone from Princess Margaret to Mick Jagger, from Jackie O to the late Claudette Colbert

Barbados

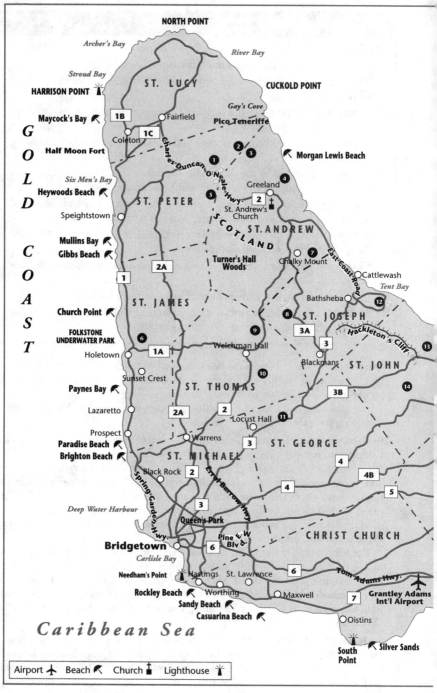

Archer's Bay

River Bay

NORTH POINT

Stroud Bay

ST. LUCY

CUCKOLD POINT

HARRISON POINT

Gay's Cove

Maycock's Bay — 1B — Fairfield

Pico Teneriffe

1C

Coleton

Morgan Lewis Beach

Half Moon Fort

1 2 3

4 Greeland

Six Men's Bay

5

Heywoods Beach

ST. PETER

2 St. Andrew's Church

ST. ANDREW

Speightstown

SCOTLAND

Mullins Bay

7 Chalky Mount

Cattlewash

Gibbs Beach

2A

East Coast Road

Tent Bay

Turner's Hall Woods

12

1

Bathsheba

Church Point

ST. JAMES

8

ST. JOSEPH

Hackleton's Cliff

FOLKSTONE UNDERWATER PARK

6

3A

9

3

13

1A

Welchman Hall

Blackmans

ST. JOHN

Holetown

Paynes Bay

Sunset Crest

10

ST. THOMAS

14

Lazaretto

3B

2A

2

Prospect

Locust Hall

11

Warrens

Paradise Beach

3

ST. GEORGE

Brighton Beach

2

ST. MICHAEL

4

Black Rock

4

4B

3

4

5

Deep Water Harbour

Queen's Park

CHRIST CHURCH

Bridgetown

6

Pine E-W Blvd.

Carlisle Bay

6

Tom Adams Hwy.

Needham's Point — Hastings — St. Lawrence

7

Grantley Adams Int'l Airport

Rockley Beach — Worthing

Maxwell

Sandy Beach

Casuarina Beach

Oistins

Caribbean Sea

South Point

Silver Sands

Airport ✈ Beach ✦ Church ⛪ Lighthouse ☀

GOLD COAST

186

Caribbean Islands

Barbados

Andromeda
  Botanical Gardens ⑫
Barbados Wildlife Reserve ❶
Chalky Mount Potteries ❼
Cherry Tree Hill ❸
Codrington College ⑮
Farley Hill National Park ❺
Flower Forest
  of Barbados ❽
Gun Hill Signal Station ⑪
Harrison's Cave ⑩
Morgan Lewis Sugar
  Windmill & Museum ❹
Sam Lord's Castle ⑰
St. James Church ❻
St. John's Church ⑬
St. Nicholas Abbey ❷
Sunbury Plantation House ⑯
Villa Nova ⑭
Welchman Hall Gully ❾

Atlantic Ocean

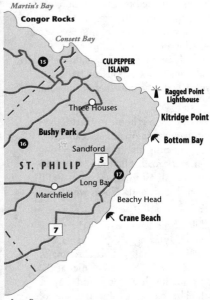

Martin's Bay

Congor Rocks

Consett Bay

⑮

**CULPEPPER
ISLAND**

Ragged Point
Lighthouse

Three Houses

Kitridge Point

Bushy Park

Bottom Bay

⑯

Sandford

ST. PHILIP

5

⑰

Long Bay

Marchfield

Beachy Head

7

Crane Beach

Long Bay

0   3 km
     1.9 mi

N

187

have passed along this coast's too-narrow highway. The parish embraces some of the best beaches along the coast and the town of Holetown, where an obelisk marks the spot where the British ship *Olive Blossom* landed the first settlers in 1627.

St. Peter Wedged between the Gold Coast to the south and seldom-visited St. Lucy parish at the top of the island, St. Peter spans Barbados and opens onto the Caribbean Sea in the west and the Atlantic Ocean in the east. Many of the finest homes on the island are found here, along with such tourist attractions as **St. Nicholas Abbey, Farley Hill National Park,** and **Barbados Wildlife Reserve,** home of the rare green monkey. It is also home to the town of **Speightstown,** once a major sugar port and now a fishing center with a bustling waterfront, old houses, and restored **Church of St. Peter's.** People in the north of the island do their shopping in Speightstown.

Christ Church South and east of Bridgetown, the southernmost parish of Christ Church embraces **Oistins,** the fishing capital of the island, and **Hastings** and **Worthing,** where you will find many of the least expensive accommodations and restaurants on Barbados. Accordingly, Christ Church attracts vacationers of more modest means than does posh St. James/Gold Coast. It has a string of white sandy beaches and a surf that lures windsurfers from around the world. The parish is also a center of commercial activity, although nothing to equal that of St. Michael.

St. Philip In the southeastern corner of Barbados, bordered by Christ Church in the west and St. John to the north, St. Philip geographically is the biggest parish in Barbados. It is a long way from Bridgetown, however, so it has been allowed to sleep. Since it borders the rough Atlantic Ocean—not the tranquil Caribbean Sea— it hasn't been overtaken by developers' bulldozers. It is visited mainly by travelers who want to see **Sam Lord's Castle,** one of the major attractions of Barbados. However, developers are coming in fast, so you'd better go now before its rural charms disappear.

St. John Site of the East Coast sugar plantations, St. John is home to **Hackleton's Cliff,** which at 1,000 feet offers some of the most panoramic Atlantic Ocean vistas. In many ways, this is the most ideal parish for wandering about, or even getting lost. There's always something to discover down every road. Highways 4 and 3B split through the parish. Follow 3B to **St. John's Parish Church,** set upon a cliff fronting the Atlantic. One of the major attractions here is **Villa Nova,** which was visited by Queen Elizabeth II and Prince Philip.

St. Joseph Windswept St. Joseph, in the middle of the East Coast, is the site of **"Little Scotland,"** with rolling hills, tiny hamlets, grazing sheep, and valleys. Its main target is the fishing village of **Bathsheba** and nearby **Tent Bay,** major destinations for both visitors and Bajans, who head here for Sunday picnics at the beach. Visitors often pass through here heading for lunch at the world-famous (although extremely modest) **Atlantic Hotel.** The parish is also the site of **St. Joseph Anglican Church,** above Horse Hill, and **Andromeda Gardens,** one of the island's choice beauty spots.

St. Thomas To the west of St. James, this landlocked parish lies in the heart of the island. It is traversed by routes 2 and 2A from St. Michael, and Route 1A coming from St. James. The major attractions here are natural wonders such as **Welchman Hall Gully** and **Harrison's Caves** (more about these attractions later). **Bagatelle Great House** is your best choice for a restaurant stopover.

St. Andrew With a small population—unique on overpopulated Barbados—this parish still maintains a lot of its rustic charm characterized by hills and dales. It lies directly northwest of St. Joseph. It has many attractions to lure visitors, including **Cherry Tree Hill** and **Chalky Mount Village,** where residents live mainly in wooden houses and earn their living making pottery.

2 Barbados Today

Although Barbados has been called "England in the tropics," change is in the air. Afternoon tea remains a tradition at many places, cricket is still the national sport, and many Bajans speak with a British accent. In spite of all that, many islanders are weighing the possibility of a divorce from the mother country. A government-appointed constitutional revision commission here is considering whether to discard Queen Elizabeth II as head of state. Such a divorce would make Barbados a republic, eliminating its formal ties to the British legal system.

There has been great dissatisfaction on the island about the Privy Council, the British high court whose members are appointed by the queen. This court is far too liberal for many local citizens, who want to break free of it. In general, Bajans favor capital punishment and find the court too lenient with criminals. Barbados has already restored the use of a whip with knotted cords to punish criminals and has widened grounds for corporal punishment in schools, all of which is against present British enforcement and law.

Crime has been on the rise in recent years, although Barbados is still viewed as a safe destination. The difference between the haves and the have-nots doesn't cause the sometimes-violent clash here that it does on some other islands, such as Jamaica.

The hotel and restaurant boom on Barbados has been phenomenal—almost too phenomenal for some, especially restaurateurs facing empty dining rooms because of the severe competition, or hoteliers with empty rooms at certain slow periods of the year.

By Caribbean standards, unemployment remains reasonably low (but don't tell that to someone out of work); the government is stable; and business is always paramount. Visitors are genuinely welcomed by most of the population, and you won't be confronted with the awful poverty of some destinations, although most Bajans are far from rich (most live in small wooden houses).

A very British but not stuffy atmosphere prevails. Only Sandy Hotel, a deluxe hotel, maintains a more straitlaced British ambience.

Barbados doesn't have the turmoil and strife of Jamaica, and certainly not the violence. For that reason, it remains in the vanguard of islands attracting visitors to its shores. Crime is on the rise, but it's mainly in the form of petty robberies and muggings. Attacks on tourists continue to be rare. Even through the island is hardly perfect or free of problems, it remains one of the more tranquil destinations in the Caribbean, especially for a nation with such a large population.

Knowing how dependent the island economy is on tourism, Barbados continues to upgrade and improve its tourist structure. Its cruise terminals were recently renovated to the tune of $6 million; today they are one of the Caribbean's finest facilities. Barbados now attracts some 450,000 to 500,000 cruise passengers every year.

The island nation has even made it easier to tie the knot. The island recently passed a law reducing the time restriction, enabling couples to marry on the day of their arrival, if they so choose. Weddings on the island have now become almost as popular as honeymoons.

3 History 101

Dateline

- 1625 First English landing on Barbados at Holetown.
- 1627 First English settlement established near Holetown.
- 1639 First legislature established.
- 1640 Sugar industry begun by Sir James Drax.
- 1751 George Washington visits Barbados on his only overseas trip; catches smallpox.
- 1766 Bridgetown destroyed by fire.
- 1834 Slavery abolished.
- 1838 Complete freedom granted to former slaves.
- 1876 Black Bajans riot.
- 1884 Franchise Act passed.
- 1905 British garrison withdraws.
- 1937 Island-wide riots erupt.
- 1938 Grantley H. Adams heads Barbados Labour Party.
- 1962 West Indies Federation dissolves after 4 years.
- 1966 Barbados becomes independent nation in the Commonwealth of Nations. Country joins United Nations.
- 1967 Barbados joins Organization of American States.
- 1973 First Barbados national currency issued.
- 1982 U.S. President and Mrs. Ronald Reagan visit Barbados.
- 1985 Prime Minister J. M. G. M. Tom Adams dies in office.
- 1986 Errol Barrow becomes prime minister for second time.
- 1987 Barrow dies in office; L. Erskine Sandiford becomes prime minister.

continues

The first known inhabitants of Barbados were the Arawak, who immigrated from South America some 400 years before the birth of Christ. They had disappeared by A.D. 1200, perhaps wiped out by the Carib, who dominated Barbados for 300 years.

All Indians had disappeared by the time the first British expedition arrived in 1625, claiming the island for England. The British found only wild hogs left by early Portuguese explorers. A Portuguese navigator, Pedro a Camoes, had come ashore in 1536 and named the island Los Barbados, "the bearded ones," after the shaggy fig trees along the shoreline. He did not establish a settlement.

On February 17, 1627, a ship called *William and John,* captained by Henry Powell, brought 80 Englishmen and 10 Africans (captured from a Spanish galleon) to the West Coast of Barbados. This landing is celebrated annually at the Holetown Festival. The early settlers imported about 40 Arawak to teach them how to cultivate Caribbean crops.

To the British, Barbados was reminiscent of the rolling downs of Cornwall and Devon. They soon turned the island into a Little England, tropical style. It became the most British colony in the New World, never having existed under any other flag. In 1639, a parliament along English lines was established, and the island was divided into the 11 parishes that exist today.

A thriving colony of Europeans and African slaves, predominantly male, turned Barbados into a prosperous land, based on trading in tobacco and cotton. By the 1640s, sugarcane production, an industry established by Sir James Drax, dominated the economy. More and more slaves were imported to work these sugar plantations.

Many English families settled here in the 18th and 19th centuries, in spite of outbreaks of yellow fever and intermittent wars. Because of the early importation of so many black laborers, Barbados is the most densely populated of the West Indian islands. No English-speaking visitor ever achieved the fame of George Washington, who arrived in 1751 on his only overseas trip. He promptly caught smallpox.

In 1766, a raging fire—a curse of the Caribbean—struck Bridgetown, destroying most of the capital. A monstrous hurricane devastated the island in 1780.

Once Barbados was the most heavily defended fortress island in the Caribbean, with 26 forts ringing its 21 miles of coast. Perhaps for that reason, the island was never invaded by another nation.

Slavery was abolished in 1834, and by 1838 complete freedom had been granted to former slaves.

■ **1989** 350th anniversary of Barbados Parliament observed.

■ **1991** 25th anniversary of independence observed.

■ **1997** Commission investigates possibilities of breaking ties with England.

Their descendants would eventually take over the island politically. Of the original English settlers, about 20 of their families dominated the island's history and economic development during the early colonial period. Descendants of many of these families still rank among the island's elite and heavily influence its cultural life. Some of their beautiful and well-preserved plantation houses bear witness to the pattern of English country life they re-created in Barbados.

Although black and white Bajans live in relative peace today, that was not always the case. For example, in the spring of 1876 riots erupted as black Bajans protested against the rule of the white "plantocracy." That riot ended with eight dead and 400 in jail. One of the injustices the Bajans protested was that only 1,300 of the island's 160,000 inhabitants were eligible to vote.

The constitution was amended in 1884 with a Franchise Act that allowed people who owned less land to vote in elections. Many of the island's nonwhites still did not qualify, however, since whites owned 90% of the land.

Barbadians emigrated to avoid the harsh conditions on the island, thousands going to Central America to help build the Panama Canal. The sugar industry had deteriorated into a depressed state by this time.

In 1905, the last of the British garrison left Barbados, although the island was still decades away from independence.

Riots in the streets continued in the years between the world wars, notably in 1937 when unrest lasted for 3 days. Fields were raided and shops broken into. These disturbances led to social change and the first lasting labor parties.

Much of the social and political change was directed by Grantley H. Adams, who from 1938 to 1945 was a spokesman for most people on the island. Adams headed the Barbados Labour Party. His first victory came in 1940, when the Labour Party won five seats in the House of Assembly.

Adams represented Barbados at the 1958 inauguration of the Federation of the West Indies, and served as its prime minister. The federation never really gained political clout, and it came to an end in 1962.

In 1961, Barbados was run by Errol Barrow, who succeeded Adams as prime minister of Barbados. His liberal Democratic Labour Party (DLP) carried out a number of public works programs.

Barrow led the island to independence on November 30, 1966. Barbados was now a sovereign state in the Commonwealth of Nations, and the little island entered the United Nations. Barrow was the first prime minister. The following year, Barbados joined the Organization of American States, and by 1973 the island issued its own currency. Barrow served for more than a decade as prime minister.

J. M. G. M. Tom Adams, son of Grantley Adams, led Barbados into the 1980s. In 1985, however, Adams died in office. Barrow became prime minister for the second time in 1986, but he died in office the following year. L. Erskine Sandiford then became prime minister. Sandiford's DLP won a strong parliamentary majority in elections in 1991, and he continued as prime minister.

In the late 1990s, Barbados has a population of about 255,000, almost all of whom are at least partly of black African descent. Barbados enjoys a 98% literacy rate, and a very high percentage of the island's youth attain a college or university education.

In the '90s, the Barbados economy continues to grow, but the unemployment rate remains high. Leading industries continue to be tourism, farming (principally sugarcane), fishing, light manufacturing (notably clothing, furniture, electronic equipment, and medical supplies), and financial services (including "offshore" financial institutions).

As Barbados faces the millennium, it is considering the unthinkable: a break from England. Like many commonwealth nations, including Australia, Barbados, through a government-appointed constitutional revision commission, is considering removing Queen Elizabeth as head of state and charting its own course as an independent nation. One of the reasons often cited for a possible break with the England is that many citizens of Barbados consider the Privy Council, the British high court, far too liberal for their tastes, especially regarding what is viewed as "leniency" toward criminals and its increasing tolerance and protection of gay rights.

4 Calypso!

Although many Bajans today listen to reggae music—most often from Jamaica—calypso is still dominant on the island. Calypso was brought to Barbados from West Africa in the early 17th century. The early songs spoke of hardships and sorrows suffered as the slaves labored in the sugarcane fields. The British overlords looked upon this music as "pagan," "barbarous," and potentially revolutionary. In 1688, the all-white English-appointed assembly passed a law banning drums or local musical instruments, as they feared it was an incitement to violence and rioting. Only through secret rituals could the slaves keep alive their music and African traditions. Even after emancipation, calypso music was still viewed with distaste by the ruling elite in Barbados, and it remained largely underground until a white Bajan group, the Merrymen, revived it in the 1960s.

Today, calypso music is heard all over the world. Much of the calypso music of Barbados was influenced early by Trinidad, which has far deeper calypso roots. But with the fervor attached to calypso by Barbados, the art form is now among the most powerful on the island.

Who judges the relative merits of a calypso artist? It's up to the crowd. Calypso performances receive wild outpourings of approval at such island-wide competitions as the Annual Crop Over Festival, where the title "Calypso Monarch" is bestowed on the performer whose music best symbolizes the spirit of calypso. Since 1995, the setting for the festival has been a natural amphitheater on the island's East Coast road. An equivalent title is "Party Monarch," which is awarded to the performer best able to energize crowds of as many as 15,000 listeners in ways that are conducive to letting the good times roll. Most visitors hear calypso as strictly entertainment, but to Bajans it is often a singing newspaper, full of social comment and political satire.

Although the titles are awarded informally, with various degrees of island politics influencing the decisions, they don't come easily, and the winners often display their trophies for many years to come. Major luminaries of the art form include The Mighty Gabby, who has emerged as the nation's premier calypso performer, thanks

Miss Rachel & the Prince

Rachel Pringle was born in 1753, the daughter of a schoolmaster from Scotland, William Lauder, and his slave mistress. According to reports of the day, Lauder was vicious to Rachel and mistreated her. Fleeing from his tyrannical household, Rachel was aided by Captain Thomas Pringle, who took a fancy to her and paid an awesome sum to Lauder for her freedom. When the captain installed his new sex toy in a house in Bridgetown, Rachel took his name.

The captain wanted a child by his new mistress but she apparently couldn't have one; their liaison remained fruitless. When Pringle sailed away on a voyage, however, Rachel decided to pretend she was pregnant. During his absence, she borrowed a child from another Bajan woman. When Pringle returned home, she presented him with "his" newborn. Pringle accepted the child as his own— until its mother showed up to reclaim her baby. Infuriated with Rachel's deception, Pringle walked out on her.

Ever resourceful, Rachel didn't waste time finding herself another guardian, a man known only as Polgreen. Taverns on the island were often run by mulatto women who were actually the paramours of the island's wealthy, so sometime in the 1780s Rachel launched the island's first hotel. Now long gone but originally on St. George Street, her ill-reputed establishment quickly became popular with the British Royal Navy.

Her most prominent guest—or should we say client—was Prince William Henry. The prince in the 1780s wasn't the staid figure he later became as King William IV. Fueled by Barbados rum, he joined in a night of hell-raising debauchery, smashing furniture and breaking the plates. At one point the future king turned over Rachel's chair, sending her sprawling onto the floor.

Before the prince sailed away, she presented his future Highness with a bill for 700 British pounds. That was an awful lot of money back then, but surprisingly, William Henry agreed to pay.

Rachel used the money to restore her establishment and renamed it the Royal Naval Hotel. Its reputation and clientele remained unchanged, but during her lifetime this hotbed hotel made the enormously fat Miss Rachel a good living entertaining the pride of the British fleet.

to his labors at revitalizing the art form, and for his designation as Calypso Monarch at four annual festivals. Gabby (his real name is Tony Carter) often mingles danceable rhythms with themes protesting Western society's social status quo. Today, he always figures high on any list that designates patriarchs of Barbados' Calypsonian forms.

His major rival today is another calypsonian, Red Plastic Bag (whose everyday name is Stedson Wiltshire), who first achieved recognition in 1982 with his "Mr. Harding Can't Burn." He rivals the Mighty Gabby in the number of times he's been designated as Calypso Monarch (four). In his case, the years were 1982, 1984, 1989, and 1996. Fifteen records have been made that feature his music.

To many, calypso music is best represented by the charismatic Eddy Grant, who was born in Antigua. This singer/producer preserves and promotes calypso music from his studio on Bayler's Plantation in the parish of St. Philip, where he has lived since 1981. Grant has been called the most charismatic singer in the entire

Caribbean Basin, and his records are widely played on Barbados. He promotes local calypsonians on his Ice Records label; Grant has been an enormous backer and promoter, both artistically and financially, of Gabby.

Final mention of a male calypsonian involves a major new talent, one of the genuine rising stars of Bajan music: Edwin Yearwood, whose musical gifts have been universally recognized since he was 14. With his band *Krosfyah,* he won the title of Party Monarch and Calypso Monarch in 1995, and was designated as Party Monarch a second time in 1996. His biggest hit, "Obadele," is still a staple on Bajan radio stations throughout the year.

Don't assume that all of Barbados' calypso stars are men: In 1997, the title of Party Monarch was awarded to a woman, Alison Hinds, whose band (Square One), is increasingly visible and talked about.

One of the most unusual blends of British and African traditions in Barbados is the tuk band. There are two divergent opinions surrounding the origin of its name: The first of these involves the sounds made by a large log drum that gives out a sound like "boom-a-tuk." The other derives from a medieval Scottish (Gaelic) word ("the touk, or beating, of a drum") that was introduced to Barbados with the fife and drum corps of the 18th-century British regiments. Originally, it included the use of a tin flute, a snare-drum, a bass drum, and a steel triangle. Originally devised as a means of keeping a phalanx of soldiers marching to the same speed and rhythm, it was later "creolized" into a broad category of syncopated music that would officially horrify any self-respecting army sergeant. Today, the Africanized musical form provides backgrounds for mock parades, where mostly male performers walk on stilts, dress as parti-colored frolicking bears or donkeys, or cross-dress as salacious, easy-going women with enormous *derrieres.* One of the island's most beloved practitioners of the art form is an artist known as Poonka (Prince Willock).

A late-breaking derivation of the tuk band tradition was developed by young Generation X-ers, members of which have invented "Ringbang." Its driving force derives partly from rhythmical chanting, equivalent in some ways to rap music as practiced in the U.S., or soca as played in Jamaica. Intended exclusively as a background for dancing, it pays little if any attention to social commentary.

With the advent of Radio Barbados in 1963, local calypso music received a greater audience, and many singers emerged from oblivion. Along came not only Mighty Gabby, as mentioned, but Mighty Dragon, Mighty Viper, Natalie Burke, John King, and Lord Summers.

For the best selection of buyable recordings of Bajan calypso, tuk, or Ringbang artists, head for the **No. 1 Record Shop,** on Independence Square, in Bridgetown (☎ **246/426-5831**). Another, less impressive, branch of this outfit lies within the Cave Shepherd Department Store on Broad Street, in Bridgetown (same phone).

5 A Taste of Barbados

Today's traveler will find an extensive selection of fine restaurants in Barbados serving French, Italian, and other continental cuisines, as do the dining rooms of the island's many hotels. If possible, however, escape the dining rooms of your hotel and sample the island's own cuisine, which is interesting but not exotically spicy. Bajan cuisine is a culinary hybrid, primarily drawn from Africa and England, but also heavily influenced by Spanish, French, East Indian, Chinese, and American cooking techniques brought to the island by visitors and immigrants.

The famous flying fish appears on every menu, and when prepared right it's a delicacy, moist and succulent, nutlike in flavor, approaching the subtlety of brook trout. Bajans boil it, steam it, bake it, stew it, fry it, stuff it, or whatever.

Try also the sea urchin, or *oursin*, which Bajans also often call "sea eggs." Crab-in-the-back is another specialty, as is langouste, the Barbadian all-tail lobster. Dolphin (the fish known elsewhere as mahimahi, not the mammal) and saltfish cakes are other popular items on the menu. Also typical are yams, sweet potatoes, and eddoes, dark-brown, thick-skinned underground parts of the taro plant. And Barbadian fruits, including papaya, passion fruit, and mangoes, are luscious.

If you hear that any hotel or restaurant is having a *cohobblopot*, or more commonly, a Bajan buffet, make a reservation. This is a Barbadian term that means to "cook up," and it inevitably will produce an array of local delicacies.

Pepperpot, stews, and curries are made with local chicken, pork, beef, and fish. The secret of the flavorful dishes, as any Bajan cook will tell you, is in the "seasoning up." It is said that seasoning techniques have changed little since the 16th century.

At Christmas, when many U.S. visitors come to Barbados, roast ham or turkey is served with *jug-jug*, a rich casserole of Scottish derivation that includes salt beef, ground corn flour, green pigeon peas, and spices. *Cou-cou*, a side dish made from okra and cornmeal, accompanies fish, especially the flying fish of Barbados.

Note: Barbados is one of the few places in the Caribbean where barracuda is a safe and acceptable food item. In other parts of the region, it is sometimes poisonous because of its diet of other fish that feed on certain kinds of plankton.

When it came time to invite a friend for a drink, old-time Bajans used to say, "Let's fire a grog. "Beer, perhaps more so than rum, has now become virtually the national drink. For many, Banks and beer are virtually the same word. Banks refers to the bottled lager that has been produced on the island since 1961. Throughout the island you'll hear Bajans ordering, "Banks thanks."

Barbados rum, including Mount Gay, the most popular brand name, has been the traditional drink of the island since the days of the planter aristocracy. Colors of rum range from clear to mahogany brown.

A drink unique to Barbados is falernum, made from rum, lime juice, sugar syrup, and various essences. Falernum, which is thick and syrupy, is often added to rum cocktails, although others prefer to drink it as a liqueur.

Mauby—colloquially "mabee"—is another traditional drink of Barbados, its flavor coming from the imported bark of a tree. In olden days, mauby vendors hawked the drink on the streets of Bridgetown, but today it comes in bottles.

Planning a Trip to Barbados

This chapter is devoted to the where, the when, and the how of your trip to Barbados—all those advance-planning tips that can ensure a smooth vacation.

Many items mentioned in chapter 3, "Planning a Trip to Jamaica," are equally applicable to Barbados. This is especially true of health and insurance, tips for travelers with special needs, and our basic consumer advice on booking package tours, airfares, cruises, and rental cars. We will not repeat these topics here, so refer to chapter 3 for more complete information.

1 Visitor Information, Entry Requirements & Customs

VISITOR INFORMATION

In the **United States,** you can obtain information before you go at the following Barbados Tourism Authority offices: 800 Second Ave., New York, NY 10017 (☎ **212/986-6516**); and 3440 Wilshire Blvd., Suite 1215, Los Angeles, CA 90010 (☎ **800/ 221-9831** or 213/380-2198). Other outlets include 158 Alhambra Circle, Suite 1270, Miami, FL 33134 (☎ **305/442-7471**).

In **Canada,** there is an office at 105 Adelaide St. W., Suite 1010, Toronto, Ontario M5H 1P9 (☎ **416/214-9880**).

In the **United Kingdom,** the Barbados Tourism Authority is at 263 Tottenham Court Rd., London W1P OLA (☎ **0171/ 636-9448**).

Once you arrive, check with the Barbados Tourism Authority on Harbour Road, in Bridgetown (☎ **246/427-2623**).

If you're interested in pursuing further information regarding Barbados via the Internet, there are thousands of sites that can assist you—from general Caribbean information to specific Bajan interests from dining to diving. We have gathered a few of them for you to help make your vacation a little easier to plan. **www. barbados.org** is the official site of the Barbados Tourism Authority, complete with information ranging from hotels to a Barbados event calendar. **www.jwg.com/land/barbados/barbados.html** is a thorough site offering a hotel map, and food, drink, and entertainment options, in addition to shopping and things to do. The site even features a 5-minute audio tour of the island. If you are undecided about which hotel to select, try **www.where2stay.com/islands/islands/barbados.html**, a relatively famous site with on-line Caribbean travelers. If you are interested in anything regarding Barbados or the rest of the Caribbean, this is one of the better places to look. If your attraction to Barbados is sports related, the sporting life is well represented on the Internet. Two sites we recommend are **www.ehi.com/travel/carib/barbados/barbtsl.htm** and **www.divefree.net/diving/coralisle.htm**, the latter of which focuses on sightseeing, island tours, and the vast array of caves and underground lakes that make Barbados a water sportsman's paradise.

ENTRY REQUIREMENTS

A U.S. or Canadian citizen coming directly from North America to Barbados for a period not exceeding 3 months must have proof of identity and national status, such as a passport, which is always preferred. However, a birth certificate (either an original or a certified copy) may also be acceptable, provided it is backed up by a photo ID. (We suggest just bringing your passport when you're going to another country just to be safe.) For stays longer than 3 months, a passport is required. An ongoing or return ticket is also necessary. Vaccinations are not required to enter Barbados if you're coming from the United States or Canada.

British subjects, Australians, and New Zealanders need a valid passport.

CUSTOMS

Allowances for goods brought into Barbados include 1 liter of wine or spirits, 200 cigarettes or 100 cigars, not exceeding 250 grams in aggregate. All articles in excess of this amount are subject to the relevant duty and tax. Personal effects are also not subject to duty, including a passenger's baggage containing apparel and articles for personal use. Visitors can bring in unlimited currency. Prohibited articles include illegal drugs, but also pornography, the nature of which is determined by the customs official. What is viewed by them as pornography may be seized, and persons attempting to import it may be liable to fines and prosecution.

For information about what you can bring home, see chapter 3, "Planning a Trip to Jamaica."

2 Money

The Barbados dollar, the official currency, circulates in $100, $20, $10, and $5 notes, and $1, 25¢, and 10¢ silver coins, and 5¢ and 1¢ copper coins. The Bajan dollar is worth about 50¢ in U.S. currency.

U.S. dollars are widely accepted, as are traveler's checks.

If you need to get cash from your own bank account, or a cash advance from your credit card, there are ATMs at the major shopping malls and at all banks. For specific locations of Cirrus machines on Barbados, call ☎ **800/424-7787.** To learn of Plus locations in Barbados, call ☎ **800/843-7587.**

If you do need to change money, most banks and hotel desks can accommodate you.

Note: Currency quotations in this guide are in U.S. dollars (U.S.$) unless specified as Barbados dollars (BD$).

3 When to Go

Our advice about traveling to Jamaica in high season vs. low season applies equally to Barbados. See chapter 3 for a full discussion.

The Bajan Dollar, the U.S. Dollar & the British Pound

The chart below gives rounded-off U.S. dollar and British pound values for Bajan prices. The chart assumes an exchange rate of $BD2 to each U.S. dollar, which has remained fixed in this position for many years. However, the British pound and the Bajan dollar fluctuate according to the same market conditions as the U.S. dollar and the British pound. At press time, that exchange rate is $BD2.80 for each British pound.

Barbados Dollars	U.S. $	U.K. £
1	.50	.36
5	2.50	1.79
10	5.00	3.57
75	37.50	26.78
100	50.00	35.70
200	100.00	71.40
300	150.00	107.10
400	200.00	142.80
500	250.00	178.50
750	375.00	267.75
1,000	500.00	357.00
5,000	2,500.00	1,785.00
10,000	5,000.00	3,570.00
25,000	12,500.00	8,925.00
50,000	25,000.00	17,850.00
100,000	50,000.00	35,700.00

THE CLIMATE   Trade winds keep humidity low on Barbados. More than 3,000 hours of sunshine mix with enough rain to produce bumper crops of fruit and vegetables.

The climate here is pleasantly tropical and varies little throughout the year. Average high temperatures in the popular winter months, November through March, range from 83° to 86°F; average lows, 70° to 73°F. Average highs April through October are 85° to 87°F; average lows, 72° to 74°F. The rainy season is June to November, when the island gets about 75% of its annual precipitation. This period is also the hurricane season.

HOLIDAYS   Bajans celebrate the following public holidays: New Year's Day (January 1), Errol Barrow Day (January 21), Good Friday, Easter Monday, Labor Day (early May), Whitmonday, Kadooment Day (first Monday in August), United Nations Day (October 7), Independence Day (November 30), Christmas Day (December 25), and Boxing Day (December 26).

BARBADOS CALENDAR OF EVENTS

Because the dates of many of the following events can vary from year to year, check with a Barbados Tourist Authority office for exact dates (see "Visitor Information," above). You might also contact the Barbados Board of Tourism, 800 Second Ave., New York, NY 10017 (☎ **800/221-9831** or 212/986-6516).

January

- **Barbados International Windsurfing.** This annual event draws some of the world's most skilled windsurfers, who consider surfing off Barbados the best this side of Hawaii. Events revolve around the Barbados Windsurfing Club. January 9 to 11.
- **Barbados National Trust Open House Program.** This program allows noteworthy houses on the island to be viewed by the public. Houses are selected by the National Trust on the basis of historical and architectural interest and decorative beauty. Call the National Trust at ☎ **246/426-2421** for more details. January 3 to April 5.
- **Barbados Horticultural Society's Open Garden Program,** Christ Church. A wide variety of exotic flowers and plants are displayed by regional horticultural societies. January 4, 11, 18, and 25.

February

- **Holetown Festival,** St. James. This weeklong event commemorates the landing of the first European settlers at Holetown in 1627. Highlights include street fairs, a Royal Barbados Police Band concert, a music festival in the historic parish church, a road race, and the crowning of a queen. February 15 to 22.

March–April

- **Sandy Lane Barbados Gold Cup,** Garrison Savannah. Horses from Barbados, Jamaica, Martinique, and Trinidad and Tobago participate in an invitational race at this historic site. March 7.
- **Oistins Fish Festival.** This festival commemorates the signing of the charter of Barbados and celebrates the life and contribution made by this fishing town to the development of the island. The program features fishing, boat racing, fishboning competitions, a Coast Guard exhibition, food stalls, arts and crafts, dancing, singing, and road races. April 10 to 13.

July–August

- ✪ **Crop Over Festival.** The island's major national festival celebrates the completion of the sugarcane harvest and recognizes the hardworking men and women of the sugar industry. Communities all over the island participate in fairs, concerts, calypso competitions, cart parades, and other cultural activities. Crop Over includes a grand costume parade and culminates in Kadooment Day, a national holiday on the first Monday in August. June 28 to August 3.

August

- **Banks International Hockey Festival.** Men's, women's, and mixed teams from many countries join Bajan clubs for a week of field hockey competition. For a listing of events and locations, contact the Barbados Hockey Federation, P.O. Box 66B, Britton Hill, St. Michael (☎ **246/423-5442**). August 23 to 30.

November

- **National Independence Festival of Creative Arts.** In 1966, Barbados became an independent country in the Commonwealth of Nations, and that achievement is marked by celebrations, with competitions and performances in dance, drama, singing, and acting. The festival begins in early November and culminates November 30, Independence Day, a national holiday. For information on the various events, contact the Barbados National Cultural Foundation, West Terrace, St. James (☎ **246/424-0907**).

December

- **Run Barbados Road Race Series.** This series is comprised of a 10-kilometer race and a 26-mile, 385-yard marathon, attracting runners from around the world. The 10k race is held in and around Bridgetown, and the marathon begins at the Grantley Adams International Airport and finishes at Heywoods, north on the West Coast. December 5 to 6.

4 Package Tours

Package tours, which usually include airfare as well as accommodations, transfers, and perhaps even meals in one total price, are really the smart way to go in the Caribbean. If you try to book your own airfare and call individual hotels directly, you'll wind up spending hundreds more than you would by buying a package. Packagers buy all these elements in bulk and pass part of the savings along to you.

It pays to shop around and compare, though. Different package tours may offer accommodations at the same hotels for very different prices. It all depends on the volume purchased by each packager. Using this book, however, you'll be able to compare the hotels offered and select the one you want.

To save time comparing the price and value of all the package tours out there, you can call **TourScan Inc.,** P.O. Box 2367, Darien, CT 06820 (☎ **800/962-2080** or 203/655-8091). Every season, the company gathers and computerizes the contents of about 200 brochures containing 10,000 different vacations in the Caribbean, The Bahamas, and Bermuda. TourScan selects the best value at each hotel and condo. Two catalogs are printed each year. Each lists a broad-based choice of hotels on most of the islands of the Caribbean, in all price ranges. (The scope of the islands and resort hotels is amazing.) Write to TourScan for their catalogs (U.S.$4 each; the price is credited to any TourScan vacation).

You can often get great package deals through the airlines. Most prominent among these is the tour desk at **American Airlines Fly-Away Vacations** (☎ **800/321-2121**). Holding an impressive array of vacant hotel rooms in inventory, American often sells Caribbean hotel bookings at prices substantially lower than similar rooms booked by an individual traveler. The packages are available only to passengers who simultaneously purchase transit to the Caribbean on American Airlines. On Barbados, there's a wide array of hotels from which to choose, often at very attractive rates.

It's best to remain flexible in your departure and return dates, because greater savings might be available to those willing to shift preferred dates slightly to take advantage of an unsold block of nights at a hotel. For details and more information, ask for the tour desk at American Airlines. (Many hotels they might offer are reviewed in this guidebook.) The telephone representative can sometimes also arrange a discounted rental car for however many days you specify.

Other leading tour operators to the Caribbean include:

Caribbean Concepts, 1428 Brickell Ave., Suite 402, Miami, FL 33131 (☎ **888/741-7711** in the U.S., or 305/373-8687; fax 305/373-8310), offering all-inclusive low-cost air-and-land packages to the islands, including apartments, hotels, villas, and condo rentals.

Consider also **Delta's Dream Vacations** (☎ **800/872-7786**), which offers customized trips to Jamaica or Barbados lasting from 2 to 20 days, including airfare, accommodations, and transfers. Tickets are refundable, and you can cancel for any reason.

From St. Louis, **Go-Go Tours** (☎ **800/821-3731**) flies package-tour customers on American Airlines to any of 30 different Bajan hotels for package-deal stays of between 3 days and a month.

Horizon Tours, 1634 Eye St. NW, Suite 301, Washington, DC 20006 (☎ **800/395-0025** or 202/393-8390; fax 202/393-1547), specializes in all-inclusive upscale resorts on both Jamaica and Barbados.

Despite the proliferation of the many bucket shops advertising special deals to the Caribbean (and Jamaica), your best bet might involve simply walking into the nearest office of North America's largest chain of travel agencies, **Liberty Travel,** whose outlets are concentrated primarily on the Atlantic seaboard. Depending on their inventory and marketing priorities at the time of your call, deals may or may not be attractive. There's no overall toll-free number for the chain, as each branch operates as a semi-independent unit. Consult your telephone directory or call directory assistance for the number of the branch nearest you. You won't get much in the way of service, but you will get a good deal.

American Express Vacations (☎ **800/241-1700**) is another option.

FOR BRITISH TRAVELERS

Caribbean Connection, Concorde House, Forest Street, Chester CH1 1QR (☎ **01244/341131**), offers all-inclusive packages (airfare and hotel) to the Caribbean and customizes tours for independent travel. It publishes two catalogs of Caribbean offerings, one featuring more than 160 properties on all the major islands, and a 50-page catalog of luxury all-inclusive properties.

Other Caribbean specialists operating out of England include **Kuoni Travel,** Kuoni House, Dorking, Surrey RH5 4AZ (☎ **01306/740-888**). **Caribtours,** 161 Fulham Rd., London SW3 6SN (☎ **0171/581-3517**), is a small, very knowledgeable specialist, tailoring itineraries to meet your demanding travel requirements.

5 Flying to Barbados

Before you try to book your own airfare and hotel separately, *be sure to read section 4, above, for important advice on package tours.* This is really the way to save serious money and avoid paying the unbelievably high rack rates at the island's resorts. See also chapter 3 for important advice on how to shop for the best airfares on the Web and through consolidators.

More than 20 daily flights arrive in Barbados from not only mainland North America and Puerto Rico, but from neighboring islands, some South American capitals, and several European hubs (notably London).

From North America, the major gateways to Barbados are New York, Miami, and Toronto. There also are flights from San Juan, Puerto Rico, the major Caribbean hub. Flying time to Barbados from New York is 4 ½ hours; from Miami, 3 ½ hours; from Toronto, 5 hours; and from San Juan, 1 ½ hours. **Grantley Adams International Airport** on Barbados is south of Bridgetown.

American Airlines (☎ **800/433-7300;** www.americanair.com) has dozens of connections passing through San Juan plus a daily nonstop flight from New York's JFK to Barbados and one from Miami to Barbados. U.S. passengers who do fly through San Juan can usually speed through U.S. Customs clearance in San Juan on their return flight rather than in their home cities, saving time and inconvenience.

Travelers via New York and Miami can opt for nonstop flights offered daily by **BWIA** (☎ 800/538-2942), the national airline of Trinidad and Tobago. BWIA also offers many flights from Barbados to Trinidad.

Canadians sometimes select nonstop flights to Barbados from Toronto. **Air Canada** (☎ 800/776-3000 in the U.S., or 800/268-7240 in Canada; www. aircanada.ca) offers the most nonstop scheduled flights from Canada to Barbados, with convenient evening departures. There are seven flights per week from Toronto in winter, plus one Sunday flight from Montréal year-round. In summer, when demand slackens, there are fewer flights from Toronto.

Barbados is a major hub of the Caribbean-based airline known as **LIAT** (☎ 246/434-5428 for reservations, or 246/428-0986 at the Barbados airport), which provides generally poor service from Barbados to a handful of neighboring islands, including St. Vincent in the Grenadines, Antigua, and Dominica.

Air Jamaica (☎ 800/523-5585; www.airjamaica.com) has increased service to Barbados from key U.S. feeder markets. Daily inbound and outbound flights link Barbados with Atlanta, Baltimore, Fort Lauderdale, and Miami through the airline's new Montego Bay hub. Additionally, Air Jamaica has added service between Los Angeles and Barbados on Saturday and Sunday, and service between Orlando and Barbados is also available Tuesday, Thursday, Saturday, and Sunday but requires an overnight stay in Montego Bay in each direction.

British Airways (☎ 800/247-9297; www.british-airways.com) offers nonstop service to Barbados from both of London's major airports (Heathrow and Gatwick).

6 Cruises

Perched directly in the path of the trade winds, in a relatively remote Atlantic position that's isolated from most of the other islands of the Caribbean archipelago, Barbados has always been a favorite destination for sailing vessels from the Americas and Europe. Here's a brief rundown on the lines that can take you there. See chapter 3 for a more complete description of the lines, their personalities, strengths, and offerings, plus tips on how to book your cruise at the best price.

Carnival Cruise Lines (☎ 800/327-9501), offering some of the biggest and most brightly decorated ships afloat, is the brashest and most successful mass-market cruise line in the world. Two of its ships, the very large *Fascination* and the smaller, more conventionally sized vessel *Jubilee,* stop at Barbados as part of their midwinter roster of cruises. *Fascination,* from a permanent base in San Juan, stops in Barbados (as well as St. Maarten, Dominica, and Martinique) as part of 7-day cruises through the Southern Caribbean. Carnival's *Jubilee* stops in Barbados as part of 10-day tours that also stop in Virgin Gorda, Tortola, Martinique, St. Lucia, and St. Thomas.

Celebrity Cruises (☎ 800/437-3111) offers the *Horizon,* which stops in Barbados as part of a 10-night cruise from Fort Lauderdale. Other ports of call include St. Maarten, St. Lucia, Antigua, and St. Thomas.

Club Med Cruises (☎ 800/4-LESHIP), as its name implies, is basically Club-Med-at-Sea, but within a more upscale, couple-oriented context than at most Club Med singles villages, and with fewer children than you'd find within any Club-Med family village. The *Club Med II,* which will be renamed the *Club Med I* sometime during the lifetime of this edition, sails the Caribbean every year between November and April. It's the largest cruise ship afloat with sails, but frankly, it benefits from wind power less frequently than you might hope for, and no one aboard shows any qualms about motoring, instead of sailing, between its home base of

Martinique and ports of call that include a stop in Barbados every other week. Other stopovers occur at isolated beaches in the Grenadines and St. Lucia.

Cunard (☎ 800/221-4770), despite whirlwinds of recent fiscal and managerial problems, and a 1997 move from its longtime New York headquarters to Miami, is famous for its British flair and its ownership of the legendary *QE2*, which makes Christmas and Easter circuits through the Caribbean, including stops at ports that include Dominica, St. Lucia, and Barbados. It also calls at Barbados as part of longer cruises that take the ship around the world.

More visible within the Caribbean are the line's smaller and more opulent vessels, *Sea Goddess I* and *II*, which resemble small but choice, and extremely expensive, private yachts when compared to a Carnival megaship. One of these, *Sea Goddess I*, defines St. Thomas, and to a lesser degree, Barbados, as its home port during part of each winter. From either of these ports, it begins transits through the Panama Canal and points throughout the central and southern Caribbean.

Holland America Line—Westours (☎ 800/426-0327) offers five respectably hefty and good-looking ships that spend substantial time cruising the Caribbean. One of them (*Ryndam*) spends the winter months on 10-day jaunts to Barbados. Originating at the port of Fort Lauderdale, other stops en route include Nassau, St. Thomas, St. Maarten, St. Lucia, and the company's private Bahamian island, Half Moon Cay.

Norwegian Cruise Line (☎ 800/327-7030) offers the *Norwegian Sea*, which has its home port in San Juan, and so gets you into the heart of the southern Caribbean sooner than vessels leaving from Florida. Ports of call, in addition to Barbados, include Santo Domingo, Dominica, St. Kitts, and St. Thomas.

Premier Cruises (☎ 800/990-7770) offers the seaworthy but not particularly glamorous *Seawind Crown*, the only major cruise ship based in the southern Caribbean port of Aruba. Most of its cruises last 7 nights, and focus on southern Caribbean islands that are too far from South Florida to be efficiently visited during an average 7-day cruise by most major cruise ships. They include stops at Barbados, as well as Curaçao and St. Lucia. Another option for passengers interested in visiting Barbados includes the *Island Breeze*, a dowager vessel built in the early 1960s that most recently belonged to Dolphin. Offering affordable 7-day cruises that depart from Santo Domingo, it leaves on tours that specialize in the Caribbean's central and southern tier. Ports of call vary on alternate weeks, but in addition to Barbados, they're likely to include Curaçao, Guadeloupe, St. Maarten, St. Thomas, Grenada, and Martinique.

Princess Cruises (☎ 800/421-0522) has a large and far-flung fleet that during the life of this edition will total between 8 and 10 megavessels. The one that most frequently stops in Barbados is the *Dawn Princess*. Based in San Juan, it visits Barbados as part of its every-other-week circuits through the Caribbean's southern tier. Other ports of call include St. Lucia, Martinique, St. Maarten, and St. Thomas.

There's also the *Monarch of the Seas*, run by **Royal Caribbean Cruise Line (RCCL)** (☎ 800/327-6700). From its year-round base in San Juan, it makes 7-night transits to Barbados as well as St. Thomas, St. Maarten, Antigua, and Martinique.

Windstar Cruises (☎ 800/258-7245) maintains a fleet of sailing ships that utilize adaptations of 19th-century designs and 21st-century materials in relatively upscale formats. In fall, winter, and spring, two of its vessels make 7-day excursions through either the Virgin Islands, and—from a base in Barbados—around the less-visited islands of the Caribbean's southern tier. Depending on the itinerary, stopovers include St. Thomas, Jost Van Dyke, Virgin Gorda, Saba, French

---

The Babe Ruth of Barbados

As in Jamaica and most other former outposts of the British Empire, cricket is the national pastime in Barbados. First made popular about 1870, the game is played by virtually every schoolboy. Some Bajans simply live for cricket.

The late cricket star Sir Frank Worrell, who might be described as the Babe Ruth of Barbados, became the country's first nonpolitical national hero. He scored 3,860 runs in 51 tests at an average of 49.48 runs—a truly outstanding accomplishment. Sir Frank died in 1967 of leukemia. Sir Garfield Sobers is another great Bajan cricket player whose name you may hear.

Cricket matches can last from a day for one inning to 5 days for two innings (obviously we're not talking about baseball innings here). If you'd like to see all or part of a local match, watch for announcements in the newspapers or ask at the tourist board.

St. Martin, Barbados, Nevis, St. Barts, Bequia, and the rarely visited Pigeon Island, a bird and marine-life sanctuary off the coast of St. Lucia. An experience aboard this company's sail-driven ships is unlike that offered by any conventional, diesel-driven cruise ship, and quite a bit more stylish.

7 Getting Around

From Grantley Adams International Airport, it costs about U.S.$20 to take a taxi to most hotels along the West Coast, and about U.S.$11 to U.S.$13 to a South Coast destination.

Once you've settled in and are ready to start exploring, you have a number of options: You can take a very inexpensive bus, hire an expensive taxi, rent an expensive car or an inexpensive bike or scooter, or stroll around sunny Barbados for free. See "The Regions in Brief" in chapter 8 for a description of the island's layout.

BY TAXI

Taxis aren't metered, but rates are fixed by the government. Taxis on the island are identified by the license plate letter "Z." One to five passengers can be transported at the same time, and the fare can be shared. Overcharging is infrequent; most drivers have a reputation for courtesy and honesty. Taxis are plentiful, and drivers will produce a list of standard rates. The rate per hour is a standard U.S.$16. Most drivers are familiar with the island and will be happy to drive you around to see the sights for an entire day.

BY RENTAL CAR

If you don't mind *driving on the left side of the road*, you may find that having your own car is ideal for a Bajan holiday.

No taxes apply to car rentals in Barbados. Extra insurance coverage, however, is recommended, at a cost of BD$10 (U.S.$5) per day.

None of the major U.S.-based car-rental companies maintains affiliates in Barbados, but a host of local companies fill the needs of the island's car-renting public. Except in the peak midwinter season, cars are usually readily available without prior reservation.

Consequently, most visitors wait until arrival to book a rental car. Lots of people pay for a taxi from the airport to their hotel, then, after settling in, arrange for their car to be delivered to them. This is a good idea, since there's often a long delay if you wait for a rental car to become available at the Barbados airport.

Many other visitors throw up their hands at the idea of driving on the left-hand side of the narrow and not-very-well-lighted island roads, and opt simply for a taxi whenever they need to get somewhere.

The island's most frequently recommended car-rental firm is **National,** Bush Hall Main Road, St. Michael (☎ **246/426-0603**), which offers a wide selection of Mokes and well-maintained cars. This company will deliver and pick up a car at your hotel. Located near the island's national stadium (the only one on the island), it is 3 miles northeast of Bridgetown. Maintaining an all-Japanese fleet of Toyotas, Mitsubishis, Suzukis, and Hondas, they charge from U.S.$55 to U.S.$90 per day for rentals of everything from open-sided fun cars to relatively luxurious cars with automatic transmission and air-conditioning. Cars will be delivered to any location on the island on request, and the driver who delivers it will carry the necessary forms to issue you a Bajan driver's license. This company is not affiliated in any way with the U.S. car-rental giant with the same name.

Other frequently recommended companies operating in Barbados, which charge approximately the same prices and offer the same services, include **Sunny Isle Motors,** Dayton, Worthing Main Road, Christ Church (☎ **246/435-7979**); and **P&S Car Rentals,** Pleasant View, Cave Hill, St. Michael (☎ **246/424-2052**). One company convenient to hotels on the remote southeastern end of Barbados is **Stoutes Car Rentals,** Kirtons, St. Philip (☎ **246/435-4456**). Closer to the airport than its competitors, it can theoretically deliver a car to the airport within 10 minutes if you call when you arrive. Stoutes rents from an all-Japanese inventory, and also offers a handful of Portuguese-manufactured Mini-Mokes.

A temporary permit is needed if you don't have an International Driver's License. The rental agencies listed above will issue you a visitor's permit or you can go to the police desk upon arriving at the airport. You're charged a registration fee of BD$10 (U.S.$5), and you must have your own valid license. The speed limit is 20 m.p.h. within city limits, 30 m.p.h. elsewhere on the island.

BY BUS

Barbados has a reliable bus system fanning out from Bridgetown to almost every part of the island. Buses run on most major routes every 15 minutes or so. Fares are BD$1.50 (75¢) wherever you go, and exact change is required.

The government-owned buses are blue with yellow stripes. They are not numbered, but destinations are marked in front. Departures are from Bridgetown, leaving from Fairchild Street for the south and east; from Lower Green and the Princess Alice Highway for the north going along the West Coast. Call ☎ **246/436-6820** for bus schedules and information.

Privately operated minibuses cover shorter distances and travel more frequently. They are bright yellow, with destinations displayed on the bottom left corner of the windshield. Minibuses in Bridgetown are boarded at River Road, Temple Yard, and Probyn Street. They, too, cost BD$1.50 (U.S.75¢).

BY SCOOTER OR BICYCLE

In spite of the bad, often potholed, roads, this could be a viable option for some adventurous souls who like to explore an island by scooter or bike. The trouble is in finding a rental agency. Most outfitters have closed down, finding it unprofitable. You can call the tourist office at ☎ **246/427-2623** to see if a rental agency has opened.

FAST FACTS: Barbados

American Express   The American Express affiliate in Barbados is located in the heart of Bridgetown. Contact the **Barbados International Travel Services,** Horizon House, P.O. Box 605C, McGregor Street, Bridgetown (☎ **246/ 431-2423**). Hours are Monday through Friday 9am to 5pm, and Saturday 9am to 1pm.

Bookstores   The island's best bookstore is **Cloister Bookstore Ltd.,** Hincks Street (☎ **246/426-2662**). It carries a full line of travel guides, history books, textbooks, and resources on island lore. Another choice is **A. S. Bryden & Sons Ltd.** (or simply Bryden's). Hours of both bookstores are Monday through Friday from 8:30am to 4:30pm and Saturday from 8am to noon.

Business Hours   Most banks on Barbados are open from 9am to 3pm Monday to Thursday and from 9am to 1pm and 3 to 5pm Friday. Stores are open 8am to 4pm Monday to Friday and 8am to noon Saturday. Most government offices are open from 8:30am to 4:30pm Monday to Friday.

Car Rentals   See "Getting Around," earlier in this chapter.

Climate   See "When to Go," earlier in this chapter.

Consulates   Contact the **U.S. Consulate,** in the ALICO Building, Lower Broad Street, Cheapside in Bridgetown (☎ **246/431-0225**); **Canadian High Commission,** Bishop Court, Pine Road (☎ **246/429-3550**); or **British High Commission,** Lower Collymore Rock, St. Michael (☎ **246/436-6694**).

Currency   See "Money," earlier in this chapter.

Dentist   Barbados might be served by more dentists than any other Caribbean island. One who is particularly well-recommended is **Dr. Derek Golding,** who maintains a busy practice with two colleagues at the Beckwith Shopping Mall, in Bridgetown (☎ **246/426-3001**). He accepts most emergency dental problems from the many cruise ships that dock in the waters off Barbados; the ships' pursers call in advance on ship-to-shore radios. The practice will accept any emergency, often remaining open late for last-minute problems. All members of the dental team received their training in the U.S., Britain, Canada, or New Zealand.

Doctor   Take your pick; there are dozens on Barbados. Your hotel might have a list of physicians on call, although some of the best recommended are **Dr. J. D. Gibling** (☎ **246/432-1772**) and **Dr. Adrian Lorde** or his colleague, **Dr. Ahmed Mohamad** (☎ **246/424-8236**), any of whom will make house calls to patients in their hotel rooms.

Documents Required   See "Visitor Information, Entry Requirements & Customs," earlier in this chapter.

Drugs   Penalties are severe for either possessing or selling drugs—heavy fines, a jail term, and most definitely deportation. Some drug pushers along the beachfronts may in fact be informants for the police.

Drugstores   Many hotels sell basic toiletries, including the much-requested suntan lotion. Medications can be obtained at the many pharmacies scattered throughout Bridgetown. One of the biggest is **Gill's Pharmacy,** Chapel Street near Tudor Street in Bridgetown (☎ **246/427-2654**), which is open Monday through Friday from 8:30am to 12:30pm and Saturday from 8:30am to 1pm. It is also open Sunday from 8:30 to 11am. Another recommended drugstore is

Connolly's Pharmacy, Prince Alfred Street at George Street in Bridgetown (☎ 246/426-4045). It is open Monday through Thursday from 8am to 5pm, Friday from 8am to 6pm, Saturday from 8am to 4pm, and Sunday from 9am to noon.

Electricity   The electricity is 110 volts AC, 50 cycles, so at most hotels you can use U.S.-made appliances.

Emergencies   The number to call in an emergency is ☎ **119.** Other important numbers include police, ☎ **112;** fire department, ☎ **113;** and ambulance, ☎ **115.**

Eyeglasses   The island's largest opticians can produce eyeglasses or contact lenses in a reasonably short time. All are in the vicinity of Bridgetown. Try **Harcourt Carter Optical,** corner of George Street and 5th Avenue in the Belleville district (☎ **246/429-5565**); or **Imperial Optical,** St. Michael's Row (☎ **246/426-4074**). Hours for both are Monday to Friday from 8am to 4pm.

Hospitals   The 600-bed **Queen Elizabeth Hospital** (☎ **246/436-6450**) is on Martinsdale Road in Bridgetown. This is the major hospital to head to on Barbados in case of an emergency. There are several private clinics as well, one of the best recommended and expensive being **Bayview Hospital,** St. Paul's Avenue, Bayville, St. Michael (☎ **246/436-5446**).

Information   See "Visitor Information, Entry Requirements & Customs," earlier in this chapter.

Laundry/Dry Cleaning   Try **Steve's Dry Cleaning,** Coles Garage Building, Bay Street, Bridgetown (☎ **246/427-9119**). It is open Monday through Friday from 7:30am to 6pm and Saturday from 7:30am to 4:30pm. A good self-service laundry near many of the inexpensive South Coast hotels is **Hastings Village Laundromat,** Balmoral Gap, Hastings (☎ **246/429-7079**). You can go there anytime from 8am to 6pm Monday through Saturday and from 8am to 2:30pm Sunday.

Liquor Laws   These are amazingly relaxed on Barbados. You can obtain a drink at virtually any time, provided a place is open for business. There seems to be no age limit, although a proprietor of an establishment would not necessarily serve drinks to a child. But some 15-year-olds—"who look older," in the words of one bartender—seem to have no problem.

Mail   Most hotel desks can attend to your mail, which takes 3 to 6 days to reach the United States. You can also use various mailboxes—painted red—throughout the island. Post offices are open Monday to Friday from 7:30am to 5pm. If you don't know where you'll be staying (not a good idea, incidentally), you can have your mail sent ℅ General Delivery, Barbados Post Office Department, Cheapside Street, Bridgetown, W.I. (☎ **246/436-4800**). At this post office, you can purchase stamps, send faxes, and mail packages. An airmail letter or postcard to the U.S. or Canada costs BD$1.15 (U.S.57¢). An airmail letter or postcard to Britain costs BD$1.40 (U.S.70¢).

Maps   At bookstores (see above), you can purchase various maps of Barbados, but one of the best, **Barbados Holiday Map,** is distributed free at many hotels. It's free because it's subsidized by advertisers. All the major roads of Barbados—not the minor ones—are shown clearly on this map, one part of which includes descriptions of major places of interest.

Money   See "Money," earlier in this chapter.

Newspapers & Magazines   The leading daily newspapers are *The Nation* and *Barbados Advocate,* both of which lean moderately to the right of the political spectrum. The *International Herald Tribune* and *USA Today* are flown in daily.

Photographic Needs   Most hotels sell film in their gift shops, and many can arrange for it to be sent out to be developed if enough time is allotted. Otherwise, you can patronize one of the three outlets of **C.L. Gibbs,** each offering photo finish 1-hour labs. They're found on the West Coast at Sunset Mall, Sunset Crest (☎ 246/432-6167); at Worthing along the South Coast (☎ 246/435-7357); and in Bridgetown on Broad Street (☎ 246/437-3497). All outlets are open Monday to Friday from 9am to 5pm and on Saturday from 9pm to 1pm.

Police   Call ☎ 112.

Post Office   See "Mail," above.

Radio   Barbados is served by three major radio broadcasters. Barbados Broadcasting Service operates an FM station; Barbados Rediffusion Service runs YESS Ten-Four (104 on the FM dial), a news and music service; and CBC Radio operates Radio Liberty FM and Radio 900, both of which broadcast news, music, and public-interest programs.

Safety   The people of Barbados seem to know that much of the island's livelihood depends on the goodwill of its tourists (the mainstay of its economy), so crimes against visitors are highly discouraged and severely punished. Nevertheless, crime has come to Barbados in recent years, because of rising unemployment among the island's youth. Purse-snatching and pickpocketing exist in Bridgetown, so take precautions. Although it's not a "crime," you still might be annoyed by the unwanted attention you get from various hawkers and peddlers on the beach. A firm and resounding "No!" should get rid of them. In any case, safeguard your possessions and never leave them unattended on the beach. And never go walking along the beach at night.

Shoe Repairs   **Harry's Heel Bar and Shoe Repair Centre,** Cowell Street, St. Michael, Bridgetown (☎ 246/427-5578), will repair most shoes, luggage, and handbags while you wait. The same company also maintains a collection point in the Gertz Shopping Plaza, Collymore Rock, St. Michael (☎ 809/436-6764), which accepts items for repair and redelivery several days later. Both branches are open Monday to Friday from 9am to 5pm and Saturday from 8:30am to 1pm.

Taxes   When you leave, you'll have to pay a BD$25 (U.S.$12.50) departure tax. By the time you arrive, the government of Barbados should have introduced a Value-Added Tax (VAT) on nearly all goods and services, including sightseeing attractions, food, and hotel rooms.

Taxis   See "Getting Around," earlier in this chapter.

Telephone, Telex, & Fax   You should have no trouble with telecommunications out of Barbados. Telegrams can be sent at your hotel front desk or at the **Barbados External Telecommunications Ltd.** Office, Wildey Main Road, St. Michael (☎ 246/427-5200), which is open from 8am to 6pm Monday to Friday, from 8am to 3pm Saturday, and 8am to 1pm Sunday. International telephone, fax, telex, and data-access services are also available at this office.

Television   CBC TV (Caribbean Broadcasting Corp.), Channel 8 on the dial, is broadcast from Barbados. News and entertainment are also imported every day on the popular TNT (Turner Broadcasting), which appears on Channel 26.

Time   Barbados is on Atlantic time, 1 hour ahead of New York (eastern standard time). Unlike Jamaica, Barbados switches to daylight savings time.

Tipping   Most restaurants and hotels add a 10% service charge, and you need not tip more unless service has been good. Many visitors or locals routinely add another 10% in those cases. Maids get about U.S.$1 per day, and bellboys are tipped from U.S.$1 per bag, porters about U.S.$1 per piece of luggage.

Transit Info   Taxis line up in front of most major hotels. If you need to call one, try **Johnson's Stables** at ☎ **246/426-5186.**

Water   Barbados has a pure water supply. It's pumped from underground sources in the coral rock, which underlies six-sevenths of the island, and it's safe to drink.

Weddings   It's relatively easy to tie the knot in Barbados, although it calls for some advance planning. Couples can marry the same day they arrive on Barbados, but must first obtain a marriage license from the **Ministry of Home Affairs** (☎ **246/228/8950**). Bring either a passport, or birth certificate and photo I.D., U.S.$100 in fees, and U.S.$25 for the revenue stamp (which can be obtained at the local post office), a letter from the authorized officiant who will perform the service, plus proof, if applicable, of pertinent deaths or divorces of former spouse(s). A Roman Catholic wedding on Barbados carries additional requirements. For more information, contact the **Barbados Tourism Authority,** 800 Second Ave., New York, NY 10017 (☎ **800/221-9831** or 212/986-6516).

10 Where to Stay & Dine on Barbados

Barbados has some of the best hotels in the West Indies. You can be pampered in elegant comfort, and enjoy an atmosphere like that of an English house party. Most hotels are small and personally run, with a quiet, restrained dignity.

The biggest recent change has been a tendency for hotels to charge all-inclusive rates. Even some that have not gone this route insist that you take two meals with them every day.

The bad news is that because of the island's popularity, especially with tour groups, its big hotels are often extremely expensive in high season. There has been little hotel development here in recent years, with few new openings, so there has been no competition to keep prices down. The price you pay for a moderately priced room here could get you a lavish suite in many parts of the world, including many U.S. cities. *Booking a package tour is just about the only way to make these rates more reasonable* (see the sections on package tours in chapters 3 and 9).

Most of our recommendations for both hotels and restaurants are at St. James Beach, the island's fashionable and expensive Gold Coast, but there should be a hotel or resort tailored for you somewhere in Barbados. Even though the upper end is very expensive, there are hostelries in all sizes and to suit most wallets—from simple inns to palatial suites or luxurious cottages. To escape $500-a-night prices at some hotels, many visitors opt for apartment rentals or time-share units. Others head south from Bridgetown to places like Hastings and Worthing where they find the best bargains, often in self-contained efficiencies or studio apartments, in which you can save by cooking some or all of your meals.

1 Where to Stay

Although rates are high in the winter, they generally drop from 20% to 60% from mid-April to mid-December. With certain variations, so-called summer rates apply from mid-April to mid-December, and winter rates are in effect from December 15 to April 15.

A 5% government tax and a 10% service charge are added to all rates.

The coming news on the hotel scene is the projected opening of one of Jamaican entrepreneur Butch Stewart's new Sandals resorts on the West Coast in the fall of 1998. This long-delayed project will be called—you guessed it—**Sandals-Barbados.** For more information and details, call ☎ **800/ SANDALS.**

ON THE WEST COAST

The rates at most of the big elegant resorts here are shockingly expensive. We've said it before and we'll say it again: Book a package deal! See chapters 3 and 9.

VERY EXPENSIVE

Almond Beach Club. Vauxhall, St. James, Barbados, W.I. ☎ **800/4-ALMOND** in the U.S., or 246/432-7840. Fax 246/432-2115. 161 rms. A/C TV TEL. Winter U.S.$470–$660 double. Off-season U.S.$400–$560 double. Rates include all meals. AE, MC, V. No children under 16.

Set on flat and sandy beach about a 2-minute walk from its more famous neighbor, Sandy Lane, this hotel lies on the island's West Coast, south of Holetown. The narrow beach here is less than ideal. An overhauled property, this was the first of Barbados's all-inclusive resorts, established in 1991 as part of a $2 million refurbishment. The accommodations are spread among seven low-rise, three-story buildings (no elevators). Pool-view units open onto three freshwater swimming pools and the gardens, planted with frangipani trees and palms; beachfront units open onto the Caribbean. Island motifs, tropical fabrics, and tile floors dominate the room decor.

Dining/Diversions: The all-inclusive program offers a dine-around option, allowing guests to consume one lunch and one dinner per weeklong stay at one of three neighboring hotels. There are two restaurants and a beachfront snack bar on the premises. The continental Almond Beach restaurant serves decent fare. Their use of sauces and seasonings is fairly unimaginative, but the meats and fish are of high quality and very fresh. The sauces are usually too sweet for our taste, with the exception of one green- and red-peppercorn sauce served over the filet of beef flambé. However Enid's, the West Indian/Bajan restaurant, is quite good. The Bajan recipes are worth trying—expect a lot of beef and pork stews, and a lot of spicy fish recipes to tingle your palate. Vegetarians should probably stick to the Almond Beach, however, where they cater more to sensitive diets and sensitive stomachs. The Rum Shop Bar evokes 19th-century colonial days and offers a sampling of virtually every kind of distilled rum on Barbados. There's lively nightly entertainment until 2am, including jazz bands, steel-drum bands, Bajan folk dancing, and contemporary music, as well as piano bar entertainment.

Amenities: Three freshwater swimming pools, tennis and squash courts, fitness center with sauna, fishing, windsurfing, waterskiing, reef fishing, kayaking, and "banana boating." Laundry and baby-sitting are available, and the guest services department can organize island tours.

Almond Beach Village. Speightstown (15 miles north of Bridgetown along Hwy. 2A), St. Peter, Barbados, W.I. ☎ **800/4-ALMOND** in the U.S., or 246/422-4900. Fax 246/422-1581. 311 units. A/C TV TEL. Winter U.S.$470–$630 double; U.S.$580–$660 suite. May–Nov U.S.$400–$530 double; U.S.$485–$560 suite. Rates are all-inclusive. AE, MC, V.

Set near a string of even more expensive hotels (referred to as the island's Gold Coast), this hotel occupies the site of a 19th-century sugarcane plantation. In 1994, it was acquired by the largest industrial conglomerate on Barbados (Barbados Shipping and Trading) and benefited from a $13 million renovation. Today, it's the most desirable all-inclusive resort on the island (with all meals, drinks, and most sports included in one net price) and a good choice for families.

Barbados Accommodations

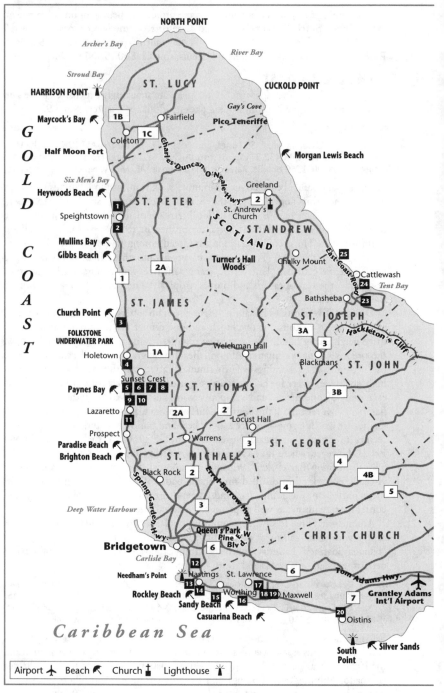

NORTH POINT

Archer's Bay

River Bay

Stroud Bay

HARRISON POINT ⚓

ST. LUCY

CUCKOLD POINT

Maycock's Bay 🏖

1B

○ Fairfield

Gay's Cove

Pico Teneriffe

1C

Coleton ○

Half Moon Fort

🏖 Morgan Lewis Beach

Six Men's Bay

Heywoods Beach 🏖

1

ST. PETER

Greeland ○

2 ✝

Speightstown ○

2

St. Andrew's Church

ST. ANDREW

G

Mullins Bay 🏖

SCOTLAND

O

Gibbs Bay 🏖

1

2A

Turner's Hall Woods

Chalky Mount ○

25

Cattlewash ○

L

D

ST. JAMES

East Coast Road

24

Tent Bay

Church Point 🏖

3

Bathsheba ○

23

C

FOLKSTONE UNDERWATER PARK

1A

Welchman Hall ○

ST. JOSEPH

Hackleton's Cliff

O

Holetown ○

3A

A

4

Blackmans ○

3

ST. JOHN

S

Sunset Crest

5 **6** **7** **8**

ST. THOMAS

T

Paynes Bay 🏖

9 **10**

Lazaretto ○

11

2A

2

Locust Hall ○

3B

Prospect ○

Warrens ○

3

ST. GEORGE

Paradise Beach 🏖

Brighton Beach 🏖

ST. MICHAEL

2

Black Rock ○

4

4B

Errol Barrow Hwy.

4

5

Deep Water Harbour

Spring Garden Hwy.

3

Queen's Park

CHRIST CHURCH

Pine Blvd.

Bridgetown ○

6

Carlisle Bay

Needham's Point ⚓

12

Hastings ○

St. Lawrence ○

6

Tom Adams Hwy. ✈

Rockley Beach 🏖

13

14

Worthing ○

17

Grantley Adams Int'l Airport

15

18 **19** Maxwell ○

7

Sandy Beach 🏖

16

Casuarina Beach 🏖

20

Oistins ○

Caribbean Sea

Silver Sands 🏖

South Point ⚓

Airport ✈ Beach 🏖 Church ✝ Lighthouse ⚓

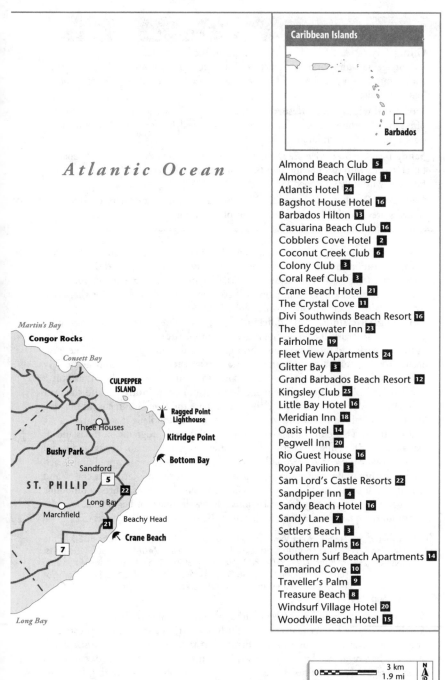

Atlantic Ocean

Caribbean Islands

Barbados

Martin's Bay
Congor Rocks

Consett Bay

**CULPEPPER
ISLAND**

Ragged Point
Lighthouse

Three Houses

Kitridge Point

Bushy Park

Bottom Bay

Sandford

ST. PHILIP   5

22

Long Bay

Marchfield

Beachy Head

21

Crane Beach

7

Long Bay

Almond Beach Club **5**
Almond Beach Village **1**
Atlantis Hotel **24**
Bagshot House Hotel **16**
Barbados Hilton **13**
Casuarina Beach Club **16**
Cobblers Cove Hotel **2**
Coconut Creek Club **6**
Colony Club **3**
Coral Reef Club **3**
Crane Beach Hotel **21**
The Crystal Cove **11**
Divi Southwinds Beach Resort **16**
The Edgewater Inn **23**
Fairholme **19**
Fleet View Apartments **24**
Glitter Bay **3**
Grand Barbados Beach Resort **12**
Kingsley Club **25**
Little Bay Hotel **16**
Meridian Inn **18**
Oasis Hotel **14**
Pegwell Inn **20**
Rio Guest House **16**
Royal Pavilion **3**
Sam Lord's Castle Resorts **22**
Sandpiper Inn **4**
Sandy Beach Hotel **16**
Sandy Lane **7**
Settlers Beach **3**
Southern Palms **16**
Southern Surf Beach Apartments **14**
Tamarind Cove **10**
Traveller's Palm **9**
Treasure Beach **8**
Windsurf Village Hotel **20**
Woodville Beach Hotel **15**

0 | 3 km
      1.9 mi

N

ⓘ Family-Friendly Hotels

Glitter Bay *(see p. 217)*   If you can afford it, the best place is Glitter Bay, with its cottagelike suites and kitchenettes. Children can play on the beach or in the swimming pool. There's a U.S.$58-per-day fee for each child sharing a one-bedroom suite with their parents.

Divi Southwinds Beach Resort *(see p. 221)*   On 20 acres, this modern resort offers two-bedroom suites with full kitchens—ideal for families. A swimming pool is reserved for children.

Sandy Beach Hotel *(see p. 223)*   Children get reduced rates at this South Coast beach resort, with its one- and two-bedroom suites, which offer a great layout for families, with fully equipped kitchenettes.

Casuarina Beach Club *(see p. 222)*   This family-run place offers reasonably priced suites with kitchenettes and a pair of swimming pools.

On 30 acres of tropically landscaped gardens and prime beachfront, its relatively isolated position makes leaving the premises awkward, although that doesn't seem to bother guests. Accommodations are clustered into seven different compounds to create something akin to a miniature, self-contained village. Exchange privileges are available with its all-inclusive twin, the Almond Beach Club (see above).

Dining/Diversions: Four different restaurants add diversity to the dining options. A specialty Italian restaurant, La Smarita, is the most formal of the lot. Although we found the decor a little boring, the food really is quite good. The meat dishes are fine, but all of the seafood pastas are excellent. In an attempt to be very formal both in atmosphere and in cuisine, some flavor is lost, but it is still a perfectly reliable restaurant. The main dining room is the Horizons, and the least formal is Enid's, for Bajan food. Other choices are the Reef, a burger-and-hot-dog joint, and a seafood restaurant where you can dine by candlelight at night.

Amenities: The resort offers one of the best children's programs on the island: It has a club just for children (with videos, Nintendo, computer lab, books, and board games), two children's playgrounds, kiddies' pool, activity center, pool and beach games, nature walks, water sports, treasure hunts, story time, arts and crafts, and evening entertainment. Other perks include five floodlit tennis courts, a nine-hole par-3 golf course (too easy for professionals but well tuned for beginners), two air-conditioned squash courts, laundry facilities, baby-sitting, and room service.

✪ **Cobblers Cove Hotel.** Road View, St. Peter, Barbados, W.I. ☎ **800/890-6060** in the U.S., 0181/367-5175 in London, or 246/422-2291. Fax 246/422-1460. 40 units. A/C MINIBAR TEL. Winter U.S.$540–$880 standard suite; U.S.$1,300 Camelot suite; U.S.$1,500 Colleton suite. Off-season U.S.$356–$506 standard suite for 2; U.S.$796 Camelot suite; U.S.$846 Colleton suite. Rates include MAP (breakfast and dinner). AE, MC, V. Closed late Sept to mid-Oct.

One of the small, exclusive hotels of Barbados and a member of Relais & Châteaux, Cobblers Cove, a former mansion, is built like a fort, in a mock-medieval style. It was erected over the site of a former British fort that used to protect vessels going into the harbor at nearby Speightstown, a 10-minute walk away. Today, after an exhaustive overhaul, the hotel is a favorite honeymoon haven, offering first-class suites housed in 10 Iberian-style villas placed throughout the gardens.

Overlooking a white-sand beach, each unit has a spacious living room, a private balcony or patio, and a kitchenette. Two of the most exclusive accommodations you can rent on all of Barbados are the Camelot and Colleton suites on the rooftop of the original mansion; they're beautifully decorated and offer panoramic views of both the beach and the garden. Meals can be delivered to your suite so you can dine in privacy. The resort contains many acres of well-developed tropical gardens and lawns.

Dining/Diversions: The open-air dining room overlooks the sea. The cuisine has won many awards and has an emphasis on Caribbean specialties from the sea— say, a fish of the day grilled or poached with Bajan seasoning, or shrimp flavored with ginger. Nearby is the resort's social center, the bar.

Amenities: Complimentary tennis day or night, swimming pool, water sports (including waterskiing, Sunfish sailing, snorkeling, and windsurfing), laundry, baby-sitting, arrangements for island tours, car rentals.

Coconut Creek Club. Derricks, St. James, Barbados, W.I. ☎ **800/223-6510** in the U.S., 800/561-1366 in Canada, or 246/432-0803. Fax 246/432-0272. 53 units. A/C TEL. Winter U.S.$372–$596 double; off-season U.S.$278–$374 double. Rates include MAP (breakfast and dinner). MC, V.

Small, intimate, and discreet, this is an elegantly informal and landscaped retreat on the West Coast, about a mile south of Holetown. Completely renovated in 1995, it resembles an exclusive country retreat in the English countryside. About half the rather small accommodations lie atop a low bluff overlooking what might be the two most secluded beaches on the island's West Coast. Many of the bedrooms are built on the low cliff edge overlooking the ocean; others open onto the pool or the flat, tropical garden. Each bedroom has a veranda or balcony where breakfast can be served. The baths are cramped.

Dining/Diversions: The restaurant, Cricketers, was modeled after an upscale English pub. Bajan buffets and barbecues are served on the restaurant's vine-covered open pergola, overlooking the gardens and the sea. The inn's food has been praised by *Gourmet* magazine. There's dancing to West Indian calypso and steel bands almost every night. Guests on the MAP are encouraged to dine at the restaurants connected to this chain's three other properties—the Crystal Cove Hotel, the Tamarind Cove Hotel, and the Colony Club—for no additional charge.

Amenities: Freshwater swimming pool, complimentary water sports (including waterskiing, windsurfing, snorkeling, and Hobie Cat sailing). Scuba diving can be arranged for an extra charge, and tennis is available nearby. There's also room service (7:30am to 10pm) and baby-sitting. The staff can book island tours and rental cars for you.

Colony Club. Porters, St. James Beach, Barbados, W.I. ☎ **800/223-6510** in the U.S., 800/561-1366 Canada, or 246/422-2335. Fax 246/422-0667. 98 units. A/C TEL. Winter U.S.$518–$622 double; U.S.$622–$704 suite. Off-season, U.S.$378–$450 double; U.S.$430–$508 suite. Rates include MAP (breakfast and dinner). AE, DC, MC, V.

Originally established by an English expatriate in the 1950s, this discreetly elegant hotel is on the island's western coast. It caters mainly to Brits. Set behind an entrance lined with Australian pines, it occupies a site a mile north of Holetown, beside one of the island's best beaches. On 7 acres of tropical gardens, the grounds contain free-form lagoon rock pools.

A complex of restored rooms looks out over shaded verandas and landscaped grounds. About a third of the rooms lie beside the sea; the others are scattered throughout the gardens. All units have either a patio or a balcony, with some extending up to the lagoon rock pools. Some rooms look a bit dowdy; others are up-to-date and spiffy. Your verdict on this resort is likely to be shaped by your room assignment; ask questions when you make your reservation.

Dining/Diversions: Set between the beachside freshwater pool and the main building is the open-sided Laguna Restaurant. The Orchids Room, the hotel's formal restaurant, offers an international cuisine. The dance floor, on an "island" in the middle of the pool, is accessed by a footbridge. There's nightly entertainment.

Amenities: Four freshwater swimming pools, hairdressing/beauty salon, complimentary water sports, chauffeured speedboat and catamaran rides, air-conditioned fitness center, two floodlit tennis courts, room service (7:30am to 9:30pm), laundry, baby-sitting, arrangements for tours and excursions.

Coral Reef Club. St. James Beach, Barbados, W.I. ☎ **800/223-1108** or 246/422-2372. Fax 246/422-1776. 69 units. A/C TEL. Winter U.S.$390–$680 double; U.S.$680–$1,200 2-bedroom suite for 2, U.S.$845–$1,150 2-bedroom suite for 4. Off-season U.S.$315–$370 double; U.S.$455 2-bedroom suite for 2, U.S.$655 2-bedroom suite for 4. Rates include MAP (breakfast and dinner). AE, MC, V. Children under 12 not accepted in Feb.

Family owned and managed, this small luxury hotel has set standards that are hard for competitors to match. It's one of the best and most respected choices on the island. Set on elegantly landscaped, flat land beside a good beach, the hotel is about a 5-minute drive north of Holetown.

A collection of veranda-fronted private accommodations surrounds a main building and clubhouse. This contains the reception area (where you'll find the staff quite helpful), a reading room, a dining area and bar, and four deluxe bedrooms on the second floor. The other accommodations are scattered about a dozen landscaped acres, fronting a long strip of white-sand beach, ideal for swimming. They open onto private patios, and some of the rooms have separate dressing rooms. Not all are in cottages. Some, not in the main building, are in small coral-stone wings in the gardens. Rental units here vary greatly.

Dining/Diversions: You can enjoy lunch in an open-air area. Dining in the evening is in a room with three sides open to ocean views. A first-class chef runs the kitchen. There's a weekly folklore show and barbecue every Thursday and a Bajan buffet on Monday evening, featuring an array of food, along with whole baked fish and lots of local entertainment.

Amenities: Freshwater swimming pool, tennis court (floodlit at night), water sports (including windsurfing, snorkeling, arrangements for scuba diving, and use of a minifleet of small sailboats), room service (during restaurant hours), laundry, massage, hair salon.

The Crystal Cove. Fitt's Village, St. James, Barbados, W.I. ☎ **800/223-6510** in the U.S., 800/561-1366 in Canada, or 246/432-2683. Fax 246/432-8290. 88 units. A/C TEL. Winter U.S.$432–$584 double; U.S.$500–$610 suite for 2. Off-season U.S.$312–$344 double; U.S.$352–$425 suite for 2. Rates include MAP (breakfast and dinner). MC, V.

This was once known as the Barbados Beach Village, but now it's The Crystal Cove, and is much better than before. It's set on a 4-acre beachfront site at Fitt's Village, 4 miles north of Bridgetown along the West Coast. The hotel has a beach, but be warned of the treacherous pilings and a lot of offshore rocks.

The Crystal Cove is a member of the Barbados-based St. James Beach Hotels, which owns some of the best properties on the island, including the Colony Club, Coconut Creek, and Tamarind Cove. Guests have access to the other hotels' combined facilities, and a water taxi is provided for transportation among the different properties. This, in fact, is one of the major reasons we recommend the Crystal Cove; if you want a change of scene, you can visit the next member of the St. James group.

If you don't like the food, you can prepare your own, as more than two dozen units have kitchenettes. The rooms are either standard, somewhat like a motel, or more upscale, with living areas separate from the bedrooms. Most of them have high ceilings as well.

Dining/Diversions: There are two restaurants. You might not drive across the island to sample the food, but it's above average. Entertainment is provided most nights.

Amenities: The Crystal Cove offers three swimming pools and two tennis courts. The hotel will provide snorkeling equipment for its guests. They will set up guided tours of the islands, as well as lessons in scuba diving, tennis, and sailing. There is no gym/health club, but guests do have access to the facilities in neighboring hotels. Services include concierge, laundry, and baby-sitting. There is no room service.

Glitter Bay. Porters, St. James, Barbados, W.I. ☎ **800/223-1818** in the U.S., 800/268-7176 in Canada, 0171/407-1010 in London, or 246/422-5555. Fax 246/422-3940. 83 units. A/C MINIBAR TEL. Winter U.S.$430–$475 double; U.S.$525–$615 1-bedroom suite for 2, U.S.$955–$1,090 2-bedroom suite for 4. Off-season U.S.$235–$300 double; U.S.$235–$365 1-bedroom suite for 2, U.S.$510–$665 2-bedroom suite for 4. MAP (breakfast and dinner) U.S.$65 per person per day extra. AE, DC, MC, V.

This carefully maintained resort has discreet charm and Mediterranean style, although it isn't as sophisticated and alluring as its next-door sibling, the Royal Pavilion (see below). But with its cottagelike suites with kitchenettes, it's a terrific choice for families (well-to-do families, that is). It lies on a 10-acre plot of manicured lowlands near a sandy beachfront a mile north of Holetown and offers a wide array of sports facilities. In the 1930s, this property was owned by Sir Edward Cunard of shipbuilding fame. The parties he gave here in the Great House were so famous that it helped make Barbados synonymous with glitter and glamour back in England.

The accommodations are in a white minivillage of Iberian inspiration, whose patios, thick beams, and red terra-cotta tiles surround a garden with a swimming pool, an artificial waterfall, and a simulated lagoon. Most units contain art, built-in furniture, louvered doors, and spacious outdoor patios or balconies ringed with shrubbery. The larger units have small kitchenettes, and some of the biggest accommodations are suitable for four to six people.

Guests here can use any of the facilities at the Royal Pavilion (see below).

Dining/Diversions: The hotel's social center is the Piperade Restaurant, beneath a terra-cotta roof and amid a garden. Offering American and international cuisine, it contains its own bar. The Sunset Beach Bar is a popular rendezvous spot. Sheltered by shrubbery and tropical trees, guests can dance on an outdoor patio and enjoy local entertainment, such as a steel band or calypso.

Services: 24-hour room service, concierge, laundry, baby-sitting, business services, and limousine service.

Amenities: Fitness and massage center, two tennis courts (complimentary for guests day and night), aerobics classes, and complimentary water sports (including waterskiing, windsurfing, snorkeling, and catamaran sailing), two swimming pools (one a shallow children's pool). Golf is available at the nearby Royal Westmoreland; horseback riding, scuba diving, and motorboating can be arranged.

✪ **Royal Pavilion.** Porters, St. James, Barbados, W.I. ☎ **800/223-1818** in the U.S., 800/268-7176 in Canada, 0171/407-1010 in London, or 246/422-5555. Fax 246/422-3940. 72 units, 3 villas. A/C MINIBAR TEL. Winter U.S.$525–$615 suite for 2; U.S.$995–$1,180 villa for 4, U.S.$1,500–$1,770 villa for 6. Off-season U.S.$275–$365 suite for 2; U.S.$470–$720 villa for 4, U.S.$715–$1,070 villa for 6. MAP (breakfast and dinner) U.S.$65 per person per day extra. AE, DC, MC, V. No children 11 and under in winter.

A spectacular place to stay, this hotel is a mile north of Holetown and sits next door to Glitter Bay, part of the same chain and sharing landscaped gardens. It's a lush pink-walled resort with lily ponds and splashing fountains. British grace and Bajan hospitality blend in this property, which became one of the finest resorts on

Barbados the moment it opened. We find it far superior to the more famous Sandy Lane (see below).

The architects created a California-hacienda style for their 72 waterfront deluxe rooms and a villa consisting of three suites in 8 acres of landscaped gardens. Guests staying here can visit the restaurants and bars at Glitter Bay and use the sports facilities there (and vice versa).

Dining/Entertainment: There are two oceanfront restaurants. Café Taboras serves breakfast and lunch. The more formal Palm Terrace, set below the seaside columns of an open-air loggia, is open only for dinner. Both restaurants offer an à la carte menu of Caribbean and international fare. On Wednesday night, there's an international buffet.

Services: 24-hour room service, concierge, laundry, baby-sitting, business service, limousine service.

Facilities: Freshwater swimming pool overlooking the ocean, massage center, fitness center at Glitter Bay, two tennis courts (complimentary for guests day and night), water-sports program (including complimentary snorkeling, waterskiing, sailing, and windsurfing), duty-free shops, beauty shop with hairdresser. Guests also enjoy privileged tee times at the nearby Royal Westmoreland.

The Sandpiper. Holetown, St. James, Barbados, W.I. ☎ **800/223-1108** in the U.S., 800/567-5327 in Canada, or 246/422-2251. Fax 246/422-1776. 45 units. A/C TEL. Winter U.S.$325–$390 double; U.S.$465–$800 suite. Off-season U.S.$195 double; U.S.$250–$370 suite. MAP (breakfast and dinner) U.S.$50 per person per day extra. AE, MC, V. No children accepted in Feb.

The Sandpiper has more of a South Seas look than most of the hotels of Barbados. Affiliated with the Coral Reef Club (see above), it's a self-contained, intimate resort near the water. The resort maintains a Bajan flavor and stands in a small grove of coconut palms and flowering trees right on the beach, a 3-minute walk north of Holetown. A cluster of rustic-chic units surrounds the swimming pool, and some have a fine sea view. The rooms open onto little terraces that stretch along the second story, where you can order drinks or have breakfast. Each unit contains a small refrigerator.

Dining/Diversions: Dining is under a wooden ceiling, and the cuisine is both continental and West Indian. Once a week in winter, big buffets are spread out for you, with white-capped chefs in attendance. There are two bars, one of which sits a few paces from the surf.

Amenities: Swimming pool, two lighted tennis courts, room service (7am to 10:30pm), laundry, baby-sitting.

Sandy Lane. St. James, Barbados, W.I. ☎ **800/225-5843** in the U.S. and Canada, or 246/432-1310. Fax 246/432-2954. 120 units. A/C MINIBAR TEL. Rates for newly renovated resort had not yet been announced at press time.

If you have to ask about the rates, you can't afford it. For years, Sandy Lane has been famous as a last remaining outpost of British colonialism on Barbados, very formal and very British. It sits a mile south of Holetown on a private white-sand beach.

But now the hotel will be closed from April 25 until September of 1998, to complete a massive $75 million renovation. The rooms will be completely refurbished to look almost new, though the plan is for them to retain the traditional Sandy Lane feel. Other construction plans include a new 45-hole golf course, 7 new tennis courts, a 16 treatment-room spa, and a children's activity center. If you're interested in staying here, call the hotel to check on the continuing progress and ask for a brochure showing the new changes.

Settlers Beach. St. James, Barbados, W.I. ☎ **246/432-0840.** Fax 246/432-2147. 22 villas. A/C TEL. Winter U.S.$450–$650 villa for 2–5. Off-season U.S.$250–$300 villa for 2–5. MAP (breakfast and dinner) U.S.$50 per person per day extra. AE, MC, V.

This collection of comfortable two-story seaside villas is located on 4 acres of sandy beachfront property 8 miles from Bridgetown, north of Holetown. Each unit has two bedrooms, two bathrooms, a spacious tile-floored lounge and dining room, and a fully equipped kitchen. The apartments are decorated in sunny colors, and were last refurbished in 1995. This resort, squeezed between larger properties, appeals to those who are independent and don't want to be coddled. It seems a bit dated, but it must be doing something right because it has lots of repeat visitors, attracting American families in summer and English visitors in winter.

Dining/Diversions: The independently run restaurant has won awards and is one of the finest on the island. A bar lies nearby.

Amenities: Swimming pool, two nearby tennis courts, room service, laundry, baby-sitting.

Tamarind Cove. Paynes Bay, St. James Beach (P.O. Box 429, Bridgetown), Barbados, W.I. ☎ **800/223-6510** in the U.S., 800/561-1366 in Canada, or 246/432-1332. Fax 246/ 432-6317. 166 units. A/C TEL. Winter U.S.$484–$510 double; U.S.$570–$688 suite for 2. Off-season U.S.$358–$372 double; U.S.$404–$466 suite for 2. Rates include MAP (breakfast and dinner). AE, DC, MC, V.

This is the flagship of a British-based hotel chain (St. James Beach Properties) and a major challenger to the Coral Reef/Sandpiper properties, attracting the same upscale crowd. Designed in an Iberian style, with pale-pink walls and red terra-cotta roofs, it occupies a desirable site beside a beautiful white-sand stretch of St. James Beach, 1½ miles south of Holetown. In 1995, a new south wing, with some 49 luxurious rooms and suites, some with private plunge pools, was added, along with a freshwater swimming pool with a beachfront terrace.

The stylish and comfortable accommodations are in a series of hacienda-style buildings interspersed with vegetation. Each unit has a patio or balcony overlooking the gardens or ocean.

Dining/Diversions: In addition to an informal beachfront restaurant, Tamarind contains two elegant choices, the more memorable of which is Neptune's, specializing in sophisticated seafood dishes. The Flamingo is the main restaurant. A handful of bars is scattered throughout the property, and there's some kind of musical entertainment every night.

Amenities: Four freshwater swimming pools, complimentary water sports (including waterskiing, windsurfing, catamaran sailing, and snorkeling). Golf, tennis, horseback riding, and polo are available nearby. There's also room service, baby-sitting, laundry, massage, and a concierge.

Treasure Beach. Paynes Bay, St. James, Barbados, W.I. ☎ **800/223-6510** in the U.S. or Canada, or 246/432-1346. Fax 246/432-1094. 29 units. A/C TEL. Winter U.S.$459–$764 1-bedroom suite for 2, U.S.$1,704 superior luxury suite. Off-season U.S.$188–$318 1-bedroom suite for 2, U.S.$647 superior luxury suite. MAP (breakfast and dinner) U.S.$32 per person per day extra. AE, DC, DISC, MC, V. No children 11 and under except by special request.

Set on about an acre of sandy beachfront land, this hotel is a minivillage of two-story buildings arranged into a horseshoe pattern around a pool and garden. Treasure Beach has a loyal following. It's small but choice, known for its well-prepared food and the comfort and style of its amenities. The atmosphere is both intimate and relaxed, with personalized service from a well-trained staff. The hotel is set on small grounds in St. James in the glittery hotel belt of Barbados, about half a mile south of Holetown. The accommodations are furnished in a tropical motif and open onto private balconies or patios. The baths are a little cramped. The clientele is about evenly divided between North American and British guests.

Dining: Even if you aren't staying here, try to sample some of the culinary specialties at the Treasure Beach Restaurant, including freshly caught seafood and favorites from the Bajan culinary repertoire.

Amenities: Sailboat rentals, a swimming pool that's too small; access to nearby golf and tennis courts. There's also room service (7:30am to 9:30pm), valet and laundry service, and safety-deposit boxes. A receptionist can arrange for car rentals and island tours.

INEXPENSIVE

Traveller's Palm. 265 Palm Ave., Sunset Crest, St. James, Barbados, W.I. ☎ **246/ 432-7722.** 16 apts. A/C. Winter U.S.$85 apt for 2. Off-season U.S.$60 apt for 2. MC, V.

Designed for those who want to be independent, this is a choice collection of simply furnished one-bedroom apartments with fully equipped kitchens, a 5-minute drive south of Holetown. It's not anything like those lavish resorts reviewed above, but the price is a whole lot more down to earth. The apartments have living- and dining-room areas, as well as patios where you can have breakfast or a candlelit dinner you've prepared yourself (no meals are served here). The slightly worn apartments are filled with bright but fading colors, and they open onto a lawn with a swimming pool. There's maid service. A handful of beaches are within a 10-minute walk.

SOUTH OF BRIDGETOWN
EXPENSIVE

Barbados Hilton. Needham's Point (P.O. Box 510), St. Michael, Barbados, W.I. ☎ **800/HILTONS** in the U.S., 800/268-9275 in Canada, or 246/426-0200. Fax 246/ 436-8946. 184 units. A/C MINIBAR TV TEL. Winter U.S.$272–$295 double; U.S.$520 suite. Off-season U.S.$175–$250 double; U.S.$282–$402 suite. MAP (breakfast and dinner) U.S.$42 per person per day extra. AE, DC, DISC, MC, V.

On more than 14 acres of landscaped gardens, this is a self-contained six-story resort, although it lies on the heavily populated southern edge of Bridgetown near an oil refinery (whose smell sometimes drifts unfortunately over its very good white-sand beach). The Hilton isn't in the island's top ranks, and it looks a bit worn and tired, but it's often packed every night. It's the favorite of business travelers and conventioneers.

Built in 1966 and overhauled and redecorated several times since then, it occupies the rugged peninsula where in the 18th century the English navy built Fort Charles. The Hilton's architecture incorporates bleached coral interspersed with jutting balconies and wide expanses of glass. The bedrooms are arranged around a central courtyard filled with tropical gardens, and vines cascade from the skylit roof. Each of the comfortable units has a balcony with a view of Carlisle Bay on the north side or the Atlantic on the south.

Dining/Diversions: The Verandah restaurant, whose backdrop is a row of diminutive clapboard Bajan houses, serves lackluster island and international specialties. The hotel has a gaming room with slot machines and both a beachfront daytime bar and snack restaurant and a nighttime bar.

Amenities: Four tennis courts (lit at night), sauna and health club; access to horseback riding and golf. Several kinds of water sports are offered on the nearby 1,000-foot-wide artificial beach, whose outermost edge is protected from storm damage by a massive breakwater of giant rocks. Also available are room service (7am to midnight), laundry, and massage.

Grand Barbados Beach Resort. Aquatic Gap, Bay St. (P.O. Box 639), Bridgetown, St. Michael, Barbados, W.I. ☎ **246/426-0890.** Fax 246/429-2400. 133 units. A/C MINIBAR TV TEL. Winter U.S.$240–$270 double; from U.S.$300 suite. Off-season U.S.$130–$160 double; from U.S.$245 suite. MAP (breakfast and dinner) U.S.$47 per person per day extra. AE, DC, DISC, MC, V.

On scenic Carlisle Bay, about a mile southeast of Bridgetown and opening onto a white-sand beach, is this well-designed eight-story resort. Like the Hilton, it's unfortunately close to an oil refinery. Set on 4 acres of grounds, it offers well-furnished but often small bedrooms with many amenities, including a minisafe and eight-channel satellite TV. The storage space for luggage is inadequate. The two top floors are devoted to executive rooms, including a lounge where a complimentary continental breakfast is served.

Dining/Diversions: At the end of a 260-foot historic pier is the Schooner Restaurant, specializing in seafood and buffet lunches. Pier One is an informal al fresco dining area, and it's also the hotel's entertainment center, where live shows are often presented.

Amenities: Water sports, a tiny outdoor swimming pool, a gym, Jacuzzi, sauna, Sunfish sailing, free use of the hotel's fitness center; complimentary day/night tennis nearby; glass-bottom boat rides. Sports, such as golf, waterskiing, and horseback riding, can be arranged. There's also room service (7am to 11pm), laundry, and an activity coordinator who can arrange tours and car rentals.

ON THE SOUTH COAST
EXPENSIVE

Divi Southwinds Beach Resort. St. Lawrence Gap, Christ Church, Barbados, W.I. ☎ **800/367-3484** or 246/428-7181. Fax 246/428-4674. 160 units. A/C TV TEL. Winter U.S.$185–$235 studio for 2; U.S.$205–$240 1-bedroom suite for 2. Off-season U.S.$120–$145 studio for 2; U.S.$140–$155 1-bedroom suite for 2. MAP (breakfast and dinner) U.S.$42 per person per day extra. AE, MC, V.

Midway between Bridgetown and the hamlet of Oistins, this resort was created when two distinctly different complexes were combined. Scattered over sandy flatlands of about 20 acres, it enjoys a loyal clientele, often young families. The showplace of the present resort is the newer (inland) buildings consisting of one- and two-bedroom suites with full kitchens. This section looks like a connected series of town houses, with wooden balconies and views of a large L-shaped swimming pool. From these buildings, visitors need only cross through two groves of palm trees and a narrow lane to reach a white-sand beach. The older, more modest, plainly furnished, but fully renovated units lie directly on the beachfront, ringed with palm trees, near an oval swimming pool of their own.

Dining: The Aquarius Restaurant, which rises above the largest of the resort's swimming pools, is the resort's main dining and drinking emporium. The food is standard; a snack/drink bar lies beside the beach, near the older units.

Amenities: Three swimming pools (one a wading pool reserved for children), sailboat rentals, snorkeling equipment, putting green, hair salon, laundry, island tours.

Oasis Hotel. P.O. Box 39W, Worthing 14, Christ Church, Barbados, W.I. ☎ **246/435-7930.** Fax 246/435-8232. 23 units. A/C TV TEL. Winter U.S.$220–$250 suite for 2. Off-season U.S.$175–$200 suite for 2. Extra person U.S.$95 each year-round. Children ages 8–12 U.S.$50 year-round in parents' room. Rates include all meals, drinks, and non-mechanized water sports. AE, DC, MC, V.

This is a well-designed, unpretentious, all-suite hotel and one of the most afford-able all-inclusives on Barbados. Small-scale, it was built on sunny flatlands in the heart of Barbados's densest concentration of hotels, restaurants, nightclubs, and pubs. Its original name was the Sichris Hotel, and despite its name change and the renovations it went through in the mid-1990s, many residents still call it by its original name. Don't expect to be dazzled by a wide array of amenities, as the resort's petite size and its original construction as a compound of self-catering holiday apartments seem to preclude the sprawling facilities you'd find at a larger resort. Each accommodation, furnished like a standard hotel room, has ceiling fans, a radio, and a safe.

Dining: The rooms all have a limited set of cooking utensils. But since meals and drinks are included as part of the all-inclusive price, very few guests opt to actually cook their own meals. The dining room serves Caribbean and international cuisine.

Amenities: There's a modestly sized swimming pool on the premises, tennis courts nearby, and—across the busy coastal highway—the sands of Rockley Beach.

Southern Palms. St. Lawrence, Christ Church, Barbados, W.I. ☎ **800/223-6510** in the U.S., or 246/428-7171. Fax 246/428-7175. 92 units. A/C TV TEL. Winter U.S.$185–$220 double; U.S.$270 suite. Off-season U.S.$112–$140 double; U.S.$162 suite. MAP (breakfast and dinner) U.S.$40 per person extra. AE, DC, MC, V.

A seafront club with a distinct personality and great value, the Southern Palms lies on the 1,000-foot stretch of Pink Beach of Barbados, midway between the airport and Bridgetown. The core of the resort is a pink-and-white manor house built in the Dutch style, with a garden-level colonnade of arches. Spread along the sands are multiarched two- and three-story buildings. Italian fountains and statues add to the Mediterranean feeling. In its more modern block, an eclectic mixture of rooms includes some with kitchenettes, some facing the ocean, others opening onto the garden, and some with penthouse luxury. Each room is a double, and the suites have small kitchenettes. The decor is the standard motel-like tropical motif. A cluster of buildings, the drinking and dining facilities, link the accommodations together.

Dining/Diversions: The Khus-Khus Bar and Restaurant serves both a West Indian and a continental cuisine. A local band often entertains with merengue and steel-band music.

Amenities: Terrace for sunning, two beachside freshwater swimming pools, sailboat rentals arranged, two tennis courts, snorkeling and scuba diving available, room service (7:30am to 9:30pm), laundry, tour desk.

MODERATE

Casuarina Beach Club. St. Lawrence Gap, Christ Church, Barbados, W.I. ☎ **800/223-9815** in the U.S., or 246/428-3600. Fax 246/428-1970. 157 units. A/C TEL. Winter U.S.$165–$180 studio for 2; U.S.$195 1-bedroom suite, U.S.$330 2-bedroom suite. Off-season U.S.$90–$100 studio for 2; U.S.$120 1-bedroom suite, U.S.$180 2-bedroom suite. Children 11 and under stay free in parents' room. AE, DISC, MC, V.

This is the best of the South Coast resorts. Set on a 900-foot coral sand beach, this unpretentious low-rise resort is Mediterranean in styling. This place is designed for those who prefer to cook for themselves. Family run, it also caters to families with reasonably priced suites. You'll approach this resort, located midway between Bridgetown and Oistins, through a forest of palm trees swaying above a well-maintained lawn. It's a pleasant place, although the staff could be a lot friendlier. Designed with red-tile roofs and white walls, the main building has a series of arched windows leading onto verandas. To get to your accommodations, you pass through the outlying reception building and beside the pair of swimming pools. These are separated from the wide, sandy beach by a lawn area dotted with casuarina and bougainvillea. Each accommodation is equipped with a ceiling fan and rattan furniture, and suites contain kitchenettes.

On the premises is an octagonal roofed open-air bar and restaurant, two floodlit tennis courts, and a fitness room. The front desk can arrange most water sports and outings through outside agencies.

Sandy Beach Hotel. Worthing, Christ Church, Barbados, W.I. ☎ **246/435-8000.** Fax 246/435-8053. 89 units. A/C TV TEL. Winter U.S.$120 double; U.S.$214 1-bedroom suite, U.S.$318 2-bedroom suite. Off-season U.S.$90 double; U.S.$130 1-bedroom suite, U.S.$177 2-bedroom suite. MAP (breakfast and dinner) U.S.$45 per adult extra. Additional person U.S.$30 extra per day in winter, U.S.$25 extra per day off-season. Children 11 and under stay free in parents' room. AE, MC, V.

Definitely not to be confused with Sandy Lane, this hotel is an unexciting but thoroughly reliable choice. It rests on 2 acres of beachfront land, 4 miles southeast of Bridgetown. The Barbadian-owned property rises around its architectural centerpiece, a soaring cone-shaped structure known as a *palapa*. Suitable for families with children, the resort contains standard motel-like double rooms, one- and two-bedroom suites, as well as 16 honeymoon suites with queen-size beds and completely private patios. All the simply decorated and spacious accommodations have fully equipped kitchenettes and private balconies or patios, and all the furniture at this informal place is locally made. Some of the ground-floor suites are suitable for guests with disabilities.

Dining/Diversions: Kolors, specializing in seafood and steaks, is under the palapa and opens onto a view of the sea and swimming pool. Every Monday, when outsiders are welcome, the resort sponsors a rum-punch party and a Bajan buffet. Entertainment is presented 3 nights a week.

Amenities: Swimming pool with tropical waterfall, children's play area, wading pool. Water sports, which cost extra, include 3-hour snorkeling trips, windsurfing, paddleboats, Sunfish, scuba lessons, and use of air mattresses, snorkels, fins, and masks. There's also room service (7:30am to 9:30pm), laundry, dry cleaning, and an activities desk to arrange island tours.

INEXPENSIVE

Bagshot House Hotel. St. Lawrence, Christ Church, Barbados, W.I. ☎ **246/435-6956.** Fax 246/435-9000. 16 units. A/C TEL. Winter U.S.$120 double; off-season U.S.$80 double. Rates include breakfast. AE, DC, DISC, MC, V.

Last renovated in 1995, this small, affordable, family-run hotel has flowering vines tumbling over the railing of its balconies and an old-fashioned, unhurried kind of charm. The hotel was named after the early 19th-century manor house that once stood on this site. In front, a white-sand beach stretches out before you. Some of the well-kept rooms boast views of the water. A sundeck, which doubles as a kind of open-air living room for the resort, is perched at the edge of a lagoon. A deck-side lounge is decorated with paintings by local artists, and a restaurant, Sand Dollar, is on the premises (see "Where to Dine," later in this chapter).

Fairholme. Maxwell, Christ Church, Barbados, W.I. ☎ **246/428-9425.** 31 units. Winter U.S.$33 double; U.S.$55 studio. Off-season U.S.$28 double; U.S.$40 studio. No credit cards.

Fairholme is a converted plantation house that has been enlarged during the past 20 years with a handful of connected annexes. The main house and its original gardens are just off a major road, 6 miles southeast of Bridgetown. The hotel is a

5-minute walk to the beach and across from its neighbor hotel, the Sea Breeze, which has a waterfront cafe and bar that Fairholme guests are allowed to use. The older part has 11 double rooms, each of which has a living-room area and a patio overlooking an orchard and swimming pool. Beside the pool is a lawn for sunbathing. More recently added are 20 Spanish-style studio apartments, all with balcony or patio, high cathedral ceilings, dark beams, and traditional furnishings. The restaurant has a reputation for home cooking: wholesome food, nothing fancy, but the ingredients are fresh. Air-conditioning, which is available only in the studios, is coin-operated: At the reception desk, you buy a brass token for U.S.$3 that you insert into your air conditioner for around 8 hours of cooling-off time.

Little Bay Hotel. St. Lawrence Gap, Christ Church, Barbados, W.I. ☎ **246/435-7246.** Fax 246/435-8574. 10 units. A/C TV TEL. Winter U.S.$100 studio for 1 or 2; U.S.$140 1-bedroom apt for up to 4. Off-season U.S.$65 studio for 1 or 2; U.S.$85 1-bedroom apt for up to 4. AE, MC, V.

This small apartment complex consists of an older core, which has been upgraded and renovated by its owners, the Patterson family. It's a peach-colored building with a tiled roof and pleasant, unfrilly accommodations with brick-tile floors, utilitarian furniture, and views over Barbados's well-developed southwestern coastline. There are ample opportunities for affordable drinking, nightclubbing, and dining within a brisk walk (or short drive). If you feel like cooking your own meals, you'll have a private kitchenette and access to several grocery stores and minimarts nearby. Italian dinners are served at Bellini's restaurant, which is vaguely associated with this hotel, for U.S.$15 to U.S.$27 per person.

Meridian Inn. Dover, Christ Church, Barbados, W.I. ☎ **246/428-4051.** Fax 246/420-6495. 12 studio apts. A/C. Winter U.S.$62 studio apt for 1 or 2; off-season U.S.$42 studio apt for 1 or 2. Children under 3 stay free in parents' studio; children 4 and over, U.S.$20 per day in winter, U.S.$12 off-season. AE, MC, V.

Close to shopping, restaurants, and nightclubs, this four-story, white-painted building right on the street is about a minute's walk to a good beach. It offers some of the least-expensive rooms on the island. They're clean and comfortable, but they'll take you back to thoughts of a 1960s Miami motel. However, they're air-conditioned, with twin beds, kitchenettes, baths, and private balconies, along with daily maid service. Each has a ceiling fan and a small fridge; TVs can be rented. Phones are in the corridors. There's no room service. Baby-sitting can be arranged. On the ground floor, a simple restaurant features fresh seafood at both lunch and dinner.

Pegwell Inn. Welches, Christ Church Parish, Barbados, W.I. ☎ **246/428-6150.** 4 units. Winter U.S.$36 double; off-season U.S.$26 double. No credit cards.

This simple but respectable guest house in a one-story, wood-sided building was built during the early 1940s. Part of the energies of its owner, Rosemary Phillips, are devoted to running a kiosk-style minimart at the back of the house, and if you arrive during business hours it might pay to go around to the back, rather than to the front, of the house. There's a laundry across the street, a swimming area (Welches Beach, which can be seen across the road), and easy access to such nearby facilities as a bank, restaurants, and shops. Each accommodation is plain; two rooms have two single beds, two rooms have one double bed each, and all rooms have a toilet, a sink, and shower.

Rio Guest House. Paradise Village, St. Lawrence Gap, Christ Church, Barbados, W.I. ☎ **246/428-1546.** Fax 246/428-2158. 9 units, 6 with private bathroom. Winter U.S.$35 double with bathroom; U.S.$55 studio. Off-season U.S.$26 double with bathroom; U.S.$45 studio. MC, V.

Built as a private home in the 1940s, this simple black-and-white two-story guest house is maintained by the resident owner, Mrs. Denise Harding. It features low rates and clean, no-frills bedrooms. None of the single rooms has a private bathroom, and these rent for U.S.$25 in winter and U.S.$20 off-season. There are no private kitchens, except in the studio. The minimarts, bars, nightclubs, and hamburger joints of St. Lawrence Gap are within walking distance, Dover Beach is within a 2-minute walk, and guests share a communal kitchen. In the kitchen, a large refrigerator is divided into compartments, each reserved more or less exclusively for one of the bedrooms, where residents can store their munchies.

Southern Surf Beach Apartments. Rockley Beach, Christ Church, Barbados, W.I. ☎ **246/435-6672.** Fax 246/435-6649. 16 units. Winter U.S.$50 double; U.S.$70 studio apt for 2. Off-season U.S.$40 double; U.S.$50 studio apt for 2. Extra person in apt U.S.$15. Children stay free in parents' studio if an extra cot is not needed; otherwise a U.S.$15 per-day surcharge applies. MC, V.

Close to the famous Accra Beach at Rockley, this is a good, serviceable choice in a centrally located complex with a swimming pool and garden. It's also convenient for nearby dining, shopping, and entertainment; this is a good choice if you don't want to rent a car. Four rooms are in the main building (the "Great House"); while the studio apartments are in a four-story concrete-block building. There are three apartments per floor, each simply but comfortably furnished, with a balcony and beach view. (Southern Surf owns the land between it and the ocean, so there's an unobstructed view of the beach.) The rooms don't have phones, but there is one for public use in the apartment block, and the only TV is in the office reception area. Rooms in the main house, although not as large, have more of an old-time Bajan feeling with ceiling fans overhead. Only the studio apartments are air-conditioned. Baby-sitting can also be arranged.

Windsurf Village Hotel. Maxwell Main Rd., Christ Church, Barbados, W.I. ☎ **246/428-9095.** Fax 246/435-2872. 48 units. Old wing, winter: U.S.$60 double, U.S.$85 studio with kitchenette for 2, U.S.$105 2-bedroom apt for 4; off-season, U.S.$45 double, U.S.$65 studio, U.S.$95 2-bedroom apt. New wing, winter: U.S.$105 studio with kitchenette for 2, U.S.$170 2-bedroom apt for 4, U.S.$275 penthouse (2-bedroom); off-season, U.S.$70 studio, U.S.$105 2-bedroom apt, U.S.$140 penthouse. MC, V.

Although this hotel assumes that windsurfers appreciate proximity to other windsurfers, many guests who don't have very much interest in the sport have been happy here, too. This is a two-story building with balconies, plus two patios so guests can mingle outdoors. It attracts a youngish, athletic crowd, and others who appreciate the lighthearted, casual setting. The bedrooms contain wooden furnishings, ceiling fans, and tile floors. A new wing with 30 units (each with air conditioner and a ceiling fan) was just added in 1998; rooms here are more expensive because they're bigger and have newer furnishings and better plumbing.

If you're watching your wallet, you'll like the location here, near the island's densest concentration of nightclubs, supermarkets, and cheap restaurants, all within an easy walk or drive. There's a snack-style restaurant on the beach. Despite the name, the hotel doesn't own or rent any Windsurfers. Instead, windsurfing enthusiasts are directed to the water-sports facilities at the nearby Club Mistral, where Windsurfer rentals are U.S.$20 per hour and lessons cost U.S.$20 per hour.

Woodville Beach Hotel. Hastings, Christ Church, Barbados, W.I. ☎ **246/435-6694.** Fax 246/435-9211. 36 units. TEL. Winter U.S.$120–$126 studio; U.S.$140 1-bedroom apt,

U.S.$180 2-bedroom apt. Off-season U.S.$85–$92 studio; U.S.$106 1-bedroom apt, U.S.$145 2-bedroom apt. AE, MC, V.

These apartments, last renovated in 1995, are one of the best bargains on Barbados, ideal for families on a budget. Set directly on a rocky shoreline 2 ½ miles southeast of Bridgetown, the hotel is in the heart of the village of Hastings, on slightly less than an acre of land. The U-shaped apartment complex is built around a pool terrace overlooking the sea. Functional and minimalist in decor, it is nevertheless clean and comfortable. The kitchenette in each accommodation is fully equipped, and a variety of rental units is offered. All have balconies or decks, and some units are air-conditioned. There are supermarkets, stores, and banks within easy walking distance. Although a handful of athletic guests attempt to swim off the nearby rocks, most opt for a 5-minute walk to the white sands of nearby Rockley (Accra) Beach. A small restaurant is open on the property, serving American and Bajan fare.

ON THE EAST COAST
MODERATE

Crane Beach Hotel. Crane Bay, St. Philip (about 14 miles from Bridgetown and a 15-minute drive from the airport), Barbados, W.I. ☎ **800/223-6510** or 246/423-6220. Fax 246/423-5343. 18 units. TEL. Winter U.S.$150 double; U.S.$250–$295 1-bedroom suite, U.S.$425 2-bedroom suite. Off-season U.S.$90 double; U.S.$150–$175 1-bedroom suite, U.S.$255 2-bedroom suite. MAP U.S.$50 per person per day extra. Honeymoon packages available. AE, MC, V.

Near the easternmost end of the island, this remote hilltop hostelry stands on a cliff overlooking the Atlantic. Crane Beach was called by one writer "the most beautiful spot on earth." At least Prince Andrew thought so when he built his clearly visible house on a nearby cliff.

Well, the location may be beautiful, but the hotel leaves something to be desired. Time-share units are hawked in the lobby, and the housekeeping appears lax. Rubberneckers, who pay an entrance fee to enter the property and use the area around the pool and the bar, often disturb the tranquillity. So it's not for everybody, but yet it is one of the most famous hotels in the southern Caribbean. Located near Marriott's Sam Lord's Castle Resorts, it opens onto one of the most scenic beaches on Barbados, which is reached by walking down some 200 steps. At times, the water can be too rough for swimming. Canopied beds and antique furnishings grace many of the bedrooms, and the views are often panoramic. Some of the units have kitchenettes, but only one has air-conditioning, which is reserved for guests in dire need of it.

Dining/Diversions: Many visitors for the day head here just to have a drink on the panoramic terrace or to order a meal. An international cuisine is served with West Indian flair. At night, the tables are candlelit; the Sunday brunch is a well-attended event.

Amenities: The Roman-style swimming pool with columns, separating the main house from the dining room, has been used as a backdrop for more fashion layouts than any other place in the Caribbean. The resort also has tennis courts, and offers room service, baby-sitting, and laundry service.

Sam Lord's Castle Resorts. Long Bay, St. Philip, Barbados, W.I. ☎ **246/423-7350.** Fax 246/423-6361. 248 units. A/C MINIBAR TV TEL. Winter U.S.$210–$245 double; off-season U.S.$145–$170 double. MAP (breakfast and dinner) U.S.$50 in winter, U.S.$40 off-season per person extra. AE, DC, DISC, MC, V.

In spite of its name, this is no castle but a Great House built in 1820 by one of Barbados's most notorious scoundrels. According to legend, Samuel Hall Lord (the "Regency Rascal") constructed the estate with money acquired by luring ships to wreck on the jagged but hard-to-detect rocks of Cobbler's Reef. Amid 72 landscaped acres, the estate has a wide, lengthy private sandy beach edged by tall coconut trees.

The Great House, near the easternmost end of the island, a 15-minute drive northeast of the airport, was built in the pirate's more mellow "golden years." Craftspeople were imported from England to reproduce sections of the queen's castle at Windsor. The decor includes the dubiously acquired but nonetheless beautiful art of Reynolds, Raeburn, and Chippendale.

Only seven rooms are in the Main House, and these are stylishly decorated with antique furnishings. Three rooms have canopied beds. The rest of the accommodations are in cottages and wings, either two or four floors high, and there are some rather tacky motel rooms with a faux-castle theme. (Some of these units evoke Miami in the '50s—no great compliment.) For privacy's sake and to get more light, try to avoid the ground-floor units if possible. The best (and most expensive) accommodations are in structures 7, 8, and 9. The staff often seems more concerned with the demands of the group traffic than with the individual traveler (the hotel is a favorite for conventions).

Dining/Diversions: Three meals a day are served in the Wanderer Restaurant, and you can order a hamburger at the Oceanus Café, right on the beach. There are many bars as well. A fiesta night in the hotel's Bajan Village is offered once a week, as is a shipwreck barbecue and beach party with a steel-drum band, a limbo show, and fire-eaters on South Beach.

Amenities: Three swimming pools, exercise room, shuffleboard, table tennis, library; sailing, horseback riding, snorkeling, fishing, and other activities can be arranged. There's also a beauty/barber shop, laundry service, baby-sitting, and a concierge to arrange island tours and outings.

INEXPENSIVE

Atlantis Hotel. Bathsheba, St. Joseph, Barbados, W.I. ☎ **246/433-9445.** 15 units. Winter U.S.$65 double; off-season U.S.$60 double. Extra adult U.S.$30 each in winter, U.S.$25 each off-season; extra child 11 and under U.S.$17 each in winter, U.S.$15 each off-season. Rates include half board (breakfast and dinner). AE.

This boxy, concrete-sided hotel has been around for years, and is a famous lunchtime spot (see "Where to Dine" for a review). It's in an isolated position on the rocky and turbulent Atlantic coast, where strong currents, winds, and undertows usually make swimming a bad idea. If that doesn't deter you, you'll enjoy the scenery in St. Joseph, which is among the most beautiful on Barbados; many botanists and nature lovers say it reminds them of the lowlands of Scotland.

The accommodations are clean but simple affairs, with white walls, carpeted floors, wooden furniture, and (in many cases) views and balconies overlooking the surging Atlantic. Mrs. Enid Maxwell and members of her family keep things running smoothly.

The Edgewater Inn. Bathsheba (13 miles northeast of Bridgetown on Hwy. 3), St. Joseph, Barbados, W.I. ☎ **246/433-9900.** Fax 246/433-9902. 20 units. Winter U.S.$105–$165 double; off-season U.S.$85–$145 double. AE, DISC, MC, V.

Built as a dramatically isolated private home on the site of a much older colonial building, and converted into a hotel in 1947, this inn is set directly on the Atlantic seacoast, a short drive southeast of the island's "Scotland District." Lying in a tropical rain forest on top of a low cliff, the property opens onto ocean views, and a nearby wildlife sanctuary invites exploration. Cozy and intimate, the small inn is decorated with beveled leaded glass windows from Asia, and furnishings reflect an island motif, with mahogany pieces handcrafted by local artisans.

The freshwater swimming pool, shaped like the island of Barbados, is the focal point of the resort. Surfers are attracted to the hotel and nonguests also drop by, either for a meal or a drink. The restaurant, serving West Indian cuisine, is open daily from 11am to 4pm for lunch and from 6 to 9pm for dinner. A Bajan buffet is staged every Sunday from noon to 3:30pm.

Fleet View Apartments. Tent Bay, Bathsheba, St. Joseph, Barbados, W.I. ☎ **246/ 433-9445.** 6 apts. Winter U.S.$40 studio apt for 1 or 2; U.S.$45 1-bedroom apt for 1 or 2. Off-season U.S.$35 studio apt for 1 or 2; U.S.$40 1-bedroom apt for 1 or 2. AE.

These apartments are an annex of the Atlantis Hotel. They're simple, with little ornamentation, and cater to independent-minded guests who don't want the fussiness associated with a traditional hotel or resort. If you have a bicycle or car, you can compensate for the isolation. Although each unit has a modest kitchen, breakfast is served across the street in the dining room of the Atlantis Hotel, and if you grow tired of cooking, the Atlantis will happily feed you. A major renovation of this property, which occurred in 1998, may lead to an increase in rates during the lifetime of this edition. For more information about the location, refer to the Atlantis listing, above.

✪ **Kingsley Club.** Cattlewash-on-Sea, near Bathsheba, St. Joseph, Barbados, W.I. ☎ **246/433-9422.** Fax 246/433-9226. 8 units. Winter U.S.$101 double; off-season U.S.$84 double. Rates include breakfast. AE, MC, V. Take Hwy. 3 north of Bathsheba.

This little West Indian inn, an exceptionally affordable gem, is far removed from the bustle of the tourist-ridden West Coast, and is often a favorite stopover for Bajans themselves. In the foothills of Bathsheba, opening onto the often-turbulent Atlantic, the Kingsley Club lies on the northeast coast. A historic inn, it offers simply furnished and very modest but clean and comfortable bedrooms. At night, you can sit back and enjoy a rum punch made from an old planter's recipe. The club enjoys a reputation for good cooking, and its Bajan food will be recommended later for those traveling to the East Coast just for the day. Nearby Cattlewash Beach is one of the longest, widest, and least crowded stretches of sand on Barbados—but be aware that swimming here can be extremely dangerous.

2 Where to Dine

Gourmet cuisine, prepared by chefs from Europe and North America, is the norm at the luxury resorts on Barbados. There has been an explosive growth in the number of new restaurants in the mid-'90s.

If you want authentic Bajan cuisine, head for the local taverns, where callaloo soup, cou-cou (a cornmeal and okra pudding), and pepperpot stew will be on the menus, all indicating the West African heritage of many Barbadians. We'll share our own favorite finds below.

Flying fish, kingfish, snapper, and dolphin (mahimahi, not the mammal) are better than most meat dishes, many of which are made from frozen meat shipped in from the north.

Most top restaurants require a reservation in the winter. It's always a good idea to call a place before trekking across the island, because of unexpected closings.

A 10% service charge is added to most restaurant tabs, but it's customary to tip more than this, especially if service has been good.

ON THE WEST COAST
EXPENSIVE

✪ **Bagatelle Restaurant.** Hwy. 2A, St. Thomas (a 15-minute drive north of Bridgetown). ☎ **246/421-6767.** Reservations recommended. Lunch U.S.$12; fixed-price dinner U.S.$45. MC, V. Mon–Sat 11am–2:30pm and 7–9:30pm. Cut inland near Paynes Bay north of Bridgetown, 3 miles from both Sunset Crest and the Sandy Lane Hotel. FRENCH/CARIBBEAN.

This restaurant is housed in one of the most historic and impressive buildings on the island. Originally constructed in 1645 as the residence of the island's first governor (Lord Willoughby), it lies in 5 acres of forest. The sylvan retreat is in the cool uplands, just south of the island's center, and retains the charm of its original buildings.

Bagatelle is one of the island's finest and most elegant choices for French cuisine with a Caribbean flair. Candles and lanterns illuminate the old archways and the ancient trees. The service is the best we've ever found on Barbados. Try the homemade duck-liver pâté, deviled Caribbean crab backs, or smoked flying-fish mousse with horseradish mayonnaise. The beef Wellington Bagatelle style with a chasseur sauce is a favorite, as is the crisp roast duckling with an orange-and-brandy sauce. The local catch of the day, the most popular item on the menu, can be prepared grilled, barbecued, or in the style of Baxters Road (that is, spicily seasoned and sautéed in deep oil). A different list of homemade desserts is featured nightly, and coffee can be served on the terrace. Cruise-ship passengers can take advantage of its light lunches before their ships sail at sunset.

Bourbon Street Restaurant. Prospect, St. James. ☎ **246/424-4557.** Reservations recommended. Main courses U.S.$20–$32.50. MC, V. Daily 6:30–10pm. Closed Mon in May–Nov. NEW ORLEANS/CREOLE/CAJUN.

Bourbon Street adds a unique option to the island's dining scene, which is dominated by Bajan menus. It aims to recreate a New Orleans dining and club atmosphere complete with spicy Louisiana food and music. For appetizers, you'll find everything from oysters on the half-shell to Bar-B-Que Shrimps à La Louisian. Main courses can be prepared as spicy as you like, and you can choose from "N'awlins" style jambalaya and crawfish to Cajun-style island cuisine like blackened red snapper or shrimp and crab Creole. Location can mean a lot to a restaurant, and Bourbon Street has everything going for it, with a view that overlooks the sea. They pride themselves on being the "house of blues and jazz" in Barbados, and they feature live music every Wednesday, Friday, and Saturday night.

✪ **Carambola.** Derricks, St. James. ☎ **246/432-0832.** Reservations recommended. Main courses U.S.$22–$50. AE, MC, V. Mon–Sat 6:30–9:30pm. Closed Aug. FRENCH/CARIBBEAN/ASIAN.

Built beside the road that runs along the island's western coastline, this restaurant sits atop a 20-foot seaside cliff 1½ miles south of Holetown. Carambola offers one of the most panoramic dining terraces in the Caribbean. However, you'll have to go early for dinner to see the view, since Carambola doesn't serve lunch. The prize-winning cuisine is creative and good, with modern French-inspired touches. The dishes may be French or continental, but they definitely have Caribbean flair and flavor, as exemplified by the fillet of swordfish or dolphin often served. A selection of savory vegetarian dishes is offered as well, and a crowd-pleasing favorite is the chicken stuffed with crab. To head to the Far East, select the spicy Thai pork tenderloin, and try to save room for one of the luscious desserts such as the lime mousse. The impressive wine list features mostly French vintages.

Barbados Dining

NORTH POINT

Archer's Bay

River Bay

Stroud Bay

HARRISON POINT

CUCKOLD POINT

ST. LUCY

Maycock's Bay

1B

Fairfield

Gay's Cove

25

Pico Teneriffe

Coleton

1C

Half Moon Fort

Morgan Lewis Beach

Six Men's Bay

Heywoods Beach

Greeland

ST. PETER

2

St. Andrew's
Church

Speightstown

SCOTLAND

ST. ANDREW

1

Mullins Bay

Gibbs Beach

2A

Turner's Hall
Woods

Chalky Mount

Cattlewash

1

Tent Bay

3

ST. JAMES

Bathsheba

23

Church Point

4

ST. JOSEPH

5

FOLKSTONE
UNDERWATER PARK

6

3A

Hackleton's Cliff

Holetown

1A

Welchman Hall

3

ST. JOHN

7

8

Sunset Crest

9

Blackmans

Paynes Bay

ST. THOMAS

10

3B

Lazaretto

11

12

2A

2

Locust Hall

Prospect

Warrens

3

ST. GEORGE

Paradise Beach

13

4

Brighton Beach

4B

ST. MICHAEL

2

Black Rock

5

4

3

Deep Water Harbour

14

Queen's Park

CHRIST CHURCH

Bridgetown

Pine Blvd.

Carlisle Bay

15

6

Worthing

6

Needham's Point

Hastings

St. Lawrence

Tom Adams Hwy.

Rockley Beach

16 17 18 19

20

7

Grantley Adams
Int'l Airport

Sandy Beach

21

Maxwell

Casuarina Beach

Oistins

GOLD COAST

Spring Garden Hwy.

Errol Barrow Hwy.

Charles Duncan O'Neale Hwy.

East Coast Road

Caribbean Sea

South
Point

Silver Sands

Airport ✈ Beach ⚲ Church ✝ Lighthouse ⚲

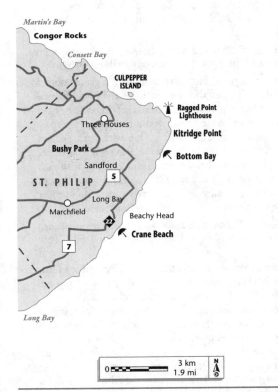

Atlantic Ocean

Martin's Bay
Congor Rocks

Consett Bay

CULPEPPER
ISLAND

Ragged Point
Lighthouse

Three Houses

Kitridge Point

Bushy Park

Sandford

Bottom Bay

5

ST. PHILIP

Long Bay

Marchfield

Beachy Head

22

Crane Beach

7

Long Bay

0 [scale] 3 km
1.9 mi

N

Caribbean Islands

Barbados

Angry Annie's
  Restaurant & Bar 8
Atlantis Hotel 23
Bagatelle Restaurant 12
Barbecue Barn 18
Bombas 9
Bourban Street Restaurant 13
Brown Sugar 15
Café Calabash 25
Café Sol 21
Carambola 9
Champers 17
The Cliff 11
The Coach House 9
Crane Beach Hotel 22
David's Place 19
The Emerald Palm 3
The Fathoms 10
Ile De France 6
Josef's 21
Kingsley Club 24
La Malson 10
Luigi's Restaurant 21
Mango's by the Sea 1
Neptune's 10
Nico's Champagne
  & Wine Bar 10
Olives Bar and Bistro 7
The Orchid Room 4
The Palm Terrace 5
Pisces 21
Pizzaz 7
Reid's 10
Ròti Hut 20
Sand Dollar 21
Secrets 21
The Ship Inn 21
Taps on the Bay 21
T.G.I. Boomers 21
39 Steps 16
The Terrace Restaurant 2
The Waterfront Café 14
Witch Doctor 21

✪ **The Cliff.** Hwy. 1, Derrick, St. James. ☎ **246/432-1922.** Reservations required in winter. Main courses U.S.$27–$37.50. AE, DISC, MC, V. Mon–Sat 6:30–10pm. INTERNATIONAL/CARIBBEAN.

Built atop a coral cliff, this open-air restaurant has a four-level dining room crafted with terra-cotta tiles and coral stone. It rests above a 10-foot cliff adjacent to the Coconut Creek Hotel, on the island's Gold Coast. Despite the fact that the English/Bajan partners who own it don't consider it exclusive, posh, or even particularly formal, it has attracted Prince Andrew and assorted titled and bejeweled clients of the nearby upscale hotels. (The prices are certainly royal, though!) Despite all this, no one will mind if you wear well-tailored shorts; the place really is surprisingly low key.

The food here was accurately praised by Frommer's reader and gourmet Dr. Stephen C. Bandy of Princeton, New Jersey, who wrote: "The Cliff offers a menu of the highest quality: the best cuts of meat, the freshest and most interesting vegetables and greens I have ever eaten on the island, and dessert confections that would not be looked down on in New York restaurants like Bouley and Lespinasse." How right he is! Menu items include grilled snapper drizzled in three types of coriander sauce (cream-based, oil-based, and vinaigrette style), accompanied with garlic-infused mashed potatoes, and Thai-style curried shrimp. Sushi is sometimes presented as a starter, complete with wasabi and portions of fresh local tuna, scallops, and snapper. As you dine, watch for manta rays, which glide through the illuminated waters below. The seas are usually calm enough to spot them, and a sighting is considered a sign of good luck.

The Emerald Palm. Porters, St. James. ☎ **246/422-4116.** Reservations required. Main courses U.S.$20–$40. AE, MC, V. Mon–Sat 6:30–9:30pm (last seating). INTERNATIONAL.

This stucco-and-tile house is 2 miles north of Holetown in a tropical garden dotted with gazebos. Go here for zesty dishes packed with international and island flavors. After passing under an arbor, you'll be invited to order a drink, served on one of the flowered banquettes that fill various parts of the house. Begin, perhaps, with a spicy cucumber soup or a succulent version of Caribbean fish soup with fresh peppers before moving on to main courses. Specialties include dishes such as roast red snapper in coconut juice with local baby spinach. The chef also manages to come up with such simple dishes as medallions of beef tenderloin in a mustard sauce. For a real taste of Barbados, try the chargrilled scallops and baby squid seasoned with a chili-pepper dressing. Meals are served on the rear terrace, al fresco style, by candlelight.

✪ **The Fathoms.** Paynes Bay, St. James. ☎ **246/432-2568.** Reservations recommended for dinner. Main courses U.S.$20–$29. AE, DISC, MC, V. Daily noon–3pm and 6:30–10pm (last order). INTERNATIONAL.

Located in a red-roofed stucco house close to the surf of the island's western coastline, this pleasant restaurant serves meals on an outdoor terrace shaded by a mahogany tree and in an interior decorated with accents of terra-cotta, wood, and pottery.

The kitchen offers a fairly ambitious menu and does itself proud with appetizers like shrimp and crab étouffée, herbed conch cakes, or blackened shrimp with mango. For a main dish, try the caramelized barracuda, grilled pork medallions, or Dorado fish Hunan, which has zesty and winning flavors. Upstairs is a Santa Fe–style tapas bar, primarily for drinks, wines, and finger foods. A pool table and board games help you pass the evening away. This attractive watering hole is open daily from 5pm until the crowd finally departs.

⊕ Family-Friendly Restaurants

The Ship Inn *(see p. 240)*   This is one of the best family restaurants, lying at St. Lawrence Gap along the South Coast, site of many budget hotels. Its all-you-can-eat carvery lunches and similar help-yourself dinners make it a favorite of the family with a lean purse and a big appetite.

T.G.I. Boomers *(see p. 240)*   Another family favorite at St. Lawrence Gap, this restaurant might be the bargain of Barbados. It offers both Bajan and American cuisine, along with the hamburgers and seafood that kids crave. It also serves the best American breakfast on Barbados.

✪ **Ile de France.** In the Settlers' Beach Hotel, Holetown, St. James. ☎ **246/422-3245.** Reservations recommended. Main courses U.S.$25–$37.50. MC, V. Tues–Sun 6:30–9:30pm (last order). CLASSIC FRENCH.

The Ile de France, located north of Holetown and 8 miles north of Bridgetown, presents the finest and most authentic French cuisine on Barbados. Place yourself in the capable hands of Michel and Martine Gramaglia, two French-born expatriates who handle their kitchen and dining room with an enviable savoir-faire. Ingredients are flown in either from France or Martinique or else obtained fresh on Barbados. Specialties might include escargots de Bourgogne, a flavorful version of fish soup with lobster, or a marinade of three fish whose exact composition depends on the catch of the day. Other dishes include tournedos with a béarnaise sauce, rack of lamb, catch of the day, shrimp, and roast lobster. For dessert, try the tart tatin, crème brulée, or banana terrine. The atmosphere is charming and traditional.

La Maison. Holetown, St. James. ☎ **246/432-1156.** Reservations required in winter. Main courses U.S.$22.50–$40. AE, MC, V. Tues–Sun 6:30–9:30pm. FRENCH/CARIBBEAN.

Located on the beach south of Holetown and open on two sides to the sea and to a flowering courtyard (whose centerpiece is a mermaid-capped fountain), this restaurant has walls of exposed coral and an intricate ceiling crafted from a Guyanan hardwood called greenheart. The award-winning cuisine is served with quiet dignity. Most diners are won over by the taste and flavor of the menu. The intriguing appetizers are likely to include blackened flying-fish fillets set on a sweet-potato salad. Main courses feature such exotica as barracuda steamed with tomato fondue and vegetable, red snapper grilled and served with a seafood sauce, mashed potatoes, and vegetables. If you don't want anything too unusual, try the grilled chicken breast with a pasta and cream sauce, or the grilled sirloin in a ragoût accompanied by sautéed fennel. The restaurant even knows how to prepare simpler dishes well. Desserts aren't neglected either, and a delectable one is fresh fruits in a tulip basket with ice cream or sorbet.

✪ **Neptune's.** In the Tamarind Cove Beach Resort, Paynes Bay, St. James. ☎ **246/432-1332.** Reservations recommended. Main courses U.S.$30–$45. MC, V. Wed–Sun 6:30–10pm. Closed Tues off-season. SEAFOOD.

This is the best seafood restaurant on Barbados but it's outrageously expensive. Count on spending well over U.S.$60 per person. Located south of Holetown, in one of the island's top resorts, it abandons the standard tropical Caribbean motif found in most of the island's other restaurants. Instead, you'll find a stylish octagonal room sheathed in faux malachite, whose emerald-green tones reflect the colors of an illuminated aquarium in the room's center. Service is impeccable.

Appetizers range from a smoked fish pâté with cucumber noodles and beetroot vinaigrette to seasoned crab claws with a bean-sprout and bok-choy salad. Neptune's catch is a selection of island fish, often served in a light orange sauce flavored with herbs. You can also order that island favorite, fillet of red snapper, or splurge on a cassoulet of lobster. A version of Bajan bouillabaisse is offered, as is a magret of duck with an onion marmalade. The dessert menu is one of the most elaborate on Barbados, ranging from a classic tiramisu to a coconut-and-mango parfait or a trio of rich chocolate mousses.

✪ **Olives Bar & Bistro.** Second St. at the corner of Hwy. 1, Holetown. ☎ **246/432-2112.** Reservations required in winter. Main courses U.S.$13–$33. AE, MC, V. Daily 6:30–10:30pm. MEDITERRANEAN/CARIBBEAN.

Run by a couple from New Zealand, this restaurant is named for the only oil used in the kitchen. Additionally, olives are the only snack served in the bar, where there's a welcome rowdiness. The street-level dining room (no-smoking/air-conditioned) spills out from its original coral-stone walls and scrubbed-pine floorboards into a pleasant garden. The cuisine celebrates the warm-weather climates of southern Europe and the Antilles, and does so exceedingly well. Even some local chefs like to dine here on their nights off. The best items include yellowfin tuna, marinated and seared rare and served on a bed of roast-garlic mashed potatoes with grilled ratatouille. You can also order roast lamb flavored with honey, garlic, and fresh herbs. More Caribbean in its flavors is a jerk tenderloin of pork. For dessert, try the toffee and walnut tart or else the Créole bread-and-butter pudding. Next door is a sandwich bar serving light luncheon fare Monday through Friday from 8am to 4pm.

The Orchid Room. In the Colony Club Hotel, Porters, St. James. ☎ **246/422-2335.** Reservations recommended. Main courses U.S.$17.50–$42.50. DC, MC, V. Winter daily 6:30–10pm. Closed 1 or 2 days a week off-season (call for times). CARIBBEAN/FRENCH.

The Orchid Room blends a plantation-house ambience with velvet-glove service and culinary finesse. It's even won the approval of the earl of Bradford, head of the Master Chefs of Great Britain, who found his last meal here "beautifully presented and perfectly prepared." Beneath sparkling chandeliers and surrounded by period furnishings, main courses are served with a dash of showmanship as silver domes are removed to reveal their treasures.

The chef brings Gallic flair to his creations, which are composed mostly of local ingredients. The appetizers are likely to include a salad of lobster with mango, delicate but full flavored. Tortellini in an herb-cream dressing is a tantalizing new addition to the menu. Your soup may be pumpkin with smoked salmon. The main courses are varied, ranging from grilled mahimahi laid on a purée of eggplant and potato and dressed with lime and olive oil to Washington state lamb fillet gift-wrapped in a cornmeal crêpe with a deeply reduced Cabernet Sauvignon sauce.

The Palm Terrace. In the Royal Pavilion Hotel, Porters (between Sunset Crest and Gibbs Beach), St. James. ☎ **246/422-5555.** Reservations required. Main courses U.S.$25–$45. AE, DC, DISC, MC, V. Daily 7–9:30pm. CARIBBEAN/EUROPEAN.

In an elegant setting on a pink-marble terrace, this dramatic restaurant opens onto the oceanfront. The Palm Terrace has a French chef who oversees a Bajan staff. Together they turn out some of the more delectable cuisine offered at any West

Coast hotel. To the sounds of music, with the trade winds sweeping in, you can sample from an alluring (and pricey menu). Starters include sea scallop ravioli with christophene and cilantro salsa; panfried foie gras with sauterne wine and grape sauce; and fresh tuna tartar with ginger and coriander. Main course selections feature grilled dorado with anchovy oil garnished with potato gnocchi and tomato coulis; panfried lobster medallions with lime and papaya salsa; and boneless lamb rack-roasted with a blend of West Indian spices and grilled smoked vegetables. Several health-conscious dishes are also available, as is a chef's nightly special.

The Terrace Restaurant. In the Cobblers Cove Hotel, Road View (½ mile south of Speightstown on Hwy. 1), St. Peter. ☎ **246/422-2291.** Reservations recommended. Main lunch courses U.S.$10–$20; main dinner courses U.S.$18–$30; fixed-price dinner U.S.$60. AE, MC, V. Daily 12:30–2pm and 7–9pm. CONTINENTAL.

This award-winning restaurant overlooks the ocean and a West Coast beach. Before dinner, guests often stop at the poolside bar to order the specialty drink, a Cobblers Cooler, an extra-tall drink blending Caribbean fruits with the rum of Barbados.

The menu changes daily to take advantage of fresh local produce. A team of French-trained chefs works in the kitchen. You might begin with gazpacho of shrimp or duck pâté with orange sauce. The catch of the day is usually featured, and it can be either poached or grilled and flavored with Bajan seasoning. A *plat végétarien* is also featured, and meat courses include Bajan ham braised with pineapple and honey in a Madeira sauce. Many guests prefer to finish their meal with an Irish coffee. Although not always exciting, the food is reliable, solid, and always perfectly prepared with first-class ingredients.

MODERATE

Angry Annie's Restaurant & Bar. First St., Holetown, St. James. ☎ **246/432-2119.** Main courses U.S.$17–$35. MC, V. Daily 6–10pm (or sometimes after midnight). INTERNATIONAL.

Don't ask "Annie" why she's angry. She might tell you! Annie and Paul Matthews, both of the U.K., run this restaurant in a new location. This cozy, 34-seat joint is decorated in tropical colors with a circular bar. Rock 'n' roll classics play on the excellent sound system. The dishes are tasty, with lots of local flavor. The place is known for ribs, the most savory on the island. We also like their garlic-cream potatoes, and their use of local vegetables whenever possible. Angry or not, Annie also turns out excellent pasta dishes, and you can also order fresh fish. Begin with a homemade soup or chicken wings, and then the night is yours, especially if you order such dishes as chicken Kiev or spaghetti bolognese. There's even a take-out service if you'd like to take something back to your studio or apartment.

✪ **Nico's Champagne & Wine Bar.** Derrick's, St. James. ☎ **246/432-6386.** Reservations recommended. Lunch main courses U.S.$8.70–$13.50; dinner main courses U.S.$11.25–$36. AE, DISC, MC, V. Mon–Sat 11:30am–10:30pm. INTERNATIONAL.

Set on the inland side of a road that bisects some of the most expensive residential real estate on Barbados (the West Coast), this is a great value, an informal bistro inspired by the wine bars of London. In a 19th-century building originally constructed in the 1800s as the headquarters for a plantation, it does a thriving business from its air-conditioned bar area. About a dozen kinds of wine are sold by the glass. Meals are served at tables protected with a shed-style roof in the garden out back. The food is flavorful and designed to accompany the wine: Examples include deep-fried Camembert with passion fruit sauce, chicken breasts stuffed with crab, red snapper, and some of the best lobster (grilled simply and served with garlic butter) on Barbados. Chris Millward and Cheryl Wiltshire, your hosts, seem to have devoted a lot of care and attention to what you eat and drink.

INEXPENSIVE

The Coach House. On the main Bridgetown–Holetown rd., just south of Sandy Lane (about 6 miles north of Bridgetown), Paynes Bay, St. James. ☎ **246/432-1163.** Reservations recommended. Dinner BD$14–$48 (U.S.$7–$24); bar snacks BD$9–$25 (U.S.$4.50–$12.50); all-you-can-eat Bajan lunch buffet BD$26 (U.S.$13). AE, MC, V. Daily noon–2am. BAJAN.

The Coach House, named after a pair of antique coaches that stand outside, is a green-and-white house said to be 200 years old. The atmosphere is a Bajan version of an English pub, with an outdoor garden bar. Businesspeople and folks who've spent the morning on the nearby beaches come here to order buffet lunches, where Bajan food is served Sunday to Friday from noon to 3pm. The price is U.S.$13 for an all-you-can-eat lunch including local vegetables and salads prepared fresh daily. The best deal here is the bar menu, which ranges from burgers and fries to fried shrimp and flying fish. Dinner is from an à la carte menu with steak, chicken, fish, curried dishes, fresh salads, and a wide range of desserts from cheesecake to banana flambé. Live music is available every night of the week, from top nightclub bands to steel bands.

Pizzaz. Hwy. 1, Holetown, St. James. ☎ **246/432-0227.** Reservations not accepted or needed. Pizzas, pastas, and salads U.S.$6–$20. AE, MC, V. Sun–Thurs 10am–11pm, Fri–Sat 10am–midnight. PIZZA.

If you're staying at one of the expensive West Coast hotels and get a sudden craving for pizza, head here to this site directly across from the Sunset Crest Beach Club. The place is new but simple. There's an unbelievable U.S.$37 pizza: the "ridiculous pie," with everything on it. Many pies aren't your typical cheese and tomato concoctions, but come with smoked mozzarella, prosciutto, smoked fish, and sun-dried tomatoes.

SPEIGHTSTOWN

Mango's by the Sea. 2 West End, Queen St. ☎ **246/422-0704.** Reservations recommended. Main courses U.S.$12.50–$32.50. MC, V. Sun–Fri 6–9:30pm. INTERNATIONAL.

Speightstown was never noted for its dining choices until the opening of this restaurant and bar overlooking the water. Run by a couple from Montréal, Gail and Pierre Spenard, Mango's offers entertainment on some nights and features daily specials. It's best known for its seafood, and the owners buy the catch of the day directly from the fisher's boats. The food is exceedingly good, and the seasonings don't overpower the flavor of the main ingredient, as they do at many Bajan restaurants. Seasonal market-fresh ingredients are used to good advantage. Grilled lobster with lime butter and white wine is also featured. If you don't want fish, opt for the 8-ounce U.S. of A. tenderloin steak cooked to perfection or the fall-off-the-bone barbecued baby back ribs. Appetizers might be anything from an intriguing green peppercorn pâté to pumpkin soup. Top off the meal with a passion-fruit cheesecake or a star-fruit torte.

BRIDGETOWN

The Waterfront Café. The Careenage, Bridgetown. ☎ **246/427-0093.** Reservations required. Main courses U.S.$12–$18. AE, DC, MC, V. Mon–Sat 10am–10pm. INTERNATIONAL.

In the turn-of-the-century warehouse originally built to store bananas and freeze fish, this cafe serves international fare with a strong emphasis on Bajan specialties. Try the fresh catch of the day prepared Créole style, pepper steak, or the fish burger made with kingfish or dolphin. For vegetarians, there's pasta primavera, vegetable soup, and usually a featured special. Some people stop by just for drinks, from beer to pastel-colored rum concoctions. Live steel-pan music is presented, with a Bajan buffet featured on Tuesday from 7 to 9pm, costing BD$35 (U.S.$17.50). If you want to see the Dixieland bands on Thursday night, make reservations about a week in advance.

SOUTH OF BRIDGETOWN

Brown Sugar. Aquatic Gap, St. Michael. ☎ **246/426-7684.** Reservations recommended. Main courses U.S.$14.50–$50; buffet lunch U.S.$17.50. AE, DC, DISC, MC, V. Sun–Fri noon–2:30pm; daily 6–9:30pm (last order). BAJAN.

Hidden behind lush foliage, Brown Sugar is an al fresco restaurant in a turn-of-the-century bungalow. The ceiling is latticed, with slow-turning fans, and there's an open veranda for dining by candlelight amid lots of hanging plants. The chefs prepare some of the tastiest Bajan specialties on the island. Among the soups, we suggest hot gun-go-pea soup (pigeon peas cooked in chicken broth and seasoned with fresh coconut milk, herbs, and a touch of white wine). Of the main dishes, Créole broiled pepper chicken is popular, or perhaps you'd like stuffed crab backs. Conch fritters and garlic pork are especially spicy options, and a selection of locally grown vegetables is also offered. For dessert, we recommend the Bajan bread pudding with rum sauce. The restaurant is known for its good-value lunches, which are served buffet style to local businesspeople.

ON THE SOUTH COAST
EXPENSIVE

Champers. Keswick Centre, Hastings, Christ Church. ☎ **246/435-6644.** Main courses U.S.$17–$32; lunch from U.S.$16. MC, V. Mon–Sat noon–3pm and 6–10pm. INTERNATIONAL.

The prices here seem high to us, but you're paying for some of the South Coast's best seafood, served at this comfortable two-story restaurant on the ocean with picture windows. You can also eat at the four tables and the bar downstairs. On Saturday there's live guitar music in the lounge. Dinner includes an excellent and well-flavored shrimp-and-mango salad or a terrine made with dolphin and salmon. You can proceed to the chicken breast served in a spinach and bleu-cheese sauce or else opt for shrimp and scallops with a shellfish coulis. The lunch sandwiches are meals unto themselves, or you can order a shrimp-and-vegetable stir-fry, perhaps ravioli with fresh mushrooms and a walnut sauce.

Josef's. St. Lawrence Gap. ☎ **246/435-6541.** Reservations recommended. Main courses U.S.$24–$35. AE, DC, MC, V. Mon–Fri noon–2:30pm; daily 6:30–10pm. CARIBBEAN/CONTINENTAL.

Set in the garden of a pink-and-white Bajan house, between the road and the sea, this is a longtime favorite. Since the menu is roughly equivalent at lunch and dinner, you'll save a bit of money by opting for a midday rather than an evening meal. Swedish specialties include meatballs in traditional gravy and Swedish-style steak. More tropical dishes include lobster, marinated breast of duck, blackened kingfish, seafood crêpes, and grilled chicken. Filet Marco Polo is made from strips of fileted beef steak floating in a pool of red-wine sauce. Although some of the Swedish fare seems heavy for the tropics, the chef can show a lighter touch. The cookery is characterized by rural good sense rather than citified refinements.

MODERATE

✪ **David's Place.** St. Lawrence Main Rd., Worthing, Christ Church. ☎ **246/435-9755.** Reservations recommended. Main courses U.S.$12–$40. AE, DISC, MC, V. Tues–Sun 6–10pm. BARBADIAN.

Owner-operators David and Darla Trotman promise that in their restaurant you'll sample "Barbadian dining at its best," and they deliver on that promise, and at mostly reasonable prices, too, with most of their selections priced at around U.S.$20. David's is south of Bridgetown between Rockley Beach and Worthing, in an old-fashioned seaside house on St. Lawrence Bay. The tables are positioned so that diners get a view of the Caribbean. Everybody's favorite, pumpkin or cucumber soup, might get you going, or you can select the more prosaic fish cakes or even pickled chicken wings. If you're afraid to venture to Baxter's Road at night, you can order Baxter's road chicken here. It's seasoned the Bajan way (that is, marinated in lime, salt, and herbs, then deep-fried). Pepperpot is a hot-and-spicy dish with beef, salt pork, chicken, and lamb. Fish steak, the best item to order, might be dolphin, kingfish, barracuda, shark, or red snapper. It's served in a white-wine sauce or deep-fried the Bajan way. Desserts are equally good: Here, at last, is a restaurant that offers that old drugstore favorite of the 1940s and 1950s, a banana split; or you might opt instead for the coconut cream pie or the carrot cake in rum sauce.

Luigi's Restaurant. Dover Woods, St. Lawrence Gap, Christ Church. ☎ **246/428-9218.** Reservations recommended. Main courses U.S.$11.50–$24.50. MC, V. Daily 6–10:30pm (last order). ITALIAN.

Since 1963, this open-air Italian trattoria has operated in a green-and-white building built as a private house. The feeling is contemporary, airy, and comfortable. Pizzas are offered as appetizers, along with more classic choices such as half a dozen escargots or a Caesar salad (when available). Half orders of many pastas are also available as starters. The baked pastas, such as a creamy lasagna, are delectable, and you can also order the fresh fish or veal special of the day, among other dishes. For dessert, try the zabaglione and one of the wide selections of coffee, ranging from Italian to Russian or Turkish.

Pisces. St. Lawrence Gap, Christ Church. ☎ **246/435-6564.** Reservations recommended. Main courses U.S.$14–$38. AE, DC, MC, V. Daily 6–9:30pm (last order). From Bridgetown, take Hwy. 7 south for about 4 miles; then turn right at the sign toward St. Lawrence Gap. BAJAN.

New restaurants come and go on Barbados, but this old favorite still hangs in. Pisces offers al fresco dining at water's edge. A beautiful restaurant with a tropical decor, it primarily serves a Caribbean seafood menu. You might begin with one of the soups, perhaps split pea or pumpkin. Other savory appetizers include flying fish Florentine and octopus salad. Seafood lovers enjoy the Pisces platter, consisting of charcoal-broiled dolphin, fried flying fish, broiled kingfish, and butter-fried prawns. You might also be drawn to seasonal Caribbean fish, which can be broiled, blackened, or panfried before it's served with lime-herb butter. Another seasonal delight is snapper Caribe, which is stuffed with shrimp, tomato, and herbs, then baked and served with a white-wine sauce. A limited but good selection of poultry and meat is offered, including roast pork Barbados with a traditional Bajan stuffing.

Sand Dollar. In Bagshot House Hotel, St. Lawrence Coast Rd., Christ Church. ☎ **246/ 435-6956.** Reservations recommended. Lunch main courses U.S.$10–$20; dinner main courses U.S.$15–$32. AE, DC, MC, V. Daily 7am–10pm. INTERNATIONAL.

Housed in a pink-walled hotel and opening onto a masonry terrace that extends almost to the edge of the water, it's less formal than it was in years past, with a modern outlook stemming from a complete renovation in 1996. Menu items include a well-seasoned pepper steak, Mount Gayribs, brochettes of jerk shrimp, chicken with a honey-rum sauce, and different versions of steak and lobster. Lunches feature a roster of sandwiches and salads that aren't available at dinner.

A wide array of salads is also featured. No one will object if you wear shorts, but bathing suits aren't allowed.

Witch Doctor. St. Lawrence Gap, Christ Church. ☎ **246/435-6581.** Reservations recommended. Main courses U.S.$12–$30. MC, V. Daily 6:15–10pm. BAJAN/AFRICAN.

The Witch Doctor hides behind a screen of thick foliage in the heart of the southern coast. The decor, in honor of its name, features African and island wood carvings of witch doctors. The place offers a fascinating cuisine with some unusual concoctions that are tasty and well prepared, a big change from a lot of the bland hotel fare. For an appetizer, try the split-pea-and-pumpkin soup, or maybe the cold, lime-soused ceviche. Chef's specialties include various flambé dishes such as steak, shrimp Créole, fried flying fish, and chicken piri-piri (inspired by Mozambique). At a sidewalk bar, you can order from the restaurant's appetizer menu and also request vegetable lasagna, small pizzas, and shrimp.

INEXPENSIVE

Barbecue Barn. Rockley, Christ Church. ☎ **246/435-6602.** Reservations not accepted. Main courses BD$20–$26 (U.S.$10–$13). MC, V. Daily 11am–11pm. BAJAN.

This basic restaurant serves simple fare often to families staying in South Coast hotels. There's a fully stocked self-service salad bar. Try the zesty barbecued chicken as a main course or in a sandwich. The menu also includes roast chicken, burgers, steak, and fried chicken nuggets. Most main courses are served with your choice of potato or spiced rice and garlic bread. A small selection of wines complements your meal.

Bombas. Paynes Bay, St. James. ☎ **246/432-0569.** Main courses U.S.$10–$16.50; lunch from U.S.$8. MC, V. Daily 10am–11pm. INTERNATIONAL.

Simple and unpretentious though it is, this place is worth a detour. Right on the water at Paynes Bay, it's so inviting that you may adopt it as your local hangout. The avocados on Barbados are said to be "ethereal," and you can find out why here, along with sampling an array of other Bajan specialties and vegetarian dishes. The drinks here are made with fresh juices and not overly loaded with buckets of sugar. The owners Gaye and Wayne, a Scottish/Bajan couple, are hospitable hosts, chalking up their latest offerings on a blackboard menu. You can visit just for a snack, perhaps enjoying roti or seasoned flying fish. Their main dishes are certainly worth trying, including the catch of the day, which can be blackened in the Cajun style or deer-fried in crispy batter and chips in the English style. They also make a wicked Bomba curry, or, for a taste of the Highlands of Scotland, will serve you sautéed chicken breast on a bed of saffron rice with a Drambuie-cream sauce.

Café Sol. St. Lawrence Gap, Christ Church. ☎ **246/435-9531.** Main courses U.S.$11–$17. AE, MC, V. Daily 6pm–midnight. TEX-MEX.

Even though this cafe has a gringo section of the menu, designed for diehard meat-and-potatoes Yankees, most savvy foodies come to this St. Lawrence Gap eatery for some of the best Tex-Mex food on the island. Burritos and tacos don't get much bigger than the ones served here. If you're looking for flavorful and zesty meals, and at a good price with oversize portions and enthusiastic service, eat here. Feast on the tostados, fajitas, nachos, and all the good-tasting beef, shrimp, and chicken dishes, each served with rice and beans or fries. As for the non-Mexican burgers, barbecued chicken, hot dogs, and steaks, you can fare better elsewhere. This is a small, comfortable place with an outside bar and patio and a medley of recorded Italian and Mexican music to entertain you.

Rôti Hut. Worthing, Christ Church. ☎ **246/435-7362.** Snacks and plates U.S.$2–$4.60; picnic box U.S.$5. No credit cards. Mon–Thurs 11am–10pm, Fri–Sat 11am–11pm. ROTIS.

The island's best rotis are served here at this little Worthing hut, an off-white concrete structure with an enclosed patio for dining. Count on these zesty pastries to be filled with good-tasting and spicy meats, or whatever. The crowd pleaser is the mammoth chicken or beef potato roti. The locals like their rotis with bone, but you can order yours without if you wish. You can also order other food items, including beef burgers, fried chicken, and beef or chicken curry with rice. This is also a good place to pick up a picnic box.

The Ship Inn. St. Lawrence Gap, Christ Church. ☎ **246/435-6961.** Reservations recommended for the Captain's Carvery only. Main courses U.S.$8–$14; all-you-can-eat carvery meal U.S.$12 at lunch, U.S.$21 at dinner, plus U.S.$9 for appetizer and dessert. AE, DC, MC, V. Sun–Fri noon–3pm and 6–10:30pm. ENGLISH PUB/BAJAN.

Come here for drinks and for big, filling portions of hearty food. South of Bridgetown between Rockley Beach and Worthing, the Ship Inn is a traditional English-style pub with an attractive, rustic decor of nautical memorabilia. (As an alternative, you can sip a rum drink and enjoy a tropical atmosphere in a garden bar.) Many guests come for darts and to meet friends, and certainly to listen to the live music presented nightly by some of the island's top bands (see "Barbados After Dark," in chapter 11). The Ship Inn serves substantial bar food, such as homemade steak-and-kidney pie, shepherd's pie, and chicken, shrimp, and fish dishes. For more formal dining, visit the Captain's Carvery, where you can have your fill of succulent cuts of prime roasts on a nighttime buffet table and an array of traditional Bajan food (fillets of flying fish, for example). After dinner, guests can listen to top local bands performing in the pub at no extra charge.

Taps on the Bay Tavern & Grill. St. Lawrence Gap, Christ Church. ☎ **246/435-6549.** Main courses U.S.$6–$20. AE, MC, V. Daily 6–10:30pm. Bar, daily 5pm–2am. CARIBBEAN/ INTERNATIONAL.

This sea-view spot is a hot dining choice in St. Lawrence. It's known for its campy decor, such as a "shooter" chair (actually, an old dentist's chair). The victim sits in this chair and gets spun around after heavy drinking. The walls are covered with items sent back by tourists, including their photos, beer ads, currency, whatever. Visitors from almost anywhere can be seen at the canopied bar. But surprisingly for a place with all these rowdy gimmicks, the food's actually pretty good, with selections such as grilled flying fish, a traditional Indian curry, crab Alfredo, and local fish prepared many ways. An extensive dessert menu features homemade pies and cakes, and you can finish off with a cappuccino or espresso. Bar snacks are also available, including steak on a bun or a cheese-cutter sandwich (cheese, lettuce, tomato, and cucumber on a bun). Thursday is karaoke night from 9pm "until," and on Friday there's a country-western band. Saturday is more Bajan authentic, as a steel band comes in to entertain.

T.G.I. Boomers. St. Lawrence Gap, Christ Church. ☎ **246/428-8439.** Reservations not required. Main courses U.S.$11–$23; lunch specials U.S.$4–$11.50. Breakfast U.S.$5.50–$7.50, Sun buffet U.S.$12.50. AE, MC, V. Daily 8am–10pm. AMERICAN/BAJAN.

Four miles south of Bridgetown near Rockley Beach along Highway 7, T.G.I. Boomers offers some of the best bargain meals on the island. Most folks come here for a belt-busting good time with tried-and-true dishes that never go out of favor. There's a hopping bar scene, where you can get a frothy pastel-colored 16-ounce daiquiri. The cook prepares a special catch of the day, and the fish is served with soup or salad, rice or baked potato, and a vegetable. You can always count on seafood, steaks, and hamburgers. For lunch, try a daily Bajan special or a jumbo sandwich.

39 Steps. Chattel Plaza, Hastings, Christ Church. ☎ **246/427-0715.** Main courses U.S.$12.50–$16. MC, V. Mon–Fri noon–3pm and 6:30–9:30pm, Sat 6:30–10:30pm. Closed Sept. INTERNATIONAL.

One of the area's most popular choices is also the best wine bar in Hastings. Diners walk the 39 steps (or whatever) to reach this convivial place where performers sometimes entertain on the sax and guitar. It's laid-back and casual, and the food and wine are not only good but affordable. Look to the chalkboard for the tasty favorites of the day. Whenever possible, the cooks use fresh, local produce. They concoct dishes that appeal to a wide cross-section, including English pub grub–style pies such as steak and kidney or chicken and mushroom. They also turn out lasagna and other pastas, along with seafood crêpes, shrimp and chicken cury, and blackened fish. The most famous dish of Barbados, flying fish, appears only on the lunch menu. They're not big on vegetables, however, serving only a mixed green salad. This pleasant restaurant and bar has lots of windows and a balcony for outdoor dining.

ON THE EAST COAST

✪ **Atlantis Hotel.** Bathsheba, St. Joseph. ☎ **246/433-9445.** Reservations required for the Sun buffet and the 7pm dinner, recommended at all other times. 2-course fixed-price lunch U.S.$12.50; set dinner U.S.$15.75; Sun buffet U.S.$18.75. AE. Daily 11:30am–3pm and at 7pm (and don't be late). BAJAN.

Here's a glimpse of old Barbados, as life used to be before all the development. The run-down Atlantis Hotel is often filled with both Bajans and visitors. It's located between Cattlewash-on-Sea and Tent Bay on the East (Atlantic) Coast. In the sunny, breeze-filled interior, with a sweeping view of the turbulent ocean, Enid I. Maxwell has been welcoming visitors from all over the world ever since she opened the place in 1945. Her copious buffets are one of the best deals on the island. From loaded tables, you can sample such Bajan foods as pumpkin fritters, peas and rice, macaroni and cheese, chow mein, souse, and/or a Bajan pepperpot. No one ever leaves here hungry, and no one has thought of adding anything new to the repertoire since World War II ended.

Café Calabash. St. Nicholas Abbey, on the St. Peter/St. Lucy border. ☎ **246/422-8725.** Creole lunch, snacks, traditional English teas U.S.$5–$20. No credit cards. Mon–Fri 10am–3:30pm. BAJAN/AFTERNOON TEA.

On the site of a Jacobean plantation Great House, this is the most romantic place on Barbados to have afternoon tea or to stop in for a Bajan lunch of Creole fare. You can eat or drink at one of the premier tourist attractions of Barbados. The cafe looks out onto one of the few remaining virgin rain forests in the Caribbean. A typical menu might include Bajan fish cakes, pepperpot stew, jerked pork chops, pickled breadfruit, and vegetarian samosas, followed by delectable desserts such as Key lime or coconut meringue pie.

Crane Beach Hotel. Crane Bay, St. Philip. ☎ **246/423-6220.** Reservations required. Lunch BD$24–$50 (U.S.$12–$25); Sun brunch BD$40.25 (U.S.$20.10). AE, DC, MC, V. Daily 7:30am–9:30pm (Sun brunch noon–3pm). BAJAN.

On a remote hilltop opening onto the Atlantic Coast, this scenic restaurant serves traditional Bajan specialties as well as a few international dishes. The dinner, costing BD$44 to BD$60 (U.S.$22 to U.S.$30), is a little too pricey to be called a real bargain, but lunches include burgers, sandwiches, and lighter fare kinder to your wallet. Sunday brunch is a good deal, too. Served buffet-style, the brunch—"a good tuck-in"—includes soup of the day (hot or cold); Bajan and international dishes, including flying fish and a baked pie made of macaroni, cream, onions, and sweet peppers; a number of side items (rice and peas, candied sweet potatoes, and plantains); an assortment of desserts, including fresh fruit; and a beverage. Either before or after brunch, guests walk down the coral-hewn stairway from the hotel's cantilevered terrace to the pink, sandy beach. The restaurant features live entertainment Tuesday and Friday until 10:30pm.

Kingsley Club. Cattlewash-on-Sea, St. Joseph (¼ mile northeast of Bathsheba, about 15 miles from Bridgetown). ☎ **246/433-9422.** Reservations required for dinner, recommended for lunch. Main courses U.S.$8–$19; fixed-price 4-course meal U.S.$25–$35. AE, DISC, MC, V. Daily 11am–3pm and 6–7:30pm (last order). BAJAN.

An historic inn amid the rolling hills of the northeastern coast of Barbados in an area called the Scotland district, the Kingsley Club also serves some of the best Bajan food on the island in a turn-of-the-century house cooled by Atlantic breezes. You're invited to enjoy your fill of split-pea-and-pumpkin soup, dolphin meunière, or planters fried chicken, followed by one of their homemade desserts, perhaps coconut meringue pie. The cuisine always struck us as what a Bajan might prepare for dinner.

Exploring Barbados

In addition to a host of water sports and other outdoor activities to keep you busy on the beach, Barbados is one of the more interesting islands in the West Indies to explore, either in your own rented car or with a taxi driver as a guide. There are formal gardens, stately Great Houses, white sandy beaches, noted museums, excellent shopping, and much more.

The principal activities on Barbados are swimming, sunning, windsurfing, and boating—all the elements of a tropical beach vacation. All these are best on the western coast in the clear, buoyant waters. You may also want to visit the surf-pounded Atlantic coast in the east, which is better for dramatic scenery than for swimming.

With visibility in excess of 100 feet most of the year, and with more than 50 varieties of fish swimming above and around its coral reefs, Barbados beckons scuba divers and snorkelers. The sea also teems with dolphin, marlin, wahoo, barracuda, and sailfish, to name only the most popular catches, making for first-rate deep-sea fishing.

1 Beaches

Barbadians say they have a beach for every day of the year. If you're only visiting for a short time, you'll probably be happy with the ones that are easy to find. They're all open to the public, even those in front of the big resort hotels and private homes. The government requires public access to all beaches, via roads along the property line or through the hotel entrance.

THE WEST COAST

Waters are calmest on the western shore, which faces the Caribbean Sea. The beaches are great here—all those lavish resorts chose this side of the island for a reason!

The major beaches border **Paynes Bay,** with access across from the Coach House or the Bamboo Beach Bar. This is a good beach for water sports, especially snorkeling. There is also a parking area. The sands can get rather crowded, but the beautiful bay somehow makes it seem worth the effort to get there. Three of the best beaches here include **Paradise Beach, Brighton Beach,** and **Brandon's Beach.**

Church Point lies north of St. James Church, opening onto Heron Bay, site of the Colony Club Hotel. This is one of the most scenic bays in Barbados, and the swimming is ideal, although the beach can get overcrowded. There are some shade trees when you've had enough sun. You can also order drinks at the beach terrace operated by the Colony Club.

Mullins Beach, a final West Coast selection, is the third most recommendable beach. Its blue waters are glassy, and snorkelers in particular seek it out. There's parking on the main road. Again, the beach has some shady areas. At the Mullins Beach Bar, you can order food and drink.

THE SOUTH COAST

Good spots here include **Casuarina Beach,** with access from Maxwell Coast Road, going across the property of Casuarina Beach Hotel. This is one of the wider beaches of Barbados, and we've noticed that it's swept by trade winds even on the hottest days of August. Windsurfers are especially fond of this one. Food and drink can be ordered at the hotel.

Silver Sands Beach, to the east of Oistins, is near the very south point of Barbados, directly east of South Point Lighthouse and near the Silver Rock Hotel. This white sandy beach is a favorite with many Bajans, who want to keep it a secret from as many tourists as possible. Windsurfing is excellent here if you're advanced. Drinks are sold at Silver Rock Bar.

Sandy Beach, reached from the car park on the Worthing main road, has tranquil waters opening onto a lagoon, a cliché of Caribbean charm. This is a family favorite, with lots of boisterous kids romping on the weekends especially. Food and drink are sold here.

THE SOUTHEAST COAST

The Southeast Coast is the site of the big waves, especially at **Crane Beach,** the white sandy beach set against a backdrop of palms that usually appears in Sunday travel magazines. The beach is spectacular, as Prince Andrew, who has a house overlooking it, might agree. It offers excellent body surfing, but at times the waters can be too rough for all but the strongest swimmers. The beach is set against cliffs, and the Crane Beach Hotel towers above it. This is ocean swimming, not the calm Caribbean, so take precautions.

Bottom Bay is one of our all-time Bajan favorites. It is north of Sam Lord's Castle. You park on the top of a cliff, then walk down steps to this much-photographed tropical beach, with its grove of coconut palms. There's even a cave. The sand is brilliantly white, a picture-postcard version of a beach with an aquamarine sea.

THE EAST COAST

There are miles and miles of uncrowded beaches along the East Coast, but this is the Atlantic side, and swimming here is potentially dangerous. Many visitors like to walk along the sands here, especially those in the Bathsheba/Cattlewash areas, enjoying the splendid rugged scenery. Waves are extremely high on these beaches, and the bottom tends to be rocky. Currents are also unpredictable. The beaches are great if you don't go into the water.

2 Outdoor Pursuits

DEEP-SEA FISHING

The fishing is first-rate in the waters off Barbados, where fishers pursue dolphin, marlin, wahoo, barracuda, and sailfish, to name only the most popular catches.

There's also an occasional cobia. **The Dive Shop,** Pebbles Beach, Aquatic Gap, St. Michael (☎ **246/426-9947**), can arrange half-day charters for one to six people (all equipment and drinks included), costing U.S.$350 per boat. Under the same arrangement, the whole-day jaunt goes for U.S.$700 (in other words, no discount).

GOLF

The Royal Westmoreland Golf & Country Club, Westmoreland, St. James (☎ **246/422-4653**), is the island's premier golf course, usurping a position formerly held by Sandy Lane. Designed by Robert Trent Jones, Jr., this $30 million, 27-hole course is spread across 500 acres overlooking the Gold Coast. It is part of a private residential community and can be played only by guests of the Royal Pavilion, Glitter Bay, Colony Club, Tamarind Cove, Coral Reef, Crystal Cove, Cobblers Cove, Sandpiper Inn, and Sandy Lane. It costs U.S.$90 for nine holes, or U.S.$176 for 18 holes, including a cart.

After the multi-million-dollar renovation that was underway in 1998 is completed at the **Sandy Lane Hotel,** St. James (☎ **246/432-1311**), on the West Coast, the resort will feature a brand-new 45-hole championship course. Call to inquire about greens fees.

A final course, **Rockley Golf Club,** Golf Club Road, Hastings (☎ **246/435-7873**), is set amid the South Coast's all-inclusive Club Rockley Resort. This course features a simple 9-hole, 18-tee layout, with a second 9 holes playable from varying tee positions. Trolleys and clubs can be rented. The charge is U.S.$34.50 for 9 holes or U.S.$46 for 18 holes.

HIKING

Most visitors spend all their time on the island's densely populated coastal plain. But much of the true beauty of Barbados can only be appreciated by hiking through the island's lush interior through such rarely visited parishes as St. Thomas and St. George (both of which are landlocked) and the Atlantic-coast parishes of St. Andrews and St. John (where the rough surf of the Atlantic usually discourages sailing and swimming).

Until recently, most visitors were asked to restrict their sightseeing in these relatively undeveloped parishes to the sides of the highways and roads. But a locally owned tour operator, **Highland Outdoor Tours,** conducts a series of tours across privately owned land. With its verdant, rolling hills and many dramatic rock outcroppings, much of the terrain might remind you of a windswept but balmy version of Scotland.

You'll have the option of conducting your tour on horseback, on foot, or as a passenger in a tractor-drawn jitney. Horseback rides and walking tours last anywhere from 2 to 5 hours. As you traverse what used to be some of the most productive sugar plantations in the British Empire, your guide will describe the geology, architecture, and historical references you'll see en route. A wide range of add-ons can be arranged as part of your experience, including barbecued dinners or picnic lunches prepared over the open hearth of an historic Bajan home.

All tours depart from the Highland Outdoor Tour Center in the parish of St. Thomas (in north-central Barbados). Transportation to and from your hotel is included in the price of horseback tours (from U.S.$60), hiking tours (from U.S.$30), and tractor-drawn jitney tours (from U.S.$30 to U.S.$60). For more information, contact Highland Outdoor Tours, Canefield, St. Thomas Parish, Barbados, W.I. (☎ **246/438-8069**).

The **Barbados National Trust** offers Sunday-morning hikes throughout the year. The program, which gives participants an opportunity to learn about the natural beauty of Barbados, are cosponsored by the Duke of Edinburgh's Award Scheme and the Barbados Heart Foundation, and attracts more than 300 participants weekly.

Led by young Barbadians and members of the National Trust, the hikes cover a different area of the island each week. Tour escorts also give brief educational talks on various aspects of the hikes such as geography, history, geology, and agriculture.

The hikes are free and open to participants of all ages. They are divided into three categories: fast, for those who wish to hike for the exercise; medium, for those wishing exercise but at a slower pace than the fast walk; and slow, fondly known as "stop and stare," for those wishing to walk at a leisurely pace.

All the hikes start promptly at either 6:30am or 3:30pm and begin and end in the same place, where parking is available. Each hike is about 5 miles long and takes about 3 hours. Visitors needing transportation should contact the Barbados National Trust at ☎ **246/426-2421.** The staff here will tell you where to meet for the hike.

HORSEBACK RIDING

A different view of Barbados is offered by the **Caribbean International Riding Centre,** ℅ the Roachford family, Auburn, St. Joseph (☎ **246/422-7433**). Maintained by Swedish-born Elizabeth Roachford and her daughters, it boards nearly 40 horses, more than most other riding stables on the island. Mrs. Roachford or one of her daughters (each trained according to the Swedish equestrian traditions) offer a variety of trail rides for equestrians of any level of experience. Their shortest ride provides a 75-minute escorted trek through tropical forests, followed by relaxation over a cool drink in the clubroom. The various rides range from the 1-hour trek for U.S.$40 to a 2½-hour jaunt for U.S.$82.50. You ride through some of the most panoramic parts of Barbados, especially the hilly terrain of the Scotland district. Wild ducks and water lilies, with the rhythm of the Atlantic as background music, are some of nature's sights viewed along the way.

SCUBA DIVING & SNORKELING

The clear waters off Barbados have visibility of more than 100 feet most of the year, and more than 50 varieties of fish are found on the shallow inside reefs. On night dives, sleeping fish, night anemones, lobsters, moray eels, and octopuses can be seen.

On a mile-long coral reef 2 minutes by boat from **Sandy Beach,** sea fans, corals, gorgonians, and reef fish are plentiful. *J.R.,* a dredge barge sunk as an artificial reef in 1983, is popular with beginners for its coral, fish life, and 20-foot depth. The *Berwyn,* a coral-encrusted tugboat that sank in Carlisle Bay in 1916, attracts photographers because of its variety of reef fish, shallow depth, good light, and visibility.

Asta Reef, with a drop of 80 feet, has coral, sea fans, and reef fish in abundance. It's the site of a Barbados wreck sunk in 1986 as an artificial reef. Dottins, the most beautiful reef on the West Coast, stretches 5 miles from Holetown to Bridgetown and has numerous dive sites at an average depth of 40 feet and dropoffs of 100 feet. The SS *Stavronika,* a Greek freighter, is a popular dive site for advanced divers. Crippled by fire in 1976, the 360-foot freighter was sunk a quarter mile off the West Coast to become an artificial reef in **Folkstone Underwater Park.** The mast is at 40 feet, the deck at 80 feet, and the keel at 140 feet. It's encrusted with coral.

The Dive Shop, Pebbles Beach, Aquatic Gap, St. Michael (☎ **246/426-9947**), offers some of the best scuba diving in Barbados (costing about U.S.$55 per

⊙ Frommer's Favorite Barbados Experiences

A Tour of the Great Houses. From mid-January through the first week of April, you can tour a different Great House every Wednesday afternoon. You can get a feel for the elegant colonial lifestyle and see plantation antiques. Watch for announcements in the local papers or call the National Trust at ☎ 246/426-2421.

An Evening at 1627 and All That. See "Barbados After Dark," later in this chapter. While dining on Bajan specialties, you can enjoy a musical celebration of the island experience.

A Nighttime Stroll Along Baxters Road. Nothing is more authentically Bajan than a promenade along this famous Bridgetown road, sampling the specialties of its food stalls (the fried chicken's terrific) and washing everything down with Banks beer. Things don't really heat up before 10pm.

Sunday Lunch with Enid Maxwell. Since 1945, Enid's Atlantis Hotel on the East Coast has set the best Sunday noonday spread on the island. Try the Bajan delicacies—pumpkin fritters, flying fish, dolphin, spinach cakes, and pickled breadfruit. Everything is homemade.

one-tank dive). Every day, two dive trips go out to the nearby reefs and wrecks. In addition, snorkeling trips and equipment rentals are possible. Visitors with reasonable swimming skills who have never dived before can sign up for a resort course. Priced at U.S.$70, it includes pool training, safety instructions, and a one-tank open-water dive. The operation is NAUI- and PADI-certified. It is open daily from 9am to 5pm. Other snorkeling and scuba diving equipment rental shops are **Carib Ocean Divers** (☎ 246/422-4414), in St. James; **Hazel's Water World** (☎ 246/426-4043), in Bridgetown, St. Michael; and **Underwater Barbados** (☎ 246/435-6542), in Christ Church (close to Bridgetown).

Good **snorkeling spots** on the West Coast include the beaches along Paynes Bay and Mullins Beach. See also the cruises and boat trips listed below; some of them include stops for snorkeling.

TENNIS

Sandy Lane, St. James (☎ 246/432-1311), has always placed more emphasis on tennis than any other resort in Barbados. When the resort opens again, as it's scheduled to in late 1998 after a major renovation, it will boast at least seven new state-of-the-art courts. Call ahead and ask about the new facilities (and fees, if you're not a guest but want to stop in and play).

The **Barbados Hilton,** Needham's Point (☎ 246/426-0200), maintains four hard-surface courts, each of which is lit for night play. Hilton's courts are not nearly as clubby or gracious as those of Sandy Lane, but they're closer to Bridgetown, and more convenient for many visitors. Guests play for free, whereas nonresidents pay U.S.$7.50 to U.S.$10 per half hour. At night, all players are charged U.S.$10 per half hour for illumination of the courts.

WINDSURFING

Experts say that the windsurfing off Barbados is as good as any this side of Hawaii, and it certainly turns into a very big business between November and April.

Thousands of windsurfers from all over the world now come here from as far as Finland, Argentina, and Japan. The shifting of the trade winds between November and May and the shallow offshore reef off **Silver Sands** create unique conditions of wind and wave swells. This allows windsurfers to reach speeds of up to 50 knots and do complete loops off the waves. Silver Sands is rated the best spot in the Caribbean for advanced windsurfing (skill rating 5–6). In other words, one needs skills similar to a professional downhill skier's to master these conditions. Nearby **Casuarina Beach** is another excellent choice.

An outfit set up to handle the demand from the hordes of international windsurfers is **Barbados Windsurfing Club,** which maintains two branches on the island. Beginners and intermediates usually opt for the branch in Oistins (☎ **246/428-7277**), where winds are constant but where the sea is generally flat and calm. Advanced intermediates and expert windsurfers usually select the branch adjacent to the Silver Sands Hotel, in Christ Church (☎ **246/428-6001**), where stronger winds and higher waves allow surfers to combine aspects of windsurfing with the conventional surfing known in Hawaii. The boards and equipment used by both branches of this outfit are provided by the Germany-based Club Mistral. Lessons at either branch cost between U.S.$40 and U.S.$65 per hour, depending on how many people are in your class. Equipment rents for between U.S.$25 and U.S.$35 per hour or U.S.$55 to U.S.$65 per half-day, depending on where and what you rent. Prices are lower at the Oistins branch than at the Silver Sands branch.

3 Seeing the Sights in Bridgetown

Often hot and clogged with traffic, Bridgetown, the capital, is an architectural hodgepodge that merits little more than a morning's shopping jaunt (see section 7 of this chapter for our specific recommendations).

Since some half a million visitors arrive on Barbados by cruise ship each year, the government has opened a $6 million **cruise-ship terminal** for them. It offers a variety of shopping options, including an array of duty-free shops, 13 local retail stores, and scads of vendors. Many of the stores stock the arts and crafts of Barbados, and cruise passengers can choose among a range of other products, including jewelry, liquor, china, crystal, electronics, perfume, and leather goods. Some shops sell Barbadian wood carvings and art, as well as locally made fashions. The interior was designed to re-create an island street scene, with some storefronts appearing as traditional chattel houses in brilliant island colors with street lights, tropical landscaping, benches, and pushcarts.

Begin your Bridgetown tour at **The Careenage,** the waterfront area whose name derives from "careening" vessels over on their sides in order to clean their bottoms. The harbor was a haven for the clipper ship, and even though today it doesn't have its former color, it's still worth exploring.

The long period of British colonization is evident at **Trafalgar Square.** The monument honoring Lord Nelson was executed by Sir Richard Westmacott and erected in 1813. The **Public Buildings** on the square are of the great, gray Victorian-Gothic variety that you might expect to find in South Kensington, London. The east wing contains the meeting halls of the Senate and the House of Assembly, with stained-glass windows depicting sovereigns of England from James I to Queen Victoria. Look for the Great Protector himself, Oliver Cromwell.

Bridgetown

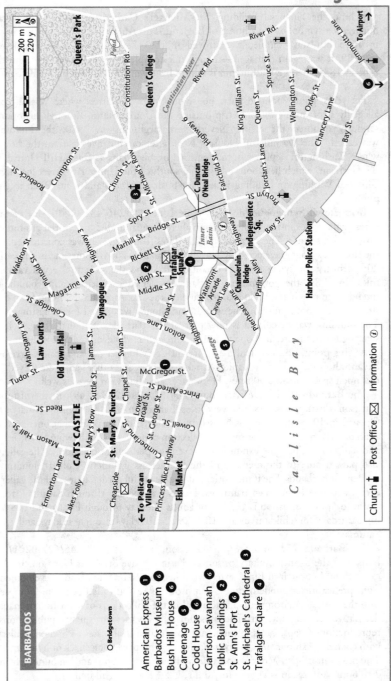

BARBADOS

○ Bridgetown

American Express	❶	
Barbados Museum	❻	
Bush Hill House	❻	
Careenage	❺	
Codd House	❻	
Garrison Savannah	❻	
Public Buildings	❷	
St. Ann's Fort	❻	
St. Michael's Cathedral	❸	
Trafalgar Square	❹	

Church ✝ Post Office ⊠ Information ⓘ

Behind the Financial Building, **St. Michael's Cathedral,** south of Trafalgar Square, is a symbol of the Church of England. This Anglican church was first built in 1655 but was completely destroyed in the 1780 hurricane. Reconstructed in 1789, it was again damaged—though not completely demolished—by a hurricane in 1831. George Washington is said to have worshipped here on his Barbados visit.

For years, guides pointed out a house on Upper Bay Street where Washington allegedly slept during his only trip outside the United States, although historians seriously doubted the claim. Nevertheless, beginning in 1910, the building was called "The Washington House." Now, after careful investigation, the house where Washington slept has been identified by historians as **Bush Hill House** in the Garrison, which lies about a half mile south of the Upper Bay Street location. This real Washington building is used for business offices and is not open to the public.

Bridgetown Synagogue, on Synagogue Lane (☎ 246/432-0840), one of the oldest synagogues in the Western Hemisphere, is surrounded by a burial ground of early Jewish settlers. The present building dates from 1833. It was constructed on the site of a synagogue erected by Jews from Brazil in 1654. Sometime in the early 20th century the synagogue was deconsecrated, and the structure served various roles. In 1983, the government of Barbados seized the deteriorating building, intending to raze it and build a courthouse on the site. An outcry went up from the small Jewish community on the island, and money was raised for its restoration. The building was saved and is now part of the Barbados National Trust; it is a synagogue once more. It is open Monday through Friday from 8am to 4:30pm.

At this point, you can hail a taxi if you don't have a car and visit **Garrison Savannah,** just south of the capital. Cricket matches and other games are played in this open space of some 50 acres. Horse races are often held here, as well.

The **Barbados Gallery of Art,** Bush Hill (☎ 246/228-0149), in the historic Garrison district, displays the very best Barbadian and Caribbean visual art. Opened in 1996, the gallery is housed in a restored old building that once served as an officers' quarters. Its permanent collection consists of 160 drawings, paintings, and sculptures. Changing exhibitions enliven the permanent collection. The gallery also pays tribute to the memory of the late actress Claudette Colbert, longtime resident of Barbados. She is memorialized in a beautiful garden here, and the gallery even owns one of her own paintings. Hours are Tuesday through Saturday from 10am to 5pm. Admission is U.S.$5 for adults Tuesday through Friday and U.S.$2 on Saturday; for children under 18, U.S.$2 Tuesday through Friday, and free Saturday.

The **Barbados Museum,** St. Ann's Garrison, St. Michael (☎ 246/427-0201), is housed in the former military prison at the impressive St. Ann's Garrison. In the exhibition "In Search of Bim," extensive collections show the island's development from prehistoric to modern times. "Born of the Sea" affords fascinating glimpses into the natural environment. There are also fine collections of West Indian maps, decorative art, and fine art. The museum sells a variety of quality publications, reproductions (maps, cards, prints), and handcrafts; it also has a children's gallery with changing exhibits. Its Courtyard Café is a good place for a snack or light lunch. The museum is open Monday to Saturday from 9am to 5pm and on Sunday from 2 to 6pm. Admission is U.S.$5 for adults, U.S.$2.50 for children.

Nearby, the russet-red **St. Ann's Fort,** on the fringe of the Savannah, garrisoned British soldiers in 1694. The fort wasn't completed until 1703. The Clock House survived the hurricane of 1831.

4 A Driving Tour Around the Island

If you can afford it, the ideal way to take this tour is with a local taxi driver who will generally negotiate a fair rate, somewhere around U.S.$50.

Of course, you can tour on your own, but you'll have to rent an expensive car, and you won't know the often unmarked roads like the locals do. If you do explore on your own, you can count on getting lost, at least several times. Although Barbados contains many signposted directions, highway authorities will often leave you stranded at strategic junctions, and it's very easy to take a wrong turn if you don't know the way—even people who live on Barbados often get confused. No clear, concise map of Barbados has yet been devised. Maps only help you with general directions; when you're looking for the route to a specific destination, they can often be most unhelpful.

Having said that, know that part of the fun of exploring Barbados is the discovery of the island. So if you do get lost a few times, and miss an attraction or two, no great harm should befall you. And the local people in the countryside are generally quite friendly and helpful.

Start: Bridgetown.
Finish: Bridgetown.
Time: 6 hours, excluding stopovers.
Best Time: Any sunny day.
Worst Time: When cruise ships are in the harbor; roads and attractions will be at their most congested.

After leaving Bridgetown (see above), head south along Highway 7, passing through the resorts of Hastings, Rockley, Worthing, and St. Lawrence, all of which contain any number of inexpensive to medium-priced hotels, as opposed to the most expensive and deluxe hotels north of Bridgetown.

After passing through Worthing (and provided that you can find this badly marked road), turn right along:

1. **St. Lawrence Gap,** which is the restaurant row of Barbados, including such favorites as Witch Doctor and The Ship Inn (see "Where to Dine" in chapter 10). There are also several budget and medium-priced hotels located along this strip, which is generally lively both day and night.

   At the end of St. Lawrence Gap, resume your journey along Highway 7 by taking a right turn. You'll bypass the town of:

2. **Oistins,** a former shipping port that today is a fishing village. Here the Charter of Barbados was signed at the Mermaid in 1652, as the island surrendered to Commonwealth forces. The Mermaid Inn, incidentally, was owned by a cousin of John Turner, who built the House of the Seven Gables in Salem, Massachusetts.

   At the signpost, take a left for Providence and the Grantley Adams airport, a continuation of Highway 7. You'll pass the airport on your right. After bypassing the airport, follow the signs to Sam Lord's Castle. At the hamlet of Spencers, leave Highway 7 and turn onto Rock Hall Road, going through the villages of St. Martins and Heddings until you come to the signposted Crane Beach Hotel.

   ⊙ **TAKE A BREAK** The **Crane Beach Hotel,** Crane Bay, St. Philip (☎ **246/423-6220**). Virtually everyone touring the South Coast stops at this remote hilltop property. The view of the Atlantic and the Roman-style swimming pool charm all the visiting cruise-ship passengers; some climb down the steep steps to Crane Beach. The house on the hill overlooking the beach is owned by Britain's Prince Andrew. There are two different entrance fees, costing U.S.$2.50 or U.S.$10. The U.S.$2.50 fee lets you hang out at the bar and is applied to your bar tab. A U.S.$10 pool package gives you greater access to the hotel's facilities, and U.S.$5 of this fee is applied to your bar tab.

After leaving the hotel, follow Crane Road east. Turn right at the signpost and continue to the end of the road to:

3. **Sam Lord's Castle** (see "Where to Stay" in chapter 10). It's a hotel but it's also one of the major sightseeing attractions on Barbados. You may want to have a drink or a snack if you didn't already stop at Crane Beach Hotel. Built by slaves in 1820, and furnished in part with Regency pieces, the "castle" is like a Georgian plantation mansion. Take note of the ornate ceilings, said to be the finest example of stucco work in the Western Hemisphere. At the entrance to the hotel are shops selling handcrafts and souvenirs. If you're not a guest, you'll have to pay U.S.$5 to enter.

After leaving Sam Lord's Castle, take a right onto Long Bay Road and continue east. Go right via the village of Wellhouse and continue along the main road that skirts the coastline but does not adjoin the coast. Turn right down a narrow road to:

4. **Ragged Point Lighthouse,** on a rugged cliff on the easternmost point of Barbados. Built in 1885, the lighthouse sends its beacon as a warning to ships approaching the dangerous reef, called "The Cobblers." The view from here is panoramic.

After leaving the lighthouse, continue straight along Marley Vale Road (don't expect proper signs). At the signpost to Bayfield, go right and pass Three Houses Park. Take a right at the signpost to Bridgetown onto Thickets Road. Take a right again at the signpost to Bathsheba. When you come to another signpost, turn left toward Bathsheba and follow a sign to:

5. **Codrington College,** opened in 1745. A cabbage-palm–lined avenue leads to old coral-block buildings. Today, the college is a training school for men and women from the entire Caribbean to enter the ordained ministry of the Anglican Church. The college is under the auspices of the Dioceses of the West Indies. Entrance is U.S.$2.50.

After leaving the college, go right, then take the next left up the steep Coach Hill Road where you'll see excellent views of the East Coast and the lighthouse you just visited. At the top of the hill, continue right and follow the signposts to:

6. **St. John's Church,** perched on the edge of a cliff opening on the East Coast some 825 feet above sea level. The church dates from 1836 and in its graveyard in the rear rests Fernando Paleologus, a descendant of Emperor Constantine the Great, whose family was driven from the throne in Constantinople (Istanbul) by the Turks. The royal relative died in Barbados in 1678.

After leaving the church, go left and then take the next right onto Gall Hill Road. Stay on this road until you reach Four Roads Junction, at which point you follow the signposts for Villa Nova, following along Wakefield Road. At the signpost for Villa Nova, turn left and then take the next right into the grounds.

7. **Villa Nova** was built in 1834 as a fine sugar plantation. It is currently closed to the public. Built in 1834 as a fine sugar plantation Great House, it's surrounded by 6½ acres of landscaped gardens and trees. Its most famous association was with Sir Anthony Eden, former prime minister of Great Britain, who purchased it from the Bajan government in 1965. In 1966, the earl and countess of Avon

Airport ✈ **Beach** 🦞 **Lighthouse** 🕯

1. St. Lawrence Gap
2. Oistins
3. Sam Lord's Castle
4. Ragged Point Lighthouse
5. Codrington College
6. St. John's Church
7. Villa Nova
8. Andromeda Botanical Gardens
9. Bathsheba
10. East Coast Road
11. Morgan Lewis Sugar Windmill
12. Cherry Tree Hill
13. St. Nicholas Abbey
14. Farley Hill National Park
15. Barbados Wildlife Reserve
16. Speightstown
17. Gold Coast
18. St. James Church
19. Holetown

entertained Queen Elizabeth and Prince Philip at the Great House. It has since been sold to private owners, who are turning it into the only exclusive, intimate luxury country hotel in Barbados. Perhaps it will open during the lifetime of this edition, if all goes well, with 11 junior suites, five one-bedroom suites, and two gourmet restaurants. When completed and finally opened, this should become one of the highlights of Barbados. Check its current status during your tour of the island.

After leaving Villa Nova, turn left and pass through the hamlet of Venture. At the next intersection, continue left until you see the signpost pointing right toward Easy Hall, another East Coast hamlet. At the next signpost, pointing in the direction of Flower Forest, go left along Buckden House Road. Take the next right and head down Highway 3, a steep, curvy road toward the ocean. Turn right toward Bathsheba and follow the signs to:

8. Andromeda Botanical Gardens, on a cliff overlooking the town of Bathsheba on the rugged East Coast (☎ **246/433-9261**). Limestone boulders make for a natural 8-acre rock-garden setting, where thousands of orchids bloom in the open air every day of the year, along with hundreds of hibiscus and heliconia. Other plants are more seasonal, including the flamboyant frangipani, jade vine and bougainvillea, lipstick tree, candlestick tree, mammee apple, and many more. Many varieties of ferns, bromeliads, and other species that are houseplants in temperate climates grow here in splendid profusion. A section is a palm garden, with more than 100 species. A simple guide helps visitors to identify many of the plants. The garden was started in 1954 by the late Iris Bannochie, on land that had belonged to her family for more than 200 years. On the grounds, you'll occasionally see frogs, herons, guppies, and sometimes a mongoose or a monkey. With an admission charge of BD$12 (U.S.$6) for adults and BD$6 (U.S.$3) for children, the gardens are open daily from 9am to 5pm; children 5 and under enter free.

After leaving the gardens, turn right and follow the signs to a great place to stop for lunch:

☕ **TAKE A BREAK The Atlantis Hotel,** Bathsheba, St. Joseph (☎ **246/433-9445**), is one of the oldest hotels in Barbados, where Enid Maxwell has been serving her favorite Bajan dishes, including flying fish and pickled breadfruit, for longer than she cares to remember. Tattered but respectable, this hotel was once a villa built by a wealthy planter in 1882. It is set directly on the seacoast, just south of the "Scotland District." It offers a set menu at lunch and features a well-attended Sunday buffet, an event among the Bajans themselves. See "Where to Dine" in chapter 10 for details.

Now continue north along the coast road to the town of:

9. Bathsheba, where ocean rollers break, forming cascades of white foam. This place has been called Cornwall (England) in miniature. Today, the old fishing village is a favorite low-cost resort for Bajans, although the waters of the Atlantic Ocean are dangerous for swimmers.

The trail north from Bathsheba takes you along the:

10. East Coast Road, which runs for many miles, opening onto dramatic views of the Atlantic. Chalky Mount rises from the beach to a height of 500 feet, forming a trio of peaks, and a little to the south Barclays Park is a 15-acre natural wonder presented as a gift to the people of Barbados by the British banking family. There's a snack bar and a place to picnic here.

Farther north, in St. Andrew, just south of Cherry Tree Hill, is the:

11. **Morgan Lewis Sugar Windmill and Museum** (☎ **246/426-2421**), typical of the wind-driven mills that extracted juice from sugarcane from the 17th to the 19th centuries, helping produce sugar that made Barbados one of Britain's most valuable possessions in the Americas. (And it was from Barbados sugarcane that rum was first made.) Admission is U.S.$7.50 for adults, U.S.$3.25 for children under 14. Open Monday to Friday from 9am to 5pm.

Now climb Morgan Lewis Hill on Highway 1 to reach:

12. **Cherry Tree Hill,** offering one of the finest views in Barbados. You can look right down the eastern shore past Bathsheba to the lighthouse at Ragged Point. The crest is about 850 feet above sea level, and from its precincts you'll see out over the Scotland District. The cherry trees from which the hill got its name no longer stand here, having given way to mahogany.

On Cherry Tree Hill, signs point the way to:

13. **St. Nicholas Abbey** (☎ **246/422-8725**), a Jacobean plantation Great House and sugarcane fields that have been around since about 1650. It was never an abbey—an ambitious owner in about 1820 simply christened it as such. More than 200 acres are still cultivated each year. In the parish of St. Peter, the structure—at least the ground floor—is open to the public Monday through Friday from 10am to 3:30pm, charging an admission of U.S.$5 per person, free for children under 13. The house is believed to be one of three Jacobean houses in the Western Hemisphere, and it's characterized by curved gables. Lt. Col. Stephen Cave, the owner, is descended from the family that purchased the sugar plantation and Great House in 1810. Light refreshments are offered for sale.

After leaving the abbey, follow the road to Diamond Corner, where you go left. Take another left onto the Charles Duncan O'Neal Highway to:

14. **Farley Hill National Park,** in northern St. Peter Parish. Farley Hill House, used in the filming of the 1950s motion picture *Island in the Sun*, starring Harry Belafonte, was gutted by fire. This movie is now largely forgotten by the world, but it still brings back many memories for Barbadians familiar with it. The park, dedicated by Queen Elizabeth in 1966, is open daily from 8:30am to 6pm. You pay a vehicular entrance fee of U.S.$1.50 for cars. After disembarking in the parking area, you can walk the grounds and enjoy the tropical flowers and lush vegetation.

Across the entrance from the park lies the:

15. **Barbados Wildlife Reserve,** a project operated by the Barbados Primate Research Center in St. Peter (☎ **246/422-8826**), standing in a mahogany forest across the road from Farley Hill National Park. From 10am to 5pm daily, for an admission charge of U.S.$10 (half price for children 12 and under), you stroll through what is primarily a monkey sanctuary. Besides uncaged monkeys, you can see wild hares, deer, tortoises, otters, caimans, wallabies, and a variety of tropical birds.

From Farley Hill Park and the wildlife reserve, backtrack to the junction of highways 1 and 2. From here, head west along Highway 1, signposted to:

16. **Speightstown,** founded around 1635. For a time it was a whaling port and is now the second city of Barbados. The community contains colonial buildings constructed after the devastating hurricane of 1831. The parish church, rebuilt in a half-Grecian style after the hurricane, is one of the places of interest. Its chancel rail is of carved mahogany.

After exploring Speightstown if you have time, turn left in the direction of the:

17. **Gold Coast,** the protected western shoreline that opens onto the gentle Caribbean. Along the shoreline of the parishes of St. James and St. Peter are the island's plushest hotels (see "Where to Stay" in chapter 10).

On Highway 1, directly north of Holetown, lies:

18. **St. James Church,** St. James, an Anglican church rebuilt in 1872 on the site of the early settlers' church of 1660. On the southern porch is an old bell, bearing the inscription of "God Bless King William, 1696." Locals still recall the 1982 visit of Ronald and Nancy Reagan. Continue south on Highway 1 to:

19. **Holetown,** the main center of the West Coast; it takes its name from the town of Hole on the Thames River in England. The first English settlers landed here in the winter of 1627. An obelisk marks the spot where the *Olive Blossom* 2 years earlier had landed the first Europeans, who did not stay. For some reason, the monument gives the date erroneously as 1605.

Chances are you may be staying in a hotel north of Bridgetown. If so, you may want to end this driving tour at your hotel. If you're staying in less expensive digs south of Bridgetown, you can continue south along the coast, passing through Bridgetown until you reach your hotel.

5 Exploring Inland

HISTORIC SIGHTS IN ST. MICHAEL & ST. GEORGE PARISHES

Tyrol Cot Heritage Village. Codrington Hill, St. Michael. ☎ **246/424-2074.** Admission U.S.$5.75 adults, U.S.$2.85 children. Mon–Fri 9am–5pm.

If you arrive at the airport, you'll recognize the name of Sir Grantley Adams, the leader of the Bajan movement for independence from Britain. This was once his home, and his wife, Lady Adams, lived in the house until her death in 1990. Once viewed as a highly prized invitation, it is now open to all who pay the admission. The date of construction was sometime in the mid-1850s, and the style was Palladian, made of coral stone. The grounds of the former political leader's home have been turned into a museum of Bajan life, including small chattel houses where potters and artists work.

Francia Plantation. On ABC Hwy., St. George, Barbados. ☎ **246/429-0474.** Admission U.S.$4.50. Mon–Fri 10am–4pm. Turn east onto Hwy. 4 at the Norman Niles Roundabout (follow signs to "Gun Hill" and Hwy. X). After going ½ mile, turn left onto Hwy. X (follow signs to Gun Hill and Francia Plantation). After another mile turn right at the Mobil gas station and follow Hwy. X past St. George's Parish Church and up the hill for a mile, turning left at the sign to Francia.

A fine home, this house stands on a wooded hillside overlooking the St. George Valley, and is still owned and occupied by descendants of its original occupants. Inside, you can explore several rooms, including the dining room with family silver and an 18th-century James McCabe bracket clock. On the walls are antique maps and prints, including a map of the West Indies printed in 1522.

Gun Hill Signal Station. Hwy. 4. ☎ **246/429-1358.** Admission U.S.$4.60 adults, U.S.$2.30 children under 14. Mon–Sat 9am–5pm. Take Hwy. 3 from Bridgetown and then go inland from Hwy. 4 toward St. George Church.

One of two such stations owned and operated by the Barbados National Trust, Gun Hill Signal Station is strategically placed on the highland of St. George and commands a panoramic view from the east to the west. Built in 1818, it was the finest of a chain of signal stations and was also used as an outpost for the British army stationed there at the time.

TROPICAL GARDENS & SPECTACULAR CAVES

✪ **Harrison's Cave.** Welchman Hall, St. Thomas. ☎ **246/438-6640.** Admission U.S.$8.75 adults, U.S.$4.35 children 3–16, free 2 and under. Daily 9am–4pm. From Bridgetown, take Hwy. 2 and follow the signposted directions.

This cave is the number-one tourist attraction of Barbados, and visitors have the chance to view this beautiful, natural, underground world from aboard an electric tram and trailer. Before the tour, a video of the cave is shown in the presentation hall. During the tour, visitors see bubbling streams, tumbling cascades, and deep pools, which are subtly lighted, while all around stalactites hang overhead like icicles. Stalagmites rise from the floor. Visitors may disembark and get a closer look at this natural phenomenon at the Rotunda Room and the Cascade Pool.

Flower Forest of Barbados. Richmond Plantation, St. Joseph. ☎ **246/433-8152.** Admission U.S.$7 adults, U.S.$3.50 children 5–16. Daily 9am–5pm. Take Hwy. 2 from Bridgetown and follow it to Welchman Hall Gully, which is signposted. The Flower Forest is nearby.

At Richmond Plantation, an old sugar estate, Flower Forest of Barbados stands 850 feet above sea level near the western edge of the Scotland District, a mile from Harrison's Cave. Set in one of the most scenic parts of Barbados, it is more than just a botanical garden, for people and nature came together here to create something beautiful. After viewing the grounds, visitors can purchase handcrafts at Best of Barbados.

Welchman Hall Gully. St. Thomas. ☎ **246/438-6671.** Admission U.S.$6 adults, U.S.$3 children 6–12, free under 6. Daily 9am–5pm. Take Hwy. 2 from Bridgetown and follow the signs.

This is a lush tropical rain forest operated by the Barbados National Trust. Here are found specimens of plants growing when the English settlers landed in 1627. Many plants are labeled—clove, nutmeg, tree fern, and cacao among others—and occasionally you'll spot a wild monkey. A series of caves were here until their roofs fell in. Breadfruit trees are claimed to be descended from seedlings brought from the South Pacific by Captain William Bligh of H.M.S. *Bounty* fame.

A RUM FACTORY & A PLANTATION HOUSE

To reach either of the sights listed below, head east from Bridgetown along Route 5. Each attraction is signposted.

Heritage Park & Rum Factory. Foursquare Plantation, St. Philip. ☎ **246/423-6669.** Admission U.S.$12. Sun–Thurs 9am–5pm; Fri–Sat 9am–9pm.

After driving through cane fields, you arrive at the first rum distillery to be launched on the island since the 19th century. Inaugurated in 1996, this factory is located in a former molasses and sugar plantation dating back some 350 years. Produced on site is a white rum, ESA Field, praised by connoisseurs. Adjacent is a park where Barbadian handcrafts are displayed in the Art Foundry (see "Shopping," below). You'll also find an array of shops and carts selling local foods, handcrafts, and products.

Sunbury Plantation House. 6 Cross Rd., St. Philip. ☎ **246/423-6270.** Admission U.S.$6 adults, U.S.$3 children. Daily 10am–4:30pm.

This 300-year-old plantation house is steeped in history, featuring mahogany antiques, old prints, and a unique collection of horse-drawn carriages. This is the only Great House in Barbados where all the rooms are open for viewing. An informative tour is given, and later guests can patronize the Courtyard Restaurant and Bar for meals or drinks; there's also an on-site gift shop. Sunbury also offers a candlelight dinner at least once a week. This is a five-course meal costing U.S.$37.50, served at a 200-year-old mahogany table. Call the number above to learn when the dinner is offered, to find out more information, or to make reservations.

6 Cruises & Tours

Barbados is worth exploring, either in your own car or with a taxi-driver guide. Unlike on so many islands of the Caribbean, the roads are fair and quite passable. They are, however, poorly signposted, and newcomers invariably get lost, not only once, but several times.

CRUISES

Largest of the coastal cruising vessels, the *Bajan Queen* is modeled after a Mississippi riverboat and is the only cruise ship offering table seating and dining on local fare produced fresh from the onboard galley. There's also cover available in case of too much sun or rain. The *Bajan Queen* becomes a showboat by night, with local bands providing music for dancing under the stars. You're treated to a dinner of roast chicken, barbecued steak, and seasoned flying fish with a buffet of fresh side dishes and salads. Cruises are usually sold out, so you should book early to avoid disappointment. Each cruise costs BD$110 (U.S.$55) and includes transportation to and from your hotel. For reservations, contact **Jolly Roger Cruises,** Shallow Draft, Bridgetown Harbour (☎ 246/436-6424). Cruises are on Wednesday from 6 to 10pm and on Saturday from 5 to 9pm.

The same company also owns two motorized replicas of pirate frigates, the *Jolly Roger I* and the *Jolly Roger II.* One or both of these, depending on demand, departs five mornings a week for daytime snorkeling cruises from 10am to 2pm. Included in the price of BD$123 (U.S.$61.50) is an all-you-can-eat buffet, complimentary drinks, and free use of snorkeling equipment, which requires a U.S.$20 refundable deposit. There's an onboard boutique on both of these boats. For information, call Jolly Roger Cruises or visit the berth at Bridgetown Harbour. They also operate a fourth boat, *Excellent,* a catamaran running on Monday, Wednesday, and Friday from 9am to 2pm and on Sunday from 10am to 3pm. The price of U.S.$55 includes a continental breakfast, a lunch buffet, free drinks, and free snorkeling gear (no deposit), plus inflatable water mattresses. Since it's a catamaran, there are fewer people, making the ambience more intimate.

Limbo Lady Sailing Cruises, 78 Old Chancery Lane, Christ Church (☎ 246/420-5418), is another touring option. Patrick Gonsalves skippers the classic 44-foot CSY yacht, *Limbo Lady,* and his wife, Yvonne, a singer and guitarist, serenades you on a sunset cruise. Daily lunch cruises are also available, with a stop for swimming and snorkeling (equipment provided). Both lunch and sunset cruises offer a complimentary open bar and transportation to and from your hotel. Lunch cruises lasting 4½ hours cost U.S.$63, and 3-hour sunset cruises, including a glass of champagne, go for U.S.$52. Moonlight dinner cruises can also be arranged as well as private charters, both local and to neighboring islands (call for more information).

Part cruise ship, part nightclub, the **M/V *Harbour Master*** (☎ 246/430-0900) is one of the island's newest attractions. A 100-foot four-story coastal vessel with theme decks, it contains a modern gallery and a trio of bars. It boasts a dance floor and a sit-down restaurant, also offering formal buffets on its Calypso Deck. On the Harbour Master Deck is found a bank of TVs for sport buffs. The showpiece of the vessel is an onboard semi-submersible, which is lowered hydraulically to 6 feet beneath the ship. This is, in effect, a "boat in a boat," with 30 seats. Lunch and dinner cruises start at U.S.$25 per person, although the semi-submersible experience costs another U.S.$5. On Friday night, the boat becomes one of the hottest night spots in the Caribbean, a venue for jazz music and dancing from 5 to 9pm, costing an entrance fee of U.S.$10, although this is redeemable for food and drink once you're inside.

SUBMERGED SIGHTSEEING

You no longer have to be an experienced diver to see what lives 150 feet below the surface of the sea around Barbados. Now all visitors can view the sea's wonders on sightseeing submarines. The air-conditioned submersibles seat 28 to 48 passengers and make several dives daily from 9am to 6pm. Passengers are transported aboard a ferry boat from the Careenage in downtown Bridgetown to the submarine site, about a mile from the West Coast of Barbados. The ride offers a view of the West Coast of the island.

The submarines have viewing ports allowing you to see a rainbow of colors, tropical fish, plants, and even a shipwreck that lies upright and intact below the surface. You're taken aboard either *Atlantic I* or *III* on two different trips, beginning with the Odyssey, which is a dive onto a reef where professional divers leave the vessel and perform a 15-minute dive show for the viewing passengers, costing U.S.$84.50 for adults or U.S.$42.25 for children. The Expedition costs U.S.$73.50 for adults and U.S.$36.25 for children. For reservations, contact **Atlantis Submarines (Barbados),** Shallow Draught, Bridgetown (☎ **246/436-8929**). It's also possible to go cruising over one of the shore reefs to observe marine life. You sit in air-conditioned comfort aboard the *Atlantis Seatrec,* a semi-submersible boat, which gives you a chance to get a snorkeler's view of the reef through large viewing windows. You can also relax on deck as you take in the scenic coastline. The tour costs U.S.$29.50 for adults; children 4 to 12 are charged half fare (not suitable for those 3 or under). A second *Seatrec* tour explores wreckage sites. Divers go down with video cameras to three different wrecks on Carlisle Bay, and the video is transmitted to TV monitors aboard the vessel. The price is the same as for the first tour. For reservations, call the number above.

RUM TOURS

Tours, with or without lunch included, are offered at **The Mount Gay Distilleries, Ltd.,** Spring Garden Highway, Brandon's St. Michael's (☎ **246/425-9066**). Founded in 1703, and today noted as the oldest rum distillery in the world, it offers 45-minute tours of the rum-making process Monday to Friday from 9am to 3:45pm, departing at 30-minute intervals. Tours cost U.S.$6 per person, and include a complimentary rum punch, access to a souvenir stand, and a highly informative tour of the distillery. A more elaborate version of the tour, which includes lunch, is available Monday to Friday for U.S.$25 per person, including free transport to and from your hotel, a tour of the distillery, a welcome rum punch, and a lunch prepared buffet style. It usually requires advance reservations.

TAXI TOURS

Nearly all Bajan taxi drivers are familiar with the entire island and like to show it off to visitors. If you can afford it, touring by taxi is far preferable to taking a standardized bus tour. The average day tour by taxi costs U.S.$50, but, of course, that figure has to be negotiated in advance.

ORGANIZED SIGHTSEEING TOURS

Instead of a private taxi, you can also book with **Bajan Tours,** Glenayre, Locust Hall, St. George (☎ **246/437-9389**), a locally owned and operated tour company. The best bet for the first-timer is the Exclusive Island Tour, costing U.S.$56 per person, with departures between 8:30 and 9am, with a return from 3:30 to 4pm daily. It covers all the highlights of the island, including the Barbados Wildlife Reserve, the Chalky Mount Potteries, and the rugged East Coast.

On Friday, for the same price, the outfit conducts a Heritage Tour, mainly of the island's major plantations and museums. And Monday through Friday it offers an Eco Tour, which takes in the natural beauty of the island. It, too, costs U.S.$56 and leaves at the same time as the above two tours. A full buffet lunch is included in all tours.

7 Shopping

Barbados merchants can sometimes offer duty-free merchandise at prices 20% to 40% lower than in the United States and Canada. But, of course, you've got to be a smart shopper to spot bargains and also be familiar with prices back in your hometown. Duty-free shops have two prices listed on merchandise, the local retail price and the local retail price less government tax. You can avoid paying the tax if you have your purchase sent directly to the airport or cruise-ship dock; otherwise, if you're using the goods while in Barbados, you must pay the tax.

Some of the best duty-free buys include cameras (such as Leica and Fuji), watches (names like Omega, Piaget, and Seiko), crystal (such as Waterford and Lalique), gold (especially jewelry), bone china (such names as Wedgwood and Royal Doulton), cosmetics and perfumes, and liquor (including Barbados-produced rums and liqueurs), along with tobacco products and cashmere sweaters, tweeds, and sportswear from Britain.

The outstanding local craft item is black coral, fashioned into attractive earrings, pendants, and rings. Clay pottery is another Bajan craft. We recommend a visit to **Chalky Mount Potteries,** where this special craft originated. Potters turn out different products, some based on designs that are centuries old. The potteries (signposted) are found north of Bathsheba on the East Coast in the parish of St. Joseph, near Barclay's Park. In Barbados, you'll find a selection of locally made vases, pots, pottery mugs, glazed plates, and ornaments.

Wall hangings are made from local grasses and dried flowers. Island craftspeople also turn out straw mats, baskets, and bags with raffia embroidery. Still in its infant stage, leatherwork is also found on Barbados, particularly such items as handbags, belts, and sandals. Cruise passengers generally head for the **Bridgetown Cruise Terminal** at Bridgetown Harbour, where there are duty-free shops and merchandise stores specializing in local and regional products.

Art Foundry. Heritage Park. ☎ **246/426-0714.**

In a historic factory building, this ground-floor gallery is a partnership between Bajan artist Joscelyn Gardner and R.L. Seale, the rum distiller. It displays some of the finest works of art on Barbados in its ground-floor gallery, while offering changing exhibitions in its upstairs galleries. Gardner's own work is for sale, as she is both a printmaker and an artist in residence.

Articrafts. Broad St., Bridgetown. ☎ **246/427-5767.**

Here John and Roslyn Watson have assembled one of the most impressive displays of Bajan arts and crafts on the island. Roslyn's woven wall hangings are decorated with objects from the island, including sea fans and coral. They make a distinctive handcrafted design. Straw work, handbags, and bamboo items are also sold.

Best of Barbados. In the Southern Palms, St. Lawrence Gap, Christ Church. ☎ **246/420-8040.**

Part of an islandwide chain of 12 stores, Best of Barbados sells only products designed and/or made here. It's the best shop on the island for local products. It was established in 1975 by an English-born painter, Jill Walker, whose prints are best-sellers. They sell coasters, mats, T-shirts, pottery, dolls and games, and cookbooks, among other items. This tasteful shop is around the corner from the entrance to Southern Palms.

A more convenient location might be the outlet in Bridgetown at Mall 34, Broad Street (☎ **246/436-1416**).

Cave Shepherd. Broad St., Bridgetown. ☎ **246/431-2121.**

The best place to shop for tax-free merchandise on Barbados is Cave Shepherd, which has branches at Sunset Crest in Holetown, Da Costas Mall, Grantley Adams International Airport, and the Bridgetown Cruise Terminal. If your time is limited and you want a preview of what's for sale on Barbados, try this outlet. It has the widest selection of goods islandwide. Cave Shepherd is the largest department store on Barbados and one of the most modern in the Caribbean. The store offers perfumes, cosmetics from the world's leading houses, fine full-lead crystal and English bone china, cameras, gold and silver jewelry, swimwear, leather goods, men's designer clothing, handcrafts, T-shirts, and souvenirs. More than 70 brands of liqueurs are sold as well as other spirits. After you finish shopping, relax on the top floor in the cool comfort of the Ideal Restaurant. You can also patronize the Balcony, overlooking Broad Street and serving vegetarian dishes with a salad bar and beer garden as well.

Colours of De Caribbean. The Waterfront Marina, Bridgetown. ☎ **246/436-8522.**

Next to the Waterfront Café, on the Careenage, this unique store has a very individualized collection of tropical clothing—all made in the West Indies—and other collections including jewelry and decorative objects. Original hand-painted and batik clothing may hold the most interest for you. The collection was assembled by owner/designer Dianne Butcher, who sees to it that her collection "reflects the music, dance, and culture" of Barbados. She answers the question of how to look elegant even though casually dressed.

Cotton Days. Bay St., St. Michael. ☎ **246/427-7191.**

Boutiques abound on Barbados, and Cotton Days is the best known and most stylish. It inventories a wide array of casually elegant one-of-a-kind garments suitable for cool nights and hot climes. The collection has been called wearable art. For inspiration, the in-house designers turn to the flora and fauna of the island and the underwater world. The sales staff is skilled at selecting whimsical accessories to accompany the dresses, blouses, and shifts sold here. Magazines such as *Vogue* and *Glamour* have praised this collection.

Earthworks Pottery/The Potter's House Gallery. Edgehill Heights 2, St. Thomas Parish. ☎ **246/425-0223.**

Some serious shoppers consider this one of the artistic highlights of Barbados. Deep in the island's central highlands, its modern building was erected in the 1970s by Canadian-born Goldie Spieler. Trained as an art teacher and ceramic artist, Ms. Spieler and her son, David, create whimsical plates, cups, saucers, and bowls whose blue and green colors emulate the color of the Bajan sea and sky. Some fans claim that a breakfast of corn flakes in a cerulean-blue porringer on a snowy stateside morning re-creates the warmth of a Caribbean holiday. Many objects are decorated with the Antillean-inspired swirls and zigzags and can be shipped virtually anywhere. On the premises is the studio where the objects are crafted and a showroom that sells the output of at least half a dozen other island potters.

Eurostyle Mall 34. Broad St., Bridgetown. ☎ **246/435-8800.**

One of Bridgetown's most modern shopping complexes offers duty-free shopping in air-conditioned comfort at several outlets. You can find watches, clocks, china, jewelry, crystal, linens, sweaters, and liquor, together with souvenir items and tropical fashions.

The Great House Gallery. In the Bagatelle Restaurant, Hwy. 2A, St. Thomas. ☎ **246/421-6767.**

Set within the airy upper floor of one of the most historic Great Houses in Barbados, this art gallery combines a sophisticated inventory of artworks with West Indian graciousness. Displayed on high white walls amid the reflected glow of an antique mahogany floor, the gallery maintains the same hours as the restaurant downstairs (see "Where to Dine" in chapter 10), adding a cultivated gloss to the rituals of dining and drinking. Established by Richard and Valerie Richings, the gallery sells oils and watercolors by Caribbean, South American, and British artists, priced from U.S.$10 to U.S.$2,000. Among them are included the award-winning works of the owners themselves.

Greenwich House Antiques. Greenwich Village, Trents Hill, St. James. ☎ **246/432-1169.**

Set within a 25-minute drive from Bridgetown, in an antique planter's house, this place evokes a genteel and appealingly cluttered private house where the objects for sale seem to have been gathered from the attic of your favorite, and slightly dotty, great-aunt. Everything within the premises was acquired on Barbados, but many items seem to be 19th- or early 20th-century and English. Your hostess, Mrs. Lorna Bishop, is the owner, and her grasp of local lore and gossip is profound. She gives the impression that at any minute, a fresh pot of tea will emerge from any of the dozens of objects that seem to fill every available inch of tabletop or display space.

Harrison's. 1 Broad St., Bridgetown. ☎ **246/431-5500.**

In addition to this main shop, Harrison's has 14 branch stores, all selling a wide variety of duty-free merchandise, including china, crystal, jewelry, leather goods, and perfumes—all at fair prices. We've been able to find good buys here on Baccarat, Lalique, Royal Doulton, and Waterford crystal. They also sell some state-of-the-art leather products handcrafted in Colombia. Harrison's is the major competitor to Cave Shepherd on the island, but we'd give the edge to Cave Shepherd.

Little Switzerland. In the Da Costas Mall, Broad St., Bridgetown. ☎ **246/431-0029.**

At this outlet you'll find a wide selection of fragrances and cosmetics from such famous houses as Giorgio, Chanel, Guerlain, Yves St. Laurent, La Prairie, and more. Fine china and crystal from European manufacturers such as Lladró are also sold, as is an array of goodies from Waterford, Lalique, Swarovski, Baccarat, and others. The shop also specializes in watches and jewelry, offering a wide range of 14- and 18-karat-gold jewelry, with both precious and semiprecious stones. Watches include Rolex, Swatch, Omega, Raymond Weil, Tag Heuer, Ebel, and others. The store also stocks the distinctive Mont Blanc pens.

Pelican Village. Princess Alice Hwy., Bridgetown. ☎ **246/427-5350.**

While in Bridgetown, go down to the Pelican Village on Princess Alice Highway leading down to the city's Deep Water Harbour. A collection of island-made crafts and souvenirs is sold here in a tiny colony of thatch-roofed shops, and you can wander from one to another. Sometimes you can see craftspeople at work. Some of the shops here are gimmicky and repetitive, although you can find interesting items.

The Shell Gallery. Carlton House, St. James. ☎ **246/422-2593.**

For the shell collector, this is the best collection in the West Indies. Shells for sale come from all over the world. The outlet features the shell art of Maureen Edghill, who is considered the finest artist in this field. She founded this unique gallery in 1975. Also offered are hand-painted chinaware, shell jewelry, local pottery and ceramics, and batik and papier-mâché artwork depicting shells and aquatic life.

Walker's Caribbean World. St. Lawrence Gap. ☎ **246/428-1183.**

Close to the Southern Palms, this outlet offers many locally made items for sale, as well as handcrafts from the Caribbean Basin. Here you can buy the famous Jill Walker prints. There's also a gallery devoted to tropical prints.

8 Barbados After Dark

Most of the big resort hotels feature nightly entertainment, often dancing to steel bands and occasionally Bajan floor shows. Sometimes there are beach barbecues.

For the most authentic Bajan evening possible, and to top off your trip to Barbados, head for **Baxters Road** in Bridgetown, a street that reaches its peak of liveliness on Fridays and Saturdays after 11pm. In fact, if you stick around till dawn, the joints are still jumping. The street is safer than it might seem to visitors; Bajans come here to have fun, not to make trouble. Entertainment tends to be spontaneous. You might hear jazz on scratchy records—certainly the voice of Billie Holiday. Some old-time visitors have compared Baxters Road to the back streets of New Orleans in the '30s. If you fall in love with the place, you can "caf crawl" up and down the street. Prices are about the same from place to place, but each has its own atmosphere.

The most popular "caf" on Baxters Road is **Enid's** (she has a telephone, "but it doesn't work"), a little ramshackle establishment where Bajans devour fried chicken at 3 in the morning. Her place is open daily from 8:30pm to 8:30am, when the last satisfied customer departs into the blazing morning sun and Enid heads home to get some sleep before the new night begins. You can also stop in for a Banks beer. In fact, if you want a totally Bajan experience, why not come here and sit yourself down at one of the oilcloth-clad tables in the dilapidated back room? You can order a complete dinner for about U.S.$8.

Beach Club. Sunset Crest, St. James. ☎ **246/432-1309.**

This bar and restaurant serves as a social hub for Sunset Crest, with many island residents happily hobnobbing with their friends and colleagues. Happy hour at the Beach Bar is from 5 to 6pm nightly, when drinks are half price. Fish fries, barbecues, or buffets are offered from 7 to 10pm daily, priced at U.S.$10 to U.S.$12.50. There's live entertainment most nights, including bands and amateur talent shows, and the club recently added a dance floor. No cover Sunday through Friday; free Saturday for diners, U.S.$10 for nondiners.

Coach House. On the main Bridgetown–Holetown road, just south of Sandy Lane (about 6 miles north of Bridgetown), Paynes Bay, St. James. ☎ 246/432-1163.

The Coach House, named after a pair of antique coaches that stand outside, is a green-and-white house said to be 200 years old. The atmosphere is a Bajan version of an English pub, with an outdoor garden bar. Businesspeople and sun worshippers on nearby beaches come here to order Bajan buffet lunches, served Monday to Friday from noon to 3pm. The price is U.S.$11 for an all-you-can-eat lunchtime assortment that includes local vegetables and salads prepared fresh daily. If you visit from 6 to 10:30pm, you can order bar meals, including flying-fish burgers, priced at U.S.$8 and up. Live music is presented most nights, featuring everything from steel bands to jazz, pop, and rock. Live music and an attentive crowd assemble together here nightly from 9pm on. Cover is from U.S.$5 (as soon as you pay it, you'll be given coupons worth U.S.$3 for drinks at the bar).

Harbour Lights. Marine's Villa, Upper Bay St., about a mile southeast of Bridgetown. ☎ 246/436-7225.

This is the most popular weekend spot on the whole island for dancing, drinking, and flirting. In a modern seafront building whose oceanfront patio allows dancers the chance to cool off, the place plays reggae, soca, and just about anything else. No one under 18 is admitted. Grilled meats and hamburgers are available from a barbecue pit/kiosk on the premises. It's open till the wee hours every night. Monday is beach party night, costing U.S.$39 including transportation to and from your hotel, a barbecue buffet, free drinks, and a live band. Cover is U.S.$6 to U.S.$15, Wednesday and Friday.

John Moore Bar. On the waterfront, Weston, St. James Parish. ☎ 246/422-2258.

This is the most atmospheric and least pretentious bar on Barbados. Although its namesake (John Moore) died in 1987, the place is owned and managed by Mr. Lamont (Breedy) Addison, whose tenure here began as a teenager. If you think this is only a watering hole, think again: It's the heart of this waterfront town, filled throughout the day and evening with the widest and most congenial group of residents in the neighborhood. Most visitors opt for a rum punch or beer, but if you're hungry, platters of local fish can be prepared, after a moderate delay.

✪ Plantation Restaurant and Garden Theatre. Main Rd. (Hwy. 7), St. Lawrence, Christ Church. ☎ 246/428-5048.

This is the island's most prominent showcase for evening dinner theater and Caribbean cabaret. Dinner and a show are presented every Wednesday and Friday. Dinner is served at 6:30pm, and a show, *Plantation Tropical Spectacular II*, is presented at 8pm. The show involves plenty of exotic costumes and lots of reggae, calypso, limbo, and Caribbean exoticism. Reserve in advance. Cover (including unlimited drinks) is U.S.$60 for dinner, the show, and transport; U.S.$27.50 for the show only.

The Ship Inn. St. Lawrence Gap, Christ Church. ☎ 246/435-6961.

Previously recommended as a restaurant, this inn is now among the leading entertainment centers on the South Coast. The pub is the hot spot. Top local bands perform every night of the week, and patrons gather to listen to live reggae, calypso, and Top-40 music. The entrance fee to the Ship Inn complex (U.S.$5 after 9pm) is redeemable in food or drink at any of the other bars or restaurants in the complex. That means that guests are actually paying only U.S.$2 for the live entertainment.

✪ **1627 and All That.** Sherbourne Centre, St. Michael. ☎ **246/428-1627.**

Nothing else on Barbados so effectively combines music with entertainment and dancing. It's the most interesting place on Barbados to visit on a Thursday night. The entertainment combines a cocktail hour, a large buffet of Bajan food, and a historic and cultural presentation. The site, Sherbourne Centre, is a conference facility. The ticket includes transportation to and from your hotel. Dinner is served at 7pm, with show time at 6:30pm, concluding at 10pm. Cover is U.S.$57.50.

The Waterfront Café. Cavan's Lane, The Careenage, Bridgetown. ☎ **246/427-0093.**

By anyone's estimate, this is the busiest, most interesting, and most animated watering hole in Bridgetown. Contained in a turn-of-the-century warehouse originally built to store bananas and freeze fish, it welcomes both diners and drinkers to its reverberating walls for Creole food, beer, and pastel-colored drinks. Live music (reggae, ragtime, rock 'n' roll, and jazz, depending on the performers) is presented Monday to Saturday from 8 to 11:30pm. Careenage Coffee, laced with various after-dinner potions, is a longtime favorite. There is no cover charge.

Index

See also Accommodations Index, below.
Page numbers in italics refer to maps.

GENERAL INDEX

Accommodations. *See also*
  All-inclusive resorts;
  Resorts; Accommodations
  Index
  Barbados, 210–28
  Jamaica, 62–67
Adams, Grantley H., 191,
  256
Airfares, 55–56, 201–2
Airlines
  Barbados, 201–2
  Jamaica, 54–55, 107
  package tours, 53,
    200–201
  Web sites, 56
Airports
  Barbados, 201–2, 204
  Jamaica, 54, 107, 135,
    156, 178
All-inclusive resorts, 8–9, 62
  discriminatory policies,
    48
  Almond Beach Club
    (Barbados), 9, 184, 211
  Almond Beach Village
    (Barbados), 7, 211, 214
  Beaches Negril (Jamaica),
    6, 52, 115
  Breezes Golf and Beach
    Resort (Runaway Bay,
    Jamaica), 130–31
  Breezes Montego Bay
    (Jamaica), 85
  Breezes Runaway Beach
    (Jamaica), 132
  Ciboney Ocho Rios
    (Jamaica), 4, 5–6, 8,
    45, 141–42, 149
  Club Ambiance Jamaica
    (Runaway Bay,
    Jamaica), 132
  Club Jamaica Beach
    Resort (Ocho Rios,
    Jamaica), 142
  Couples Ocho Rios
    (Jamaica), 8–9, 142
  Enchanted Garden
    (Ocho Rios, Jamaica),
    6, 142–43
  FDR (Franklyn D.
    Resort) (Runaway Bay,
    Jamaica), 7, 51, 131
  Goldeneye (Oracabessa,
    Jamaica), 143

Grand Lido (Negril,
  Jamaica), 8, 115–16
Grand Lido Braco
  (Trelawny, Jamaica),
  133
Grand Lido Sans Souci
  (Ocho Rios, Jamaica),
  144
Hedonism II (Negril,
  Jamaica), 2, 48, 116
Jack Tar Grand Montego
  Beach Resort (Jamaica),
  86
Jamaica Grande
  Renaissance Resort
  (Ocho Rios, Jamaica),
  144–45
Negril Inn (Jamaica),
  116–17
Oasis Hotel (Barbados),
  221–22
Poinciana Beach Hotel
  (Negril, Jamaica), 52,
  117
Sandals Dunn's River
  (Ocho Rios, Jamaica),
  5, 145
Sandals Inn (Montego
  Bay, Jamaica), 86–87
Sandals Montego Bay
  (Jamaica), 5, 8, 87
Sandals Negril
  (Negril, Jamaica),
  117–18
Sandals Ocho Rios Resort
  & Golf Club (Jamaica),
  145–46
Sandals Royal Jamaican
  (Montego Bay,
  Jamaica), 87–88
Swept Away (Negril,
  Jamaica), 118
American Express, 39, 54, 206
Andromeda Botanical
  Gardens (Barbados), *187*,
  188, *253*, 254
Aquatic Gap (Barbados), 221,
  237, 245, 246–47
Arawak Indians, 18–19, 190
Art galleries, 11
  Barbados, 260–62
  Jamaica, 71
    Kingston, 11, 175–76
    Montego Bay, 99–100
    Ocho Rios, 151

Asta Reef (Barbados), 3, 246
Athenry Gardens (Portland,
  Jamaica), *155*, 163
Atlantis Hotel (Barbados),
  227, 228, 241, 254
Atlantis Submarines
  (Barbados), 259
ATMs, 38, 197

Bajan buffets, 7, 195, 215,
  223, 228, 237
Bajan Queen (Barbados),
  258
Barbados Gallery of Art
  (Bridgetown), 250
Barbados Hilton (Barbados),
  220–21, 247
Barbados Museum
  (Bridgetown), 185, *249*,
  250
Barbados National Trust,
  199, 246
Barbados Wildlife Reserve,
  187, 188, *253*, 255, 260
Barbados Windsurfing Club,
  199, 248
Bargaining, 71–72
Barnett Estates (Jamaica),
  96–97
Barnett Plantation (Montego
  Bay, Jamaica), 89
Barrett family, 97, 134–35
Bathsheba (Barbados), 188,
  252, *253*, 254
  accommodations, 227–28
  restaurants, 241
Baxters Road (Bridgetown,
  Barbados), 12, 247, 263
Beaches, 1–2
  Barbados, 184–85,
    243–44
  Jamaica, 43
    Miskito Cove Beach,
      98
    Montego Bay, 1, 43,
      94
    Ocho Rios, 148–49
    Port Antonio, 2, 43,
      162
    Runaway Bay, 134
  nudist, 2, 7, 73, 159
Bellfield Great House
  (Jamaica), 96–97
Berwyn (Barbados), 246
Bicycling, on Barbados, 205

Bird watching
    Barbados Wildlife
        Reserve, *187*, 188,
        253, 255, 260
    Jamaica, 43, 44, 126–27
        Port Royal, 174
        Rocklands Wildlife
        Station, 98
Black River (Jamaica), 16,
    104, 123, 124, 181
    boat tours, 4, 45, 123,
        124
Black River (town; Jamaica),
    35, 104, 123
    accommodations, 124–25
    restaurants, 125–26
Blackwell, Chris, 7–8, 143,
    168, 182
Bloody Bay (Negril, Jamaica),
    52, 106, 110, 112, 115
Bluefields (Jamaica), 123
Blue Harbour (Port Maria,
    Jamaica), 140, 151
Blue Mountain coffee
    (Jamaica), 15, 34, 44, 70,
    180–81
Blue Mountain-John Crow
    Mountain National Park
    (Jamaica), 17, 44, 180
Blue Mountain Peak
    (Jamaica), 17, 44, 181
Blue Mountains (Jamaica),
    15, 17, 180–83
    accommodations, 7–8,
        10, 181–83
    tours, 44–45, 181
Boat tours. *See also* Cruises
    Barbados, 258–59
    Jamaica
        Black River, 4, 45,
            123, 124
        Montego Bay, 11–12,
            98
        Port Royal, 174
Bond, James, 3, 95, 129,
    135, 143, 150
Bonney, Ann, 106, 112
Booby Cay (Negril, Jamaica),
    2, 106, 116
Boston Beach (Port Antonio,
    Jamaica), 2, 162
Bottom Bay (Barbados), 244
Brandon's Beach (Barbados),
    2, 243
Bridgetown (Barbados), 185,
    248, 250
    history of, 190–91
    nightlife, 12, 247, 263
    restaurants, 236–37
    shopping, 11, 194, 261,
        262, 263
    sightseeing, 248, 250
    visitor information, 196

Bridgetown Synagogue
    (Barbados), 250
Brighton Beach (Barbados),
    2, 184, 243
Brimmer Hall Estate (Port
    Maria, Jamaica), 150–51
British colonialism, 19–23,
    190–91, 218
British travelers
    airlines, 55, 202
    customs regulations, 37
    disabled, 48
    High Commissions, 72,
        206
    information sources, 35,
        196
    money, 38, 198
    package tours, 54, 201
Browning, Elizabeth Barrett,
    97, 135
Buccaneer Scuba Club (Port
    Royal, Jamaica), 2–3, 45,
    178, 180
Bucket shops, 53, 55–56, 201
Buses, 62, 205
Bush Hill House
    (Bridgetown, Barbados),
    249, 250

Cabs. *See* Taxis
Calendar of events
    Barbados, 198–200
    Jamaica, 41–43
Calico (Montego Bay,
    Jamaica), 11–12, 98
Calypso, 11, 30, 192–94
Canadian travelers
    airlines, 55
    customs, 36–37
    High Commissions, 72,
        206
    information sources, 35,
        196
Carambola (Barbados), 10,
    229
Cardiffall Lot Public Beach
    (Jamaica), 134
Careenage, The (Bridgetown,
    Barbados), 185, 236–37,
    248, *249*, 259, 265
Carlisle Bay (Barbados), 221,
    246, 259
Carnival, in Jamaica, 41–42
Car rentals
    Barbados, 204–5
    Jamaica, 60–61, 107, 156
Casuarina Beach (Barbados),
    222–23, 244, 248
Cattlewash-on-Sea
    (Barbados), 228, 242
Caves, 4–5, 163, 188, 257
Chalky Mount Village
    (Barbados), *187*, 189, 260

Chandler, Muriel, 102
Cherry Tree Hill (Barbados),
    187, 189, 255
Children, 50–52
    best resorts with, 6–7,
        51–52, 214
    restaurants, on Barbados,
        233
Christ Church Parish
    (Barbados), 188
    accommodations,
        221–26
    restaurants, 237–41
    special events, 199
Chukka Cove Farm and
    Resort (Jamaica), 131, 134
Church Point Beach
    (Barbados), 244
Clara's Heart (film), 154
Cliff, The (Barbados), 10,
    232
Climate
    Barbados, 198
    Jamaica, 40–41
Codrington College
    (Barbados), *187*, 252, *253*
Coffee, Blue Mountain
    (Jamaica), 15, 34, 44, 70,
    180–81
Coke Methodist Church
    (Kingston, Jamaica), *166*,
    175
Columbus, Christopher, 19,
    123, 129, 130, 150
Columbus Park Museum
    (Discovery Bay, Jamaica),
    134–35
Condo rentals, in Jamaica,
    66–67
Consolidators, 55–56, 201
Consulates, 72, 206
Cornwall Beach (Montego
    Bay, Jamaica), 1, 94
Coward, Noël, 129, 135,
    136, 138, 140, 143, 152
    Firefly (Jamaica), 150,
        151
Coyaba River Garden and
    Museum (Jamaica), 151
Crafts. *See* Handcrafts
Crane Bay (Barbados), 226
    restaurants, 241–42
Crane Beach (Barbados), 2,
    244, 252
Cricket, in Barbados, 189,
    204, 250
Croydon Plantation
    (Jamaica), 98
Cruises. *See also* Boat tours
    to Barbados, 202–4
    to Jamaica, 57–60
Crusoe's Beach (Navy Island,
    Jamaica), 162

Crystal Springs (Ocho Rios, Jamaica), 42, *155*, 163

Cuisine
  Barbados, 194–95, 228. *See also* Bajan buffets
  Jamaica, 33–34

Currency and exchange
  Barbados, 197, 198
  Jamaica, 37–38, 72

Customs regulations, 36–37, 197

Daniels River (Jamaica), 4, 164

Deep-sea fishing. *See* Fishing

Derricks (Barbados), 215, 229, 232, 235

Devon House (Kingston, Jamaica), *166*, 173, 176

Dinner theater, on Barbados, 12, 264

Disabled travelers, 47–48

Discovery Bay (Jamaica), 129, 130

Dive Shop (Barbados), 3, 245, 246–47

Diving. *See* Scuba diving/snorkeling; Shipwrecks

Doctors, 72, 73, 206

Doctor's Cave Beach (Jamaica), 1, 43, 75, 94
  accommodations, 81–84

Donald Sangster Airport (Jamaica), 54, 107, 135, 156

Dottins Reef (Barbados), 246

Drug laws, 29, 206

Drugstores, 72, 206–7

Dunn's River Falls (Ocho Rios, Jamaica), 4, 129, 135, 152

East Coast (Barbados), 188
  accommodations, 226–28
  beaches, 244
  driving tour, 252, 254–55
  restaurants, 241–42

East Coast Road (Barbados), *253*, 254

Edinburgh Castle (Lydford, Jamaica), 149–50

Elizabeth II, Queen of England, 26, 59, 78, 96, 188, 189, 192, 255

Embassies, 72. *See also* Consulates

Emergencies
  Barbados, 207
  Jamaica, 73

Enid's (Barbados), 9, 12, 247, 254, 263

Entry requirements
  Barbados, 197
  Jamaica, 36

Fairy Hill Beach (Winnifred, Jamaica), 162

Falmouth (Jamaica), 7, 42, 75, 101–3

Family travel. *See* Children

Farley Hill National Park (Barbados), *187*, 188, *253*, 255

Fashions, 11, 100–101, 261

Fern Gully (Jamaica), 149

Festivals
  Barbados, 198–200
  Jamaica, 41–43

Firefly (Jamaica), 150, 151

Fishing
  Barbados, 244–45
  Jamaica, 43
    Montego Bay, 94
    Ocho Rios, 149
    Port Antonio, 162–63
    tournaments, 42, 43, 162

Fitt's Village (Barbados), 216–17

Fleming, Ian, 129, 135, 136, 150
  Goldeneye (Jamaica), 143, 150

Flower Forest of Barbados, *187*, 257

Flynn, Errol, 5, 17, 129, 136, 150, 151, 159, 163
  Navy Island, 7, 156, 159, 161, 162

Folklore, Jamaican, 27–29

Folkstone Underwater Park (Barbados), 246

Folly Great House (Port Antonio, Jamaica), *155*, 164

Food. See Cuisine

Fort Charles (Port Royal, Jamaica), 179

Francia Plantation (Barbados), 256

Frenchman's Cove Beach (Jamaica), 162

Ganja. *See* Marijuana

Gardens
  Andromeda Botanical Gardens (Barbados), *187*, 188, *253*, 254
  Athenry Gardens (Jamaica), *155*, 163
  Coyaba River Garden and Museum (Jamaica), 151

Flower Forest of Barbados, *187*, 257

Prospect Plantation (Jamaica), 151–52

Garrison Savannah (Barbados), 185, 199, *249*, 250

Gay and lesbian travelers, 48–49

Giddy House (Jamaica), 180

Gold Coast (Barbados), 185, 188, *253*, 256. *See also* St. James Parish

Goldeneye (Jamaica), 143, 150

Golf, 3
  Barbados, 3, 245
  Jamaica, 3, 43–44
    Mandeville, 44, 45, 126
    Montego Bay, 3, 43–44, 95
    Ocho Rios, 44, 149
    Runaway Bay, 134

Grant, Eddy, 193–94

Grantley Adams International Airport (Barbados), 201–2, 204

Great House Gallery (Barbados), 262

Great Houses
  Barbados, 247
    open house, 199
    Francia Plantation, 256
    St. Nicholas Abbey, *187*, 188, 255
    Sunbury Plantation House, *187*, 257–58
    Tyrol Cot Heritage Village, 256
    Villa Nova, *187*, 188, 252, *253*, 254
  Jamaica, 96
    Barnett Estates, 96–97
    Bellfield Great House, 96–97
    Folly Great House, *155*, 164
    Greenwood Great House, 97
    Marshall's Pen (Mandeville), 106, 126
    Rose Hall Great House, 97–98
    Seville Great House, 135

Great River (Jamaica), 96

Greenwood Great House (Jamaica), 97

Gun Cay (Jamaica), 174
Gun Hill Signal Station
  (Barbados), *187*, 256–57

Hackleton's Cliff (Barbados),
  188
Haile Selassie, 24, 26, 173
Half Moon Golf, Tennis &
  Beach Club (Montego Bay,
  Jamaica), 5, 51, 75, 78
  recreational activities,
    3–4, 43, 45, 46,
    95, 96
  restaurants, 91–92
Handcrafts, 11
  Barbados, 260–61, 263
  Jamaica, 70
    Kingston, 176
    Montego Bay,
      99–100
    Ocho Rios, 153
Harmony Hall (Ocho Rios,
  Jamaica), 151
Harrison's Cave (Barbados),
  4–5, *187*, 188, 257
Hastings (Barbados), 188
  accommodations,
    225–26
  golf, 245
  restaurants, 237, 241
Health concerns, 46
Heritage Park & Rum
  Factory (Barbados), 257
High season
  Barbados, 197
  Jamaica, 39, 55
Hiking
  Barbados, 245–46
  Jamaica, 44–45
    Blue Mountains, 44,
      181
History
  Barbados, 190
  Jamaica, 18–25
Holetown (Barbados), *253*,
  256
  accommodations, 218
  restaurants, 233–36
Holetown Festival (Barba-
  dos), 190, 199
Holidays
  Barbados, 198
  Jamaica, 41
Holland Estate (Jamaica),
  124
Honeymoons
  best resorts for, 5–6
  marriages
    in Barbados, 189, 209
    in Jamaica, 50
Horseback riding
  Barbados, 246
  Jamaica, 45

Horse racing, on Barbados,
  199
Hospitals, 73, 207
Hurricanes, 24, 40–41, 198

Information sources
  Barbados, 196–97
  Jamaica, 35–36
Institute of Jamaica
  (Kingston), *166*, 175
Insurance, 46–47
Island in the Sun (movie),
  255

Jamaica House (Kingston,
  Jamaica), *166*, 173
Jamaica People's Museum of
  Craft & Technology
  (Spanish Town), 178
James Bond, 3, 95, 129,
  135, 143, 150
Jewelry stores, 11, 153–54,
  262
John Crow Mountains
  (Jamaica), 16
Jolly Roger (Barbados), 258
Jumbie, 27, 28

Keswick Centre (Barbados),
  237
King's House (Kingston,
  Jamaica), *166*, 174
Kingston (Jamaica), 15, 17,
  165
  accommodations, 165,
    168–70
  art galleries, 11, 175–76
  history of, 23
  Meet-the-People
    program, 71
  nightlife, 177
  restaurants, 170–73
  shopping, 175–77
  sightseeing, 173–75
  special events, 42
  tours, 45
  visitor information, 35

Language, 26–27. *See also*
  Patois
Limbo Lady (Barbados),
  258
Lime Cay (Jamaica), 174
Lord, Samuel Hall ("Regency
  Rascal"), 226–27, 252
Lovers' Leap (Southfield,
  Jamaica), 124

Maiden Cay (Jamaica), 174
Mallards Beach (Jamaica),
  148
Manchester Country Club
  (Jamaica), 44, 45, 126

Mandeville (Jamaica), 16,
  104, 126–28
  accommodations, 127
  golf and tennis, 44, 45,
    126
  restaurants, 128
Manley, Norman Washing-
  ton, 18, 25, 174
Marijuana, 28–29
Markets, in Jamaica
  Kingston, 176
  Port Antonio, 154
  Spanish Town, 178
Marley, Bob, 25, 30, 31
  Birthday Bash (Montego
    Bay), 41
  Museum (Kingston,
    Jamaica), *166*, 173
  recordings, 32
  Tribute (Ocho Rios), 41
Maroons, 20, 21, 22, 41
Marriage laws
  in Barbados, 189, 209
  in Jamaica, 50
Marshall's Pen (Jamaica),
  106, 126–27
Martha Brae River (Jamaica),
  102
Mavis Bank (Jamaica), 17,
  182–83
Maxwell, Enid, 9, 12, 227,
  241, 247, 254, 263
Meet-the-People program
  (Jamaica), 71
Mico College (Kingston,
  Jamaica), *166*, 175
Middle Quarters (Jamaica),
  124
Milk River Mineral Bath
  (Jamaica), 127
Miskito Cove Beach
  (Jamaica), 98
Money
  Barbados, 197, 198
  Jamaica, 37–39
Montego Bay (Jamaica), 16,
  75–101
  accommodations, 5,
    75–88
  all-inclusive resorts, 8,
    85–88
  beaches, 1, 43, 94
  boat tours, 11–12, 98
  nightlife, 11–12, 101
  recreational activities,
    3–4, 43–44, 45, 46,
    94–95, 96
  restaurants, 9, 88–94
  shopping, 11, 99–101
  sightseeing, 96–98
  special events, 41, 42–43
  tours, 98
  visitor information, 35

Morgan, Henry, 20, 178, 179
Morgan Lewis Sugar Windmill and Museum (Barbados), *187*, *253*, 255
Morgan's Harbour (Port Antonio, Jamaica), 174, 178–79, 180
Motorbikes, in Jamaica, 62
Mount Gay Distilleries (Barbados), 259
Mullins Beach (Barbados), 244
Museum of Craft & Technology (Spanish Town, Jamaica), 178
Music. *See also* Reggae, in Jamaica
  Barbados, 194
  calypso, 11, 30, 192–94
  festivals
    Barbados, 192–93
    Jamaica, 41–43
    Jamaican, 29–33

National Heroes Park (Kingston, Jamaica), *166*, 174
National Library of Jamaica (Kingston), *166*, 175
National parks
  Blue Mountain-John Crow Mountain (Jamaica), 17, 44, 180
  Farley Hill (Barbados), *187*, 188, *253*, 255
National Stadium (Kingston, Jamaica), *166*, 174
Nature reserves
  Barbados Wildlife Reserve, *187*, 188, *253*, 255, 260
  Marshall's Pen (Jamaica), 106, 126–27
  Welchman Hall Gully (Barbados), 4, *187*, 188, 257
Nature tours, in Jamaica, 43, 174
Navy Island, 7, 156, 159, 161, 162
Needham's Point (Barbados), 185, 247
  accommodations, 220–21
Negril (Jamaica), 16, 104, 106–23
  accommodations, 48, 107–18
    for children, 6, 51–52
  all-inclusive resorts, 8, 115–18

beaches, 1–2, 43, 106
nightlife, 123
restaurants, 118–22
scuba diving/snorkeling, 2, 45, 122
traveling to, 54, 107
visitor information, 35
Negril Beach (Jamaica), 1–2, 106, 109
Negril Coral Reef Preservation Society (Jamaica), 122
Negril Lighthouse (Jamaica), 106
Negril Scuba Centre (Jamaica), 2, 45, 122
Nelson, Horatio, 21, 22, 178, 179, 248
New Kingston Shopping Centre (Jamaica), 177
Newspapers, 73, 208
Nightlife, 11–12. *See also* Music
  Barbados, 263–65
    Baxters Road (Bridgetown), 12, 247, 263
    dinner theater, 12, 264
  Jamaica
    Kingston, 177
    Montego Bay, 11–12, 101
    Negril, 123
    Ocho Rios, 154
Nonsuch, Cave of (Portland, Jamaica), *155*, 163
Norma at the Wharfhouse (Montego Bay, Jamaica), 9, 88
Norman Manley Airport (Kingston, Jamaica), 54, 156, 179
North Coast (Jamaica), 16, 129–64
Nudity. *See also* Beaches, nudist
  in Jamaica, 16, 73

Obeah, 27, 97, 98
Ocho Rios (Jamaica), 16, 129, 135–54
  accommodations, 5–6, 136–46
  all-inclusive resorts, 8–9, 141–46
  beaches, 148–49
  car rentals, 136
  nightlife, 154
  recreational activities, 4, 44, 45, 149
  restaurants, 9–10, 146–48
  shopping, 152–54

sightseeing, 149–52
special events, 41, 42
traveling to, 135–36
visitor information, 35
Off-season
  Barbados, 197
  Jamaica, 39–40, 55
Oistins (Barbados), 188, 199, 251, *253*
Old Fort Craft Park (Montego Bay, Jamaica), 99
Old King's House (Spanish Town, Jamaica), 178
Orange Bay (Negril, Jamaica), 45, 106, 122
Orchid Room (Barbados), 10, 234
Organized tours. *See* Tours
Outfitters, 2–3, 246–47. *See also specific activities*

Package tours
  Barbados, 200–201
  Jamaica, 52–54
Palmer, Annie (White Witch of Rose Hall), 91, 97–98
Paradise Beach (Barbados), 2, 134, 243
Paradise Village (Barbados), 224–25
Parishes, of Barbados, 185, 188–89. *See also specific parishes*
Patois, 26
Paynes Bay (Barbados), 243, 247
  accommodations, 219–20
  restaurants, 232, 233–34, 236, 239
Pier 1 (Montego Bay, Jamaica), 90–91, 101
Pineapple Place Shopping Centre (Jamaica), 152–53
Piracy, 19, 106, 112, 129, 156, 174, 178, 179
Plantations, of Jamaica. *See also* Great Houses
  Brimmer Hall Estate, 150–51
  Croydon Plantation, 98
  Holland Estate, 124
  Prospect Plantation, 151–52
  tours, 98
Port Antonio (Jamaica), 17, 129, 130, 135, 154–64
  accommodations, 5, 156–60
  beaches, 2, 43, 162
  recreational activities, 162–63
  restaurants, 160–62
  sightseeing, 163–64

special events, 42, 43
traveling to, 156
visitor information, 35
Porters (Barbados), 217–18,
232, 234–35
Portland (Jamaica), 42, 163
Port Maria (Jamaica), 150–51
Port Royal (Jamaica), 7, 165,
174, 178–80
history of, 20–21, 179
scuba diving, 2–3, 45,
178–79
Pottery, on Barbados, 260,
261–62
Pringle, Rachel, 193
Prospect Plantation (St. Ann,
Jamaica), 151–52
Public Buildings
(Bridgetown, Barbados),
248, 249
Puerto Seco Beach (Jamaica),
129

Rackham, Jack (Calico Jack),
112
Rafting. See River rafting, in
Jamaica
Ragged Point Lighthouse
(Barbados), 252, 253, 255
Rain forest: Welchman Hall
Gully (Barbados), 4, 187,
188, 257
Rap music, 29, 31–32
Rastafarianism, 13, 24–31.
See also Marley, Bob
Reading (Jamaica), 99–100
Reggae, in Jamaica, 11, 13,
27, 29–31. See also
Marley, Bob
festivals, 41, 42
Montego Bay, 101
Negril, 123
recordings, 32–33
Reggae Sumfest (Montego
Bay), 42
Reggae Sunsplash (Jamaica),
41, 42
Rental properties, in Jamaica,
63, 66–67
Resorts, 63. See also
Accommodations Index
all-inclusive. See All-
inclusive resorts
best honeymoon, 5–6
for families, 6–7
Barbados, 214
Jamaica, 51–52
Restaurants, 9–10
Barbados, 228–42
dinner theater, on
Barbados, 12, 264
Jamaica, 67–70

Richmond Plantation
(Barbados), 257
River rafting, in Jamaica
Great River, 96
Martha Brae, 102
Montego Bay, 96
Port Antonio, 163
Rio Grande, 163
Rocklands Wildlife Station
(Jamaica), 98
Rockley Beach (Barbados),
222, 225, 239
Rocky Point Riding Stables
(Jamaica), 45, 95
Rodney Memorial (Jamaica),
178
Rose Hall Beach Club
(Jamaica), 94
Rose Hall Great House
(Jamaica), 97–98
Royal Westmoreland Golf &
Country Club (Barbados),
3, 245
Rum, 34, 195
Heritage Park & Rum
Factory (Barbados),
257
Mount Gay Distilleries
(Barbados), 259
Sangster's Old Jamaica
Spirits (Jamaica),
176–77
Runaway Bay (Jamaica), 16,
129, 130–35
accommodations and
restaurants, 7, 130–33
beaches, 134
recreational activities,
131, 134
sightseeing, 134–35

Safety
Barbados, 208
Jamaica, 73–74
Sailing
Barbados, 258
Jamaica
Montego Bay, 41, 94
Port Royal, 180
regatta, 41
St. Andrew Parish
(Barbados), 189, 245,
254–55
St. Ann (Jamaica), 42, 43,
151–52
St. Anne's Bay (Jamaica), 50,
129, 130, 131, 134, 136,
150
St. Ann's Fort (Bridgetown,
Barbados), 249, 250
St. Elizabeth (Jamaica), 41
St. George (Barbados), 245,
256–57

St. Jago de la Vega (Spanish
Town, Jamaica), 177–78
St. James Beach (Barbados),
2, 215–16, 219
St. James Parish (Barbados),
185, 188
accommodations, 211,
215–20
driving tour, 256
golf, 3, 245
restaurants, 229, 232–36
special events, 199
St. James Parish Church
(Barbados), 187, 256
St. John Parish (Barbados),
188, 245
St. John's Parish Church
(Barbados), 187, 188, 252,
253
St. Joseph Anglican Church
(Barbados), 188
St. Joseph Parish (Barbados),
188, 257
accommodations, 227–28
horseback riding, 246
restaurants, 241, 242
St. Lawrence Gap (Barbados),
251, 253
accommodations, 221–25
nightlife, 264–65
restaurants, 233, 237–41
St. Michael Parish
(Barbados), 185
accommodations, 220–21
restaurants, 237
sightseeing, 256
special events, 199
St. Michael's Cathedral
(Bridgetown, Barbados),
249, 250
St. Nicholas Abbey
(Barbados), 187, 188, 255
St. Peter Parish (Barbados),
188, 255
accommodations,
214–15
restaurants, 235
St. Peter's Church
(Barbados), 188
St. Philip Parish (Barbados),
188, 251–52, 257–58
accommodations, 226–27
restaurants, 241–42
St. Thomas Parish
(Barbados), 188, 229,
245, 257
Sam Lord's Castle
(Barbados), 187, 188,
226–27, 252, 253
Sandals Golf & Country
Club (Ocho Rios, Jamaica),
149
Sandals of Barbados, 211

Sandals of Jamaica, 5, 48, 50.
See also Accommodations
Index
Sandy Beach (Barbados), 3,
244, 246
Sandy Lane (Barbados), 6,
185, 218
  Barbados Gold Cup,
  199
  recreational activities, 4,
  245, 247
San San Beach (Port Antonio,
Jamaica), 43, 158, 162
Scooters, 62, 205
"Scotland District"
(Barbados). *See* St. Joseph
Parish
Scuba diving/snorkeling. *See*
Shipwrecks; *and specific*
reefs
  Barbados, 3, 243,
  246–47
  best outfitters, 2–3
  Jamaica, 45
    Montego Bay, 45,
    94–95, 95
    Negril, 2, 45, 122
    Ocho Rios, 149
    Port Antonio, 162
    Port Royal, 2–3, 45,
    178–79
    Runaway Bay, 134
Seasons
  Barbados, 197
  Jamaica, 39–40, 55
Senior citizen travelers, 49
Seville Great House
(Jamaica), 135
Shell Gallery (Barbados),
263
Shipwrecks
  Berwyn (Barbados), 246
  Stavronika (Barbados),
  246
  Texas (Jamaica), 3, 45,
  178
Shopping. *See also specific*
items
  Barbados, 260–63
    Bridgetown, 11, 194,
    261, 262, 263
  bargaining, 71–72
  best buys, 10–11
  duty-free
    Barbados, 260, 261
    Jamaica, 100
  Jamaica, 70–72
    Kingston, 175–77
    Montego Bay, 11,
    99–101
    Ocho Rios, 152–54
Silver Sands Beach
(Barbados), 244, 248

1627 and All That
(Barbados), 12, 247, 265
Ska music, 30, 31
Slavery, 20, 21, 22, 27, 30,
135, 191, 192. *See also*
Maroons
Snorkeling. *See* Scuba diving/
snorkeling
Somerset Falls (Port Antonio,
Jamaica), 4, 155, 164
South Coast (Barbados),
188
  accommodations,
  221–26
  beaches, 244
  restaurants, 237–41
South Coast (Jamaica), 16,
104, 123–26
Southfield (Jamaica), 124
Spanish Town (Jamaica), 17,
165, 177–78
Special events. *See* Festivals
Speightstown (Barbados),
188, 253, 255
  accommodations, 211,
  214
  restaurants, 236
Spices, Jamaican, 70
Stavronika (Barbados), 246
Strawberry Hill (Blue
Mountains, Jamaica), 7–8,
182
Submarine tours, on
Barbados, 259
Sugarcane, 20–21, 22, 190,
192, 245
  Morgan Lewis Sugar
  Windmill and Museum
  (Barbados), 187, 253,
  255
Sunbury Plantation House
(Barbados), 187, 257–58
Sunset Crest (Barbados),
220, 263–64
Sunsplash festival (Jamaica),
41, 42
SuperClubs (Jamaica)
  Breezes Montego Bay,
  85
  Grand Lido (Negril), 8,
  115–16
  Grand Lido Sans Souci
  (Ocho Rios), 144
  Runaway Golf Club, 44,
  134

Taxes
  Barbados, 208
  Jamaica, 74
Taxis
  Barbados, 204, 209,
  259–60
  Jamaica, 62

Tennis, 3–4
  Barbados, 4, 247
  Jamaica, 45–46
    Mandeville, 44, 45,
    126
    Montego Bay, 3–4,
    46, 96
    Ocho Rios, 4, 45,
    149
Tent Bay (Barbados), 188
Texas (Jamaica), 3, 45, 178
Theater, dinner, on Barbados,
12, 264
Things Jamaican, 11, 72,
100, 176
Tipping, 74, 209
Tourist information. *See*
Visitor information
Tours. *See also* Boat tours;
Package tours
  Barbados, 259–60
    hiking, 245–46
    submarine, 259
  Jamaica
    Blue Mountains,
    44–45, 181
    Kingston, 45
    Montego Bay,
    11–12, 98
    nature, 43, 174
    plantations, 98
Trafalgar Square
(Bridgetown, Barbados),
248, 249
Traveler's checks, 38–39
Traveling
  to Barbados, 201–2
  within Barbados,
  204–5
  to Jamaica, 54–60
  within Jamaica, 60–62
Treasure Beach (Barbados),
219–20
Treasure Beach (Jamaica),
2, 16, 104, 124
  accommodations,
  7, 125
Trelawny (Jamaica), 133–34
Trembly Knee Cove
(Navy Island, Jamaica), 7,
159
Tryall Golf, Tennis & Beach
Club (Montego Bay,
Jamaica), 79
  recreational activities, 3,
  4, 43, 46, 95, 96
Tuk bands, 194
Turtle Beach (Jamaica), 139,
142, 148
20,000 Leagues Under the Sea
(film), 106
Tyrol Cot Heritage Village
(Barbados), 256

Underwater Park, Folkstone (Barbados), 246
University of the West Indies (Kingston, Jamaica), *166*, 174

Venture (Barbados), 254
Villa Nova (Barbados), *187*, 188, 252, *253*, 254
Villa rentals, in Jamaica, 63, 66–67
Visitor information
    Barbados, 196–97
    Jamaica, 35–36

Walter Fletcher Beach (Jamaica), 43, 94
Washington, George, 184, 185, 190, 250
Water, tap, 46, 74, 209
Waterfalls
    Dunn's River Falls (Ocho Rios, Jamaica), 4, 129, 135, 152
    Somerset Falls (Port Antonio, Jamaica), 4, *155*, 164
    Y.S. Falls (South Coast, Jamaica), 123, 124
    "Y's Waterfall" (Blue Mountains, Jamaica), 45, 181
Weather
    Barbados, 198
    Jamaica, 40–41
Web sites
    Barbados, 196–97
    Jamaica, 36
    travel, 56
Weddings
    in Barbados, 189, 209
    in Jamaica, 50
Welches (Barbados), 224
Welchman Hall Gully (Barbados), 4, *187*, 188, 257
West Coast (Barbados), 185, 188
    accommodations, 211–20
    beaches, 243–44
    restaurants, 229, 232–36
    scuba diving/snorkeling, 246–47
"White Witch of Rose Hall," 91, 97–98
Whitfield Hall (Jamaica), 44, 181, 182–83
Wildlife Reserve, Barbados, *187*, 188, *253*, 255, 260
Windsurfing
    Barbados, 247–48
    International Windsurfing, 199
    Jamaica's Montego Bay, 94

Wood carvings, Jamaican, 70, 153
Worrell, Frank, 204
Worthing (Barbados), 188
    accommodations, 221–22, 223
    restaurants, 237–38, 240
Wyndham Rose Hall Golf & Beach Resort (Montego Bay, Jamaica), 51, 80–81, 101
    recreational activities, 3, 4, 43, 46, 95, 96

Yachting. *See* Sailing
Y.S. Falls (South Coast, Jamaica), 123, 124
"Y's Waterfall" (Blue Mountains, Jamaica), 45, 181

ACCOMMODATIONS INDEX

Almond Beach Club (Barbados), 9, 184, 211
Almond Beach Village (Barbados), 7, 211, 214
Atlantis Hotel (Barbados), 227
Bagshot House Hotel (Barbados), 223
Banana Shout (Negril, Jamaica), 111
Barbados Hilton (Barbados), 220–21, 247
Beaches Negril (Jamaica), 6, 52, 115
Belvedere, The (Montego Bay, Jamaica), 82
Blue Cave Castle (Negril, Jamaica), 111–12
Blue Harbour (Port Maria, Jamaica), 140, 150
Blue Harbour Hotel (Montego Bay, Jamaica), 82
Bonnie View Plantation Hotel (Port Antonio, Jamaica), 159–60
Boscobel Beach Resort (Ocho Rios, Jamaica), 51
Breezes Golf and Beach Resort (Runaway Bay, Jamaica), 130–31
Breezes Montego Bay (Jamaica), 85
Breezes Runaway Beach (Jamaica), 132
Caribbean Isle Hotel (Runaway Bay, Jamaica), 132–33
Casuarina Beach Club (Barbados), 214, 222–23

Caves, The (Negril, Jamaica), 107
Charela Inn (Negril, Jamaica), 108
Chukka Cove Farm and Resort (Runaway Bay, Jamaica), 131, 134
Ciboney Ocho Rios (Jamaica), 4, 5–6, 8, 45, 141–42, 149
Club Ambiance Jamaica (Runaway Bay, Jamaica), 132
Club Jamaica Beach Resort (Ocho Rios, Jamaica), 142
Cobblers Cove Hotel (Barbados), 214–15
Coco La Palm Resort (Negril, Jamaica), 108
Coconut Creek Club (Barbados), 215
Coconuts (Little Bay, Jamaica), 108–9
Colony Club (Barbados), 215–16
Comfort Inn & Suites (Montego Bay, Jamaica), 51–52, 81, 89
Coral Cliff Hotel (Montego Bay, Jamaica), 82–83
Coral Reef Club (Barbados), 216
Couples Ocho Rios (Jamaica), 8–9, 142
Courtleigh Hotel (Kingston, Jamaica), 169
Coyaba (Montego Bay, Jamaica), 6, 79–80
Crane Beach Hotel (Barbados), 226
Crowne Plaza Kingston (Jamaica), 165, 168
Crystal Cove, The (Barbados), 216–17
Crystal Waters (Negril, Jamaica), 109
De Montevin Lodge Hotel (Port Antonio, Jamaica), 160
Devine Destiny (Negril, Jamaica), 112
Divi Southwinds Beach Resort (Barbados), 214, 221
Doctor's Cave Beach Hotel (Montego Bay, Jamaica), 81, 94
Dragon Bay (Port Antonio, Jamaica), 158
Drumville Cove Resort (Negril, Jamaica), 113
Edgewater Inn (Barbados), 227–28

El Greco Resort (Montego Bay, Jamaica), 83

Enchanted Garden (Ocho Rios, Jamaica), 6, 142–43

Fairholme (Barbados), 223–24

FDR (Franklyn D. Resort) (Runaway Bay, Jamaica), 7, 51, 131

Fern Hill Club Hotel (Port Antonio, Jamaica), 157

Firefly Beach Cottages (Negril, Jamaica), 113

Fleet View Apartments (Barbados), 228

Foote Prints (Negril, Jamaica), 113

Forres Park Guest House (Blue Mountains, Jamaica), 181–82

Glitter Bay (Barbados), 3, 214, 217

Goblin Hill Villas at San San (Port Antonio, Jamaica), 158

Goldeneye (Oracabessa, Jamaica), 143

Good Hope (Falmouth, Jamaica), 7, 102

Grand Barbados Beach Resort (Barbados), 221

Grand Lido (Negril, Jamaica), 8, 115–16

Grand Lido Braco (Trelawny, Jamaica), 133

Grand Lido Sans Souci (Ocho Rios, Jamaica), 144, 149

Half Moon Golf, Tennis & Beach Club (Montego Bay, Jamaica), 75, 78

Hedonism II (Negril, Jamaica), 2, 48, 116

Hibiscus Lodge Hotel (Ocho Rios, Jamaica), 138

High Hope Estate (Ocho Rios, Jamaica), 136, 138

Holiday Inn SunSpree (Montego Bay, Jamaica), 51, 85–86, 101

Home Sweet Home (Negril, Jamaica), 113–14

Hotel and Gallery Joe James (Trelawny, Jamaica), 133–34

Hotel Astra (Mandeville, Jamaica), 127

Hotel Four Seasons (Kingston, Jamaica), 169

Hotel Mocking Bird Hill (Jamaica), 160

Indies Hotel (Kingston, Jamaica), 170

Invercauld Great House & Hotel (Black River, Jamaica), 124

Irie Sandz Hotel (Black River, Jamaica), 124–25

Jackie's on the Reef (Negril, Jamaica), 109

Jack Tar Grand Montego Beach Resort (Jamaica), 86

Jake's (Treasure Beach, Jamaica), 125

Jamaica Grande Renaissance Resort (Ocho Rios, Jamaica), 144–45

Jamaica Inn (Ocho Rios, Jamaica), 5, 136

Jamaica Palace (Williamsfield, Jamaica), 158–59

Jamel Jamaica Hotel (Jamaica), 140–41

Kingsley Club (Barbados), 8, 228

Le Meridien Jamaica Pegasus (Kingston, Jamaica), 168

Lethe Estate (Montego Bay, Jamaica), 80

Little Bay Hotel (Barbados), 224

Little Pub Inn (Ocho Rios, Jamaica), 139

Mandeville Hotel (Jamaica), 127, 128

Meridian Inn (Barbados), 224

Morgan's Harbour Hotel & Beach Club (Port Royal, Jamaica), 180

Navy Island Marina Resort (Port Antonio, Jamaica), 7, 159, 161

Negril Beach Club Hotel (Jamaica), 109–10, 122

Negril Cabins (Jamaica), 110

Negril Gardens Hotel (Jamaica), 110

Negril Inn (Jamaica), 116–17

Negril Tree House (Jamaica), 110

Oasis Hotel (Barbados), 221–22

Ocean Edge Resort Hotel (Negril, Jamaica), 114

Ocean View Guest House (Montego Bay, Jamaica), 83

Parkway Inn (Ocho Rios, Jamaica), 139

Pegwell Inn (Barbados), 224

Pineapple Hotel (Ocho Rios, Jamaica), 139

Pine Grove Mountain Chalets (Jamaica), 170

Plantation Inn (Ocho Rios, Jamaica), 138

Poinciana Beach Hotel (Negril, Jamaica), 52, 117

Point Village Resort (Negril, Jamaica), 52, 111

Reading Reef Club (Montego Bay, Jamaica), 81–82

Richmond Hill Inn (Montego Bay, Jamaica), 83

Ridgeway Guest House (Montego Bay, Jamaica), 83–84

Rio Guest House (Barbados), 224–25

Rock Cliff Hotel (Negril, Jamaica), 114

Rockhouse (Negril, Jamaica), 114

Round Hill Hotel and Villas (Montego Bay, Jamaica), 78–79, 91

Royal Court Hotel (Montego Bay, Jamaica), 84

Royal Pavilion (Barbados), 6, 217–18

Runaway H. E. A. R. T. Country Club (Runaway Bay, Jamaica), 132

Sam Lord's Castle Resorts (Barbados), 226–27

Sandals Dunn's River (Ocho Rios, Jamaica), 5, 145

Sandals Inn (Montego Bay, Jamaica), 86–87

Sandals Montego Bay (Jamaica), 5, 8, 87

Sandals Negril (Jamaica), 117–18

Sandals Ocho Rios Resort & Golf Club (Jamaica), 145–46

Sandals Royal Jamaican (Montego Bay, Jamaica), 5

Sandals Royal Jamaican (Montego Bay, Jamaica), 87–88

Sandpiper, The (Barbados), 218

Sandy Beach Hotel (Barbados), 7, 214, 223

Sandy Lane (Barbados), 6, 218

Seasplash Resort (Negril, Jamaica), 108, 123

Settlers Beach (Barbados), 219

Shaw Park Beach Hotel (Cutlass Bay, Jamaica), 141

Southern Palms (Barbados), 222

Southern Surf Beach Apartments (Barbados), 225

Strawberry Hill (Blue Mountains, Jamaica), 7–8, 182

Sundance Resort (Montego Bay, Jamaica), 84

Swept Away (Negril, Jamaica), 118

Tamarind Cove (Barbados), 219

Tamarind Tree Hotel (Runaway Bay, Jamaica), 139–40

Terra Nova Hotel (Kingston, Jamaica), 168–69

Thrills (Negril, Jamaica), 114–15

Traveller's Palm (Barbados), 220

Treasure Beach (Barbados), 219–20

Treasure Beach Hotel (Black River, Jamaica), 7, 125

Trident Villas & Hotel (Port Antonio, Jamaica), 5, 157

Tryall Golf, Tennis & Beach Club (Montego Bay, Jamaica), 79

Turtle Beach Towers (Ocho Rios, Jamaica), 140

Verney House Resort (Montego Bay, Jamaica), 84–85

Wexford Court Hotel (Montego Bay, Jamaica), 82

Whitfield Hall (Blue Mountains, Jamaica), 182–83

Windsurf Village Hotel (Barbados), 225

Winged Victory Hotel (Montego Bay, Jamaica), 85

Woodville Beach Hotel (Barbados), 225–26

Wyndham Kingston Hotel (Jamaica), 169

Wyndham Rose Hall Golf & Beach Resort (Montego Bay, Jamaica), 80–81

FROMMER'S® COMPLETE TRAVEL GUIDES
(Comprehensive guides with selections in all price ranges—from deluxe to budget)

Alaska
Amsterdam
Arizona
Atlanta
Australia
Austria
Bahamas
Barcelona, Madrid & Seville
Belgium, Holland &
   Luxembourg
Bermuda
Boston
Budapest & the Best of
   Hungary
California
Canada
Cancún, Cozumel & the
   Yucatán
Cape Cod, Nantucket &
   Martha's Vineyard
Caribbean
Caribbean Cruises &
   Ports of Call
Caribbean Ports of Call
Carolinas & Georgia
Chicago
China
Colorado
Costa Rica
Denver, Boulder &
   Colorado Springs
England
Europe
Florida

France
Germany
Greece
Hawaii
Hong Kong
Honolulu, Waikiki & Oahu
Ireland
Israel
Italy
Jamaica & Barbados
Japan
Las Vegas
London
Los Angeles
Maryland & Delaware
Maui
Mexico
Miami & the Keys
Montana & Wyoming
Montréal & Québec City
Munich & the Bavarian Alps
Nashville & Memphis
Nepal
New England
New Mexico
New Orleans
New York City
Nova Scotia, New
   Brunswick &
   Prince Edward Island
Oregon
Paris
Philadelphia & the Amish
   Country

Portugal
Prague & the Best of the
   Czech Republic
Provence & the Riviera
Puerto Rico
Rome
San Antonio & Austin
San Diego
San Francisco
Santa Fe, Taos &
   Albuquerque
Scandinavia
Scotland
Seattle & Portland
Singapore & Malaysia
South Pacific
Spain
Switzerland
Thailand
Tokyo
Toronto
Tuscany & Umbria
USA
Utah
Vancouver & Victoria
Vermont, New Hampshire &
   Maine
Vienna & the Danube Valley
Virgin Islands
Virginia
Walt Disney World &
   Orlando
Washington, D.C.
Washington State

FROMMER'S® DOLLAR-A-DAY GUIDES
(The ultimate guides to comfortable low-cost travel)

Australia from $50 a Day
California from $60 a Day
Caribbean from $60 a Day
England from $60 a Day
Europe from $50 a Day
Florida from $60 a Day
Greece from $50 a Day
Hawaii from $60 a Day
Ireland from $50 a Day

Israel from $45 a Day
Italy from $50 a Day
London from $70 a Day
New York from $75 a Day
New Zealand from $50 a Day
Paris from $70 a Day
San Francisco from $60 a Day
Washington, D.C., from
   $60 a Day

FROMMER'S® MEMORABLE WALKS

Chicago
London

New York
Paris

San Francisco

FROMMER'S® PORTABLE GUIDES

Acapulco, Ixtapa/
   Zihuatenejo
Bahamas
California Wine
   Country
Charleston & Savannah
Chicago

Dublin
Las Vegas
London
Maine Coast
New Orleans
New York City
Paris

Puerto Vallarta, Manzanillo
   & Guadalajara
San Francisco
Sydney
Tampa Bay & St. Petersburg
Venice
Washington, D.C.

FROMMER'S® NATIONAL PARK GUIDES

Grand Canyon
National Parks of the American West
Yellowstone & Grand Teton

Yosemite & Sequoia/
   Kings Canyon
Zion & Bryce Canyon

THE COMPLETE IDIOT'S TRAVEL GUIDES
(The ultimate user-friendly trip planners)

Cruise Vacations
Planning Your Trip to Europe
Hawaii

Las Vegas
Mexico's Beach Resorts
New Orleans

New York City
San Francisco
Walt Disney World

SPECIAL-INTEREST TITLES

The Civil War Trust's Official Guide to
   the Civil War Discovery Trail
Frommer's Caribbean Hideaways
Israel Past & Present
New York City with Kids
New York Times Weekends
Outside Magazine's Adventure Guide
   to New England
Outside Magazine's Adventure Guide
   to Northern California

Outside Magazine's Adventure Guide
   to the Pacific Northwest
Outside Magazine's Guide to Family Vacations
Places Rated Almanac
Retirement Places Rated
Washington, D.C., with Kids
Wonderful Weekends from Boston
Wonderful Weekends from New York City
Wonderful Weekends from San Francisco
Wonderful Weekends from Los Angeles

THE UNOFFICIAL GUIDES®
(Get the unbiased truth from these candid, value-conscious guides)

Atlanta
Branson, Missouri
Chicago
Cruises
Disneyland

Florida with Kids
The Great Smoky
   & Blue Ridge
   Mountains
Las Vegas

Miami & the Keys
Mini-Mickey
New Orleans
New York City
San Francisco

Skiing in the West
Walt Disney World
Walt Disney World
   Companion
Washington, D.C.

FROMMER'S® IRREVERENT GUIDES
(Wickedly honest guides for sophisticated travelers)

Amsterdam
Boston
Chicago

London
Manhattan

New Orleans
Paris

San Francisco
Walt Disney World
Washington, D.C.

FROMMER'S® DRIVING TOURS

America
Britain
California

Florida
France
Germany

Ireland
Italy
New England

Scotland
Spain
Western Europe

YOU TRAVEL, *H*ELP IS NEVER FAR AWAY.

From planning your trip to

providing travel assistance along

the way, American Express®

Travel Service Offices are

always there to help.

American Express Travel Service Offices are found in central locations throughout Jamaica and Barbados.

Travel

http://www.americanexpress.com/travel